Understanding Community Economic Growth and Decline

This book presents a fully comprehensive look at what all communities—large and small, urban and rural—can do to grow and sustain their local economic bases. It examines the causes of economic decline for localities as well as the economic "product" being marketed to employers, the process of growth, and the means of sustaining economic growth over time. Drawing on the experiences of hundreds of communities and hundreds of leaders around the United States, *Understanding Community Economic Growth and Decline* also outlines the various strategies that have or have not worked to enable or support a general local economic recovery. Exploring many facets of growth and re-growth following periods of economic decline, and offering practical, real-life tactics that have been successfully employed in local and regional economies across the US, this book is required reading for community planners and administrators, those currently working in public administration, and students studying regional planning or economic development.

Gerald L. Gordon is President and Chief Executive Officer of the Economic Development Authority in Fairfax County, Virginia, USA.

Understanding Community
Economic Growth and Decline

"Gordon provides an extraordinarily wise and compelling take on the complexities of economic planning in our time. In order to thrive, his research demonstrates, we must learn to account for eventualities we can't anticipate. How? Implicitly, the book is an argument for education that prepares the next generations to recognize the astounding dynamism and interconnectedness of our world."

– **Zofia Burr**, *George Mason University, USA*

"This book addresses a timely issue that impacts all communities, presenting the findings of extensive research and years of practical experience. It is a great choice for both the scholar and the practitioner seeking answers to modern day questions in economic development. A thoughtful exploration of the topic that is also an interesting read weaving together theory and real-life examples."

– **Kendra Stewart**, *The College of Charleston, USA*

"In a time when federal and state funding for localities is declining, it's imperative that these communities take a proactive and strategic approach to economic growth. Jerry Gordon's book is a must read for those studying economic development and those practitioners living it on a daily basis."

– **Dr. Matt Shank**, *Marymount University, USA*

Understanding Community Economic Growth and Decline
Strategies for Sustainable Development

Gerald L. Gordon

Routledge
Taylor & Francis Group

NEW YORK AND LONDON

First published 2018
by Routledge
711 Third Avenue, New York, NY 10017

and by Routledge
2 Park Square, Milton Park, Abingdon, Oxon, OX14 4RN

Routledge is an imprint of the Taylor & Francis Group, an informa business

Library of Congress Cataloging-in-Publication Data
Names: Gordon, Gerald L., author.
Title: Understanding community economic growth and decline : strategies for
sustainable development / Gerald L. Gordon.
Description: New York, NY : Routledge, 2018. |
Includes bibliographical references and index.
Identifiers: LCCN 2018002018| ISBN 9781138556249 (hardback : alk. paper) |
ISBN 9781315149936 (ebook)
Subjects: LCSH: Community development—United States. |
Sustainable Development—United States. | Urban economics. |
Regional economics—United States.
Classification: LCC HN90.C6 G67 2018 | DDC 307.1/40973—dc23
LC record available at https://lccn.loc.gov/2018002018

ISBN: 978-1-138-55624-9 (hbk)
ISBN: 978-1-315-14993-6 (ebk)

Typeset in Sabon
by Florence Production Ltd, Stoodleigh, Devon, UK

Dedication

I have had the extraordinary privilege of working for the Fairfax County Economic Development Authority for more than 34 years. Over that time, the FCEDA has been recognized by organizations within the county and around the nation. I have had opportunities to do things and visit places that are the result of the enormous successes that have come to this community. And, I have learned through those many experiences the lessons that are reflected upon in this book.

Every time I have personally been recognized, selected, or thanked, it has been stunningly clear to me that it was happening because I sit in the chief executive's chair. It is certainly not because I alone had accomplished those things for which the recognition was being offered. It has always been a shared success.

I have had the gratifying experience of working for and with some extraordinary men and women literally for decades and, *together*, we have helped to build this incredible community and *together* we have learned what makes communities grow. A dedication in this book is woefully inadequate to recognize the contributions of so many people for so many years. The real evidence of our collective hard work and diligence is the extraordinary community of Fairfax County, Virginia. We all humbly share that accolade.

Contents

viii *Contents*

Contents

Illustrations

Tables

About the Author

Virginia Business Magazine named Dr. Gerald L. Gordon the 2010 "Virginia Business Person of the Year," and has for the past seven consecutive years named him as one of the Fifty Most Influential Virginians. Leadership Fairfax, Inc. named Dr. Gordon the recipient of its 2011 Northern Virginia Regional Leadership Award.

Dr. Gordon is the President and Chief Executive Officer of the Economic Development Authority in Fairfax County, Virginia, one of the largest office space markets in the United States. He has been with the FCEDA since late 1983. In that time, office space in the county grew from 32 million square feet to nearly 120 million square feet and jobs in the county grew from 243,000 to about 600,000. As a result, the real estate tax rate has decreased from $1.47 to $1.13.

In 2005, the FCEDA was included by *Site Selection Magazine* in the Top Ten Economic Development Organizations in North America and, in 2007, *Time* magazine called Fairfax County "one of the great economic success stories of our time." In 2011, the *Washington Post* wrote that "Fairfax County remains the economic wunderkind of Virginia and . . . of the Washington area."

Dr. Gordon has served as an Adjunct Professor at the Catholic University of America, the University of Maryland, George Mason University, and Virginia Commonwealth University. He has consulted with numerous city and state governments throughout the United States as well as the governments of the Republic of Poland, the island of Vieques in Puerto Rico, and the island nation of Yap, which is one of six nations in the Federated States of Micronesia. He has served as a consultant to various government agencies, the US Navy, businesses and nonprofits, associations, colleges and universities, and the United Nations.

Holding a bachelor's degree from The Citadel, a master's degree from George Washington University, and a doctorate in international economics from the Catholic University of America, he is also the author of 13 books and numerous articles on strategic planning, and economic development. His most recent books were published by CRC Press and include *The Economic Survival of America's Isolated, Small Towns* (2013), *Reinventing Local and Regional Economies* (2011), and *The Formula for Economic Growth on Main Street America* (2009).

Dr. Gordon is a recipient of the prestigious Israel Freedom Award of the Israel Bonds organization (2003) and was the first American (2006) to address the All-Parliamentary Exports Group in the British House of Commons. In 2007, he received a Fulbright Senior

Scholarship and, also in 2007, was named a Fellow of the International Economic Development Council. He is the recipient of the James Rees Award of the Fairfax County Chamber of Commerce and the Jeffrey A. Finkle Lifetime Achievement Award of the International Economic Development Council; and, in 2012, was named the Trendlines Trendsetter of the Year for the Washington, DC metropolitan area.

Preface

For nearly 45 years, I have had the privilege of working for two northern Virginia communities as well as serving in a consultative capacity for dozens of cities and counties across the United States and around the world. I have always been struck by the dramatic distinctions in the circumstances of these communities and yet the commonality of many of the principles that underlie both their economic growth, their economic development, and even their economic decline.

These communities are seemingly as different as can be imagined: from rural Caithness and Sutherland Counties in the northern-most reaches of Scotland to the rural small town of Kinston, North Carolina to the truly isolated communities of Yap in Micronesia and the island of Vieques, Puerto Rico, to the densely populated suburban areas of Snohomish County, Washington and Poznan, Poland.

I was invited to Caithness County as a Fulbright Senior Scholar because the nuclear power generating facility in Dounreay was being de-commissioned and the community had neither a plan to provide alternative employment for those not engaged in agricultural pursuits in the region nor a means of retaining the more than 1000 computer, engineering, and other technical workers who had been employed there. If that workforce were lost, the region would lose its primary asset for attracting new employers.

Kinston, North Carolina had suffered through two devastating floods that had destroyed farming in the region and had convinced local officials that other businesses should be attracted to, or grown in the area to provide a more diverse economy for its residents. They needed to pursue economic development that would remain constant over time, despite uncontrollable forces.

Snohomish County, Washington is north of Seattle and King County, situated in a beautiful area along the Puget Sound. Its economy was clearly overly dependent upon the Boeing Corporation and its suppliers. They also sought a more diversified economic base.

Vieques is an island that is part of Puerto Rico. It is a lovely location that had a growing business community on the western third of the island. On the eastern side of the island, there was a park and numerous natural wonders to enjoy that attracted visitors. However, in the center of the island sat Camp Garcia, the United States Navy's only live bombing range in the world. Navy pilots needed the area to practice their bombing runs, but the people of the island objected and President Clinton authorized the Viequensies to vote either to allow the Navy to stay or to be relocated. If the vote was to send the Navy elsewhere, the question became: How can we build an economy that will replace all that the Navy currently contributes to the local economy, both directly and indirectly?

Poznan, Poland had, only a few years before my visit, left the Soviet orbit and was in need of more than a new economy. They needed to understand business and strategic planning from the beginning. Strategic planning for the Poles had, until then, meant that they produced whatever their Soviet masters told them to produce, demand and supply notwithstanding. A team recruited by the United States Information Agency (USIA), the Polish Foundation in Support of Local Democracy, and the United Nations were sent to help the Polish government (and the government of Poznan, in my case), as well as the fledgling businesses understand the means of evolving from communism to democracy as well as from socialism to capitalism.

All of these situations were vastly distinct from the others. But, every one of them had some commonalities and some clear and consistent lessons. These experiences, coupled with my professional positions, led me to assemble my thoughts and begin to consider what was worth sharing. What of the many lessons I have learned along the way might be of value to others? How many other communities across the United States are confronting similar concerns? How many of those communities are worried about losing their employment base or have already lost a portion of it? Will they attempt to recover using the same strategies that have already been tried, and failed? Can a strategy that was successfully implemented in one city or county also bring success in another?

In writing previous books, and interviewing mayors and council chairs and business people and university presidents and other community stakeholders, one point that became immediately and thoroughly clear was that community leaders often get so bogged down in their immediate problems that they can lose sight of the fact that their peers in other locations are asking the same questions and worrying about the same types of events and similar obstacles to their economic development. When I discussed with them what their peers had discussed, they seemed to express a level of relief that they were not alone in facing these challenges. In short, I was aware that there was value in what I had learned in my work and my discussions with community leaders across the United States.

The first phase of sharing these concepts was in the classroom. This was a great experience—probably much less so for the students than for me because I taught in the graduate programs of several extremely diverse universities with students from around the world. As they shared with me their experiences in their own communities, my lessons were refined and sharpened. It was that focus that led me to a series of books, published by CRC Press, that related to how the economic bases of communities grow and contract. I started with some general notions and then applied those to a variety of settings: large cities and regions, micropolitan communities, and finally, to small, isolated towns. The underlying presumption was that communities of such divergent situations would lead to distinctly unique lessons and that those would not be clearly transferrable primarily to peer communities.

As I look back on the lessons learned in the research leading to those volumes, I now realize that I was wrong. Certainly, size and location yield unique considerations, but the degree of commonality of lessons learned, and recommendations for, all communities became increasingly clear. This book then purports to consider an overarching approach of economic growth and development as well as the regrowth of communities that have suffered economic setbacks. It is intended to be a resource for planners and community leaders and other stakeholders across the United States and around the world as they work to sustain or rebuild economic growth and to ensure a standard of living for their residents. This, I believe to be the core mission of communities and their elected and appointed leadership.

Introduction

Economic fortunes for individuals are ever-shifting. They can be won, they can be lost, and they can be regained. The same can be said for communities. Regardless of size, geographic location, or whether they are best classified as urban or suburban or rural, cities, counties, and regions have economies that continuously self-adjust to reflect the global, national, and local pressures that are brought to bear.

Over time, the economies of cities, counties, and regions experience growth, stasis, and decline. Most of these fluctuations are the result of larger economic forces and the resetting of local economies and industries to adjust to these impacts. As such, the impacts on the local employment and tax bases can be *comparatively* minor. Some of the pressures that affect local and regional economies can be seen as they approach in time; others are much stealthier in their approach and result in surprises for which the community may not be either well prepared or prepared at all. In some cases, communities simply did not believe the warning signals until it was much too late to respond effectively. In other situations, the community was so overwhelmed by the unanticipated losses that they were frozen, unable to respond at all and a long-standing sense of economic security was replaced by a feeling of hopelessness and a general course of inaction.

In many instances of imminent economic decline, cities and regions have been so planted in years—or even decades—of consistent growth and economic stability that the leadership was able to observe and understand the warning signals on the horizon but simply could not believe they really foretold the collapse of that stability. In Detroit, leaders saw foreign competition and cheaper labor rates yielding lower automobile prices for imports. They saw the increasing demand across the United States for smaller, more efficient automobiles but never really believed that the American public would shift their allegiance to foreign manufacturers. Surely, they believed, the smaller foreign cars could not substantially replace the traditional, large American luxury cars.

In the Seattle of the early 1970s—primarily a one-industry town built around the Boeing Corporation and aerospace—the winding down of the war in Southeast Asia prefaced a reduced demand for military aircraft. At the same time, the combination of double-digit inflation and double-digit unemployment destroyed the Phillips curve and its assertion that it would be mathematically impossible to have both occur at the same time. The result was that expendable incomes were down and commercial airliners were not purchasing aircraft either. The implications for Boeing and the City of Seattle, and, in fact, the entire Puget Sound region, was that the lack of diversification in the regional economy was about to become a serious problem. Yet, only slowly were efforts made to diversify the economic base away from aviation, Boeing, and its sub-contractors.

Readers should not get the impression that this refers only to the impacts on large cities such as Seattle, Pittsburgh, or Charlotte, in each of which predominant industries or employers brought down the entire region's economy as they declined. The same lessons apply to smaller towns. Longworth wrote in *The American Midwest* (2008) that Illinois had been the home to 35,000 jobs before Maytag moved jobs to Mexico and the city lost 7000 jobs in seven years. As the jobs were outsourced, it became clear that the process of moving jobs away—in this case, to Mexico—hurts the poorest and least well-educated among us. Many cities Longworth considered in the mid-west were simply "in denial" and many sizeable cities, including Gary, Indiana, Flint, Michigan, and East St. Louis, Illinois "died in the Rust Belt era and many never revive" (p. 30).

This absence of "vision" applies not only to large cities; small, rural towns, larger regions, and others can also be subject to these same inabilities to understand approaching economic forces sufficiently. But, for one moment, let's imagine a world in which community leaders are not only capable of envisioning these incidents but also of understanding their impacts. Would that help to avoid the negative consequences of regional economic decline? Well, it certainly would help; but, it isn't going to eliminate fully the effects of economic fluctuations. The truth is that some of those changes in the basic economy that influence various areas around the country simply cannot be controlled. In other words, even if local leaders see those forces coming at them, and even if they fully comprehend them, and even if they want to act quickly, they may still not be able to influence what is about to happen to them and their constituents.

The great problem here is that the impacts of such economic decline are not always understood, even after-the-fact. The focus of research and press coverage is often about the first wave of impacts. These include the loss of jobs, the loss of expendable income, and the eventual loss of labor force, the support economies, and even the community's overall quality of life. While those are all very real effects of regional or local economic decline, they do not tell the entire story. The aftershocks include the loss of community pride and spirit, the loss of the very assets required to rebuild, and the inability to find alternative employers and industries to replace the old ones. The tax bases from which local public services are provided decline and the community takes on a different feel. Services decline at the very time when the demand is increasing from the jobless and the underemployed. Yet, it is also a time when the resources necessary to respond to the renewed demand have been dramatically reduced. Community institutions and the loss of renown as a good place to live, work, or visit round out this rather unattractive picture in cities, counties, and regions.

For these are cities that have lost their sole or the primary employer or industry and have been unable to attract replacement jobs, the obvious consequences are the loss of jobs, security, wealth, and tax base. But there are many other devastating consequences that often get overlooked by students of municipal economic growth and development.

When the sole or primary employer leaves town, those who were employed and have lost their jobs will seek opportunities elsewhere. The ones who are most able to find alternatives in other locations are the most employable. When they leave, often the highest-skilled adults have some of the community's best students, and they leave with them. The resultant "brain drain" means that the city no longer has the primary asset needed to attract employers to replace the jobs that have been lost.

Second, when the best and brightest are lost, the remaining populace are those who are less employable and who are now unemployed or, at best, underemployed. This means that the community has a diminished tax base from which to pay public services to a constituency that is increasing its demand for services and transfer payments. This "double whammy" places pressures not only on families but also on communities.

The initial wave results in people taking part-time jobs or positions with far less pay than they had been accustomed to and for which they are qualified. Reductions in expendable income mean that higher-priced items are the first to go. This is immediately reflected in home sales, automobile purchases, and more. All of that trickles down to the next level of purchasing, and so on. And, when employers leave town, restaurants, retailers, and others also suffer.

For communities in the initial stages of decline, the ideal solution is to attract one or more new companies to re-employ the workforce and jump-start the economy. However, just at the very time that the need for business attraction is at its most critical, outside businesses will see a community in distress. The advantages it will be able to offer are an available labor pool and vacant facilities.

But, prospective employers will also see a downtown with vacant store-fronts and public services that have been reduced or eliminated due to declining tax revenues. They may see classrooms that are over-crowded and they may see increasing crime rates. In some cases, they would have seen a school building that has been boarded up while children are bussed to another community or neighborhood. These business prospects may see a local post office that is no longer in service or a hospital that is closed while individuals in need have to travel long distances for medical treatment or a bank that has closed due to lack of customers or loan applicants. Those prospects whose business is in retail will observe the lack of the purchasing power their store requires to be profitable. In short, at the very time that a new employer coming to town would be more important than ever, the community will be at its least likely position to attract one.

Such communities may be in a downward spiral from which they cannot extricate themselves. As people and families move away in order to find new employment elsewhere, the community loses its best and brightest—those most likely to find alternative employment. This results in a loss of tax base and the inevitable decline in the quantity and quality of public services. The result of such declining elements of the basic quality of life is that more people move away when they can, and the cycle restarts.

The community remains because there are many people who, for a variety of reasons, cannot or will not move away. They remain in place and their collective demand for assistance increases. More food stamps, more welfare, and other forms of public support become evident, but the tax base from which these services would come is depleted. Greater demands from a lower-level work force and families in greater need tend to create an inhospitable environment for new employers. The cycle repeats itself.

In many communities experiencing hard times, neighbors, churches, and non-profits step in to help offset some of the needs that the city cannot cover. However, when the sole or primary employer leaves town, those organizations are stretched beyond their capacities to serve. This is especially true in locations where the non-profit organizations and churches that would normally be involved are experiencing revenue shortfalls because their support was funded by the individuals and companies that have departed. The same decline in support is felt by local scouting groups and little leagues that also depended on the generosity of the local employer/sponsor that is no longer in town.

One unseen loss is the inability of families to send their children to college which, in turn, diminishes the value of the local labor force asset. Worse, it can also cement the loss of community-wide and individual self-esteem. Ultimately, communities can even lose the very important institutions that make it a community: the local school, the local press, local health care, and more. We will consider several examples of this in subsequent chapters.

At this point in the history of such a downward spiral, the city faces a revenue crisis. In some states, municipalities constitute their local General Fund appropriations primarily on the basis of income tax generation. The decline in those revenues mirrors the decline in public services. In states where municipalities are more dependent upon the real estate tax base for General Fund expenditures, the loss of primary employers yields vacant buildings and lower overall assessments for real property which translates into declining revenues.

Ironically, the very efforts of those who remain in such communities to make ends meet for their families can help to paint an inaccurate picture of the depths of the needs. This is because many federal support programs distribute funding on formula bases that include the local unemployment rate. On the surface, this may seem to make sense but the consequences often force second wage-earners to accept jobs and others to accept jobs either with lower pay or fewer hours. These are the "underemployed," who are not often counted in the unemployment rates that trigger public support programs at both the federal and state levels. The underemployed, however, constitute a loss for a community. They may often be hidden from the view of business site location executives who review the data about available workforce, thereby diminishing a potential and very valuable economic development asset. They often have to take more than one position to make what they once made in their prior single job. The underemployed are often in part-time occupations rather than being full contributors to the production levels of the local economy. In short, they are underutilized, overworked, and under-contributors.

Several theories have been offered in the existing literature to provide a construct for how and why city and regional economies either grow or decline. These theoretical structures are valuable to students of city planning, public administration, and economics because they establish the logic behind was has happened in America's regions, cities, and towns.

Further, much has been written about *individual* communities across the United States and how they have either developed or revitalized their local economies over time. The focus in such volumes has typically been on the specific causes of economic decline and what strategies have been successful for those individual cities, counties, and regions around the country. When considered in the aggregate, that research may constitute a broader understanding of what communities facing similar challenges today may, or may not, find to be effective responses to similar challenges.

To gain a thorough understanding of how best to react to local economic decline, present and future community leaders must first understand clearly the causes of the reversals in their economic fortunes. Further, one must understand the means by which communities' best potential assets for growth can be identified and exploited to the greatest potential.

The analyses of cities and their economic histories, within the context of the theoretical foundations available are at the heart of this research. They will be supported by examples from a variety of US communities of varying sizes and circumstances to buttress the awareness of students and practitioners to the inherent conclusions. These case studies were the bases for my previous four books with CRC Press and number over two hundred communities that represent locations across the United States. They include regions, large cities, micropolitan communities, and small, isolated towns.

While all communities are unique, what distinguishes this book is that it presents a comprehensive look at what all communities—large and small, urban and rural—have learned; and, what they must and can do to grow and sustain their local economic bases. It will examine the causes of economic decline for localities as well as the economic "product" being marketed to employers, the process of growth, and the means of sustaining economic growth over time. In short, it will present real-life situations and their successes and failures which can bring the theoretical literature to life.

The objective of this book is to outline a comprehensive approach to understanding what happens as communities grow or contract, how best to turn these negative situations around, and how best to sustain strong economic growth over time. Drawing on the experiences of hundreds of communities and hundreds of leaders around the United States, this book also outlines the various strategies that have or have not worked to enable or support a general local economic recovery.

As a comprehensive approach, the intention is to address all of the many conditions for community growth and decline, whether they are urban or rural, large or mid-sized cities and regions, or small, isolated towns. Many of the conclusions that will be addressed will apply to communities across-the-board; others may be particularly relevant to specific settings. In the end, cities and regions across America—and their leadership—should find the basic tenets that can help guide their future planning for economic development.

There are many indicators that the national and global economies are, at present, on the rebound and that is good news for the nation and the world. For some localities across the United States, such positive trends are resulting in new jobs, growing wealth, and enhanced public services.

Not all cities, however, have been created as equals. Since 2010, ten US municipalities have declared bankruptcy. Lower-cost communities and business-friendly policies are enticements to businesses making location decisions. Bankruptcy does not mean that the obligations of the municipality will be forgiven. It only means that outside counselors will be making the decisions about how the local budget—and services—can be reduced and debts resolved. Yet, municipalities are declaring bankruptcy more frequently than ever before, always as a result of an inadequate business community to help offset the cost of public services for residents and always because the lack of local employment opportunities translates into reduced commercial and residential property values and a reduced tax base.

The variations from one municipality or one region to the next are often stark and the nation runs the risk of the "have" localities distancing themselves even further from the "have-nots" or, at least, the have-less communities. Even within a given area or region, these distinctions can become clear. This has led local leaders to pursue a variety of tactics quite often aimed at resolving the immediate demands of their constituencies: jobs opportunities, public services, and more.

The need to address the immediate needs of one's residents is an essential focus for municipal leaders. However, even as they address the short-term needs of their communities, they must retain a focus on the longer-term solutions required to sustain economic growth into the future and to set the stage for the continued enhancement of the quality of life in their communities.

This means that elected officials need to retain a focus on the future of their communities beyond their individual terms of office. I have recently completed the last of four books on the topic of how regions and cities of all sizes and environments grow or regrow their economies (2009, 2011, 2013, 2015, CRC Press, New York). I have interviewed hundreds of mayors and elected board chairs, as well as appointed officials, newspaper reporters, local college presidents, economic development professionals, business people, and other local stakeholder leaders in cities and towns across America. The result has been a series of "lessons learned" by those who actually lived through the processes of growth, perhaps decline, and even regrowth. These lessons yield potential strategies and tactics for other municipal leaders in similar situations across the country to consider.

There were three types of interview outcomes. The first and most prominent group expressed new ideas, community-wide collaboration and planning, and great expressions of hope for the future. They were working toward a new economy or a strengthening of the existing business base. They saw the value of—or, at least, the need for—a growing commercial sector to help offset the cost of residential public services, and the community was largely behind the vision and the strategy.

A second grouping reflected uncertainty in terms of whether the city or town in question would be able to recover fully. This group is the ideal target for the lessons learned from the first group. There was lingering doubt about the potential to rebuild the area's economic base. Perhaps they had reacted too late and too slowly, or perhaps there was not sufficient local support for the approach. Perhaps they had simply lost the work force or other key assets that were needed to rebuild. In some cases, the loss of the traded natural resource or global competition or the success from more competitive regions of the country were at the basis of the decline and the comeback was not likely to occur without dramatic restructuring of the local economy.

The third grouping—albeit considerably smaller than the others—is the subject for this essay. These are leaders in cities and towns in which either the leadership or the citizenry or both have given up. They either feel that their cities cannot or will not recover, or that they will only recover to an unacceptable degree and thereby never become what they once were. This often occurred after a length of time during which there was no growth and the community, as one, simply quit trying. These are cities that have generally lost their sole or primary employer or industry and have been unable to attract replacement employers. The obvious consequences are the loss of jobs, security, wealth, and tax base. But there are four other devastating consequences that often get overlooked.

When the sole or primary employer leaves town, those who were employed and have lost their jobs will seek opportunities elsewhere. The ones who are most able to find alternatives in other locations are the most employable. When they leave and perhaps the best local students leave with them, the resultant "brain drain" means that the city no longer has the primary asset needed to attract other employers.

Second, when the best and brightest are lost, the remaining populace are those who are less employable and who are now either unemployed or underemployed. This means that the community has a diminished tax base from which to pay public services to a constituency that is increasing its demand for such services, transfer payments, and more. This "double whammy" places pressures not only on families but also on communities. And, of course, when employers leave town, restaurateurs, retailers, and others also suffer.

In many communities experiencing hard times, neighbors, churches, and non-profits step in to help offset some of the needs that the city cannot provide. However, when the sole or primary employer leaves town, those organizations are stretched beyond their capacities to serve. This is especially true in locations where the non-profit organizations and churches that would normally be involved are also experiencing revenue shortfalls because their programs were funded by the individuals and companies that have departed. The same decline in support is felt by local scouting groups and little leagues that also depended on the generosity and sponsorship of the local employer who is no longer in town.

Ironically, the very efforts of those who remain in such communities to make ends meet for their families can help to paint an inaccurate picture of the depths of the needs. This is because many federal support programs distribute funding on formula bases that include the local unemployment rate. On the surface, this may seem to make sense but the consequences often force second wage-earners to accept jobs and others to accept jobs either with lower pay or fewer hours. These are the "underemployed," who are not often counted in the unemployment rates that trigger public support programs.

Communities face the travails of creating and sustaining economic growth forever. The task is never fully completed and the potential for losing employers and jobs is ever-present. Indeed, the economic development practice of marketing does, at least in part, mean that a community may gain an employer or a facility, while another loses it. Communities must be ever-vigilant to grow and retain the momentum in their economic base. As a consequence, many lessons have been learned that can assist other communities where there are similar situations and challenges. Those lessons can be most instructive to others: even the greatest challenges can be overcome. Economies can be rebuilt or replaced; it requires vision, creativity, and community-wide determination. The fact that seemingly intractable situations have indeed been reversed should serve as encouragement to communities and officials that they can do it too. But, the efforts need not start from scratch; there are lessons that can be learned from those who have been through all of it before!

References

Gordon, Gerald L. *The Economic Survivability of America's Isolated Small Towns.* New York: CRC Press, 2015.
Gordon, Gerald L. *The Economic Viability of Micropolitan America.* New York: CRC Press, 2013.
Gordon, Gerald L. *The Formula for Economic Growth on Main Street America.* New York: CRC Press, 2009.
Gordon, Gerald L. *The Reinvention of Local and Regional Economies.* New York, CRC Press, 2011.

Part I
An Examination of Existing Theories of Community Economic Growth and Decline

The causes of economic growth and decline have intrigued political scientists and economists for centuries. The pursuit has been directed at a structural model that could explain what happens and why, with the expectation that, once those causes could be identified, they could also either be controlled or used to guide community responses.

Consultation with dictionaries yields definitions of "theory" that employ such terms as hypotheses, abstract, and uncertainty. One very clear definition is drawn from the online Merriam-Webster: "an ideal or hypothetical set of facts, principles, or circumstances." The point is that theories, even by their very definition point to the ideal. Theories enable thinkers, planners, and leaders to analyze what is happening within a model that shapes their thinking for them.

To what extent do theories actually apply to a real situation in which municipal leaders struggle to find solutions to very un-hypothetical factors impacting very real people and their very real livelihoods and their real families? Can theories of economic growth actually help to forecast what will come next in the life of a community or its economy or its residents? If one acknowledges that such cannot be the case—certainly for every municipal application across the country—what value can be placed by mayors, chairs, and appointed leaders on theoretical guidance?

It is, of course, unfair—and unwise—to dismiss such models and the centuries of thought behind them, simply because they don't neatly fit onto today's problems in hundreds of cities and regions across this nation. In truth, such theoretical models do offer valuable insights into how larger forces are impacting communities—large and small, urban and rural, dense and isolated. In short, theoretical models do provide the basis for a basic understanding of what has happened to local economies, why, and what actions to take to initiate or sustain growth or to reverse the economic misfortunes of communities.

This section will provide a very brief summary of relevant economic theories. Many volumes go deeply into these models and can provide the quantitative constructs that have been developed for these theories. Other volumes represent attempts to provide single theories incorporating the elements of many others in an effort to unify those approaches. One excellent such work comes from Aghion and Howitt (*Endogenous Growth Theory*,

1999). There is no need to replicate such works; what is needed is to extract the best of the lessons from the many theories that have been offered over time.

These theories of economic growth purport to represent the reasons for growth and decline and the insights into why such trends occur and how they can be foreseen, or even avoided. One must certainly wonder, however, how a single construct can forecast for, and provide counsel to, economists working to grow and sustain the economies of Cleveland and the Washington, DC metropolitan area; or even Detroit and Lynchburg, Virginia. Every city, town, or region exists in a vastly different set of circumstances with vastly different cultures and leadership, and facing both similar and dissimilar challenges against the backdrop of different times.

What is the conclusion to be drawn from this statement? Are we to believe that theories of economic growth and decline are not constructs for students and practitioners to review? Of course not; the message is that one single theory that is universally applicable to all settings at all times is unrealistic and misleading. Even those who have presented new theoretical models do so for one reason: either the existing models don't suit all situations or they believe that those constructs are flawed in some way (or ways).

One volume that is widely held in high regard is that of Shaffer, Deller and Macouiller (2004). They maintain that growth theory considers which forces are behind economic growth and what measures can best lead to sustainable growth. But, they also offer that, "While economic theory can provide insights into these questions, often more questions are raised than are answered. Ideas and concepts that were accepted as 'truth' thirty years ago are now questioned."[1]

Most importantly, much of the theory that has been available for study over the years makes presumptions that, if not accurate, throw the entire construct into a tailspin. Communities, especially smaller communities do not always have either perfect knowledge or the means of interpreting data or the inherent trends. Perhaps one of the greatest criticisms of several of the available growth theories is that they assume that, once community leaders understand the implications of data and trends, they have the power to govern accordingly. This is absolutely untrue, as we will review in this volume. Many of the trends that are impacting local economic growth and decline—even those of major cities and regions across the United States—are completely out of the control of local elected officials. The economic forces impacting communities today—large and small—are increasingly finding their origins in the relationships between nations, the labor rate advantages of other countries, and the rapidly increasing growth of technology.

All of these questions about the existing growth theories will be examined. None of those theories will be judged to be universally applicable to all situations. Nonetheless, students and practitioners must continue to review and comprehend these theoretical structures because they do provide insight into what happens and why. They are, quite simply, models into which real people and real communities and real events can be better understood.

Shaffer et al. note that the literature of growth can be broken into two approaches: "deductive, which focuses heavily on theoretical modelling and attempts to establish paradigms that explain how the economy grows; and inductive, which tends to focus on empirical observation to gain insights to help explain the growth process."[2]

This volume is about one part deductive and nine parts inductive. The great value will be to see where those lines cross, and to what purpose.

From this review, it will be possible for the reader to gain a sufficient appreciation for the theories of economic growth as they apply to communities across the United States. With that as preface, an examination of America's small, medium, and large city experiences can be better understood. That examination will follow in this volume, with the ultimate intent of offering several additional foundations to be considered when analyzing community economic growth and decline.

Notes

1   Ron Schaffer, Steve Deller, and Dave Marcouiller. *Community Economics: Linking Theory and Practice.* (Ames, IA: Blackwell, 2008): 29.
2   Ibid., 30.

1 Competing Theories of Community Economic Growth and Decline

Numerous theoretical foundations have been offered for why growth occurs in one area and not others. Over time, with the ever-changing environment for commerce and trade, theories not only proliferated but contradicted each other. This should not be surprising: technology and capital inputs alone have been in a constant state of change, and these are now considered to be the primary ingredients for sustainable economic growth and economic development, a distinction that will be discussed in the coming pages.

Initially, theoretical constructs for forecasting economic success and/or economic decline were fairly basic. The first economic growth theory of renown was that of Thomas Malthus, who noted that population growth occurred in locations where people had expendable resources for non-essential items. At the other extreme, Malthus maintained that population growth would be controlled by poverty, disease, famine, and warfare. Over time, most of the early economic growth theories presumed the most vital factor of growth to be transportation and cost minimization. By locating near rivers or other means of getting products to market, production could more readily lead to sales.

If one could not move their product from the point of manufacture, the enterprise could not be successful. That is why so many firms located near rivers, thus creating jobs that, in turn, generated population growth and the expenditures of incomes that led to the creation of support services and personal services and general community growth.

To locate bases of operations further away from transportation routes only added to the costs of moving products to the point from which they could be moved downstream. This was the first consideration of theories that place cost minimization at the heart of the location decisions of that time. In addition to the costs of transporting products from the point of production, there were the costs of moving the raw material inputs of the manufacturing process to the company's location. Other costs were also a consideration, depending upon the type of good being produced, including the costs of labor in cities versus more rural areas.

Regardless of the type of costs involved in the overall process, they were the prime consideration for location decisions. It was really quite simple: businesses locate in ways that enabled greater profits with the least costs. Bingham and Mier summarized this conclusion as follows: "Location theory evolved from the simple transportation cost minimization models . . . In general, studies prior to 1960 indicated that basic cost factors were the dominant determinants of industrial location patterns." The most significant factors included transportation, access to markets, access to material inputs, and the availability and costs of labor. "The list of locational factors has been lengthened ... technical competence of the labor force, state and local taxes, regional business climate, quality of life factors, and other regional differences have been found to exert influence on business location decisions."[1]

The environment for businesses and the process of site-location decision-making has, of course, become much more intricate and complex over time, and so has the practice of attracting businesses to specific communities. With that, the theories that purport to explain such decisions have also gained in complexity.

Many factors have gained or declined in relevance for location decision-making. Transportation alone has seen significant changes: rivers are no longer the only—and frequently not the best—means of bringing materials to the point of production or for moving the final product to market. Highway travel and air cargo can provide substantially greater alternatives to manufacturers. For those manufacturers who allowed the waste from the manufacturing processes to leak into the navigable waterways to which they were proximate, social movements and legal changes have nullified that particular advantage for some of their riverside locations. Air transport has also changed the nature of global competitiveness as will be discussed later.

Central place theory extends the transportation cost minimization approach by considering the ranges that the transportation modes reach. That is to say that consumers of goods and services will travel up to the distance of a given range for certain types of products or services. In this theoretical approach, sellers require a certain density to be successful in promoting sales. With less density, only certain types of sellers will be able to survive. As the density of the areas increases, there are more people likely to buy certain types of products. The further that density spreads from the core, the greater the number and variety of products that can be sold because there will be sufficient demand.

There are further considerations that amend central place theory, most notably the demographics and economic tastes of the population. For example, Coca Cola adjusts the sweetness of its products depending on an area's demographics. Density is not the issue in that case. Starbucks knows precisely the economic characteristics of the area that would support their stores. Again, density—at least not density alone—is not the sole issue they will consider in making location decisions for stores.

More modern theories of economic growth and location suggest that the two primary inputs for economic growth are advances in technology and the availability of capital for research and growth. As those factors become increasingly available in a community, such theories maintain, a corporate base will grow. While that may be generally true, it leads to the conclusion that such a theoretical approach does not apply to every situation and every company in every location.

Before looking at the most useful bits of each theory that has been offered, a review of the various theoretical constructs that have been offered over time has significant merit. This can provide an overall understanding of why companies are making location decisions today, some of which are surprising to many of those in the field. For example, in 2014 Cadillac was split off from General Motors and moved its corporate headquarters from Detroit to New York City. The announcement surprised a great many people because it did not fit neatly into the previous experiential construct.

Cadillac's move was designed to create a greater image for the automobile manufacturer. In that sense, they felt that Detroit was not the location they needed. New York—more specifically, the very trendy SoHo area on the lower east side of Manhattan—gives the company the potential to create for itself a much different image than it has possessed in the past. There is absolutely no theoretical model that could possibly have predicted such a decision.

The current locational theories purport to forecast the types of locations that companies will select, and why. They emphasize the availability of capital and the advances being made in technology. Clearly, those are two primary factors, although they do not represent everything needed by companies today. Of course, companies will require the necessary types of, and availability of, labor pools; while theorists argue that the labor force needed will come to where the companies are being most successful but that causes a chicken-and-egg situation. Will employees select a location from which they attract the necessary workforce, or will they only consider locations where the workforce presently exists? Capital is another difficult factor to pin down: capitalists often expect the companies in which they invest to relocate to a place close to them so they can stay easily involved. Theories cannot account for the specific capital source; they can only surmise that capital is an important input and that it will help dictate where a company will look.

Another, more recent practice that is a contrary factor to location theories is location incentives. This is a practice whereby localities or states offer a company cash grants, buildings, land leases, tax abatements or other financial arrangements in exchange for location decisions, investments, and job creation. Clearly, location theories can assert that such programs can help attract or retain a business, but they cannot specify which location will win an incentives bidding war between many communities competing for a given site location decision.

In short, theories can only go so far in predicting location decisions. They can only highlight the necessary factors needed by communities to become or remain competitive with other locations seeking the same business decision. Other, less quantifiable factors are also important in site-location decisions, including the presence of unions, the quality of life (which has a different meaning for every decision-maker), and more. All of these variations should be kept in mind when reviewing the advantages and usefulness of the various theories of economic growth. Herrick and Kindleberger state that "The theory conceived and delivered in the ivory tower frequently gasps and expires in the chill of the real world."[2]

As noted above, many locational models asserted that companies located and, by extension, economies grew, where there was a disruption in transportation grids. This explains many of the older business locations, such as Chicago, St. Louis, New Orleans, and more. At some point in time, this model grew to include midpoints in highway transport. That resulted in the growth of numerous markets in the central part of the United States. Today, shipping can go by air and sea ports to distant markets and that has generated growth around port cities on the east coast and airports around the borders of the United States from which external markets can be reached most efficiently.

Regional theorists offered explanations for how regional markets grew. They maintain that firms either produced for local consumption or for the exportation of their goods to outside markets. Further, the assertion is made that the latter is critical for a variety of reasons: first, the exportation of product yields an importation to the community of capital and that capital generates incomes, expenditures, and the growth of secondary markets such as retail and personal and business services. This may be considered to be particularly vital in a small town setting where the influx of even small amounts of capital are spent and re-spent throughout the community, supporting the development and growth of expendable incomes and commerce in general.

Engel's Law states that, as incomes increase, people will become increasingly likely to spend a greater proportion of their incomes on non-essential goods and services. This, in turn, creates growing demand for greater production, leading to increases in productivity, and efficiency, and even the overall quality of life in the community. However, in order to attract businesses, a community must possess (or obtain) those supports that firms in a given industry need in order to succeed. It must build highways, rail and air connections, port facilities, warehouses, office space, and more. Kumar concurs that the political, social, cultural, and economic environment must be favorable if significant growth is to happen.

> There must be a banking and credit system capable of financing growth. There must be a legal system that establishes the ground rules of business behavior. There must be a tax system that does not discourage new investment and risk-taking ... a government that is sympathetic to economic expansion.[3]

To ensure that all of these things are in place, communities must be willing to spend their resources on these components rather than others. This also means that the area must be able to attract capital.

It is important at this juncture to note that the impact of an influx of capital, technology, and employment to a community has the exact same force when it leaves a community. Upon its arrival, earnings are spent and re-circulated throughout the community—again, most notably in smaller communities. The cycle includes the development of a commercial sector and the growth of incomes that lead to greater taxes, enhanced public services, improved educational opportunities due to specific corporate skills requirements, and a generally improved quality of life. When jobs and capital depart from a community, the reverse occurs: the diminishment of public services and the overall quality of life in the community. This will be discussed at greater length in a later chapter under the heading of secondary and tertiary effects of local economic growth and decline.

As a final impact, the loss of businesses leads not only to the decline of public services and the general quality of life, it also means that the community loses some of the appeal it will need in order to attract replacement employers and jobs. For this reason, it is critical that communities react quickly to the loss of employers and develop the outreach efforts to market the community as will be discussed further in a later chapter.

As relates to the impacts of companies on the economic growth of communities, two theoretical approaches are of note. Economic Base Theory concentrates specifically on issues related to the demand side of municipal economies and planning for their further development. This relates to the essential business functions that support the existing community and by attracting cash flow to the community, thus generating retail demand, cash circulation, and local tax generation as described above. It may include manufacturers or agricultural pursuits that sell to distant markets, but may also include businesses that attract people from outside of the region, such as hospitals, theme parks, colleges and universities, or natural attractions, large events, shopping, and more.

One criticism of this point of view is that these are all industries that are subject to economic, social, and political forces that are entirely out of the control of the local leadership. For example, a global recession will negatively impact leisure travel, the internet damages travel to outlet malls, and weather will influence the attendance at events and parks. Such businesses are also referred to in the literature as "basic" industries. Their counterparts—the so-called "non-basic" industries—react to local demand for products and services. This grouping will include retailers, personal services, and local government employees.

Clearly, the growth of the basic sector, which generates demand for everything from school teachers and firefighters to barbers and cooks, is entirely dependent on the local demand that is generated by the basic industries. As those businesses grow, there is an increasing demand for the non-basic businesses in the community. It absolutely must be kept in mind, however, that the reverse is also true. When primary employers are lost to a community, so are the secondary and tertiary employers. So too is the tax base that provides the funds for the school teachers and firefighters mentioned above. This makes the Economic Base an incomplete explanation either for community growth or decline.

It is critical to recognize however that, when firms are in their decline phase, there is sometimes a tendency for individuals who were formerly in their workforce to remain in the community and take the opportunity to create new enterprises. This is much more likely to occur where greater population densities are found because the size of the population may imply a greater demand for the services or goods being produced than one would find in a smaller community. Additionally, new enterprises might be able to take advantage of the remaining workers and abandoned plants. One challenge is for the new start-ups to be enterprises that require the same general skill sets that are already present and available in the community.

This theory further suggests that businesses in a given community will develop in that location because there is an alignment of comparative advantages between the company and the community. Companies will produce in a given field because "they can specialize in the activities which it can produce more efficiently than in other regions."[4]

The lesson suggested by Economic Base Theory is that communities with an interest in attracting or growing businesses in a given line of work must provide them with the assets and amenities they require to be successful. This may include opportunities for local, relevant skills training for industry-specific skills; or, it may imply that the communities need to develop office parks or industrial parks that prepare land and buildings for the identified industry segment.

Proponents of the Economic Base Theory maintain that a community must have land and/or facilities in place in order to attract companies and indeed many communities have done so by preparing industrial parks and shell buildings to appeal to employers for positive location decisions. This is a clear chicken-and-egg conundrum. Regarding this as an investment, many communities have invested in the development of such business parks and some have successfully lured employers to them. On the other hand, many of these business parks have been lying largely vacant for many years with little or no return on the municipality's investment.

Such large-scale investments on the part of anxious communities must be made with extremely careful consideration. "Build it and they will come" strategies often work better in the movies and can sometimes backfire in real life economic development. The Economic Base Theorist might argue that, although painful, such investments are the only way to attract or grow businesses. The counter to this theory is not simply that there is insufficient return on the investment. Moreover, there is always concern about how that investment could have otherwise benefitted the community had it not been spent on a vacant business park: better schools, safer neighborhoods, and lower taxes are often offered as part of the counter-argument, and the extension of that reply is that better schools, safe neighborhoods, and lower taxes are better ways to attract businesses to a community than available space for businesses to occupy.

Much of the supply-side theories can be classified as Neoclassical Theory. This approach suggests that communities require certain characteristics in order to attract, build, and sustain a vibrant economic base, among which are understood to be the availability of capital that is comfortable with investments in the industries in question, a constant influx of technology and the educational and business components that support it, and appropriate workforce for the selected industries. As already noted, however, the conundrum posed by this assertion is whether businesses want to locate where those factors already exist, or whether one needs a critical mass of those businesses to attract such inputs.

Another concern with Neoclassical Theory is offered by Product Cycle theorists who point out that change in technology is a constant. As such, a community produces a certain product only to have the advance of newer technology render that item obsolete. Thus, communities must constantly seek not the improvement of the invention, but the next generation of technology in that area, or the next iteration of other technological advance. For example, Romer's "central contribution is the construction of a model that highlights how concepts and ideas can drive economic growth." Human beings, Romer says, possess

> a nearly infinite capacity to reconfigure physical objects by creating new recipes for their use . . . new technologies like biotech . . . demolish the specter of diminishing returns, which led Ricardo and Keynes to suppose that growth had limits . . . new technologies create increasing returns, because new knowledge, which begets new products, is generated through research.[5]

Thus, human ideation is seen not only to be never-ending, but to have the ability to generate an infinite supply of technologically minded workers and researchers as well as a constant flow of the investment dollars that help to spawn new ideas and new companies that will ultimately also tend toward obsolescence. Clearly, and in a general sense, urban areas, which tend to have greater densities of the required inputs, will find greater success in attracting such businesses and in sustaining local economic development.

Shaffer et al. maintain that economic growth "really hinges on technological innovation. When one looks historically at how the economy makes major strides forward, it is based on radical new innovation. The neoclassical model cannot handle (i.e., predict) advances in technology or innovation." Barro and Sala-i-Martin concur: "Although some discoveries are serendipitous, most technological improvements reflect purposeful activity, such as research and development (R & D) carried out in universities and corporate or government laboratories."[6] Thus, neither the time, place, certainty, or success of research, nor the influx of technology into a given community, can be modeled. As growth theory itself evolved to require greater empirical evidence, many of these models proved to be less and less predictive.

A further objection relates to seeing the input of technology as having an impact upon an economy that is independent of other factors. The insertion of technological advances may indeed spur overall economic growth, but it may also eliminate a wide range of employment functions through replacement of human workers by machines or process improvements.

Furthermore, the relative amount of inputs can have relatively differing levels of impact. Cortright notes, for example:

> If we assume that knowledge creation is central to growth ... small events at key times can reshape the direction of economic growth and the geographic pattern of economic activity. In this view, economic growth is deterministic, but is chaotic, unpredictable, and shaped by the choices made by economic actors.[7]

This suggests that communities may be able to determine the course of their futures by attracting or creating small and manageable—but constant—increments of technology and innovation, but that the degree of change thus created cannot be assumed or confidently forecasted. "Inventions may allow producers to generate the same amount of output with either relatively less capital or relatively less labor input."[8]

The assumed ability to grow new technologies with relatively less capital flies in the face of such classical theorists as David Ricardo and Adam Smith who believed that growth came largely from capital accumulation. The ratio of capital to the other factors of production was, for them, a constant. The Harrod-Domar Model furthers that position by asserting that, while labor can be inserted into a system, it must be done at a constant ratio to the capital that already exists within that system.

Robert Solow did not agree with the classical theorists' position that the ratio of capital to the other factors of production must remain in a given balance. Rather, Solow believed that, if labor grew faster than the available capital, the costs of wages would simply decline. And, if the growth of capital outpaced that of labor, the resultant seller's market would result in higher wages generally. However, this does not consider, as many economic growth theories did not consider until recently, that the imbalance of the factors of production may simply result in firms relocating to areas where the proper balance and availability of those factors can be found. Further, as Herrick and Kindleberger point out, "Modern neo-classicists focus mainly on the difficult allocation of a given set of resources and, largely ignore social and political factors."[9]

Neoclassicists assume that all factor sets and all reactions are consistent and do not react to the essential differences in factors "among the various sectors of the economy on the basis of any natural differences among them."[10] But, factors, industries, and locations all do have distinctions. The uncertainty of the factor effects is matched by the question of the mobility of the production factors. Factor Price Equalization Theory is based on the assumption that capital and labor are mobile and will relocate to find their greatest returns. More recent experience shows, however, that most capital tends to be invested in companies in close proximity to the source of funding. If capital finds a more distant investment, it is much more likely that the business will become mobile—and move closer to the source of investment—than it is that the capital would be mobile. It is also note-worthy that, while goods can be transported, services are more difficult to transport. Aghion and Durlauf further point out that services can also be much more "vulnerable to various governmental barriers to trade, such as professional licensing requirements . . . domestic content requirements in public procurement or poor protection of intellectual property rights."[11]

Certainly these factors are as, or more, related to global than domestic trade; many American communities that exist on the borders or coasts do conduct a great deal of trade outside of the country. Where those border communities have service economies, their factor mobility has additional layers of consideration. Aghion and Durlauf quite correctly note that advances in technology and software standardization alleviate the need to move some of the factors of production, such as capital and technology, in favor of combining them, while they remain in separate locations, into a single production process.[12]

Workforce can be viewed from both perspectives. On the one hand, individuals will move to locations where their skills sets are in demand. On the other hand, communities can use the asset of a relevant workforce as an inducement for companies to relocate to that community.

One supply-oriented theory relative to the labor input is known as the Human Capital Theory, which points out that increased productivity enhances labor market competitive-ness. What is of even greater importance is that technology can override the productivity value of the labor force if it has the ability to replace workers by performing the same functions more efficiently. Further, as pointed out by Shaffer et al., technology change can increase productivity output by shifting resources from lower to higher productivity applications.

> Community growth and decline are largely due to differential growth rates based on the particular composition of industries the community hosts and the competitiveness of those industries in relation to those of other regions. Both of these considerations are greatly influenced by the prevailing utilization rate and the rate of change.[13]

Another approach to a theory of internal factors that govern growth is the Marshall-Arrow-Romer Model which purports that a concentration of like industries in a given location creates "spillovers" and that, when those "externalities are internalized, innovation and growth speed up." Jacobs argued in the late sixties, however, that it is the knowledge transfers between diverse industries that result in innovation and growth rather than the clustering of similar industry segments. Jacobs argued that diversification was key to growth whereas both the Marshall-Arrow-Romer Model and Porter's theories of cluster-ing posited that growth would come as the result of the same industries co-locating and sharing common advances and workforce.[14]

The two sets of theories also differ in another sense. The Marshal-Arrow-Romer Model maintains that the sharing of one firm's innovations causes them to reduce research and development because it will likely be stolen by others in the community. This serves to slow local economic development. Porter, however, asserts that those technological advances are then improved upon, thereby creating new discoveries and new growth. "Porter would argue that local competition is good because it fosters imitation and innovation."[15]

Many internal (to communities) factors can alter the future of economic growth, including individual attitudes and cultures, the social environment, traditional beliefs, racial and ethnic diversity, and rural and urban distinctions. The external forces affecting community growth and development can be even more impactful. Exogenous theories generally point out that many of the factors that influence local economic development are outside of the control of the local authorities. Their references largely relate to national and global forces impacting local economies, such as business cycles, exchange rates, and the comparative costs of labor. The sequester enacted by Congress in 2011 is an unusual but certainly impactful event that could not be controlled in any way by state or local leadership. For communities with higher than average federal expenditures in their economic bases, sequestration was one such uncontrollable event.

The neoclassical model leads communities to gather in place the assets that firms expect in their locations of choice. Some regions, for example, have had success in building clusters of related firms and support services as a means of attracting industries for which those assets are critical to success. This clustering effect is the basis for Agglomeration Theory. Some of the business clusters that can be found across the United States are quite elaborate in the depth and breadth of the related industries found within, while others include only a few of the basic components of what helps a particular industry segment thrive.

Shaffer et al. explain clusters as "an array of linked industries and other entities important for competition . . . they can be trade associations and universities, standards-setting agencies, think tanks, and vocational training providers." Even governments, Shaffer et al. explain, have roles in helping these clusters grow, "removing obstacles, relaxing constraints . . . eliminating inefficiencies in productivity."[16] Many of the local governments' leaders previously interviewed had contributed to cluster growth simply by eliminating burdensome regulations and onerous municipal ordinances. By so doing, they not only enabled growth and commerce within the cluster, they also demonstrated to the various components of the cluster that the community was a willing and active participant in its success.

By clustering all of these like businesses with relevant support organizations, communities have seen accelerated exchange of ideas, companies partnering on projects where both bring unique but compatible skill sets to the effort, and a building energy and enthusiasm for the industry. In many cases, firms report growing reluctance to leave the cluster as it had become such a comfortable and encouraging, mutually supportive environment for the firm and for its workforce and their families.

Clusters are said to involve linkages that reach both backward and forward, the former enabling easier access to inputs and the latter making the transport away from the cluster to other markets more efficient. Ideally, the cluster incorporates all the components necessary to conduct business, prepare for the future of the industry, and to connect with external markets and other clusters. In such a case, a firm need not look outside the cluster for any service or connection it needs. And, when a new requirement is identified, rather than going elsewhere to acquire the good or service, the cluster becomes a powerful economic development asset for attracting that good or service or support institution to join the cluster, thereby strengthening its foundation even further.

In the long run, because industries and industry segments evolve over time, a vital cluster will naturally change to accommodate shifts in the industry. It will acquire new technologies that are relevant, it will attract educational institutions, and it will spawn the next generation of activities from within the cluster. Thus, the vital cluster becomes an innovative laboratory for the envisioning and creation of new concepts that will further strengthen the cluster and the industry and, by extension, the community.

The literature is full of examples of the benefit of like businesses clustering together because they can buy their needed goods and services collectively, generating savings for all by buying in bulk. The public sector can facilitate the growth of clusters through permitting and land use policies, tax policies, research facilities, and the creation of relevant training programs. Favorable laws relating to anti-trust matters, the protection of intellectual property, and employee oversight have also contributed to the success of clusters. Local governments also have a role in promoting the existence of the cluster, usually in the context of business attraction.

In part due to the cohesiveness of industry clusters, their demise can be particularly destructive for their host communities. Part of what was observed in the fall of steel in Pittsburgh, aerospace and aviation in Seattle, and cluster environments elsewhere was that the loss was not only of jobs, but of community, of economic security, all of that resulted in a sense of hopelessness for the next generation who had expected to follow in the employment footsteps of their parents and their grandparents by working in the same industry and even for the same employer or same facility.

Such agglomerations had a strong theoretical basis. And, for many years, the theory had been consistent with reality . . . but reality had changed for those regions. It is unquestioned that theoretical approaches to economic growth can be useful as constructs to help us better understand reality. Today, the region of Seattle and the Puget Sound area have multiple clusters: in this case, information technology, the life sciences, higher education, and aerospace and aviation. Pittsburgh is another multi-cluster region today, including clusters in energy, telecommunications, financial services, the life sciences and health care, and information technology. Another excellent example is Fairfax County, Virginia, which has moved its economy away from being home to a cluster of government contractors to have great strengths in, and the enabling support systems around it, for clusters in information technology, translational medicine and cancer research, cyber security, cloud computing, data analytics, and software.

Still, while agglomeration theory and clustering are good examples of theories that have practical application to growing a local economic base, not all theoretical approaches are as useful to the economic development practitioner. As the 1987 Nobel Laureate in Economics, Robert Solow, wrote. Any theory that

> says something about the real world is likely to have implications for policy . . .
> I described the aggregative theory of growth as a parable. You expect a parable to
> have a moral, but hardly to contain concrete instructions for the conduct of life.[17]

Categorizing Economic Growth Theories and Identifying Case Studies

Table 1.1 itemizes the economic growth theories that have been summarized. In today's global economy, the most valuable lessons about local and regional economic growth are more experiential and observational than purely theoretical.

Table 1.1 Components of Economic Growth Theories

Location and Growth Theories/Principles

Cost-Minimization Theories
    transportation
    labor/unionization
    taxes

Neoclassical Theories
    workforce appropriateness
    capital availability
    infusion of new technologies

Exogenous Theories
    rate of Savings (Harrod-Domar Model)
    technological advance (Solow Model)

Endogenous Theories
    public policies to promote growth
    factors outside of local control

Product Cycle Theories
    technology becomes obsolete
    constant influx of new technologies required

Factor Price Equalization   Mobility of labor and capital
Human Capital Theory   technology overrides of capital requirements

Economic Base Theory
    communities put assets into place
    basic and non-basic industries

Agglomeration Theories   clustering of support functions

Notes

1 Richard D. Bingham and Robert Mier. *Dilemmas of Urban Economic Development: Issues in Theory and Practice.* (Thousand Oaks, CA: Sage, 1997): 20.
2 Bruce Herrick and Charles P. Kindleberger. *Economic Development.* (New York: McGraw-Hill, 1983): 19.
3 John F. McDonald. *Urban America: Growth, Crisis, and Rebirth.* (Armonk, NY: M.E. Sharpe, 2008): 66.
4 David L. Barkley. Employment Generation Strategies for Small Towns: An Overview of Alternatives. (September 2001). http://ageconsearch.umn.edu/record/113339
5 Michael Luis. *Century 21 City: Seattle's Fifty-Year Journey From World's Fair to World Stage.* (Medina, WA: Fairweather, 2012): 13.

6   Robert J. Barro and Xavier Sala-i-Martin. *Economic Growth*, 2nd ed. (Cambridge, MA: MIT Press, 2004): 23, 52.
7   Joseph P. Cortright. *Making Sense of Clusters: Regional Competitiveness and Economic Development*. (Washington, DC: Brookings Institution, March 26, 2006): 26.
8   Ibid.
9   Herrick and Kindleberger, 50.
10   Ibid., 50.
11   Phillipe Aghion and Steven N. Durlauf. *Handbook of Economic Growth Theory*. (Cambridge, MA: MIT Press, 2005): 1473.
12   Ibid., 1491.
13   Shaffer et al., 143.
14   Jane Jacobs. *The Death and Life of Great American Cities*. (New York: Random House, 1992).
15   Edward L. Glaeser, Hedi D. Kallal, Jose A. Scheinkman, and Andrei Shleifer. Growth in Cities. *The Journal of Political Economy*, vol. 100, no. 6, Centennial Issue. (December, 1992): 1127, 1131.
16   Shaffer et al., 52.
17   Robert Solow. *Growth Theory: An Exposition*. (Oxford: Oxford University Press, 2000): 71.

References

Aghion, Phillipe and Durlauf, Steven N. *Handbook of Economic Growth*, vol. 1B. San Diego, CA: Elsevier, 2005.

Barkley, David L. *Employment Generation Strategies for Small Towns: An Overview of Alternatives*. Clemson, SC: Clemson University, September 2001.

Barro, Robert J. and Sala-i-Martin, Xavier. *Economic Growth*. Cambridge, MA: MIT Press, 2004.

Bingham, Richard and Mier, Robert. *Dilemmas of Urban Economic Development: Issues in Theory and Practice*. New York: Sage, 1997.

Cortright, Joseph. *New Growth Theory, Technology, and Learning*. Washington, DC: United States Department of Commerce, 2001.

Glaeser, Edward. *Triumph of the City: How Our Greatest Invention Makes Us Richer, Smarter, Greener, Healthier, and Happier*. New York: The Penguin Press, 2011.

Herrick, Bruce and Kindleberger, Charles P. *Economic Development*. New York: McGraw Hill, 1983.

Jacobs, Jane. *The Death and Life of Great American Cities*. New York: Random House, 1992.

Jacobs, Jane. *The Economy of Cities*. New York: Random House, 1969.

Luis, Michael. *Century 21 City: Seattle's Fifty Year Journey from World's Fair to World Stage*. Medina, WA: Fairweather, 2012.

McDonald, John F. *Urban America: Growth, Crisis, and Rebirth*. Armonk, NY: M.E. Sharpe, 2008.

Shaffer, Ron, Deller, Steve, and Marcouiller, Dave. *Community Economics: Linking Theory and Practice*. Ames, IA: Blackwell.

Solow, Robert. *Growth Theory: An Exposition*. Oxford: Oxford University Press, 2000.

2 A Brief History of Economic Growth and Decline

When one considers the various theories of economic growth, economic development, and economic decline sequentially, it is possible to observe an historical trend-line. Initially, human production had no purpose other than to feed oneself and one's family. Over time, it was realized that, if one person or one group was a better producer of one item and others produced other items, trade could take place that meant everyone could share in the production and trading and the sharing of multiple items, in an increasingly efficient system because individuals are now needed only to produce that which they can produce and deliver more efficiently than their competitors.

As various items grew to acquire perceived value, trading of those items for those of lesser perceived value led to levels of exchange wherein some producers were able to receive greater returns for that which they produced and traded. Over time, this equated to pricing practices that, in turn, led to the acquisition of wealth. Of course, where there was wealth accumulation by a few, there was also a larger group that had to produce more and receive relatively less. Ultimately, those who managed to possess the means of production for the more highly valued items—or, who could trade for them from other locations—became increasingly wealthy and powerful.

In order either to acquire valuable products for possession or resale, or to take the most highly valued producers to market, producers needed to move their items over increasing distances to the markets best suited for their sale. The costs of transporting such goods over distances—and even overseas—led manufacturers and producers to seek means of doing so while expending the minimal costs possible. The characterization of that process and the benefits thus derived led to the Cost Minimization Model of economic growth.

This process also led producers, whenever feasible, to move closer to the navigable waterways they used to transport their goods. This eliminated the costs of getting their products to the points of departure. As is evident even today, those locations meant that smaller conurbations began to locate near rivers and on the coastlines where easier access to ports could reduce the costs of transport to market. Over time, as more producers located nearby, cities grew.

Even today, cities and towns remain in the places where they were originally established. This includes resource production and extraction, agriculture, mining, or timber. Many communities have discovered that conserving and restoring natural resources for outdoor recreation and tourism can be ways to revitalize an economy and to contribute to a more diversified base. As such, they have managed to convert historic strengths that were lost into new economic drivers.

Even today, one can observe those initial patterns of growth by viewing the higher densities in such areas. In the United States, the greatest density of population is found on the eastern seaboard, followed by the west coast. Great cities also exist along the great rivers of the country, such as the Mississippi, Arkansas, and Missouri River. "Pittsburgh," it is pointed out, "did not begin as a manufacturing city but as a depot." And, Chicago "handled and processed goods, mainly flour and timber, shipped to eastern markets through the Great Lakes and on the new railroads, and it served as a distribution point for products from the east shipped to the mid-west."[1]

As technology advanced to the point of enabling transportation through other means, the process was frequently reversed. Rather than locating near points of transport departure, much of today's means of product transport have moved toward the producers, including rail lines, major highways, and air freight. As a result of this history—and consistent with the theory of cost minimization—companies that must transport goods over larger distances now make their location decisions with shipment access and costs in mind. And, communities that are interested in attracting producers develop and improve those facilities for that purpose. This also includes the development of air service for companies that do not have a product to move but who must ship their personnel over greater distances to their respective markets.

The advance of transportation technologies enabled producers to ship their products in new, more efficient ways. The result, in part, was that the small towns that were built up around rail lines and that were substantially dependent upon that line for their economic stability, "suffered the unintended consequences."[2] As those rail lines became less useful, the small towns around them became less relevant. Small town institutions, such as banks and restaurants and retailers, left next, and a downward spiral may have begun, sometimes leading to the demise of the town. Wood explains that "most small farm towns in rural areas are becoming an endangered species, unable to retain, let alone attract, population, and they are facing losses of even rudimentary services." An examination of the plight of these small rural towns will be revisited in a later chapter, along with strategies that enabled many of them to rebuild upon new economic development strengths.[3]

As mid-sized and larger cities grew over time, they developed the broad sets of skills that were appropriate to the firms that were located therein. Smaller producers moved to smaller towns where their more specialized products called for a greater specialization in the workforce. Neoclassical theorists point out that, in both cases, it became necessary to attract the specific types of workers the production processes required. But, the larger cities also imported a greater array of support functions, including those that brought the raw materials in and shipped out the finished products, but also those who provided goods and services to the workforce. This resulted in cities becoming much more diversified over time in both workforce and product components. The requisite investments came to these locations as well because it was a place where the returns would be greater than the amounts invested.

Such wealth for some and expanded incomes for others created varying degrees of incomes that were in excess of the costs of life's necessities. The expendable income beyond the level of necessities became available for the so-called luxury purchases. As the Harrod-Domar model illustrates, there is a point reached at which such luxury purchases attract additional businesses to the city and the workforce becomes still more diversified and the location increasingly attractive to those who can afford to be more selective about their choice of locations.

Following the conclusion of World War II, the nation's demand for such luxury items grew substantially. People wanted to own automobiles, household appliances, and more. Fueling the growth of those industries was a dramatic expansion of the population—the so-called baby boom. Between 1946 and 1964, 76.4 million people were born in the United States.[4] As communities grew to accept these new residents and to attract and create the companies building and transporting those products, new inputs of capital and technology were required. This is an instance in which the third factor—workforce—created a demand for the other two. This may be especially apt in the current age of innovation.

The Factor Price Equalization Model supports the notion that the largest of these cities evolved further but also allows that smaller cities and towns could develop as well based on the acquisition of the same inputs of labor and capital, where there was a reason for their attraction. The mobility of these factors, as well as technology, enables any location to develop if it has a sufficiency of one of the factors, which thus gives it the ability to attract enough of the others.

A strong workforce may be sufficient in today's world to attract investors if the workforce is in the areas of technology that are in greatest demand. One of the great attractions of the Research Triangle Park in North Carolina has been the presence of a highly trained workforce coming from the many universities in the region. A technological advance can similarly attract firms and workforce to an area if it can demonstrate a strong return-on-investment. Cities that have developed new methods of medical treatment have been able to attract both workers and capital to places such as Baltimore (Johns Hopkins University), Kansas City (the Stowers Institute), and Philadelphia. Capital can be an attraction as well as young firms in need of growth investors; firms may come to the source of financing. This has been part of the reason for growth in areas such as northern California, Seattle, Boston, and elsewhere.

Of course, one cannot assume that all areas will develop and that the development can be sustained over lengthy periods of time. Endogenous growth theorists point out that many of the factors that determine the fate of products and services in today's world are far beyond the control of the firms' management, or even of business in general. An early demonstration of the endogenous theory and the many factors that are beyond the control of communities and firms came from Malthus who posited that population growth would not continue unabated; rather, floods, famine, fires, warfare, and disease would control growth in uneven and unpredictable occurrences.

A modern example of this was the passage of the North American Free Trade Act, or NAFTA. Many businesses and many industries lobbied hard against the passage of the bill because it feared the lower labor costs elsewhere in the Americas would take business and jobs away from American companies and workers. The outcome however, was the passage of the bill and a demonstrated inability of cities, towns, regions, and even whole industries to control their own futures.

Cities and regions that did possess the needed factors of labor, capital, and technology—or land in the case of agricultural production, or oil or mineral extraction—could evolve by continuing to replenish those factors as needed. Economic Base Theorists maintain that areas without the necessary attractive features for business attraction could bring them to their communities or develop them from within. This has brought us to modern-day economic development specialists who market their communities (the product, in business terms) to prospective business clients. In many cases, the city or region in question seeks to attract or grow a variety of assets that are all attractive to a type of industry or an industry segment. By so doing, they have created a range of supportive companies, associations, institutions, and more to grow a single, specific industry. This is summarized in Chapter 1 as Agglomeration Theory, or clusters.

Over time, the nation's population was increasingly drawn into more urban areas. This evolution gives us a chance not only to observe how economic growth theory impacts people and places, but also to consider new theoretical constructs for growth, development, and decline in other locations. It begins to give us a more complete understanding of how communities initiate and sustain economic development.

Glaeser reported that, in 2010, 243 million Americans lived in the urban areas of the nation.[5] Firms moved to these cities to gain access to the labor force it needed for production. The benefits of that immediate access are presumed to offset the relatively greater costs of both land and labor in cities. This influx of both capital and jobs created a dynamism in urban places that made them even more attractive to workers which, in turn, attracted more businesses.

In the era following World War II, however, urban residents—including those returning from their service overseas—sought neighborhoods, single-family homes, and yards of their own. Enabled by the spread of private automobile ownership, sub-urban communities grew quickly to accommodate the subsequent baby boom (1946 to 1964). As those with the funds to move did so, companies were forced to follow the best and most skilled workers to where they lived. The benefit of less expensive land for their offices and production facilities also made the suburbs more attractive to commerce.

The urban crisis was the focus of all discussions about central cities,

> with persistent poverty, . . . racial tension, rioting, school desegregation . . . The prevailing view of suburbs shifted as well . . . were not seen just as unattractive, bland, socially empty places, as the 1950s critics observed, but were now seen as the destination of "white flight" and, therefore, complicit in the crisis.[6]

The political and social divide between central cities and their neighbors became increasingly strained.

Eight of the top ten most populous cities of the 1950s had, by 2010, lost 20 percent or more of their population bases.[7] Many cities have been left behind as the nation's economy boomed, and they have suffered from the losses of their economies in a great many ways. "The exodus of urban manufacturing . . . posed a mortal threat to the world's industrial cities."[8]

This mobility of a primary production factor (labor) meant that the others followed; capital investments and technological advances and inputs followed, facilitating even greater divergences between cities and suburbs. The impacts of that mobility are deep and both indirect as well as direct and obvious, as will be covered in greater depth in a later chapter. Suffice it to say here that a primary result has been that the levels of poverty and the unemployment rates in the city centers became much higher than in their suburban neighbors. This leads us to question whether that trend can be reversed at all through the relocation of some of the factors in question: labor, capital, and technology.

The final key theory that contributes to our understanding of economic growth, economic development, and economic decline in today's local economies is the Product Cycle Theory, which suggests that technology never stands still; it is ever-changing and, as such, cities, regions, and other communities cannot stand still. They must continually seek to attract or develop the next technology to produce. To do so means a continuous influx of capital and the continuous attraction and improvement of the local workforce.

Many have examined the case of Detroit and automobile manufacturing as an example of a region that lost its way because it failed to seek a continuous influx of one of the prime factors, in their case, technology. As the Big-Three automobile manufacturers ignored domestic demand for smaller, more efficient cars, they continued to produce the styles that had come off of the assembly lines for generations. Instead, they argued for Congressionally approved protections against foreign producers with the "unfair" advantage of cheaper labor rates. Such protective tariffs further increased the cost of American-manufactured automobiles and created a growing domestic demand for the smaller, more efficient, and less expensive Japanese vehicles.

Without dramatic advances in the technology component, no amount of capital or labor could sustain the industry or the community. Jane Jacobs observed that "the past development of a city is no guarantee of future development because the city can stop vigorously adding new work into the economy and thus can stagnate."[9] So went Detroit and the region surrounding it. So went the steel industry in Pittsburgh and the areas surrounding it, reaching as far as the Great Lakes to West Virginia, Pennsylvania, and Ohio. The technology factor was not enhanced sufficiently to offset the loss of advantage in terms of the labor factor.

Clearly, these economic theories do not always apply to every time and every place. In today's world, there are thousands of communities across the United States that want to develop their economic bases and that are, therefore seeking the same assets. There is a limited amount of investment capital available. There is a limited workforce, although retraining can expand the existing numbers. What is infinite, however, may be the development of new technologies.

A further assist in the decline of the entire region had been the weakening of the labor input. Between the demands of the unions for higher wages and benefits and the extremely lower relative costs of labor in other countries, the industry in the region was unable to compete. As we will be reminded in a later chapter, the mere presence of these inputs is not sufficient to sustain either economic growth or economic development. It is their timely and strategic deployment and interaction that will help sustain an industry and its local economy over time. Of course, the same result occurred in the steel mills and related industries around Pittsburgh and elsewhere. In those cases, other endogenous factors were both domestic and foreign. The decline in American automobile production was as much of a contributing factor to the decline in demand for American steel as were union demands for that industry and comparative price competition from overseas producers. These cases will be revisited in later chapters as well.

What is indeed most certain in the current stage of the history of economic growth is that nothing is certain. In the 1980s and 1990s, businesses wanted (and developers built) office parks with treed acres and distances between buildings with walking trails and picnic benches that were once highly prized corporate locations. In the new millennium, companies no longer want such isolation. They want to be in multi-use areas where employees can work outside or have lunch together and meet their peers from other companies nearby.

The millennial generation of workers is helping to drive some of these changes because much of their interest lies in collaboration and interaction. Given the universal shortage of IT workers, employers are willing to configure their space to be attractive to the workforce they need so desperately.

Globalism is certainly having an impact on how business is conducted today across the United States. Price controls from nations and continents away impact the ability of American firms to produce and to meet marginal revenue expectations here in the United States. Global politics feed into the ability of American businesses to sell abroad or to import products from elsewhere. These events and trends impact local economies in the United States and can be devastating both to the businesses and to communities—large or small—that may be dependent upon the products and industries involved.

In today's business world, employers and communities need constantly to be vigilant to assess coming trends and to adjust before they are impacted by those changes. The alternative is to be comparatively less desirable than competitor communities and to lose their employment base as well as the commercial contributions to the local tax base that enable communities to provide quality, quantity, and scope of public services to their constituents without needing them to bear the full burden of the costs.

Notes

1   Nora Johnson, Adhir Kackar, and Melissa Kramer. *How Small Towns and Cities Can Use Local Assets to Rebuild Their Economies: Lessons From Successful Places.* (Washington, DC: Environmental Protection Agency, May 2015).
2   Jane Jacobs. *The Economy of Cities.* (New York: Random House, 1969): 130, 156.
3   Richard E. Wood. *Survival of Rural America: Small Victories and Bitter Harvests.* (Lawrence, KS: University of Kansas Press, 2008).
4   Michael Luis.
5   Glaeser, 8.
6   Ibid., 51.
7   Laura Bliss. A New Way to Rank Economic Growth in America's Metros. (January 28, 2016) www.citylab.com
8   Ibid.
9   Jacobs, 122.

References

Bliss, Laura. A New Way to Rank Economic Growth in America's Metros. January 28, 2016. www.citylab.com

Glaeser, Edward. *Triumph of the City: How Our Greatest Invention Makes Us Richer, Smarter, Greener, Healthier, and Happier.* New York: The Penguin Press, 2011.

Jacobs, Jane. *The Economy of Cities.* New York: Random House, 1969.

Johnson, Nora, Kackar, Adhir, and Kramer, Melissa. *How Small Towns and Cities Can Use Local Assets to Rebuild Their Economies: Lessons From Successful Places.* Washington, DC: Environmental Protection Agency, May 2015.

Luis, Michael. *Century 21 City: Seattle's Fifty Year Journey from World's Fair to World Stage.* Medina, WA: Fairweather, 2012.

Wood, Richard E. *Survival of Rural America: Small Victories and Bitter Harvests.* Lawrence, KS: University of Kansas Press, 2008.

3   Growth versus Development

Quite often, the concepts of local economic growth and local economic development are confused for one another. Furthermore, in efforts to distinguish the two, the literature has frequently over-simplified the manner in which they vary. Growth is characterized as being simply "more of the same" whereas development is said to mean advances throughout the community from which everyone benefits.

Growth and development have one thing in common: they both mean very different things in the contexts of different locations. Is growth the same—even conceptually—in Miami as it is in Danville, Virginia; or, development in Denver and Raton, New Mexico?

Often, the literature represents growth as being a bad thing because it is "just" more of the same. In a community that has just lost its primary employer, growth can be a life-saver for the community and its people, and may even be a sufficient backfill of jobs and tax base to support the community until development can occur. Consider Pittsburgh, for example. After the steel industry overseas forced local producers out of business in the seventies, there were precious few jobs left for those who wanted to stay in the region. Any employment that would have helped people live and stay in their homes until new employers and new industries could be attracted would have to be considered welcome.

Steven Deller makes the distinction between local economic growth and economic development by illustrating the needs of the community for both. A statement about growth might be, according to Deller, "We want jobs," whereas the same statement for proponents of development would be "We want quality of life." In other words, Deller posits that development provides jobs that are more advanced and pay more and are more challenging and long term, thereby yielding a greater general quality of living throughout the community. This notion of forward-looking jobs in growing sectors of the economy is reflected further in the comparative statements, "We want business" and "We want economic security." The summary statements offered by Deller summarize the economic impacts of both concepts and the community expectations and needs that lead to both: "Any growth is good" and "We want balanced growth."[1]

The eminent urbanist, Jane Jacobs saw this as early as the 1960s: "developing new work is different from merely repeating and expanding efficiently the production of already existing goods and services."[2] The truth is that, for many communities across the United States, beggars cannot be choosers (at least in the short run). Indeed, any growth is good for a community that is dying or that has double-digit unemployment and is losing its core public services. Certainly, in the long run, any community wants better jobs that will have quality of life spin-offs. But, what people really want right away are jobs, income, and a community that functions well.

Other components of development that are cited in the literature include sustained progress and progressive change. Beall and Fox found that, as cities grew, the primary benefits of growth accrued largely to the urban areas at the expense of rural areas. As the economy became increasingly diverse in a region, more complex production led to centralization of the production functions. As such and at a macro level, development needs consciously to focus on a more equitable distribution of the economy across an entire community or region. This, they maintain, is an important component of development that is absent in mere growth.[3] A different way of viewing equity in economic development is offered by Shaffer: "Development is more focused on equity than equality . . . Equity means that everyone has a fair chance, not that everyone has an equal chance."[4]

A general consensus can be drawn that growth is a more quantitative consideration whereas development has a qualitative component as well. This does not however mean that an equitable distribution of the effects of development must be shared by all. One could assert that the evolution of the quality of the economy and the community as a whole should be accessible to all but that does not imply that its effects will be equitably spread throughout the community as a result. As the community or the region develops, the improvements in the quality of life and the opportunities to advance will enable the economic evolution to benefit all who have the drive. As Widdison indicates, the distinction turns on such considerations as greater choices in the job market, greater choices of consumer goods and services, and, potentially, improvements in the social and natural environments. And, Herrick and Kindleberger concluded that "Development goes beyond growth to include change in the composition of outputs and the relative sizes of the contribution of the various inputs to the production process."[5]

In a simplistic statement, much of the literature refers to growth as more and development as making things better. Others, including Diffen, have restated the phrase as quality versus quantity but the essence is the same.[6] To the extent that "better rather than just more" is the standard applied to differentiate between growth and development, one must accept that production for export is an element of development as it brings additional revenues into the community that support improved services, both public and private.

A 2016 report by the Brookings Institution noted that, between 2009 and 2014, the vast majority of US metropolitan areas reflected economic growth but that only 63 percent showed increases in per capita prosperity. Thus, "growth doesn't necessarily equate with prosperity." In fact, only 37 percent of the nation's largest metros "showed consistent and continuous improvements in productivity, average annual wages, and the standard of living, starting from before the recession across a ten-year period (2004–2014)."[7]

Consideration of economic growth on the national level has often been attacked by those who consider the practice to be destructive of communities. There has been for many years an assertion in the literature on economic development that the practice of attracting companies to a community represents little more than a zero-sum game. By moving jobs from one community to another, there is no net gain. Fifty jobs lost here and 50 jobs gained there; all-even in the macro sense.

While there are many cases in which that has likely been the case, that argument does not paint a complete picture. There are many reasons that a company may leave one location and go elsewhere. If an employer is unhappy in one location and has decided to relocate, the loss of jobs does not represent a zero-sum gain and loss, but rather a necessary loss from which someone will benefit—the community to which it relocates.

Moreover, companies often leave one location for another because the current site is limited or because they cannot find enough qualified workers in that community or because the quality of life has declined or because the tax rates have become too high or for a myriad of other reasons. In all of those cases, the relocation to another site can enable the business to become more efficient as a producer of goods or services. Lower taxes make it possible to put more money back into research and development. A more accessible or more effective workforce can make the company more efficient as well.

Greater efficiency in business operations generally yields greater output and higher profits. This, in turn, can result in a growing workforce requirement which means that there is greater gain in one location than there was loss in the previous location. In such instances, there are gains at the macro level.

Depending upon the circumstances of the community in question, either growth or development can advance the cause of employment, economic stability, and the overall quality of life. In so many cases, growth is embraced by the leadership of communities where the city and its people are merely trying to survive. If, over time, the requisite assets for development can be acquired, and development complements the growth, so much the better, but the most immediate needs of the community and its citizens are to obtain long-term employment, enhance local spending, and generate the tax base that pays for the public services that ultimately do equate to an improved quality of life.

Generally speaking, economic development has greater impacts on a community than does simple economic growth. Incomes tend to be greater, generating greater spending in the secondary and tertiary markets and yielding greater tax revenues. For local officials, this also means a diminished requirement for tax hikes because the revenues per person rise and the ability to provide quality public services is enhanced. Greater tax revenues also can mean a diminished need to borrow funds for the local government, thus keeping municipal bond ratings more favorable and the interest rates lower for when borrowing is necessitated. "A study by the University of Washington's Economic Policy Research Center shows that every job that Microsoft creates, supported 5.81 jobs elsewhere in the region—from bakers to butchers."[8] For some types of positions, the ration is lower; for others, it can be even greater. Estimates for the new fields of translational medicine have ranged as high as eight-or-nine-to-one.

Notes

1 Steven Deller. *Community Economic Development*. (Madison, WI: University of Wisconsin, Cooperative Extension): 10.
2 Jacobs, 1969.
3 Jo Beall and Sean Fox. *Cities and Development*. (New York: Routledge, 2009): 70.
4 Shaffer et al., 4.
5 Herrick and Kindleberger, 21.
6 Diffen. 2007. Economic Growth vs. Economic Development. www.diffen.com

7 Brookings Institution. *Metropolitan St. Louis Export Plan*. (Washington, DC: Brookings Institution, 2010).
8 University of Washington Economic Policy Research Center. (Seattle, WA: University of Washington: 2009).

References

Beall, Jo and Fox, Sean. *Cities and Development*. New York: Routledge, 2009.
Brookings Institution. *Metropolitan St. Louis Export Plan*. Washington, DC: Brookings Institution, 2010.
Deller, Steven. *Community Economic Development*. Madison, WI: University of Wisconsin, Cooperative Extension.
Diffen. Economic Growth vs. Economic Development. 2007. www.diffen.com
Herrick, Bruce and Kindleberger, Charles P. *Economic Development*. New York: McGraw Hill, 1983.
Jacobs, Jane. *The Economy of Cities*. New York: Random House, 1969.
Shaffer, Ron, Deller, Steve, and Marcouiller, Dave. *Community Economics: Linking Theory and Practice*. Ames, IA: Blackwell, 2004.
University of Washington, Policy Research Center. Seattle, WA: University of Washington, 2009.

4 In Search of a New Understanding

Economic theories and economic history provide structures within which we can better understand what is happening to local economies today and how best to ensure sustained local economic growth. So much of the growth theory that was developed over the years contradicted earlier constructs. Barro and Sala-i-Martin maintained that "Probably because of its lack of empirical evidence, growth theory effectively died as an active research field in the early 1970s."[1] Theoretical approaches cannot address the issues of economic decline and how to respond to them. Consider, for example, the relatively recent series of municipal bankruptcies.

Cities across the United States have declared bankruptcy with varying outcomes. Their lessons are instructive to others who are faced with the same dilemma of not wanting to declare bankruptcy but feeling it may be the best way forward. Neal Conan is the host of "Talk of the Nation" on National Public Radio. He interviewed Phil Batchelor, an administrator experienced in helping towns recover after declarations of municipal bankruptcy. The most recent city to find itself in that position at the time of the broadcast in July of 2012 was San Bernardino, California which could not pay its bills and faced a deficit of nearly 50 million dollars.

Batchelor pointed out that a declaration of municipal bankruptcy does not excuse the locality from its financial obligations: "you still have the obligation to get your fiscal house in order. You still have to balance the budget. You still have to settle with claimants . . . and you still have to deal with your unfunded liabilities."[2] But, the city had 6 million dollars with which to settle 382 million dollars in outstanding claims. The city felt it had no choice but to file for municipal bankruptcy.

The real advantage for a municipality is that it gives more time to accomplish those matters. If the city and the creditors cannot agree on a partial payment schedule, the state can send in an administrator to take over or the courts can make the decisions for the parties involved.

Clearly, there are downsides to declaring municipal bankruptcy. "One is they abdicate responsibility for their own destiny."[3] Further, there are still budget cuts to be made and outsiders will be making those decisions from a purely fiscal perspective. Elected officials have that same requirement but they also have a greater appreciation of the needs of the community. That element of the decision-making process for budget cuts may be forfeited.

The City of Vallejo, California declared bankruptcy and the resultant budget cuts were severe. They lost three of their eight fire stations, 72 percent of their sworn police officers, trash collectors, and more. City positions were reduced across the board as were salaries and benefits, including pensions for past employees. Preventive maintenance of the city's infrastructure and equipment was either eliminated from the budget or postponed, meaning that the costs of repair would be even greater when funds do become available. Most importantly, perhaps, for a community in that kind of distress, Batchelor notes the highly negative impact on the community's psyche: "You couldn't manage your own business . . . It destroys morale."[4] What employers will want to locate an office or a factory in a community in such a situation?

In a 2010 survey of the nation's cities, the National League of Cities learned that economic development was the most critical issue cited; it was noted as vital by 66 percent of all respondents and out-polled public safety (at 64 percent). All other responses were cited by fewer than 50 percent of all respondents, including infrastructure, housing, education, environment, health, and other factors.[5] In subsequent surveys (2014, 2015, 2016, and 2017), economic development topped the list each time. And, it was the top issue cited by cities of fewer than 50,000 residents, 50,000–100,000 residents, 100,000–300,000 residents, and more than 300,000 residents.[6]

Within the general concept of economic development, the key sub-issues cited were job creation, business attraction, downtown development, employment, and arts and culture. Clearly, the futures of cities across America are seen by their leadership to be intensely tied to economic development. What is the best way for city leaders to understand how to advance the cause of economic development in their respective communities?

We can learn so much more from those who have already experienced the same issues and either failed or succeeded than we can from theoretical constructs that endeavor to explain all reactions in all communities with the same presumptions of causality and effect. Many mayors, chairs of locally elected boards, and public administrators across the country have tried a wide range of strategies and tactics to advance the economic growth or economic development of their cities, towns, and regions. In the process, they have learned a great deal about what does and does not work, and why or why not. And, they always seem to be prepared to share that knowledge.

As experience is the best teacher, the remainder of this volume will examine the experiences of hundreds of local leaders across the United States as they attempted to develop or resuscitate their respective economic bases. They come from small towns, large cities, and regions, rural areas, suburban communities, and micropolitan regions. There is no one-size-fits-all economic growth theory. Experience will lead us to a better understanding of economic development, economic decline, and economic recovery at the local level. Subsequent chapters will examine such experiences in large metropolitan regions and small, rural towns. Within the context of theoretical foundations, we can allow experience to become our teacher.

Notes

1   Robert J. Barro and Xavier Sala-i-Martin, *Economic Growth*. (Cambridge, MA: MIT Press): 18.
2   Neal Conan. What Happens When a City Declares Bankruptcy? (July 11, 2012) www.npr.org
3   Ibid.
4   Ibid.

38   *Existing Theories*

5   Trevor Langan and Brooks Rainwater. *State of the Cities, 2017* (Washington, DC: National
     League of Cities, 2017): 2.
6   Ibid.

References

Barro, Robert J. and Sala-i-Martin, Xavier. *Economic Growth*. Cambridge, MA: MIT Press, 2004.
Conan, Neal. What Happens When a City Declares Bankruptcy? July 11, 2012. www.npr.org
Langan, Trevor and Rainwater, Brooks. *State of the Cities, 2017*. Washington, DC: National
     League of Cities, 2012.

Part II

Why Local Economies *Must* Grow
Causes of Increasing Demand

Many communities across the United States resist growth and development. They see more people, more traffic, more competition for the available services in their communities. They see it as a loss of traditional ways and the traditional values of their communities; and, indeed it may be. But, the overriding question is not always whether one wants growth and the change that comes with it. Rather, the guiding principle may be whether a community can actually stop the growth, or whether it can realistically survive without development and change.

The quality of life factors in any community rest on a base of public services, including public education, public safety, human services, public works, libraries, parks, and more. In the absence of business revenues, community residents must absorb all of the costs themselves and do so through increased real estate, sales, income, and other taxes and fees. Employers help to offset those costs for residents through the payment of their taxes but, if they move away because the community is not sufficiently supportive of business growth, the residents are faced with a rising tax burden and/or the loss of valued public services.

Can they remain in place while others around them, as well as the local, regional, national and global environment in which they exist, change continuously? Do communities that want to stay in one place (in an economic sense) really have that option? Or, must they change to keep pace with the changing times and the very nature of competition for economic development amongst cities, states, and regions?

5   Economic Stasis

"We Don't Want to Grow; We Want to Stand Still"

A frequent comment made by community leaders in my previous research was that we don't want to grow any further; we want to remain a small community. And, while the importing of additional revenues and additional tax base would be positive, we don't want more people here, and we certainly don't want more congestion here. We're happy just as things are. That is often a great dream. If only it could be.

But this kind of attitude does not always reflect reality. Communities do not exist within a vacuum. They are in constant competition—even if that competition is not obvious—with other similar communities. Even if a locality does not wish to attract new employers, they must be ever-vigilant to retain the ones they have. And, completely flat job growth or population expansion is unlikely because times and industries and peoples' needs are constantly changing, the result of which is that people come and go. And, companies come and go, whether because they relocate or because they close their doors. And, whole industries come and go, or simply disappear from the United States. These include lumber operations, much of the textile industry, steel, and more.

The communities that have, in the past, lost textile manufacturers or steel plants or other industries, have all too often faced the serious possibilities of municipal bankruptcy, excessive unemployment rates, high levels of underemployment, the loss of the tax base from which public services are paid, and even the very sense of community. In short, the community and its very quality of life are, in such situations, in serious jeopardy. To presume that such changes will never occur is to ignore reality and run the risk of municipal decline. In major cities, that ignorance of such change has resulted in the loss of economic sustainability and the overwhelming loss of status as a desirable place in which to live, work, and visit. Witness Detroit, Cleveland, Youngstown, and others.

Even in regions dominated by farming and other agricultural pursuits or natural resource extraction, the economies have been changing—and will continue to do so—as big businesses take over the land and markets, and can be operated much more efficiently due to technological advances and economies of scale; or, as global market prices rise and fall due to totally uncontrollable forces. Albrecht, for example wrote that rural communities and regions that lose jobs to mega-farming become no longer self-sufficient. "Even major farm states like Iowa now imports the vast majority of their food."[1]

Albrecht further notes that rural communities can recover more quickly by forming clusters of collaborative communities within a given region. By doing so, they can increase budget efficiency and enhance public service provision without raising taxes. Such an approach is critical if rural areas are to transform the region's agricultural workforce into an attractive asset for today's economy: "Public education is primarily funded by property taxes and rural areas have lower property values and a lower tax base . . . rural schools have problems with economies of scale. Many technologies or programs have a substantial initial cost, whether . . . used by ten students or five thousand students."[2]

Even communities that do nothing and actually endeavor to stand still will be in relatively changing positions because everyone else around them is moving on. So, why would communities expect to be able to stand put rather than making efforts to move forward? Is it really all about their reluctance to accept change or is there a deeper-seated reason? University of Michigan professor John Austin concluded that a culture of expectation and entitlement

> grew around the success of the mass production economy. A sense that this relative prosperity would always endure, that the region always could reap good wages without education and continuing innovation stilled the dynamic of entrepreneurialism and economic diversity that built the region. It's a deep-seated malaise.[3]

Communities that do try to control the forces of growth will also learn that not all of the dynamics in place can be directed through policy or action. Cities remain dynamic and are constantly experiencing change. Pagano and Bowman discuss how product cycle progressions and changing consumer tastes can impact the local economies not only of the production center but also the communities around it. "Cities either adapt to their changing environments or succumb to the invisible hand of the marketplace."[4]

The conclusion of attempts to hold a city or region in place is that it will be overwhelmed by the impacts of advancing technologies and other uncontrollable forces. Notwithstanding the desire not to attract additional businesses to locate in the city or region, the existing businesses are at risk of being lured away by cities and regions that are perceived as being more business-friendly and supportive of growth. This is more than just attitudinal; such locations will prepare by creating the new technology and infrastructure, workforce, and other factors that will be desirable to the businesses considering relocation.

If one defines "staying in place," the community must at least develop and evolve with changing technology and other amenities. Growth may not be the target of many politicians and many of their constituents, but the option may not be standing still——ultimately it will be economic decline.

The macro economy can often be finite in nature: as such, growth in one community can easily portend decline for their neighbors. Increasingly, the forces that generate local and regional economic changes will be global in their origins, meaning that global wins could yield local losses. Localities with an interest in maintaining a static economy will find it harder and harder to stay in place and more and more likely to decline.

Lightbourn and White observed that "Cities never stand still. They are constantly in motion, constantly evolving. From generation-to-generation, the people are different, the industries are different."[5] The vast majority of jobs in America today can be found in small and medium-sized businesses. The vast majority of those are young—fewer than five years since their inception. This is, in part, due to the forces outside of the control of the business owners. They can control how hard they work and how much they charge but they have no governance over factors outside their immediate borders. Smick remarked that the lives of working Americans and their families have become "intertwined with the uncertainties of global trade and financial systems. Most Americans have become pawns in the global financial system."[6] He further asserts that deflationary economies make it difficult for small and mid-sized businesses to succeed because pricing stability is minimal. Sudden drops in prices for the goods and services of these companies result in revenue losses, job reductions, and business deaths. Companies seek to locate in places where that which is controllable is managed as well as possible, including that which falls into the domain of state and local lawmakers and administrative officials.

Business location decisions are based not on today's needs alone. Companies want to locate in communities that have a history of consistent pro-business strategies, rhetoric, and policies. Flipping from pro-business to slow-business to no-business and back again will create, at the very best, uncertainty. Businesses and executives do not like uncertainty; they expect taxes, zoning, infrastructure, and other relevant decisions to be made in a way that favors their growth and cost-minimization strategies. If they do not, they can easily relocate to any of several communities where they do. Executives translate these kinds of decisions into "wanting" their business. Like people, if they feel unwanted, they will move on.

The ideal location for a business in this regard is the community that unashamedly goes out of their way both in expressing their pro-business philosophies and in implementing public policy that is consistent. Further, the ideal community for a business location is one that can demonstrate that their history has been pro-business. If a city or town has been pro-business and is still pro-business, one might be able to assume that they will continue to be in the future. If the community has not been pro-business or has been inconsistent in its policies, no amount of rhetoric will convince business site location decision-makers to believe it will change.

The conclusion must be that a community cannot stand still: its existing businesses are always subject to being relocated, and their neighbors may be passing them in their growth, thus changing their relative economic position. No community, large or small, urban or rural, in today's economy can reasonably expect not to change. The challenge for local leadership is to control and channel that change over time in directions that are as positive and desirable as can be managed. Considering some of the cities that encountered these kinds of issues can help to demonstrate the outcomes.

1   Houston

In 2015, oil prices dropped and held for a sufficiently long period to induce the giant corporations in Houston—Haliburton, ConocoPhillips, and others—to announce massive layoffs. Experts expressed uncertainty that a recovery was coming soon and that the situation could even worsen. "In Houston, fifty proposed multi-family (housing) projects have been postponed indefinitely or killed outright since oil plummeted."[7] More than one million square feet of office space was dumped back onto the market to be sub-leased, reflecting the general decline of growth plans by Houston businesses across the spectrum of industries. "Every Houstonian—from the steelworker at the Port of Houston to the

doctor at the massive Texas Medical Center to the engineer in a new office tower . . .—
is talking about the collapse of oil prices and knows what it could mean."[8]

Does this mean that the Houston area's economy is not diversified? No, the economic
base of the city and the region is less dependent than ever on oil. Today, energy constitutes
38 percent of the overall economy, whereas in the eighties, estimates placed that dependency
to be as high as 75 percent. The issue of dependency in Houston is simply that dramatic
fluctuations in the prices that control that 38 percent, while better, is still high enough to
affect the entire economy of the region, and even the State of Texas.

For example, at the time of this writing, speculative office construction in the region
is on indefinite hold; expenditures are down while savings are increasing. Still, a third
transportation loop around the city of Houston is being planned and will mean that there
will be massive new areas open for development when the demand is re-established in the
oil industry and elsewhere throughout the region.

The petroleum and petrochemical industries have been large parts of the Houston
economic base since the early part of the twentieth century. In recent years, health care,
manufacturing components, aerospace, and professional services have been added to the
economic base of the city and the region. Much of the job growth in recent years has been
of exportable commodities that have resulted in an influx of dollars to the city.

It was not always thus, however, and the region's economy suffered dramatic swings
as external forces lashed the oil industry and affected global prices. At a time when the
economy of the region was overly dependent upon that industry, the impacts on the region
were significant. This was greatly apparent in the sixties when 80 percent of the region's
jobs were in the oil industry, and again in 1982, when the global oil bust was so substantial
that the area's construction and manufacturing sectors were also deeply affected. Bivins
described the rises and falls in the region's economic condition due to oil as "a dark blot
(that) casts a shadow over Houston's economy."[9]

In the 1980s, as oil prices reached a low of ten dollars per barrel, Houston was "robbed
of 220,000 jobs over a four year period. Waves of foreclosures rolled in and Houston
home prices plummeted. Hundreds of Texas banks and savings and loans institutions
failed."[10] The situation devolved clearly into one such as that which was described in an
earlier chapter; the decline of the primary economy sent ripples of economic difficulties
through the region's secondary and tertiary economies. The city's leaders needed to get
past their sense that "it will come back—it always does." This time was different. The
trough was too deep and too sustained. Local leaders needed to begin to diversify
the economic base.

Even as the city and the region began to diversify their economy, the oil industry
remained such an overwhelming anchor in the base that changes in world oil prices were
sufficiently impactful to control the overall economy. Lomax noted that "many of the
rumors concerning Houston's diversification have been greatly exaggerated—the economy
is little more diversified than it was in the days of Ronald Reagan."[11] In the mid-1980s,
health care's share of the Houston economy was 5.3 percent. "It had risen by 2013 to
6.7 percent at the same time that the oil and gas industry's share of the region's economy
increased from 10 percent to nearly 14 percent." Further, by 2015, 22 of the 25 Fortune
Five Hundred companies headquartered in Houston were in the oil and gas industry.[12]

The lack of substantial diversification in the Houston economy took a toll in the summer of 2014, when there were precipitous declines in the world's oil prices, including a 10 percent drop overnight in the late fall and a drop in "the benchmark price for US crude oil fell from a high of $1.08 per barrel in June to below $45 by January 2015."[13] As the oil prices dropped, the rest of Houston's oil production cluster also suffered. Rig operations were down a full third from the previous year. Fifty proposed multi-family housing projects were stricken from the plans. In the early part of 2015, 1 million square feet of downtown Houston Class A office space was put back on the market, empty.[14] Professors at the University of Houston forecasted in 2015 that the region could, in the worst case scenario, "probably face several years of subpar growth."[15]

Still, there were those who believed that the problems of the Houston economy being based on its homogeneity were overstated. Rines, for example, wrote that

> calls for the imminent collapse of the Houston economy were due in part to a misreading of how the economy is structured. The makeup of the Houston economy is more complex than simply energy and the derivatives thereof ... Houston is predominately growing its services sector.

Yet, even those observers, including Rines, felt that the economic base needed to be broader. "Instead of celebrating the survival of the local economy, Houston should double down on its diversification."[16]

The *Houston Chronicle* reported in 2016 that Houston's economy was not at all sufficiently diversified and still was overly dependent upon oil. Tomlinson wrote that "When more than 50 percent of the jobs in Houston are either directly or indirectly tied to oil and gas, as some claim, then lower-for-longer prices will have an impact."[17] He concludes his article with the admonition that "Waiting around for another oil boom to solve the city's problems would be a huge mistake."[18]

DePillis, another *Chronicle* reporter, noted that the impact of global oil prices are "starting to hold back sectors that appeared to have been chugging along. Some, such as law firms, bars and restaurants, and educational services, have already reversed direction, stalling job growth in Houston."[19] Many of the city's architectural firms, engineers, specialized software designers, and consultants to the oil industry laid off employees in 2016, totaling as many as 13,000 individuals.[20] Further, with a glut of both commercial and residential real estate, thousands of construction workers are unemployed and departing for cities with growth presently under way.

Bob Harvey is the President and CEO of the Greater Houston Partnership, which is a collaborative group representing the entire greater Houston MSA (Metropolitan Statistical Area)—some 30 counties, plus two counties that are proximate but not formally part of the MSA. The function of the Partnership is to promote the region and to generate prospect interest for the area. The information about those economic development prospects are then shared with the relevant jurisdictions within the region and with state economic development officials. The state is particularly important because it is the source of incentive programs that help to encourage the companies to select the greater Houston area as a location.

Harvey is a native Houstonian, who returned to the region following graduate school in the early eighties. He had led the Partnership for the five years leading up to the interview. He defines the region's economy as being cyclical rather than having structural issues. That is to say that, there are certain cycles in any industry that can cause economic downturns for areas that are overly-dependent upon it for their economic stability. Because there had been cyclical variations in the energy industry repeatedly over preceding years, the people of Houston were not surprised in 1982 when it declined again. The business and political leadership, as well as the residents, seemed to be convinced that it would all come back. There was always an underlying sense that things would return too "normal."

But, in the 1980s downturn, things were different: one in seven jobs in the Houston MSA was lost and, during the height of the problems of the mid-eighties, the city's job base lost a net 6000 jobs while the population continued to grow. And, when it became clear that the industry was not going to bounce right back, the city began to rally and think seriously about diversifying the region's economic base. Fortunately, the city's elected officials had always been very strongly pro-business, so they were able to move forward relatively quickly with a united front. Another positive was that people did not leave the city in droves as had happened in some other major metropolitan areas. Part of this may have been due to the fact that people still expected the industry to bounce back more quickly than it did.

The Partnership was formed to facilitate the development of the commercial tax base and the entire region was included. The industries the Partnership elected to focus on included the use of energy manufacturing talents to become involved in manufacturing in different segments of the economy. Also targeted were international logistics management through the port and the life sciences, which utilized their outstanding medical facilities and research programs. Today, the medical sector in the region accounts for 108,000 jobs and the life sciences more broadly for a total of 300,000 jobs.

But, Harvey is not satisfied that the region now has a sufficiently diversified economic base. "Every downturn in the energy business reminds us that we need to do more." Houston is striving to be more of an international community and has set its sights on being acknowledged as the "Americas hub" as well as a region that plays host to corporate headquarters operations. The Partnership is also focused on creating an "environment of innovation" that includes the attraction of the venture funding necessary to grow new start-ups as well as other assets that will help grow new businesses and help them to thrive. This is a very serious issue for the region because, according to Harvey, the city now ranks in surveys in the mid-twenties for the growth of new start-ups and he regards this as an important matter for the region's future economic development.

The venture capital needs of the region's businesses are not being satisfied, but its strengths in the life sciences area are not truly ripe for venture capital investment because the delivery time to market for products and services is so long that investors must be very patient. Instead, there is greater interest expressed in areas of new technology such as cyber security, virtual reality, or information technology. The universities in Houston— and in many other regions across the United States—are prime contributors to new start-up businesses that can attract new investments and create both jobs and wealth.

In Houston, there are two excellent institutions of higher learning; however, Rice University was, until recently, solely an undergraduate institution, and today has an enrollment of only about 5000. The University of Houston is now considered a Tier 1 university for research but, due to that being a recent accomplishment, remains toward the lower end of the list of the top one hundred. The Partnership thus also reaches out to the University of Texas in Austin and to Texas A & M, only 90 miles away, for new business start-up opportunities.

In terms of the lessons that have been learned in Greater Houston and that can be useful to other regions across the United States, several thoughts were offered by Harvey. His first lesson offered was that regionalization of economic development efforts, where feasible, are valuable because businesses are not, at first review, concerned about which specific jurisdictions they locate in, with the exception of variances in tax policies or other related matters. Second, Harvey noted that economic development is a highly competitive business and therefore, communities that expect to be successful must be prepared to put adequate resources into the budgets of their economic development organizations. Otherwise, the competition will be more active and their messages more widely heard. Elected officials must, therefore, understand why economic development is important and must be constantly kept apprised of activities.

An additional lesson offered was that communities must present to business prospects a favorable location for doing business. The assets that are important to businesses must be in place and the pro-business attitude must be constant and pervasive. Finally, Harvey opined that economic development does not generate overnight returns. Elected officials and others must accept this proposition from the start and take a long-term view toward the returns on investments that can be reasonably anticipated.

Summary: Lessons from the Houston Case Study

Houston's is an economy that, prior to some diversification in recent years, has always been controlled by forces beyond local control. Oil prices governed what happened in the city and throughout the region. When prices dipped below a certain level, jobs were lost; expendable incomes declined; and, employers in the secondary and tertiary economies suffered and laid off their workers. Retailers, home builders, automobile sales all suffered. The tax base shrunk and public services declined in both quantity and quality.

The diversification into other areas of technology as well as health care and higher education have helped to balance the situation but dramatic shifts in oil prices still have rather immediate and, often, prolonged effects. Even after the world prices rise and the jobs are restored, the fears linger and that affects spending and re-spending. It can also slow the pace of innovation and entrepreneurialism as individuals may be reluctant to take such risks.

The conclusion here must be that cities and regions must take steps to diversify their economic bases while they are on top rather than waiting for a crisis to which they have to respond; build momentum and economic development before the growth curves indicate impending issues. In short, some diversification is not sufficient. A well-balanced economic base is vital to future stability. To facilitate the diversification of their economies, cities such as Houston must encourage the development of an environment that encourages innovation not thwarts it. Entrepreneurs can be not only encouraged but also supported by local programs and by counsel from businesses and the region's universities.

The attraction of venture capital is another way that communities can stimulate the growth of start-up business and later-stage companies. Universities have demonstrated not only the ability to help businesses start up and flourish, but typically have a great interest in helping their home communities improve the economic development of their cities and regions.

2   Tulsa, Oklahoma

An example from a somewhat smaller setting than Pittsburgh, Seattle, or Washington, DC will be instructive to emphasize that the need for industry diversification in a local or regional economy is critical. Consider Tulsa, Oklahoma: oil is to Tulsa—and to much of the State of Oklahoma—what automobiles were to Detroit and aerospace was to the Puget Sound Region. In the same manner, local leadership did not expect the employers and the jobs related to the oil industry ever to be in jeopardy. And, in the same way as officials in other cities, they were as ill-prepared when it did happen.

The oil industry in general, and the drilling in the region, had always represented a somewhat inconsistent employer, but the peaks and valleys in the demand had never reached the point where dramatic layoffs had occurred. External impacts, such as oil prices for barrel, the demand for smaller and more gasoline-efficient vehicles, and other factors impacted the local employers and the overall economy regularly but the community survived and prepared for the next comeback.

In the early 1970s, the Organization of Petroleum Exporting Countries (OPEC) acted to restrict world supplies in a successful effort to drive up prices. In and around Tulsa, oil wells were activated to help offset these losses. The boom peaked in the early 1980s and, by 1987, Tulsa's boom appeared to have played itself out.

The next blow to the industry came as oil companies became increasingly engaged in offshore drilling and moved the bases of their operations closer to those sources. Citgo moved its headquarters to Houston and it became clear that the city and the region needed to develop core strengths in industries other than oil. This is not to say that the energy industry is no longer a vital component of the Tulsa economy. As recently as 2013, the MSA (Metropolitan Statistical Area) was home to more than 56,000 jobs. A multiplier for the industry has been calculated that estimates a total regional employment base that is supported by the oil industry of nearly 190,000, with nearly 13 billion dollars in labor income and more than 31 billion dollars in local value added.[21]

One of the targeted industries that also satisfied a growing need in the state was health care and the related businesses that constitute a cluster for the region. The presence of the University of Oklahoma and the Oklahoma State University, both of which have associated teaching hospitals, helps to create a substantial cluster in the area around health care and wellness. And, as goes Tulsa, so goes the State of Oklahoma, so this cluster has grown fairly quickly and had a natural catchment area for patients.

Growth of other industry segments followed, including higher education, entertainment, seed production, aerospace, and more. The non-connectivity of industries also meant that a negative external impact on one would not damage the fortunes of the economy or the employment base as a whole. Although oil remains the largest segment of the economy, the balance is stabilizing.

Still, the city is susceptible to a general recession because so many of the region's businesses are small businesses and because many are in fields that are non-essential and the first to be cut out of individuals' and families' expendable incomes. These include entertainment outlets and retailers. And, although there are tens of thousands of local employees of hundreds of aviation-related businesses in the region, their economic impact, coupled with that of the remaining companies still working in the oil sector do not equal the previous level of contributions from the oil industry alone.

Information technology in the Tulsa area has begun to grow significantly as well, in part because the quality of life is perceived to be very high and the cost of living is relatively very low when compared to other areas where there are a lot of firms and jobs in the IT sector. The location of these technology businesses in the region has also spawned increasing focus on the part of the region's economic development professionals in growing those sectors through attraction of new firms as well as the growth of new local businesses.

And, the numbers of creative workers are increasing in Tulsa, which, theoretically, enables the growth of technology companies. According to a report by the New York-based firm, Resonance, Tulsa has nearly 114,000 creative workers, and increasing at the rate of roughly 10 percent per five-year period.[22] The evolution of the city center, with arts venues and other cultural opportunities, helps to grow the creative group of workers in the city. The city can now boast of having its own Symphony Orchestra, Ballet troop, and Opera company. Further, between Oral Roberts University and the University of Tulsa, the city is home to about 8000 undergraduate and graduate students, which also increases the creative nature of the area.[23]

Plans called for an innovation park to be created wherein young companies could be started, incubated, funded, encouraged, and generally nurtured until they become ready to move on to other commercial office space. Key partners included the two major area universities with a directive to engage in a collaborative research, both with each other and with corporate and individual tenants of the park.

To complement the research institutions and start-up firms, the park engaged several sources of commercial and venture investments that would accelerate the research and its commercialization. In this way, albeit unwittingly, the park was to mimic the theoretical constructs reviewed in Chapter 1 by injecting workforce, capital, and technology. Additionally, however, the park included a fourth input not discussed in the theories of earlier decades: a mechanism for the transfer of technology to the local and external marketplaces. As such, the use of the inputs were maximized and ensured of greater returns.

The State of Oklahoma has been focused on what happens in Tulsa and has contributed substantial funds to programs in the city to further diversify the economy. This makes sense as the city and the region (seven surrounding counties) constitutes roughly one-fourth of the state's population and one-third of the state's economic output. True, what is good for Tulsa is good for Oklahoma; similarly, however, when Tulsa struggles, the state feels their pain, largely in terms of declining income tax revenues.

Since World War II, the city has engaged in an aggressive expansion plan. This meant that, what were initially suburbs became incorporated into a greater whole. In 1949 alone, more than 60 annexations were approved that expanded the city's reach by more than six square miles and to reach more than 7500 new residents. The city's land area doubled again in the 1950s. "City Commissioners annexed 25.89 square miles in that decade, increasing the size of the city from 24.04 square miles to 49.93 square miles."[24] In 1966, the city tripled its size again.

The central issue for the City of Tulsa and the region became jobs for its population and that issue extends today to whether, despite the broader range of economic sectors represented, and despite the efforts to grow and attract new and creative businesses to the area, the community will still be overly (even though not as dramatically) dependent upon oil for their future economic stability. With strengths in telecommunications, tourism, finance, retail operations, aviation, and various other forms of technology, the hope for the city was to foolproof itself from rises and falls in the world price of oil.

Mike Neal, the CEO of the Tulsa Regional Chamber of Commerce; Jim Morgan, the Chamber's Senior Vice President for Communications; and, Brien Thorstenberg, their Senior Vice President for Economic Development, conducted a joint interview for this research. The city and the region have had a succession of five-year plans, beginning with the first plan that covered the timeframe from 2001 to 2005.

The genesis of these plans was, first, an awareness that the region's oil-dependent economy was insufficient to sustain growth well into the future. But, there was also a realization on the part of community leaders who, as they traveled for their respective companies, realized that Tulsa was falling behind other parts of the country where the economies were advancing and diversifying. At that point in time, Tulsa had lost more than 27,000 jobs. A leader of leaders stepped up to take charge in the form of the Bank of Oklahoma, Mr. Stan Lybarger.

The group sought to raise funding from the public and private sectors to support an economic development program. More than 9 million dollars in private donations was raised for a five-year program and the group then encouraged both the city and the Chamber of Commerce to contribute 1 million dollars apiece. This yielded a pot of more than 11 million dollars and the beginnings of a highly effective public–private collaboration for the region. A singular goal was established: create 10,000 high-value jobs in Tulsa over the ensuing five-year period. Around that time, Mr. Neal arrived from Memphis to manage the program.

Toward the conclusion of the first five-year plan, a second plan was needed for the next period of time. Atlanta-based Market Street Services was engaged to develop the next plan. The recommendations included proposals to broaden the goals and metrics for the program, as well as to broaden the scope in order to cover growth for the entire region. Only as a region would the marketing efforts be able to demonstrate sufficient land, buildings, and workers to be attractive to the companies being pursued. As a result, the coverage area moved from one county to sixteen municipalities plus three other important groups—the Cherokee, Osage, and Muskogee nations. The expansion also meant that the coverage area now encompassed the nation's largest industrial park. Clearly, the messages now had more depth and could garner greater attention from cite-location decision-makers.

At the same time, the group was able to attract more investors into the fold, moving up to 120 private businesses and 28 municipalities. The second iteration of planning for economic development in Tulsa called for specific industries to be targeted, including energy, aerospace, Information Technology, transportation and logistics, and health care. New metrics for success included 1 billion dollars in new capital investment (the outcome was nearly 2 billion dollars) and the growth of more jobs.

The third iteration of planning (also prepared by Market Street Services) called for additional goals and metrics to be added to the plan. These placed renewed emphasis on workforce development, support for entrepreneurialism and commercialization of new products and services, community development, and the attraction of Tulsans graduating from colleges and universities outside of the area to return to Tulsa. Four pillars were approved for the five-year period from 2016 to 2020. These are shown below, including some of the metrics established for each of the pillars:

1   a prosperous future—job attraction and retention, including manufacturing jobs for the more rural parts of the region;
2   a skilled future—workforce issues designed to increase the numbers of Bachelor's degrees, Associate's degrees, and technical degrees;
3   an innovative future—programs to support entrepreneurs and commercialization of goods and services;
4   a livable future—community development, downtown development, and walkability.

The community is now working on "Vision 2025," for which the voters of the county approved 550 million dollars. This plan includes numerous projects that will enhance the quality of life for people in Tulsa and throughout the region. Vision 2025 was approved by the voters and includes a tax increase of one cent, 60 percent of the proceeds of which are being used for projects such as two new low-water dams on the Arkansas River, with plans for two more, improvements to the downtown area, health care facilities, projects on all of the higher education campuses in the region, expansion of the convention center, infrastructure at the airport, parks, and river projects to take full advantage of the beauty of the riverfront areas. In addition to the development of the projects, the residents are finding a great sense of pride in the new projects and in their revitalized city and county.

As for the original purpose for the program—the diversification of the region's economy away from an over-dependence on oil—Mr. Neal stated that "Energy has rebounded some but it is not fully back by any means." The community, however, has evolved as well as advanced its economic fortunes as the business community does diversify. The lesson to be learned from Tulsa's experience is that the leadership must be collaborative from both the public and private sectors. Businesses and elected officials are all in the effort together.

The efforts have reaped benefits. Tulsa has been recognized by *Forbes* magazine as one of the top ten places in the United States for the overall cost of living as well as high ratings for income growth, commuting times, job development, and more.

Summary: Lessons from the Tulsa Case Study

One lesson from the Tulsa experience relates to the roles that universities can play in building and rebuilding a local or regional economy. From skills training to lending faculty resources to the planning process to the operations of research parks, universities can offer substantial support for local economic development. And, they typically want to be heavily involved as they, too, are part of the community.

A second lesson that can be transferable to some other large cities or metro areas is that, if the community is the only significant conurbation in a large region, it likely has the services sector that people and businesses further away require. In the case of Tulsa, health care for their entire section of Oklahoma is one example of a service that attracts people from many miles to spend money in the city. This can help drive the growth of hospitality and retail sectors in the area as well.

Although, development and re-development generally need the entire community to come together, both public and private representatives, to generate change, Tulsa demonstrates the impetus that a single, well-respected, high-energy individual can provide to getting the process started and to motivating others to participate in the vision process, planning, fund-raising, marketing, and more. Once again, it is always about leadership!

Tulsa is fortunate to be located along the Arkansas River, but there are many, many examples of riverfronts that have been left in disrepair or are not being used for their best purpose. Tulsa has made the best use of its riverfront, a lesson from which others can learn. Unique and beautiful features of a community should be used to their maximum potential to help drive economic development.

3   St. Louis

The area in which St. Louis is located was originally acquired by the United States as part of the Louisiana Purchase, consummated by President Thomas Jefferson in 1803. Its great value was its position on the Mississippi River, which meant that it was a vital point in the transshipment of goods from north to south. When the railroads became a dominant form of transportation in the United States, the river-to-railroad connection became vital and St. Louis grew in importance to the commerce of the rest of the nation. Later, as the nation expanded even further west, St. Louis was a critical jumping-off point for that movement. Given its geographic position, St. Louis today sits within 500 miles of about one-third of the population of the United States, making the region a great place for distribution facilities and companies.

The geography of St. Louis makes it a perfect location for logistics, warehousing, light assembly, and distribution. The city sits at the confluence of the Mississippi River, other navigable waterways, major interstate highways, more than 4000 miles of railroad track, linked by six rail lines, two large airports, and the second largest inland port in America. In short, any portion of the continental United States is accessible by air within a few hours from the St. Louis region.

The area boasts a large and active Foreign Trade Zone (FTZ) in which goods can be stored and assembled without incurring any duties until shipped out of the zone to the ultimate markets. Because of the city's location, manufacturers and importers and exporters can use the FTZ to save money while preparing—or, just storing—their products for the next shipment.

With the advent of World War II, St. Louis became an important center for the manufacture and testing of military aircraft. As a result, the end of the war meant that aircraft production was a potential growth industry for the city and the region. Many of the planes—or parts—that were built and tested there were for military applications but the available skills in the workforce allowed for civilian aircraft production to expand as well.

Based in part on the growth of the aircraft manufacturing business, by 1960, the region's population had risen to more than 2 million people, making the St. Louis metropolitan area the ninth largest American metro region. The rate of growth was also significant, as the population in 1960 exceeded that of the region in 1950 by more than 20 percent.

However, by 2017, the population of the City of St. Louis had dipped to fewer than 3000 people, the losses being "traceable to the exodus of manufacturing jobs. Everywhere you look in the city and inner suburbs, there are signs of industrial decay."[25]

In 2017, the Boeing Corporation indicated that, if it were to receive the contract for the manufacture of the T-X aircraft, it would construct large sections of the fuselage and wing assemblies at their facility near St. Louis. If that should come to fruition, the region will gain as many as 1400 jobs for engineers and assemblers and an additional 400 support positions as well. Of course, those 1800 positions have high skill requirements and pay very well. They will also spin off anywhere from two to four additional positions in the secondary and tertiary economies for everything from sales clerks to home builders to school teachers to firefighters and police officers. The contributions by these well-paid employees to the state and local tax bases will be significant if the T-X contract is granted to Boeing. The sale of homes, cars, and other larger-ticket items will increase and that will generate larger shares of expendable incomes that will be spent and re-spent throughout the community.

An additional opportunity for the city and the region, should Boeing receive the contract, will be in the ability to attract the parts suppliers, finishers, and other small businesses that will provide input into the development of the aircraft.

Between 2001 and 2011, the region lost nearly 45,000 jobs, a number that equated to more than 3 percent of its workforce, at a time that other regions were experiencing population and job growth.[26] Between 2007 and 2009, the region lost nearly 6 percent of its total employment base.[27] There were five industries that constituted the bulk of the job losses in that period of time: manufacturing accounted for approximately 47 percent of all job losses; financial services accounted for 11 percent; and, pharmaceuticals, transportation/distribution, and personal services accounted for 7 to 8 percent apiece.[28] And, Swenson reported in 2012 that "the region has 75,000 fewer jobs than at its pre-recession peak."[29]

The major employers that each cut at least 250 jobs include some of America's best-known corporate names: Daimler-Chrysler, Anheuser-Busch, General Motors, Lear, Monsanto, Pfizer, Hyatt, Western Union, Wachovia, and Macy's. The tax base impacts of those job reductions were made clear when the St. Louis Board of Education was added to the list of organizations that had eliminated at least 250 positions in that time period.

Most importantly, these prominent corporations represent a wide range of industries, which means that the causes were not industry-specific but more structural in nature, and therefore more difficult to reverse and to restart economic growth and development in the region. Largely for this reason, the St. Louis metropolitan area emerged from the so-called Great Recession slowly. Its rate of recovery was ranked fifty-fifth among the top

100 large metro areas in the United States. By April of 2011, the region's unemployment rate had reach 8.5 percent and the nearly 123,000 people were out of work.[30]

The RCGA is the Regional Chamber and Growth Association. It reported at the time that "uncertainty is the most certain aspect of what lies ahead."[31] This challenge, and the unemployment statistics cited above, is somewhat misleading. Indeed, there were tens of thousands of people who were out of work. However, there were also a great many openings available to those with the requisite skills. The problem was that there was a great mismatch between the skill sets required in the demand and those represented in the workforce supply. Forty-six percent of the post-recession job openings were in health care or computer fields. Given the inability of the resident workforce to qualify for those positions, the availability of opportunities did little to encourage the unemployed or to create a positive outlook about the potential for new development and a brighter tomorrow around the region. In a survey conducted by RCGA, a mere 43 percent of all respondents agreed that the economic outlook of the region was better than one year prior to the survey.[32]

Output in the region has grown 40 percent slower than in the rest of the country and wages have increase 14 percent slower than in the rest of the United States. Strauss' conclusion: "The St. Louis economy clearly has been stagnating for some time."[33]

Part of the basis for the re-growth of the St. Louis economy may fall on the growth of immigration to the region. A 2012 paper by Jack Strauss, the Simon Chair of Economics at St. Louis University, noted that the metropolitan area is home to more than 126,000 immigrants, or nearly one in five of the region's total population. He maintains that "The region's relative scarcity of immigrants largely explains our poor economic growth."[34]

A 2015 survey was based on focus groups and discussions with more than 1100 employers in St. Louis across 24 distinct industry segments. Four of every ten respondents expected to increase hiring in the coming year while only one in ten expected to decrease their complement of positions.[35] Workforce shortages consisted of both having too few workers seeking employment and a mismatch of skill sets available relative to the types of positions available. More than four out of every five employers in the survey noted that they had to hire people who were unprepared for the positions they had open, and train them on the job. This equates to time lost, an absence of quality on the job, and a loss of revenues.[36]

The clear tactic for the city's planners would be to outline the types of jobs available and the specific skill sets required, and then to design training programs to supply the necessary workers for the local employers. The danger of not doing so is to have those companies find locations in other cities that could satisfy their demands for skilled workers.

But, will this be effective in St. Louis? "no city which achieved the scale of a half million residents has lost a larger percentage of its population in peacetime than St. Louis."[37] The Between the years 1950 and 2009, the region had gained more than one million residents but those gains were largely in the outer rings of the region. From 1950 to 2009, the city and the inner rings of the suburbs declined to about two-thirds of the region's total. From 2000 through 2015, the city and the inner rings of the suburbs added about 10,000 residents to the total while the middle rings added more than 130,000 people.[38] Much of the new employment growth is located in the middle and outer rings.

In order to encourage the growth of the city of St. Louis and the inner rings of the suburbs, the region's leadership must work collaboratively to provide the necessary transportation networks that will bring inner city residents to the jobs growing in the middle and outer suburbs. One bright spot for the city and the region—and, its employers—has been the net addition of 30,000 immigrants who have come to the region and settled largely in the city and the inner rings of suburbs. "In the late 1990s, an influx of Bosnian refugees to St. Louis led neighborhood heading toward 'ghost town' status" into areas "teeming with new residents and new economic activity. 'Industrious Bosnians' ended up transforming a crime-ridden area into a 'decent quarter.'"[39]

While not sufficient by itself to offset the losses that came from domestic out-migration, the immigrants can be a boon to the region's economic development. Local leadership needs to ensure that they receive language and skills training where appropriate and can access the jobs growing in the outer rings of the suburbs. If that can be done effectively, they will contribute to the region's development and, as will be reviewed later in this text, will be likely to create new businesses at greater rates than the existing population.

Strauss further concludes that, if the region had experienced immigration growth equivalent to other major cities of its size, their income growth would be 4 to 7 percent greater and their overall economy would be between 7 and 11 percent higher. Of course, Strauss bases his assessment on the assumption that the additional, theoretical immigrant population would possess similar education levels and work ethics as the existing immigrant group in the region. The existing foreign-born population in the region earns 25 percent more than the average American-born individual, at 83,000 dollars. Further, they are "44 percent more likely to have at least a college education and 130 percent more likely to have an advanced degree."[40]

The conclusion for St. Louis and the surrounding region must be to develop a plan to attract more immigrants to the region. He points to other cities that have already done so, including New York, Columbus, Chattanooga, Indianapolis, Louisville, Philadelphia, and others.

The Brookings Institution feels that one opportunity for St. Louis is to increase its regional exports, thereby bringing more expendable income to the city and the region. In 2014, it reported, the region's exports represented a total value of more than 16 billion dollars, the twenty-second highest total for any US metropolitan area.[41] That amount represented more than 11 percent of the region's GDP, up from 2003 when the percentage was just slightly more than 8 percent. Brookings estimated that the number of direct jobs created by the export trade totaled more than 44,000 and that the grand total, including those jobs created indirectly by exporting activities, totaled about 95,000 around the region.

Still, between 2008 and 2014, a mere 1 percent increase was measured in exports from the region. This ranked seventy-third among the top 100 metropolitan areas in the United States; and 22 percent of that growth was in the automobile and aerospace industries. This implies that there is an opportunity to enhance the export trade from the St. Louis region, thereby creating jobs, generating wealth, and expendable income, creating community spending and re-spending, enhancing the state and local tax bases, and enhancing the overall quality of life in the community.

Summary: Lessons from the St. Louis Case Study

The City of St. Louis and the entire region not only lost jobs, but lost jobs across a rather wide range of industries. In the process, they lost the diversity in the economic base that might otherwise have sustained them through the loss of a single employer or a single industry segment. The lesson from the St. Louis case study must certainly be that, as a region rebuilds its economy, it must ensure that it either has or can attract or train the required workforce for the jobs of tomorrow.

St. Louis now possesses a workforce and many job vacancies but the two do not match up. One option is to attract the companies for which the workforce presently exists; another is to prepare the available workers for the types of companies the community wants to attract. St. Louis may need to address this issue through the in-migration of individuals to the community. This is something that the region has not managed successfully to date.

Notes

1 Don E. Albrecht. *Rethinking Rural: Global Community and Economic Development in the Small Town West.* (Washington, DC: Washington State University Press, 2014) 145.
2 Ibid., 176–7.
3 Richard C. Longworth. *Caught in the Middle: America's Heartland in the Age of Globalism.* (New York: Bloomsbury, 2008.)
4 Michael A. Pagano and Ann O'M. Bowman. *Cityscapes and Capital: The Politics of Urban Development.* (Baltimore, MD: Johns Hopkins University Press, 1995): 2.
5 George Lightbourn and Sammis White. Moving Milwaukee Forward. WPRI Reports. (June 3, 2008).
6 David M. Smick. *The Great Equalizer: How Main Street Can Create an Economy for Everyone.* (New York: Public Affairs, 2017): 144–5.
7 Ralph Bivins. Falling Oil Prices Temper Houston's Economic Surge. (May 7, 2015) http://urbanland.uli.org
8 Ibid.
9 Ibid.
10 Ibid.
11 John Nova Lomax. Houston's Real Estate Market Feeling the Effects of Oil's Price Drop. (October 1, 2015) www.texasmonthly.com
12 Ibid.
13 Bivins.
14 Ibid.
15 Roger W. Gilmer and Adam W. Purdue. Houston and Low Oil Prices: An Update on the Economic Outlook. (March 18, 2015) www.bauer.uh.edu
16 Sam Rines. Houston's Economic Success Isn't Just About Energy. (December 21, 2016) http://chron.com
17 Chris Tomlinson. Houston's Economic Diversity Isn't So Diverse: Brexit Will Only Complicate Matters. (June 27, 2016) www.houstonchronicle.com
18 Ibid.
19 Lydia DePillis. The Deceptive Diversity of Houston Beyond Oil: Energy Downsizing Stating to Affect Growth in Other Industries.(June 25, 2016) http://houstonchronicle.com
20 Ibid.
21 Russell Evans. *Tulsa's Energy Industry in 2012. Industry Definition and Economic Impact.* (Oklahoma City, OK: Oklahoma City University, 2012): 3.

22 Resonance. Opportunities for the Tulsa Region in Creative Age. (New York: Resonance, February 22, 2016): 4.
23 Ibid., 7.
24 History of Tulsa. www.wikipedia.com
25 Loren Thompson. Boeing's T-X Could Be Good News for Struggling St. Louis Economy. (May 16, 2017) www.forbes.com
26 Jack Strauss. *The Economic Impact of Immigration on St. Louis.* (St. Louis, MO: St. Louis University, April 2012).
27 Regional Chamber and Growth Association (RCGA). *Talent: The Future of St. Louis in the Knowledge Economy.* (St. Louis, MO: RCGA, 2010): 2.
28 Kyle Swenson. Post-Recession Cleveland is in Worse Economic Shape than Detroit. (February 26, 2016) http://clevelscene.com
29 Regional Chamber and Growth Association, 5.
30 Ibid., 5.
31 Ibid., 8.
32 Strauss, 10.
33 Ibid, 2.
34 STLCC. 2015. State of St. Louis Workforce. www.stlcc.edu
35 Ibid.
36 Wendell Cox. Shrinking City, Flourishing Region. (January 27, 2011) www.newgeography.com
37 Ibid.
38 La Corte, Matthew. Refugees Are Revitalizing Some Great American Cities Facing Decline. (June 21, 2016) https://niskanecenter.org
39 Strauss, 2.
40 Brookings Institution. Metropolitan St, Louis Export Plan. (Washington, DC: Brookings Institution, 2010): 2.
41 Ibid., 7–8.

References

Albrecht, Don E. *Rethinking Rural: Global Community and Economic Development in the Small Town West.* Pullman, WA: Washington State University Press, 2014.
Bivins, Ralph. Falling Oil Prices Temper Houston's Economic Surge, May 7, 2015. http://urbanland.uli.org
Brookings Institution. *Metropolitan St. Louis Export Plan.* Washington, DC: Brookings Institution, 2010.
Cox, Wendell. Shrinking City, Flourishing Region. January 27, 2011. www.newgeography.com
DePillis, Lydia. The Deceptive Diversity of Houston Beyond Oil: Energy Downsizing Starting to Affect Growth in Other Industries. June 25, 2016. www.houstonchronicle.com
Evans, Russell R. *Tulsa's Energy Industry in 2012: Industry Definition and Economic Impact.* Oklahoma City, OK: Oklahoma City University, 2012.
Gilmer, Roger. Houston's Payroll Employment Revisions Confirm No-Growth Scenario: But the Local Economy Shows Resilience in the Face of Oil Market Damage. March 16, 2017. www.bauer.uh.edu
History of Tulsa. www.wikipedia.com
La Corte, Matthew. Refugees Are Revitalizing Some Great American Cities Facing Decline. June 21, 2016. https://niskanecenter.org
Lightbourn, George and White, Sammis. Moving Milwaukee Forward. WPRI Reports, June 3, 2008.
Lomax, John Nova. Houston's Real Estate Market Feeling the Effects of Oil's Price Drop. October 1, 2015. www.texasmonthly.com

Longworth, Richard C. *Caught in the Middle: America's Heartland in the Age of Globalism*. New York: Bloomsbury, 2008.

Pagano, Michael A. and Bowman, Ann O'M. *Cityscapes and Capital: The Politics of Urban Development*. Baltimore, MD: The Johns Hopkins University Press, 1995.

Regional Chamber and Growth Association. *Talent: The Future of St. Louis in the Knowledge Economy*. St. Louis, MO, 2010.

Rines, Sam. Houston's Economic Success Isn't Just About Energy. December 21, 2016. http://chron.com

Smick, David M. *The Great Equalizer: How Main Street Can Create an Economy for Everyone*. New York: Public Affairs, 2017.

STLCC. State of St. Louis Workforce. St. Louis. 2015. www.stlcc.edu/STLWorkforce

Strauss, Jack. *The Economic Impact of Immigration on St. Louis*. St. Louis, MO: St. Louis University, April, 2012.

Swenson, Kyle. Report: Post-Recession Cleveland is in Worse Economic Shape than Detroit, Or Anywhere Else. February 26, 2016. www.clevescene.com

Thompson, Loren. Boeing's T-X Could Be Good News for Struggling St. Louis Economy. May 16, 2017. www.forbes.com

Tomlinson, Chris. Houston's Economic Diversity Isn't So Diverse: Brexit Will Only Complicate Matters. June 27, 2016. www.houstonchronicle.com

6 Global Forces on Local Economies

There was a time in this country when local economies were subject, more or less, only to their own capacities and capabilities. Occasional impacts from outside the community could have an impact on the local economic base. For example, a new rail line or a new highway could change the ability of local producers to export their products from the community as well as the ability of others to import their products into the community. In time, communities could expect their economies to be affected by national events and decisions that were uncontrollable locally and could have a deleterious effect on their ability to sustain economic development or growth into the future. Some of those impacts are permanent or, at least, long term, while others could be more temporary than extended.

Times have changed. As Schaeffer and Loveridge characterized the change:

> With increasing globalization of the economy, it is no longer safe to assume that an industry that is viable today will continue to be healthy next year ... an investment decision made in a distant boardroom can make local manufacturing facilities obsolete.[1]

The nature of global impacts on local economies can be relative to inputs, political decisions, or changing patterns of taste and product demand. In Houston, for example, "dependence on the upstream energy industry made it particularly vulnerable to economic downturns determined by energy prices, the national economy, and the value of the dollar against foreign currencies" (city-data). The impacts can be potentially devastating for a local economy, large or small. Applebaum wrote that "the costs of globalization have been greater and more enduring than expected."[2]

Perhaps the greatest economic concern with globalization is that the "haves" benefit while the "have-nots" can lose further ground. The disparity between the two becomes greater than ever and that can mean strained relations between various parts of the world and even between the urban and rural areas of this country. "There is mounting evidence," wrote Applebaum, "that the benefits of globalization have accrued disproportionately to upper-income households, while the costs have fallen heavily on the less affluent, contributing to the rise of economic inequality."[3]

For communities that benefit from global economic connections, planners need to take maximum advantage of such opportunities by enhancing trade and specialization in that for which local employers enjoy global competitive advantages. For the areas that lose jobs and employers in the industries for which they no longer enjoy such competitive advantages, the local leadership needs to convert production into areas for which a competitive advantage can be regained and exploited, and in which they can sustain global forces more effectively.

Communities around the world are today subject to global forces, global financial systems, and the constant rolling of the economic successes and failures of other nations and their businesses. Smick points out that "It is impossible to measure the effect of a global innovative culture, open to levels of risk, firing on all cylinders on a million fronts."[4] Community officials and their economic development professionals will seek employers that fit the current economic base and for whom the existing labor force is relevant. At the same time, they will pursue industries that can provide more sustainable growth and then pursue the assets necessary to attract them. As new industries, and even new technologies, are being pursued, the community must keep an eye on a wide array of local, national, and global forces that will affect their evolution because that will affect their business community, their citizenry, the local tax base and public services, and the general quality of life for all.

1   Overseas Labor Costs

One of the primary assertions of the price equalization models addressed in Chapter 1 is that many of the factors affecting production are global and not local. Aghion and Durlauf explain that what trade always does is to "create a global market in which only the most competitive producers of the world can survive. Trade forces high-cost industries to close down and offers low-cost industries the opportunity to grow."[5] This further implies that, as world trade grows—especially with emerging regions of the world—efficient production and delivery systems will determine rates of productivity and sustainability.

Congress and other legislative bodies have, in order to protect their industries and producers that are less competitive, enacted numerous protective measures. Although these practices will have the effect of sustaining US firms and community economies, they also have the effect of raising the costs of the most efficient firms rather than lowering the costs of the least efficient. Ultimately, the costs are passed along to the consumer. It is a difficult call for Congress to make: protect consumer purchasing power or protect the industries and businesses and jobs—and even communities—they represent?

American cities and regions that have lost jobs to Mexico or Asia bemoan the fact that their cheaper labor was unfair and that Congress needed to protect their jobs by imposing quotas on Mexican or Asian imports to offset the lower wages. This would not, however, have been sufficient to balance the tab. Longworth wrote that, in part due to the union activities in the United States, Ford and General Motors trucks produced in the United States cost $1,300 per vehicle more to manufacture. And, when Electrolux left Greenville, Michigan, they removed jobs that cost the company $22.99 in wages and benefits and placed them in Mexico at the cost of only $3.65 per job.

Still, it became a more attractive approach to some legislators to impose import fees on foreign products because their constituents did not want to look for different jobs or acquire different skills. They wanted the same types of jobs they had always had and those men and women voted. So, they trundled along trying to please them.

Many small, rural towns have economies that were once based on natural resources and they, too are susceptible to the lower prices from overseas producers. The economy in and around Bend, Oregon, for example, has been based on the timber industry for well over one hundred years. When the Oregon Woodworking Company shut down its Bend-based operations in 2007, laying off 130 employees, the cause was clear: "We cannot compete with the competition coming from China, period. We have a great product. We just can't compete on price."[6]

Even in agricultural pursuits, the small American family farm was put out of commission by mega-farms that needed far fewer employees but were vastly more efficient. And, to make matters worse, these mega-farms don't even use local suppliers.

As Austin (University of Michigan) wrote, "Many towns are going to die. It's hard to say that to them, but it's true." He further asserted the result of many decades of easy economic growth was low ambition. "Neither ambition nor innovation had been needed for a century. Now, they are crucial and no one knows where to find them."[7]

Dayton, Ohio presents a prime example. Once the source of great manufacturing know-how, Dayton was the home in the 1970s to high-paying manufacturing jobs with a future. As overseas options became available to US firms, Dayton lost 40,000 jobs at General Motors, 2000 at Dayton Tire, and 3000 at Dayton Press.[8] Labor economists generally acknowledge that one primary job generates two to three additional jobs in the secondary and tertiary economies. Thus, the loss of these 45,000 jobs could actually account for more than 150,000 to 180,000 jobs. If the typical family contains three or four members, the total of individuals impacted could conceivably reach nearly three-quarters of a million people.

Many of the extra-national forces that impact economic growth are related to the cost of labor in the United States relative to other global markets. This has affected numerous products in which the United States possessed long-term market dominance and upon which many smaller communities across America had depended for their economic stability. In some product lines, the numbers of jobs lost can be stunning.

According to the United States Department of Agriculture's Economic Research Service, the United States is no longer the primary consumer of domestically produced cotton.

> As textile and apparel trade liberalized over the last few years, productions shifted to countries with lower wages . . . Many US textile and apparel plants closed; some firms went out of business. The United States lost more than 900,000 textile and apparel jobs from 1994 to 2005.
>
> (USDA/ERS)

US mills that had once bought 10 to 11 million bales of cotton per year have been reduced to less than half of that amount.[9]

Rural communities were disproportionately impacted by these losses, notably in the American southeast, which had been home to countless mills. The intention of creating freer trade with other countries had the unintended consequence of putting those mills out of business, damaging the small towns in which they were located, and putting nearly one million American workers out of their jobs. And the US trade deficit in textiles and apparel generally jumped dramatically between 1994 and 2006 from 28 billion dollars to 77 billion dollars.[10]

Especially hard-hit was the State of North Carolina, which, in 1940, had 40 percent of its employment in the textiles industry. By 2013, only slightly more than 1 percent of all North Carolina-based jobs were in the industry. In part, this decline has been due to dramatic increases in technology-based positions. However, the small towns that were home to the textile industries are not generally benefiting from the increase in technology-based employment in the state. This leaves those communities far behind others and with little chance of catching up.

> The timber industry is but one example of an industry that has been hit hard by jobs and markets lost to overseas competitors. The conversion of open spaces to the status of public lands, as well as environmental concerns and endangered species legislation (e.g., that which applies to the preservation of the spotted owl in Oregon), have combined to result in the loss of jobs in the timber industry; again, these are jobs that existed in small towns and rural communities.[11]

This is not a condemnation of such legislation nor of the need to protect endangered species. It simply is a statement of the unintended consequences for many of the rural areas that have been negatively impacted and that need to rebuild their employment bases, their tax bases, and their public services to help their families and their communities.

One of the nations' smallest states, the State of Maine, was disproportionately hit by losses in the timber industry. In 1980, there were 25 paper mills in the State of Maine and today, less than one-third of those are still operating. Only 4000 of the 17,000 jobs that were associated with those operations in 1990 remain.[12] Additionally, technology has replaced many of the jobs as well, not only mill jobs but also in terms of developing new materials that can be as efficiently, or more so, used to replace timber in various uses. Again, this is not to be critical of such advances but simply to cite the unintended consequences they have on communities across the nation.

The North American Free Trade Agreement (NAFTA) accelerated the loss of US jobs as well: an estimated 683,000 in total.[13] Many of those job numbers are the same jobs counted above in the timber and textiles industries; still, community impacts were substantial. In 2010, the number of new jobs in the automobile manufacturing sector in Mexico—more than 30,000—exceeded the growth of the entire US auto industry.[14]

The loss of jobs seems to have been more as a result of factories and mills becoming more efficient rather than from foreign competition. A study by professors at Ball State University in Indiana concluded that fully 87 percent of those losses were the result of increased technology-driven efficiency while only 13 percent resulted from foreign competition. This, too will be considered in later chapters.

2   Politics and Unrest

Political strife worldwide can wreak havoc on local economies across the United States. When this occurs in large cities and metropolitan areas, it may be less impactful on the overall economic base of the community. When it occurs in a smaller city or town, it can have a severe impact on the economy. Because such situations are highly volatile, surprises can and do occur, meaning that communities halfway around the globe may be caught unprepared for any implications to their local well-being.

Not all such impacts come from outside the country. Congressional dictates and Executive Orders can be equally impactful around the nation. President Obama's 2016 calls for a 15 dollar minimum wage made it difficult for some companies around the country to retain the same levels of workforce. President Trump's use of Executive Orders to halt immigration from certain areas of the world yielded profound reactions from many of the nation's businesses. More importantly perhaps, the image of a different, non-welcoming United States may cause reluctance on the part of the world's business community to remain in, come to, or engage in commerce with the nation.

In a world that is as interconnected as we are today, events in a city in Europe or the Middle East or Latin America can affect the economic viability of cities and towns in the United States. Events that impact trading partners, buyers, resource providers, competitors, and travel overseas can have an impact on those selling, manufacturing, representing, and developing travel plans to overseas markets. Sir Isaac Newton's third law of physics is that, for every action, there will be an equal and opposite reaction. In today's world of global politics, Newton's third law applies to the economy. Although the reactions may not be equal, they will certainly occur. Businesses and communities need to be ever-mindful for the potential of global events to impact their local economies.

The impacts of some of a President's actions, as well as global conflicts, will also be reflected in prices on stock markets and exchanges around the world. What can communities do to protect their individual economies in the face of global actions over which they have no control? National business organizations, such as the US Chamber of Commerce, the International City Management Association, and others spend a great deal of time and money studying these matters and advising their constituents about what may happen and how best to react. Business executives and economic development leaders need to keep abreast of such potential impacts constantly as well.

Oil prices are an area that is particularly sensitive to world political activities. This is largely due to the pricing that is a result of the global supply, which is largely from the Middle East, an area of consistent and long-term unrest. A paper by the Federal Reserve Bank of Dallas highlights the historic fluctuations in oil prices, starting from the October 1973 war between Arab nations and the State of Israel. OPEC lowered the production of oil by 5 percent until Israel withdrew to its 1967 borders and embargoed oil shipments to the United States to force it to pressure Israel to do so. Throughout that decade, oil supply to the United States was affected by pipeline breaks and revolution in Iran. These events were entirely outside of local control but had dramatic effects on local economies. Other uncontrollable incidents for localities result from a variety of outside influences, most notably external competition.

3 Pure Competition

Of course, one of the most serious challenges to local economies comes from overseas competition. Lower prices as a result of lower wage rates represent only one form of competitive advantage. In some cases, the mere increase in the numbers of global competitors has had the effect of increasing the supply of a given product. While global demand remains constant, any increase in the supply will lower the cost and damage companies' abilities to retain their workforces.

Another challenge is the research and development that is being done by firms overseas. For example, one of the reasons for the decline of the American automobile industry was the realization by Japanese automobile manufacturers that smaller, more fuel-efficient cars were in great demand in the American markets due to fuel prices and to the congestion in American cities where parking larger vehicles was becoming increasingly difficult. While the foreign producers were selling small, fuel-efficient cars across the United States, the Big Three manufacturers in Detroit were in denial that the days of the larger vehicles were rapidly declining. The Japanese—and other—manufacturers had simply done their research and acted upon it.

Once they realized that US auto manufacturers were not responding to the market changes, the Japanese manufacturers increased their production levels to fill the gap in supply. Rather than changing their design and cost factors, the US manufacturers appealed to Congress for protective tariffs that had the effect of increasing prices of the imported models. The American people lost first, then the American industry lost. And, in its wake, the City of Detroit and others in the region also lost. Those who manufactured the steel or supplied the seat covers or the tires—they all lost. In places such as Detroit, the retailers, restaurants, home builders, and more all lost.

Pharmaceutical manufacturing is another area in which pure global competition has reduced the share of the US markets that American companies had enjoyed. After years of American firms dominating the US marketplace, German, French, British, Japanese, and other manufacturers became increasingly competitive. Oil extraction and distribution is also an industry in which global forces have had negative impacts on local economies throughout the United States, and the list goes on. As Bivins explained, "The prospects are solid for energy in the United States because risk and uncertainty surround energy production in Russia, Mexico, and Brazil."[15] This, of course, works both ways; as will be discussed in a later chapter, US businesses as well as American communities and their constituents have been severely damaged by global powers collaborating to manipulate oil prices or managing the supply of petroleum that is available to the United States.

Of course, the potential for increasing global trade is very important to many communities, especially on the American coasts. "The growth of the Pacific Northwest helped propel Seattle to its current stature and the economic expansion of the Pacific Rim is likely to sustain Seattle's growth well into the future."[16] For this reason, US policy towards the protection of American industries needs to be applied very carefully. Quotas and restrictions on various products, and tariffs applied to imports can sometimes be an effective way to protect American industries but it can also create trading wars in which other nations implement similar tariffs on US exports. That can have the effect of protecting one industry but hurting another, or of one benefitting one community while damaging the economic base of another.

Those who argue against such protectionist policies do not always make their case for those reasons. Often, the "free markets" proponents do so for more theoretical reasons. The argument relies on the benefits of a laissez-faire economy and posits that free trade, without barriers or protections, accrue to the benefit of the consumers who have greater choices and therefore lower, more competitive prices. While this is so, the impacts of protectionism are not always considered by policymakers other than within the context of entire industries.

Do we place tariffs on the import of foreign automobiles in order to protect the US automotive industry? Yes, that industry is vital to our economy and to numerous major cities. Do we place protectionist measures on the import of foreign shoes? Perhaps not; the US industry is small and few communities in the country are dependent upon shoe production and sales. This may make sense at the national level but can also damage those cities and businesses for which the domestic sales of their footwear, as well as their export, may be a critical component of their economy. Businesses and communities need to be ever-vigilant in their assessment of the competition and the changing world economic environment. Everyone is subject to global competition and no one can foresee every coming change or impact. At the risk of redundancy, competitive assessments need to be conducted constantly. Again, placing these ideas into the context of actual situations can be very instructive for both students and practitioners who may someday find themselves with similar challenges.

4 Pittsburgh

Steel was Pittsburgh and Pittsburgh was steel. One report shows that, in 1978, Pittsburgh's factories produced nearly 17 million tons of steel annually, employed 90,000 workers, and represented 10 percent of all the employment opportunities in the region.[17]

The mid-1970s brought foreign competition to the steel industry that Pittsburgh had dominated since its inception. In return, the industry dominated the city and the surrounding region, and the local economic base. Like automobile production in Detroit and aerospace in Seattle, no one in Pittsburgh ever even considered that their dominance of the industry would ever be challenged, and certainly no one believed that such competition, if it did ever come, would come from overseas.

The *New York Times* reported that,

> In the early 1980s, the city (Pittsburgh) was being talked about the way Detroit is now. Its very survival was in question. The number of steel workers in the Pittsburgh area dropped from 90,000 in 1980 to 44,000 in just four years. By 2000, employment in the primary metals industries had declined to less than 2 percent of the region's total job base.[18]

Pittsburgh did not confront these levels of joblessness alone. The impacts were felt throughout the region as the unemployment rate in neighboring Beaver County reached an astronomical 28 percent.[19]

Overseas competition came from countries and producers with such relatively low labor rates that, even after the transport from Asia to the United States, the costs per ton were still dramatically less. As the US automobile industry was similarly impacted by foreign (Asian) competition, the domestic demand for tonnage of steel from the Pittsburgh producers also declined slowly at first and then much more dramatically toward the end. Detroit had been Pittsburgh's biggest customer and Detroit was no longer buying.

Compounding the problems of foreign competition and non-competitive wage rates for the industry, union demands exacerbated the issues. The United Steelworkers' demands for higher wages and ever-increasing benefits for their worker-members made it difficult for employers to negotiate. Both sides took inflexible positions from which compromise became increasingly difficult. As the industry began its slide, railroads, mines, engineering shops, and more also felt the pinch. The very nature of the region's economy had to change.

The city was left with a skyline comprised of disused steel plants and dilapidated factories. Potential employers were not greeted to Pittsburgh by attractive and welcoming scenes. Views of Pittsburgh like that shown in Figure 6.1 were all too common in the 1970s.

"Deindustrialization in Pittsburgh was a protracted and painful experience."[20] Leaders in the region believed that the steel industry would re-emerge in the city and the region and that the former prosperity would be recaptured. It took many years for a full acceptance that the industry was not returning to its glory days and that new industries had to be pursued to ensure economic growth.

The changes in the city that resulted from the loss of the steel industry and the resultant layoffs affected the community in a deep and impactful way. "The shutdown of the steel

Figure 6.1 Dirty Pittsburg
Source: Shutterstock

industry in the Pittsburgh region involved more than jobs. Swept away was an inter-generational way of life that provided a sense of continuity, family cohesion, and communality."[21] It also meant that, with lower general levels of expendable income, other employers in the region also suffered. Retailers sold fewer goods, restaurants and diners did less business, new home and new car sales stopped.

Local governments in the city and throughout the region also felt the impacts of the loss of the steel industry; they received smaller and smaller payments to the tax bases from which they provided public services. The quality of life in the region took a nosedive: "National Guard units were being mobilized, not to face an external threat, but to deal with domestic discord due to the dire economic conditions."[22] When the general realization did finally occur to—and was finally accepted by—the city and regional leadership that the changes to the steel industry were permanent, local planners decided not just to pursue the growth of the former industries but the development of new industry segments that would not only create new jobs, but would help to advance the community in a variety of ways.

In the decade of the 1990s, Pittsburgh was among the country's top 30 cities to lose population, declining 1.5 percent. Pittsburgh was, in 2001, also near the bottom of rankings of large metropolitan areas for the amount of annual immigration to the area and the percentage of foreign-born workers in its labor force. Without more immigrants, experts said, "Pittsburgh companies will have problems filling new jobs. Without new jobs, Pittsburgh will have problems attracting immigrants."[23]

At the same time economic development professionals were trying to attract new jobs for the region's anxious workforce, city planners began to focus less on the growth of job opportunities and more on the development of the economic base of both the City of Pittsburgh and the region surrounding it. The region was certainly not without strengths to offer to new employers. Surveys indicated that surviving firms offered a wide variety of engineering services equipment operations and raw material management. Linkages could be built from those areas to clusters other than steel and the primary metals industry.

Part of the city's recovery plan called for the major universities in the city to conduct research in areas such as software and biotechnology using state appropriations. The leaders of the day created a "vision of the two universities [the University of Pittsburgh and Carnegie Mellon] marshalling their joint intellectual and infrastructural resources to make these institutions active partners in stimulating the region's economy by spearheading the Pittsburgh BioVenture initiative."[24]

The State of Pennsylvania was able to add funding to the university coalition because it had funds available from the tobacco settlement. Between the institutions and the state, the industry began to evolve, in large measure because the universities were able to assess their respective strengths and make determinations about which university would exercise their competitive advantages in which areas. They were thus able to consider their respective strengths as complementary rather than competitive.

> The University of Pittsburgh has outstanding Departments of Psychiatry, Neurology, Neurological Surgery, Neurobiology, and Neuroscience. Carnegie Mellon University has recognized expertise in neuroscience in the Departments of Computer Science, Psychology, and Statistics.[25]

Ultimately, the University of Pittsburgh and its Medical School advanced in the area of research while Carnegie Mellon advanced on the clinical side of the bio-technology business. The practice of doctors and scientists interacting on a regular basis yielded results. The addition of a strong robotics industry to the region added an additional factor to support the growth of bio-science research in the city.

The recovery plan for the city and the region also included connecting the research and development labs of the great companies that were seeking new lines of production—Alcoa, Westinghouse, US Steel, Rockwell, and others—with these great universities in the region. By then supporting their interconnected research functions with public funding and support for entrepreneurialism, they believed the growth of new products and new economic development would occur. And, indeed many new ideas and new companies were created and commercial success was realized.

Numerous organizations emerged to exercise leadership for the region's recovery and evolution to new markets and new industries. One such group, drawing for its leadership on both public and private executives, was the Alleghany Conference on Community Development; it and other such groups worked to plan for the new industries by connecting the public and private sectors with the universities and other institutions to create the assets that would make the city and the region more attractive to new employers. They were further able to attract the necessary investment dollars to re-create the downtown as well as connect it better by multi-modal transportation lines to the suburban areas of the region.

Today, reportedly, restaurants are full, concert venues are well-subscribed, and the residents of the city have regained the pride of place exhibited by earlier generations. People are attracted to Pittsburgh to live and raise families, and to work and start up new firms, and the city has been cited as one of the Best Places to Live. "Today, the region is home to 10,000 tech firms employing nearly 300,000 people, with a total payroll of $20.7 billion—roughly one-third of the region's total wages."[26]

Pittsburgh has also been fortunate to be the home of a number of large foundations, such as the R.K. Mellon Foundation, the McCune Foundation, the Heinz Endowments, and others. These foundations have been strong contributors, not only in dollar terms but as sources of counsel and input as well as providing an apolitical, impartial meeting place. The significance in terms of size and substance has been a major factor in the city's and the region's ability to recover and to diversify its economy away from its previous over-dependence on the production of steel and other metals. In 1996,

> thirty local businesses, foundations, and individuals contributed 40 million dollars to a private fund (the Strategic Investment Fund) that will invest in local job-creating projects, complementing similar funds set up by the city and Alleghany County. Today, there are approximately fifteen venture capital firms in the Pittsburgh area—in 1980, there were two.[27]

The Pittsburgh region was also able to capitalize substantially on the presence of several major universities. The University of Pittsburgh and its Medical School are major factors in the growth of the life sciences industries and research throughout the region. Carnegie-Mellon University has developed strong programs in robotics that have resulted in the city becoming a renowned international hub for companies engaged in robotics design and applications.

The Robotics Institute at Carnegie-Mellon University now includes two facilities of greater than 100,000 square feet for research as well as 40 acres of testing fields. The Institute now includes more than 500 faculty, staff, and students who are eyeing the worldwide robotics market which, according to the Pittsburgh Technology Council, has reached more than 300 billion dollars and includes nearly nine million operating robots doing things that are either unsafe or dangerous for human beings. These robots possess artificial intelligence that allow them to "think" and act as programmed. The market for military ground robots has exceeded 44 billion dollars and other robots are working in various advanced medical procedures, a global market that the Pittsburgh Technology Council estimates has reached more than 14 billion dollars.[28]

The entire region immediately benefitted from the resurgence of business and the diversification of its economic base. Companies in Alleghany, Beaver, Butler, Fayette, Washington, and Westmoreland Counties have added more than 85,100 workers between 1994 and 2001 alone, according to Fitzpatrick.[29]

Is Pittsburgh still overly dependent upon a relatively few industries? The health care and life sciences sectors are indeed very strong but the question persists as to whether it is lasting enough to sustain the economic base of the city and the region. One report concluded "Probably not."[30] The author of the 2008 report, "Pittsburgh's Future," further observes:

> We should not make the same mistake we made in the 1970s—ignoring the warning signs of over-concentration in an industry that is known to have significant inefficiencies . . . so we can become truly diversified and better able to weather any storm in a particular economic sector.[31]

A good warning and the city has taken to heart the further diversification of its general industry base.

Robert Hurley is the CEO of the Alleghany County, Pennsylvania Department of Economic Development. Robert is atypical in one sense: he grew up in the area and then left but returned. He noted that many of his generation left and have not returned to the region. Individuals and families worked either in the metals industry directly or in the businesses that supported the industry. People grew up expecting to do so because their fathers and their fathers had before them. Complicating the issue for the city and the region are slow in-migration rates and death rates that exceed birth rates. In short, the city is declining in population (see Chart 6.1, The Post-World War II Population of Pittsburgh, Pennsylvania) and that creates concerns for employers that might become concerned about attiring a sufficient workforce. Generally speaking, the population has become increasingly younger over time; however, the decline in population over the 15 year period from 2000 to 2015 reached nearly 9 percent.

The region is somewhat complex and that has made it difficult to coordinate economic development efforts over time. The region is comprised of ten counties and Alleghany County alone comprised of 130 municipal governments, including the city of Pittsburgh which, with 300,000 residents, is the largest. The overall population of Alleghany County is about 1.25 million.

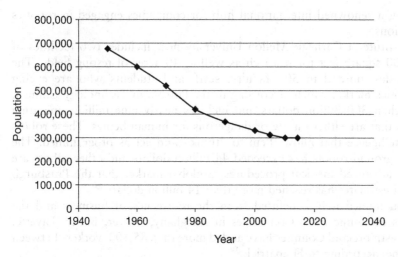

Chart 6.1 Post-World War II Population of Pittsburgh, Pennsylvania

Despite the dispersion of leadership over so many municipalities, the region was able to pull together to plot a revival of the economic base following the loss of the steel industry. Much of the leadership for that movement came from the philanthropic foundations that have resided in Pittsburgh for many years and that foresaw a need to pull together to rebuild the economy and the region. Complementing that leadership was the support of the universities, without which Hurley notes, the economic recovery of the city and the region would not have been possible. At a minimum, it would have taken a considerably longer period of time. There are many colleges and universities in the region and many were active in the recovery process but the two most impactful are, and continue to be, Carnegie-Mellon University and the University of Pittsburgh and its Medical School.

The universities were important, first because they attracted strong professionals to the region. That enhanced the income levels and the potential for new company growth. The University of Pittsburgh's greatest strengths have been in the life sciences and engineering. These were complemented, not overlapped, by Carnegie-Mellon's strengths in software and robotics. Further, the University of Pittsburgh helped drive new growth in a very large area on the east side of the city by building new classrooms and dormitories. This created jobs, higher incomes, and individual and family expenditures that circulated and re-circulated throughout the community. Collectively, the universities in the region account for as many as 60,000 undergraduate students, not to mention those engaged in graduate studies at the region's colleges and universities.

Carnegie-Mellon has been especially successful in spinning off new companies into the community from university research. Combined with the impact of employment in the region by major companies, such as Google, Amazon, and others, the income levels have begun to rise and the demand for new technology workers has been growing. People who have been attracted to the city to work for those companies and who have subsequently been offered transfers have declined to accept them because they have come to enjoy living and working in the city and in the region (Figure 6.2).

Figure 6.2 Revived Pittsburg
Source: Shutterstock

Recent discoveries of oil in the shale around the region have resulted in the attraction of workers from other communities with shale production. These too are high-paying jobs and help the economic base although people are aware that they cannot rely on such employment over the long term.

The region is not without challenges. As is the case with any region in the United States, there are very wealthy areas and pockets of poverty. The collective minority population has not generally fared as well as others, and that has caused severe issues for the city and the region. Mr. Hurley feels that minority leaders need to be more engaged in the city and the region in terms of planning and leadership. "We have diversified the economy and we need to diversify the community and its leadership. We need minority groups to be involved."

Another challenge is the development of a regional transportation plan. In part due to the proliferation of municipalities, the region has not always worked well on such difficult issues. The exception to that may be the airport which has grown its direct flights listing from 37 direct connections three years ago to 68 today. Also, in an effort to make the city and the region a more attractive place for the millennial generation to work, bicycle trails have been built in recent years at a substantial pace.

Industry targets for the region include the life sciences, advanced manufacturing, and autonomous vehicle systems. It is important to note that each of these industries is consistent with the strengths and offerings of the two major universities. Shell oil and GE have both opened facilities with large employment bases in the last few years.

The current directions for the City of Pittsburgh and Alleghany County are embraced by the community and Hurley notes that the region does have the political will to the move the area forward economically. Some of the county's many municipalities have begun to buy services from others (including Police protection, Fire services, and public education) in a move to create greater efficiencies, and there is legislation in the state legislature that would facilitate disincorporation of some of those municipalities.

Hurley does have some possible lessons to offer other areas that find themselves in similar circumstances. Inclusivity is critical, he asserts, because everyone must benefit from economic development or the community is not advancing together. Second, every institution must become engaged in the process, including colleges and universities, political leadership from both parties, and both large and small communities. His most emphatic conclusion was that the economic stability of both the city and the region are far more diverse and protected than ever before, and moving in the direction of even greater economic diversification and, therefore, long-term sustainability and growth.

After the steel industry collapsed and more and younger people departed the region, the remaining populace was, on average, much older. That, too, slowed the recovery. For this reason, and despite the reports by many analysts and academics that Pittsburgh had undergone a significant Renaissance, two University of Pittsburgh economics professors, Frank Giarratani and David Houston, wrote that "It would be very optimistic to say that the region is on the road to recovery."[32] The conversion to a technology and services economy will take longer. In this regard, Craig wrote that a particularly difficult challenge comes in the form of the urban core of the city, "where the population stood at slightly more than 900,000 in 2006, down from a 1950 high of 1.6 million."[33]

Since that time, however, the education and health care sectors have helped to drive the growth of jobs in the city and in the region, creating jobs that are high-paying and that are not likely to depart the city. Furthermore, jobs in health care and medical research have a much higher than average multiplier effect. That is, these jobs create more jobs in the secondary and tertiary economies than do jobs in other industries. This trend has begun to reverse the slow population growth of the region and has also begun to reduce the average age of the workforce. Finally, jobs in health care help the region's business community to interact with the many excellent universities in the region and, in turn, help the universities grow as well.

Summary: Lessons from the Pittsburgh Case Study

Pittsburgh is another great example of a city and a region that advanced its economic cause through development rather than simple growth. It is also a region that has done so through dramatic diversification of the economic base, from a steel town to a town with an economy based on information technology, health care, and a very strong university community.

On the other side of the coin, Pittsburgh also demonstrates what happens to a city and a region when the secondary and tertiary impacts of job loss come home to roost. All too often, people think of the positive aspects of secondary and tertiary impacts when an economy grows. Economies that decline also experience secondary and tertiary impacts: the loss of support businesses, vital assets and organizations, and rising crime rates, especially in downtown areas where the lowest education levels, the highest levels of unemployment, and lowest income levels are found. This is complicated by the growth of the new job base in the suburban areas that are more attractive to employers and close to the residential areas where the more educated workforce lives.

Ultimately, Pittsburgh and its region reversed the trend of suburban economic success and urban challenges. The regional economic development organization that was formed incorporates all of the cities and towns that surround the city, in collaborative spirit with the inner city itself. They believe that, in this way, an equitable pattern of growth will extend to the entire region, including the center city, and that reduced distinctions in opportunity will contribute to more equitable life styles, school performance, lower crime rates, and more. In other words, there is a recognition that such social ills are not based on background or personal characteristics but on economic opportunity and the types of neighborhoods that result from such opportunity. There has also been a key realization that the minority groups in the city and the region have too long been absent from the planning process and from future development, and that they need to be included in order to move forward collectively.

Pittsburgh's planners also recognized that the effort to develop an economy further should not be seen solely as the responsibility of the local governments in the region. The planning for, and implementation of, economic development requires strong involvement from the public sector (both elected and appointed) as well as the business community, local institutions, colleges and universities, key individuals, and other key stakeholders. This may be especially the case for the Pittsburgh region, which has so many renowned universities and faculty, well-established and long-time resident foundations, and public and private research laboratories to help in the region's future development.

Finally, Pittsburgh also illustrates the damage that population loss can do to a region. Plans are being put into place to retain the region's best minds while importing more people from across the United States and from around the world.

5 Detroit

As was the case in Seattle, civic and corporate leadership failed to accept that their industry—automobile production—was susceptible to overwhelming external factors that would spell its decline, and that of the city and the region with it. In the late 1960s and early 1970s, Japanese cars began entering US markets. Their size and costs were so much different than the products of the Big Three that they had appeal for American buyers. Their fuel efficiency—never an issue for US consumers who loved their big beautiful cars—also began to take hold in the American demand. As Maynard asserted, "Either Detroit wasn't paying attention, or if it did notice, the center of the automotive universe plodded on blindly in a state of denial."[34] Smick was even more emphatic: "A foreign car tidal wave was coming, yet the Chrysler guys hadn't a clue . . . Within less than two years, Chrysler was desperate for a federal bailout."[35]

The issue should have been clear: the US manufacturers' share of global automobile production had actually begun to decline in the seventies and eighties, and was paralleled by an obvious increase in foreign production and imports into the United States. From 1937 to 1985, General Motors maintained a global market share of just below 50 percent. It ranged from a high average of 49.7 percent in 1961 to 1965 timeframes to a pre-1986 low average of 41.8 percent in the early thirties and forties. Ford maintained a very constant average of the global market share from 1937 through 2000, ranging from a low period average of 17.8 percent between1981 and 1985 to a high average of 26.2 percent between 1961 and 1965. Chrysler held a steadily declining average that ranged from the 1937 high of slightly more than 25 percent to 10.7 percent by 1990. The issue was clearly obvious long before the Detroit manufacturers reacted. There was a state of denial: certainly this was just an aberration.

But, it was very real—and, lasting. Foreign production, which registered a mere 0.2 percent in 1937, climbed steadily through 2007, the year in which it topped US production with 52 percent of the world's market share. There can be no arguing that the American manufacturers were not aware of their changing fortunes because the foreign market share climbed steadily and consistently, without any loss in share for more than 60 years. That consistency is illustrated in Chart 6.2, Foreign Automobile Production, Share of the Global Market. Beginning with virtually no share of total automobile sales in the early 1950s, the foreign manufacturers represented more than half of all sales by the 2006 timeframe.

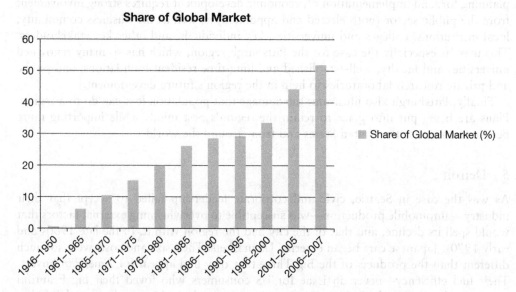

Chart 6.2 Foreign Automobile Production, Share of Global Market, 1937 to 2007

Source: Hughes, Jonathan and Cain, Louis. 2007. *American Economic History*, 8th ed. New York: Addison-Wesley, p. 600

In prior periods of fluctuating demand for vehicles, the solution of Detroit's manufacturers was "simply to shut down its plants to keep its vehicle inventories in line with sales, laying off workers for months on end."[36] Union representatives ultimately ended expectations of hikes in prices and demanded greater job security to go along with higher wages and improved benefits packages. These agreements made it even more difficult to compete with foreign-produced automobiles that had been produced with much lower labor inputs.

Newly-applied fuel mileage requirements and emissions standards that had been imposed by Congress exacerbated Detroit's problem and sales of foreign cars—now both cheaper to purchase and cheaper to operate—increased at the expense of the domestic industry; and, at the expense of Detroit and its workers. Other external, and considerably less controllable, events followed that would make Detroit's product even less appealing to the American consumer. Ultimately, as Maynard wrote, "it shows that the Big Three do not understand them (the American consumers) and do not genuinely respect them."[37] In contrast, foreign companies, notably the Japanese automobile manufacturers, took a much different approach to their business: "the 'Toyota Way' has been refined into two main principles: continuous improvement and respect for people."[38]

Following the Egyptian and Syrian attacks on Israel in 1973, and the subsequent takeover of lands by the Israeli armed forces, OPEC reduced the supply of oil in a successful effort to drive up world process and to punish the United States for arming and re-arming the Israeli forces. "In 1973, the American automakers churned out 12,637,000 cars and trucks. Two years later, they sold 8,985,000 vehicles, a 29 percent decline, mostly in passenger cars."[39]

The city's economy had been diversified in the same way that Seattle had diversified its economic base. The economy was dominated by automobile manufacturing but was also home to a thriving community of suppliers to the Big Three producers; the interconnectivity of the "diverse" industry base meant only that both the suppliers and the producers constituted the economic base. When the collapse of one began, the rest quickly followed suit.

"Today, the boomtown is bust. It is an eerie and angry place of deserted factories and homes and forgotten people . . . Its downtown is a museum of skyscrapers . . . Coyotes are here."[40] As the jobs left, so did those residents who had the financial ability to relocate and the skills to find employment elsewhere. By 2013, Detroit's population had, over decades, declined to a level of 688,000 people, down from nearly 2 million in the 1950s.[41] In 2010, one of every three residents of the city lived in poverty. "In 2009, the city's unemployment rate was 25 percent, which was nine percentage points more than any other large city and more than two and one-half times the national average."[42] In the massive areas of total vacancy, "Estimates had placed the number of roaming dogs in the city in the tens of thousands."[43]

And, with joblessness and poverty, comes crime. *Forbes* Magazine ranked Detroit as the most dangerous city in the United States, based on an unimaginable 1,220 violent crimes per 100,000 residents, and 90,000 fires. This was a substantially greater number than other major cities, such as New York, which all had much higher population levels. "The city had more murders in the year before its bankruptcy than Milwaukee, Cleveland, Pittsburgh, and St. Louis combined: 386 to 329."[44]

Figure 6.3 Detroit in Decline
Source: Shutterstock

The once-proud city had, physically, become a wasteland with "90,000 buildings left abandoned. Indeed, huge swaths of the city's 140 square miles were poised on the cusp of returning to nature."[45] Thirty percent of Detroit's area of 40 square miles was vacant. By comparison, the entire City of San Francisco is 47 square miles. It got so bad that a local journalist proclaimed that "Detroit Firefighters Have Their Own Name for Foreclosed Homes: Fuel."[46] Perhaps the worst observation of all: "Visiting Detroit is the closest Americans can come to viewing what appears to be a war-torn city without leaving the US."[47] In April 2012 "it became clear that Detroit, drowning in 12 billion dollars of debt, would have to accede to some form of state control."[48]

As Detroit struggled to recover, it was unable to capture even a single one of the newly announced foreign manufacturers' US production location decisions. This has been variously attributed to different reasons but high among them would certainly have to be the different approach to business attraction of the southeastern states and the different assets they have to offer these manufacturing firms from outside of the United States. For example, being right-to-work states means that they are not unionized. Foreign producers are well aware of the history of Detroit and the negotiations with the unions that resulted in burdensome salary, benefits, and security packages. "Of the five automobile assembly plants that were up for grabs in recent years, Alabama landed three . . . Collectively, the state's automotive workers have an annual payroll of three billion dollars."[49]

Management of the city and its finances had compounded the problems facing the entire region by the time the State of Michigan brought in external auditors and managers to help resolve the many and varied issues. One such financial expert reported being "stunned by what he found: an additional seven billion dollars in retiree health costs that had never been reported, or even tallied up."[50] These problems were not of recent making: they had been becoming greater and greater over decades, including "hoping that deep-rooted structural problems would turn out to be cyclical downturns that might melt away as the economy picked up."[51]

Years of neglect, over-spending, failure to reduce spending, amassing enormous debt, corruption, and ignorance of the depth of the problems brought Detroit to the point where it simply could not come back. No one could identify the number of police officers, although public safety accounted for more than half of the city's budget. For years, the city had increased the pay to its employees by pegging the annual increments to those of the United Auto Workers union. The city's bond reached junk bond status and the city could no longer borrow money. And, finally, employees' pensions are under-funded and over-committed, leaving a problem for the future of substantial proportions.

To compound the problems further, Detroit faced "a human capital challenge. Upwards of one half (47 percent) of all Detroit adults (2009) . . . lack basic reading and writing skills needed to obtain and hold good-paying jobs that could sustain them and their families."[52] There has been some movement:

> In the first decade of the twenty-first century, corporations began to relocate their offices into Detroit's downtown central business district from the suburbs. Information technology companies including Compuware Corp., Quicken Loans, Inc., and GalaxE Solutions, Inc., have clustered in the city.[53]

At the present, office space is both available and relatively inexpensive. This serves as an attraction for businesses to continue that trend. The city's leadership hopes that others will follow by bringing jobs back to the city.

Rod Miller is the CEO of the Detroit Economic Growth Corporation. His perspective is not only on the City of Detroit and the region in which it is located, but on urban markets more broadly. His previous positions included posts in New Orleans, Baton Rouge, and Phoenix. Mr. Miller believes that urban leaders need to look first for where their specific opportunities lie. That is precisely where the City of Detroit began its recovery process: What opportunities exist for us to begin re-building using the strengths that we do possess? How can we leverage our strengths?

Detroit does have numerous assets that make it attractive to businesses considering a location in the city. Detroit has always been a place that makes things and that expertise is still in the city and in the region. Given the history of manufacturing and shipping automobiles, Detroit also has a world-class ability in terms of the logistics of warehousing and shipping. The transshipment of materials into, and finished product from, Detroit is an opportunity for automobile and other types of manufacturing, most notably transshipments in and out of Canada.

The historic and present concentration of automobile manufacturers in Detroit still represents strengths for the city and the region. However, competitive areas for new automotive manufacturing are today primarily in the American southeast. Foreign automobile manufacturers have elected to locate their plants recently in states such as Alabama,

Tennessee, and South Carolina. Miller notes that those locations have "heavy arsenals of incentives to offer." They are also able to market the fact that they are Right-to-Work states, which appears very attractive to the manufacturers who recall that, in Michigan, which is not a Right-to-Work state, part of the problem stemmed from the high cost of labor and benefits that were negotiated by the relevant unions for the workers in the automotive industry. The result was higher unit process that made their products less competitive with Asian imports.

Miller felt that Detroit's 2014 formal declaration of bankruptcy was a vital step for the city because it enabled Detroit to move forward with a "cleared slate." It allowed the city to plan its recovery and its budget without the pressure of the overwhelming debt that had been incurred by a city of 2 million and left to be paid by a city of 700,000. The bankruptcy also enabled the Mayor and City Council to begin designing and providing public services to the remaining residents in a way that would help bring both people and companies back to the city.

When the efforts toward an economic recovery began in a sustained way, the Mayor and a relative few business leaders came together. The absence of more of the community's business leadership was glaring and made it difficult to move forward at a more accelerated pace. There was also a clear reluctance on the part of the neighboring suburban jurisdictions to be involved as well. This was not a new problem as the suburban communities and the city had not worked well together for some time. That challenge continues today, driven by the very distinct difference between the City of Detroit and its suburban neighbors: the city is 85 percent African American and the suburbs are 80 percent Caucasian, and the city has a very poor population while there is substantial wealth in the suburbs. Finally, because the city's public services are paid for predominantly by real estate taxes, the ability to attract people and businesses back to the center city is made difficult by the quality and quantity of those services and, as a result, the overall quality of life.

Miller explains that the city is now "pivoting." It is building on its traditional strengths in manufacturing and logistics, as well as the automotive history generally, to develop an economy around such related sectors as automotive manufacturing, software, new materials, and research on new innovations such as driverless cars. The city is focused on pivoting around its core strengths. But, new economic sectors have grown and are evolving as well, including robotics, information technology, medical services and research, and lower-tech industries, such as food preparation and sales. In most of these areas, Detroit finds its competition is coming from cities in the Rust Belt, such as Milwaukee, Indianapolis, Cleveland, and Minneapolis. The key, according to Miller, is to remain focused on where industry is headed and to stay ahead of those changes.

In terms of lessons learned that might benefit other cities in similar situations, needing to recover their economic base, Miller offers the following:

1   It is important to come together throughout the entire community. This means businesses, races, suburbs and the city, and political parties. Everyone needs to be part of the process.
2   Efforts must be made to bring people back to the city. People with the needed skills to support business growth and people who want to help rebuild need to come back to Detroit and become engaged in the process.

3   The caliber of public services needs to be raised. Otherwise, it will be harder to attract
new businesses to the city.

Another lesson to be learned from the Detroit experience is that the universities can be
extremely valuable partners. In Detroit, the local campuses of the University of Detroit
and Wayne State University have not only been engaged in the process, but they have
helped to drive it. They have built housing and classrooms for students in the city. The
area's largest technology business incubator, Techtown, is a university project. The University of Detroit has been the primary anchor in one section of the city and has been key
in the stabilization of that corridor. Miller noted that "This is the first time I have been
in a community where the universities are so well engaged and so effective in their partnership with the city." Miller's conclusion: "When disaster strikes, it is not just a crisis; it is
an opportunity."

Summary: Lessons from the Detroit Case Study

The greatest lesson that can be learned from the well-documented troubles of the Motor
City relates to the fact that the leadership of the business community and of the city simply
could not accept what was happening to them. They believed it was a temporary occurrence
and that the Big Three automobile dealers would recover their pre-eminent position as
the world's leading car manufacturers. The city delayed responding because they too felt
the problems would go away. When they did not go away, the community sat in shock
far too long before responding by trying to rebuild and refocus the economic base. The
lesson is to monitor trends and ensure that they are fully understood and appreciated,
and to react before the trend lines start their rapid descent.

The trend to smaller, more efficient cars was fully appreciated by their foreign competitors but not by the leadership in Detroit. Fuel efficiency, driven in part by OPEC price
manipulation, was mirrored by a growing demand for energy efficiency. The traditional
large-sized family cars were being replaced by smaller, more fuel efficient Japanese vehicles.
Detroit either didn't see any of this or refused to accept that it was a permanent change
in their economic base and, when they finally did acknowledge it, they could not seem to
comprehend it. And, when they finally did acknowledge that change was needed, their
ability to respond was severely hampered by union contracts that were highly restrictive.
The real lesson here is not about reaction times or disbelief but rather about not getting
into such restrictive situations in the first place. A diversity of industries was needed in
Detroit long before the crisis in automobile manufacturing. Cities and regions need to
keep abreast of global economic forces and trends.

Detroit's decline was ultimately so deep that the city experienced extremely high crime
rates and was, at one point, known as "the murder capital of the world." Slums and
dilapidated neighborhoods were all that was left of a once-proud city. The city's elected
officials were corrupt and federal money was squandered on projects that did not
advance the economic development of the city. Given this ineffective local government,
the region's business leaders were unwilling to interact on planning for a recovery for
many years. Such public–private collaboration is a vital component of economic development in any city.

Detroit still has the facilities and skills to recover in many diverse areas of the economy. Strengths in logistics and shipping remain. This is one area that can be exercised to help return Detroit to its former position of economic strength. All of the area's leaders must pull together to make this happen, however, including elected officials, business executives, the schools and colleges and universities, faith-based organizations, and more. If some successes can be demonstrated, people may come back into the city to live. They will pay taxes that will enable the local elected officials to provide better schools and other public services that, in turn, will help bring more people and more companies back into the city.

6   What Do These Case Studies Teach Us?

When one considers each issue, the relative importance of each to these case study cities becomes evident. Of the 11 cities considered, eight were situations in which external factors played the primary role in initiating the economic decline they experienced. Whether that means the end of a war or prices set elsewhere around the world or overseas competition from markets with relatively low labor costs or decisions made in Washington, DC, the ability to control the situation was taken out of the hands of the local elected leadership and the business executives in the region. Those outside factors, however, were exacerbated by disbelief that what had happened was not soon going away. That type of insistence and either a reluctance to respond to what was seen as a short-term matter or a form of collective shock that made action impossible for too long a time, compounded the problem by causing delays that resulted in the further loss of jobs, prestige, and community cohesion and positivity. Once the decline began, inaction often accelerated its course.

In most cases, an inadequate diversity in the economic base was responsible for the decline in the first place. Whether the strength was in aerospace or oil or steel or a military installation or federal contracting, the pre-decline expectation was that their city was golden because "certainly" those industries are never going away. Those beliefs were so firmly entrenched that, when the events that brought them down first occurred, it was assumed that it was simply a temporary problem. Oil prices will come back up. Those small foreign cars will not appeal to American buyers. The feds will always procure goods and services from the private sector. The lessons learned from these historic economic changes were that: 1) nothing is forever in a global economy except for change; 2) examining today's markets is an important business process but, without understanding those of tomorrow, such analysis is not entirely useful; and, 3) when you see what is coming, react before it occurs rather than waiting for the negative consequences before responding.

Impacts on the secondary and tertiary economies, both when scaling the growth curve and when sliding down its slopes, have underestimated impacts. The impacts on suppliers, retailers, personal services, public services, and community organizations don't seem to be fully appreciated until the impacts have hit. An important lesson for municipal leaders is that, once the primary sector announcements have been made, start immediately to prepare for the secondary affects. They will certainly be in the way.

After the full impacts of these events have been realized, the city is in for more shocks to its economic system. Those who can leave—that is, those who can find employment elsewhere take off for stronger markets. Population decline means that the local retailers, personal service providers, public schools, and others lose their customer base. And, there are more layoffs. Population decline also means the loss of workforce; and, not just any workforce, but those who can find employment elsewhere: typically the most educated, skilled, and experienced. Now, the community has a diminished ability to attract new employers.

It means that neighborhoods decline in appearance, main streets decline in attractiveness, and that school scores go down while crime rates go up. And, that, in turn, has meant that neighborhoods where there are no residents are the sites of the most fires in a city. There will be more demand coming for unemployment insurance and other transfer payments while the tax base from which they are paid is in freefall. Crime will increase as the localities' ability to provide police and fire protection rapidly declines. It means that cities that were once commercial leaders can fall to the bottom of the list very, very quickly.

The lesson should have been learned: this could happen to our community. We should be ever-scanning the commercial horizon and we should be further diversifying the local economic base. But, every time an economy that is overly dependent on a single industry or a single employer is impacted by these types of losses, surprised looks appear.

The final ignominy for these cities and regions is the loss of a reputation as a great place to do business. Companies are reluctant to locate in Detroit; it is too crime-ridden. Buffalo is too cold, Houston too hot. Perhaps Washington, DC's economy is not seen as being diverse enough. Why go there? There is nothing to attract us there. For this reason, much of the focus of these case study reviews was on how to recover.

One recovery requirement has already been mentioned: the need to react with speed and certainty: this is not coming back, we must get our act together, design a strategy, and put our plan into motion immediately. When that realization has been reached, it cannot be seen as solely a public sector responsibility. This city is everyone's city, so its problems are everyone's problems. The public sector, businesses, institutions, and organizations and all the people around the community must be involved in the solutions.

Community-wide approaches are ignored to the area's detriment. Perhaps some will concur because ensuring that everyone can advance as the economy is rebuilt is simply the right thing to do. Forget propriety; think selfishly if you must. To leave some behind, or to leave some neighborhoods or inner cities behind as growth is propelled is making problems for future leaders to address. Low incomes relate directly to high crime. Low educational attainment is directly related to greater public service costs. Workforce development is essential in rebuilding economies, especially where there are available jobs and high rates of unemployment. Preparing people for those jobs and enabling them to access them by public transportation is, if nothing else, an accelerator for economic growth.

Several of the cities examined herein have cited difficulties in bringing back those who have departed as well as historically low levels of in-migration. Immigrant populations and new residents from other US cities are key ways to build the workforce and create the kind of workforce assets that are attractive to potential future employers.

The success in using a region's geographic position as an economic asset has been noted as well. Whether that means proximity to a riverfront or a position as the only large conurbation with many miles, plans should exercise the assets that are naturally provided. Unlike oil prices and labor rates, the river will always be there.

As economic development has occurred in cities on the rebound, several components have been cited as necessary assets. Those communities that look forward to developing jobs in the business sectors of the future consistently cited the absolute need to encourage innovation and entrepreneurialism. The latter concept refers to the willingness of individuals to take risks in establishing new businesses. The concept of innovation is related to seeing new ways of doing things and then creating a commercial entity to provide such goods and services. Communities can support the growth of these businesses through local ordinances, tax policies, the creation of incubation facilities, the creation of bridges from the local universities to the businessperson or aspiring businessperson, and the attraction or creation of local venture capital funds to help support risk.

There are many other ways that local economies can be rebuilt, but the consistent reference of the case study communities to the factors cited above highlight their relevant importance. Moreover, the fact that all of these cities have begun steady climbs back up the economic growth curve is an indicator that, once down, communities *can* climb back up.

Notes

1 Peter V. Schaeffer and Scott Loveridge. *Small Town and Rural Economic Development: A Case Studies Approach*. (Westport, CT: Praeger, 2000): 57.
2 Binyamin Applebaum. This is the Bust in the Boom Town That Banks Built. (October 21, 2009) www.washingtonpost.com
3 Ibid.
4 Smick, David M. *The Great Equalizer: How Main Street Can Create an Economy for Everyone*. (New York: Public Affairs, 2017).
5 Phillipe Aghion and Steven N. Durlauf. 2005. *Handbook of Economic Growth*, vol. 1B. (San Diego, CA: Elsevier, 2005): 1453.
6 Chuck Chiang. Bend Plant to Close: Thirty to Lose Jobs. (May 26, 2007) www.bendbulletin.com
7 Longworth, Richard C. *Caught in the Middle: America's Heartland in the Age of Globalism*. (New York: Bloomsbury, 2008).
8 *Delta Farm Press*. 2016. Aurora, Illinois.
9 United States Department of Agriculture/Economic Research Service. 2005. US Textile and Apparel Industries and Rural America. www.ers.usda.gov
10 *Delta Farm Press*.
11 George Wuerthner. Why Is Logging Dying? Blame the Market. (June 15, 2016) http://hen.org
12 Maxwell Strachan. US Economy Lost Nearly 700,000 Jobs Because of NAFTA. (May 12, 2011) http://huffingtonpost.com
13 Ibid.
14 Patrick Gillespie. Rise of the Machines: Fear Robots, Not China or Mexico. (January 30, 2017) www.money.cnn.com
15 Ralph Bivins. Falling Oil Prices Temper Houston's Economic Surge. (May 7, 2015) http://urbanland.uli.org
16 Seattle Office of Economic Development, Trends. www.seattle.gov
17 Carey Treado and Frank Giarratani. *Intermediate Steel Industry Suppliers in the Pittsburgh Region: A Cluster-Based Analysis of Regional Economic Resilience*. (Pittsburgh, PA: Center for Industry Studies, University of Pittsburgh, December 2008): 3.
18 Ibid., 2.
19 Christopher Briem. It Was Twenty Years Ago Today. (February 16, 2003) www.post-gazette.com
20 David Streitfeld. For Pittsburgh, There's Life After Steel. (*New York Times*, January 7, 2009).

21 Roy Lubove. *Twentieth Century Pittsburgh: The Post-Steel Era.* (Pittsburgh, PA: University of Pittsburgh Press, 2004): 8.
22 Ibid.
23 Dan Fitzpatrick. Job Growth in Pittsburgh: Is the Glass Half-Full or Half-Empty? (July 15, 2001) www.post-gazette.com
24 Briem.
25 John F. McDonald. *Urban America: Growth, Crisis, Rebirth.* (Armonk, NY: M.E. Sharpe, 2008): 2.
26 Ibid., 4.
27 Dennis B. Roddy. Welcome to New Pittsburgh: A City Transformed. (January 22, 2015) www.pittsburghmagazine.com
28 Pittsburgh Technology Council. Robotics in the Pittsburgh Region. Pittsburgh, PTC. (June 12, 2014).
29 Fitzpatrick.
30 John G. Craig. Pittsburgh's Recovery Can Serve as a Lesson for Detroit. (March 22, 2009) www.washingtonpost.com
31 Pittsburgh (weather any storm).
32 Craig.
33 Ibid.
34 Ann Maynard. *Where the Buffalo Roam.* (New York: Weidenfeld, 1992): 13.
35 Smick, 114–5.
36 Lawrence J. White. "The Automobile Industry," in Adams, Walter, Ed. *The Structure of American Industry*, 6th. ed. (New York: MacMillan, 2008).
37 Maynard, p. 17.
38 Ibid. 31.
39 Ibid. 65.
40 Scott Martelle. *Detroit: A Biography.* (Chicago, IL: Chicago Review Press, 2012): 206.
41 Charlie LeDuff. *Detroit: An American Autopsy.* (New York: Penguin, 2013): 5.
42 Nathan Bomey. *Detroit Resurrected: To Bankruptcy and Back.* (New York: W.W. Norton, 2016): 2.
43 Edward Glaeser. *Triumph of the City: How Our Greatest Invention Makes Us Richer, Smarter, Greener, Healthier, and Happier.* (New York: Penguin, 2011): 40.
44 Mark Binelli. *Detroit City Is the Place to Be: The Afterlife of an American Metropolis.* (New York: Metropolitan Books, 2012): 8.
45 Bomey, 3.
46 Binelli, 9.
47 Ibid., 27.
48 James Moreland. Detroit is an Example of Everything that Is Wrong with Our Nation. (August 18, 2016) www.economyincrisis.org
49 Binelli, p. 243.
50 Maynard, p. 203.
51 Monica Davey and Mary Williams Walsh. For Detroit, a Crisis of Bad Decisions and Crossed Fingers. (March 11, 2013) www.nytimes.com
52 Davey and Walsh.
53 Lewis D. Solomon. *Detroit: Three Pathways to Revitalization.* (New Brunswick, NJ: Transaction, 2014): 7.

References

Aghion, Phillipe and Durlauf, Steven N. *Handbook of Economic Growth*, vol. 1B. San Diego, CA: Elsevier, 2005.
Applebaum, Binyamin. Perils of Globalization: When Factories Close and Towns Struggle, May 17, 2015. www.nytimes.com

Binelli, Mark. *Detroit City Is the Place to Be: The Afterlife of an American Metropolis.* New York: Metropolitan Books, 2012.

Bivins, Ralph. Falling Oil Prices Temper Houston's Economic Surge, May 7, 2015. http://urbanland.uli.org

Bomey, Nathan. *Detroit Resurrected: To Bankruptcy and Back.* New York: W.W. Norton, 2016.

Briem, Christopher. It Was Twenty Years Ago Today. February 16, 2003. www.post-gazette.com

Chiang, Chuck. Bend Plant to Close: Thirty to Lose Jobs. May 26, 2007. www.bendbulletin.com

Craig, John G. March 22, 2009. Pittsburgh's Recovery Can Serve as a Lesson for Detroit. www.washingtonpost.com

Davey, Monica and Walsh, Mary Williams. For Detroit, a Crisis of Bad Decisions and Crossed Fingers. March 11, 2013. www.nytimes.com

Delta Farm Press. Aurora, Illinois, 2016.

Fitzpatrick, Dan. Job Growth in Pittsburgh: Is the Glass Half-Full or Half-Empty? July 15, 2001. www.post-gazette.com

Gillespie, Patrick. Rise of the Machines: Fear Robots, Not China or Mexico. January 30, 2017. www.money.cnn.com

Glaeser, Edward. *Triumph of the City: How Our Greatest Invention Makes Us Richer, Smarter, Greener, Healthier, and Happier.* New York: Penguin, 2011.

LeDuff, Charlie. *Detroit: An American Autopsy.* New York: Penguin, 2013.

Longworth, Richard C. *Caught in the Middle: America's Heartland in the Age of Globalism.* New York: Bloomsbury, 2008.

Lubove, Roy. *Twentieth Century Pittsburgh: The Post-Steel Era.* Pittsburgh, PA: University of Pittsburgh Press, 2004.

McDonald, John F. *Urban America: Growth, Crisis, Rebirth.* Armonk, NY: M.E. Sharpe, 2008.

Martelle, Scott. *Detroit: A Biography.* Chicago, IL: Chicago Review Press, 2012.

Maynard, Micheline. *The End of Detroit: How the Big Three Lost Their Grip on the American Car Market.* New York: Random House, 2004.

Moreland, James. Detroit is an Example of Everything That is Wrong With Our Nation. August 18, 2016. www.economyincrisis.org

Pittsburgh Technology Council. Robotics in the Pittsburgh Region. Pittsburgh, PA: Pittsburgh Technology Council, June 12, 2014.

Roddy, Dennis B. Welcome to the New Pittsburgh: A City Transformed. January 22, 2015. www.pittsburghmagazine.com

Seattle Office of Economic Development, Trends. www.seattle.gov

Shaeffer, Peter V. and Loveridge, Scott. *Small Town and Rural Economic Development: A Case Studies Approach.* Westport, CT: Praeger, 2000.

Smick, David M. *The Great Equalizer: How Main Street Can Create an Economy for Everyone.* New York: Public Affairs, 2017.

Solomon, Lewis D. *Detroit: Three Pathways to Revitalization.* New Brunswick, NJ: Transaction, 2014.

Strachan, Maxwell. US Economy Lost Nearly 700,000 Jobs Because of NAFTA. May 12, 2011. www.huffingtonpost.com

Streitfeld, David. For Pittsburgh, There's Life After Steel. *New York Times.* January 9, 2009.

Treado, Carey and Giarratani, Frank. *Intermediate Steel Industry Suppliers in the Pittsburgh Region: A Cluster-Based Analysis of Regional Economic Resilience.* Pittsburgh, PA: Center for Industry Studies, University of Pittsburgh, December 2008.

White, Lawrence J. "The Automobile Industry," in Walter Adams, Ed., *The Structure of American Industry,* 6th ed. New York: MacMillan, 2008.

Wuerthner, George. Why Is Logging Dying? Blame the Market. June 15, 2016. http://hen.org

7 National and State Forces that Impact Local Economies

As companies and residents left the Rust Belt to find warmer climes and more comfortable places to raise families and grow companies, one lesson became clear. As Glaeser wrote, "America's deserts and mountain ranges aren't densely inhabited for a good reason: few people want to live in such harsh places."[1]

Federal policies are often enacted to benefit the many rather than the few. Often they are enacted to benefit an industry-wide need or a federal budgetary need or other considerations that have far-reaching consequences. In some cases, such measures can have results that were never anticipated, yielding the expression, "the law of unintended consequences." As has already been discussed, when moving to implement nation-wide, industry-wide, or regional protections, Congress cannot always consider the impacts on local economies. Aghion and Durlauf point out that "migration, trade policy, national investment in communications and transport infrastructure have profound impacts on the urban system, migration patterns, regional economic development, and the like."[2]

State, and even regional, policies can inhibit growth and development although the policies are never intended to do so but, at times, they can inadvertently have that effect. For example, the City of Portland, Oregon has, for decades, existed under growth control policies that limited both residential and commercial growth within urban growth boundaries, concentric circles designed around the city. The intended purpose was to protect certain greenbelt areas and to control the population growth while directing any such growth into specific growth corridors.

The actual impact of the limitations on growth was called into serious question however when, in the late 1990s, the largest employer in Oregon, Intel, which already had 4000 employees in the state, announced their desire to increase their workforce substantially. A law was on the books that limited new employers to the state, and existing employers in the state, from creating more than 1000 jobs at a time. Of course, the law was intended to restrain unfettered growth and sprawl; new jobs meant new residents as well. The law allowed for Intel to create up to 1000 additional jobs on its campus before incurring excessive fines for each job over that limit.

The sense in the city at the time was that, if Intel had not already been located in Oregon, and approached the leadership with a plan for 5000 jobs, they would have been turned away. In other perhaps ill-considered legislative maneuvers, the largest employers were assessed impact fees. These are fees based on the assumptions that thousands of employees place greater demands on local infrastructure than do hundreds or tens of employees.

While the theory is sound, such policies are not friendly to large businesses and likely kept many large potential economic development prospects away from considering Oregon locations. And, although Intel tolerated these kinds of legislative policies, neither is it a good strategy if one wants to retain existing businesses. Moreover, such growth-constricting policies at the state, regional, and local levels create an image, in this case one of a state that is not pro-business and that will not support companies if they do locate there. Notwithstanding whatever prospects Oregon lost, and whatever existing businesses they were unable to retain, there were, no doubt, numerous additional business prospects that refused even to consider business locations in Oregon for these reasons.

In another inexplicable move, the City of Portland and surrounding Multnomah County passed ordinances to impose new taxes on the net incomes of the highly successful venture capital companies in the region. Although the ordinances were subsequently repealed, the venture capital businesses had already moved away. In an effort to obtain greater tax revenues from them, they ended up losing all of what they already had.

Controls on the free-market economy often do have unintended consequences for the localities or states involved; not all of the consequences of such decisions are clearly anticipated. The urban growth boundaries in Oregon had the result of the majority of office construction taking place downtown while most of the jobs resided in the suburbs. In an attempt to control sprawl and direct growth, there arose a mismatch between where the building took place and the preferences of the business community as to location.

Another set of economic impacts from the federal level for Oregon affected the timber industry in the state. As the management of federal lands grew, Oregon became largely federal owned. Samuels points out that the federal government now owns 53 percent of all the land in the state and has dramatically reduced grazing and logging on those lands in recent decades. These restrictions seriously damaged two of the larger industries in the state.[3]

It is not always clear that growth restriction ordinances are serving either the best interests of the people or the intentions for which they were actually designed. Also in the late 1990s, the State of Maine became concerned about the national chain retailers that were entering the state and driving out the local, so-called "mom-and-pop" stores. The enabling legislation that was passed with that intent gave the localities throughout the state the ability both to deny permits to new "big-box" chain retailers as well as to close down and send away existing chain retailers if the community felt it would thereby protect small, home-grown retailers.

Three communities in the state exercised that option and sent existing chain stores out of the community. In the interest of protecting dozens of jobs, hundreds were lost. Further, the tax bases of those localities were decimated and the state's revenues were also negatively impacted. It is unclear whether those results were anticipated by the state and local decision-makers or whether they were simply willing to accept the consequences. Of course, only three localities exercised the option, so it is quite possible that other localities throughout the state did realize the potential hazards of doing so.

Another example of state policies that negatively affect fiscal stability in municipal governments was revealed in research for a previous book. The Mayor of Chambersburg,

Pennsylvania expressed his frustration at being a public servant who was trying to do the best for his constituency while the state legislature constantly over-regulated what municipalities can or cannot do. He noted that the neighboring State of Maryland had roughly one legislator for every 12,000 people while the State of Pennsylvania had about one for every 4000 residents.

The legislature had enacted legislation that was designed to attract pensioners to retire in the Keystone State. The draw for the retirees was that the state would not tax their pension income and the consequence was that local governments receive no revenues from such individuals although they still demand public services; and, their demand for health care, recreational facilities, and more was even greater than the existing population in many communities. The well-intentioned legislation may have had some benefits for both the state and the individuals, but it had serious, negative unintended consequences for cities and towns across the State of Pennsylvania.

In the State of Ohio, changes in the state's tax code severely impacted how cities can collect revenues and pay for public services. Gary Norton, the Mayor of East Cleveland, reluctantly led his city into municipal bankruptcy proceedings. In addition to suffering the whiplash of economic decline in the regions core city (Cleveland), the smaller city had revenues taken by the state. The state removed the local government revenue fund. "It is essentially all the taxes . . . collected by the State of Ohio. Revenues like sales tax, and income tax, and property tax . . . generated in the cities" had been redistributed by the state to cities as a form of revenues sharing. The state halved the amount to be shared. "Twenty percent of the city's budget had come from the local government revenue fund. When that was halved," said Norton, "that's cutting 10, 12 percent of your budget. That's what happened to us."[4]

One more clear and very recent example of how national political decisions can affect local economies relates to the Trump administration's position on Deferred Action for Childhood Arrivals (DACA). This legislation, approved in the Obama administration, allowed young men and women to stay who were brought to this country illegally by their parents when they were quite young and had no control over what happened to them. Now, decades later, many are adult students and employees. To the extent that communities and employers are home to these individuals, their success is, in part, dependent upon the retention of these employees.

The Trump administration, however, in September of 2017, decided to revoke the DACA program and flip the issue back to Congress for a final decision on how to treat these individuals. If a bill is not passed that allows them to remain in the United States, they will potentially have to return to the respective nations of their birth. Many of these people have no recollection of those places and do not speak any language other than English. But, the real losers could be the companies and communities that have housed and employed them. This could be an especially difficult challenge for smaller towns that have higher percentages of such people in their workforces. And, yet they have little control over what happens to these individuals and it could have a potentially devastating effect on both businesses and the economic futures of entire communities.

The lesson to be learned here is that communities must keep a constant eye on what is happening in Washington, DC and around the world. In the instance of DACA, it means that cities and towns need to marshal their collective forces to deliver repeated messages to their representatives in the state capitals and through their senators and representatives in Congress. Their decisions could damage businesses and wreak havoc in cities, towns, and regions across the country.

Communities must be diligent in notifying their state legislators about the potential local impacts of proposed state legislation. Of course, some enactments may benefit some parts of a state while having less positive impacts on others. At that point, it may not be possible to muster enough votes to protect one or more cities and towns. Constant local impact analyses of state policies and laws can be promoted through state chambers of commerce and municipal leagues. Local leadership and economic development professionals need to be intensely aware of proposed changes in state codes and the best means of communicating their concerns.

1   Federal Cutbacks and Other Budgetary Causes

It is self-evident to state that not all of the forces affecting local economic development are controllable by a community's leaders. It is equally obvious to assert that communities are always able to find relief from all of the external winds buffeting local economic progress. However, some of those forces can be seen, understood, and prepared for by localities before they strike. When that occurs, the community can prepare itself and thus be more likely to recover more quickly; and in some cases, never even skip a beat.

One such external force comes to communities and regions that are proximate to military installations. Communities may carry on for years, living off the commerce that is conducted around and on the base. Soldiers eat, shop, and participate in local communities. In many cases, local leaders expressed no serious concerns about losing the base and the nearby businesses that supply. Much like automobiles in Detroit, steel in Pittsburgh, and aviation and aerospace in Seattle, many areas couldn't believe that their installation would ever be moved.

The Base Realignment and Closure—better known as BRAC—process of the federal government is designed to sustain the nation's preparedness while being efficient by consolidating like commands into single locations. The results have not been even across all communities; there are winners (those that gain in employment and investment by the military) and losers (those in which the installation has been moved and bases deserted).

In the most recent round of BRAC, the command relocations just within the northern Virginia portion of the greater Washington, DC region had tremendous and varied impacts on the area's counties. Fairfax County is home to Fort Belvoir, which received more than 16,000 new positions—in various commands—on the base. This meant that there was a new demand for public schools on the base. That is the responsibility of Fairfax County, not the Army or the federal government. This also meant increased traffic on the already congested Route One Corridor (Historic Richmond Highway), again for which the county received no additional funding.

There was also a positive element of these relocations. The commands that moved onto Fort Belvoir had multiple private sector contractors who either wanted to or needed to (under contract) move closer to their contracting commands. This resulted in a greater demand for office space within a specific distance from the base. The resultant new construction did increase revenues to the county's tax base, which provides public services essentially from real estate taxes (64 percent of expenditures from the General Fund for public services come from the real estate tax base).

Neighboring jurisdictions to Fairfax County did not fare quite as well. While Fairfax County was a net job recipient under that round of BRAC, Arlington County was a net loser of positions and, as a result, sub-contractors. One area in the county in which they were dominant was Crystal City. As that area lost tenants, the vacancy rates in the county's office space reached as high as 25 percent. This typically has the result of lowering commercial assessed values and impacting a real estate tax base that, again, was the source of funding for local public services.

Another neighboring jurisdiction, the City of Alexandria, saw an entire building purchased by the Army. While this resulted in new jobs in the city, there was no demand for new housing by employees because they already lived in the region and simply had new commuting routes. However, the primary impact was the purchase of the building, meaning that it came off of the tax rolls of the city because the federal government does not pay taxes to states or localities. Further, the location of the building is such that the increased traffic and the shifting patterns of commuting traffic caused significant congestion.

The loss of a military unit can be devastating to the region in which it resides. This can be especially so for smaller regions, even when the unit so affected is also relatively smaller. When the potential bases slated for consideration under BRAC are announced, communities often do spring into action. The Letterkenny Army Depot near Chambersburg, Pennsylvania was a strong contributor to the local economy. It was such an important feature of the local economic landscape that the municipalities and the State of Pennsylvania spent large sums of very scarce funds to improve the roads around the Depot. This was in hopes of demonstrating the local support for making Letterkenny successful and comfortable.

The Pennsylvania efforts were rewarded; not only was the Depot left in place, but 166 new positions were added. This is unusual; more likely to be the case is that community actions to save a base may be considered irrelevant—decisions are made for reasons of national-level efficiency and strategic implications for the military. The result is that the decisions move into the political realm. When a base or facility is added to the BRAC list and the list is made public, political forces—local, state, and federal—are marshalled to argue on behalf of retention. Community impacts are cited and infrastructure support is offered but, in many instances, those with influence attempt to bring it to bear to save the units in question.

These efforts pit two types of logic against one another: community interests and the needs of the military. While those discussions continue, communities have often begun a parallel process of awareness and planning. This comes from the realization that the region is about to have returned to it frequently a vast area to be used and marketed for commerce. It often includes roads and utility infrastructure and, on occasion, advanced technology infrastructure. There will be buildings that have been used for offices or residences, possibly supported by everything from proving grounds and testing facilities to stores and conference facilities to movie theaters and bowling alleys. Surely, the realization dawns, there are alternative uses from which we can benefit and build new types of economic activity. In short, if such external decisions are seen coming, they can be used as positive economic assets for future growth. This will be examined in depth in the case study of Plattsburgh, New York.

Of course, not all losses to an area's economic development—or even its very sustainability—can be recovered from as positively as described above. External forces that affect local growth may include newly-competing markets in which labor costs are so dramatically lower that regions cannot come back without a complete overhaul of their industrial base, workforce, and facilities.

This may be particularly difficult for small cities and towns. In previous research, discussions were held with the mayor of Tifton, Georgia which, following the implementation of the North American Free Trade Act (NAFTA), lost jobs in the local textile mills. In a somewhat isolated community, the loss of 550 jobs in a single decision was devastating. Notwithstanding platitudes about leadership and pulling one's self up by one's bootstraps, there is often little that can be done. In the case of Tifton, some ground was recovered but, as was covered in an earlier interview, 50 new jobs this year and 20 more next year—while they help—do not replace the loss of more than 500 jobs in an employer that had been part of the community for decades. Compounding the sense of loss was the frustration that there was absolutely nothing that the community could have done to prevent the loss. The forces that caused it came from overseas.

Interestingly, not all of the national-level forces that impact local economies are actions taken. In some instances, the impacts are due to national-level decisions not being taken. In an interview conducted for previous research with the leadership in Gillette, Wyoming, the point was made and remade that the absence of a comprehensive national energy policy was damaging the economic growth of that region. Without a national policy on the mining of coal, opportunities were being lost in parts of the world that had expressed significant demand: India and China. As such, external forces were diminishing the opportunities for growth locally.

The first budget proposed by the newly elected Donald Trump resulted in a considerable uproar because every one of the programs being proposed for cuts had constituencies that bemoaned the attempts to reduce the federal support for their individual causes. In fairness, none of the complaints were outrageous, and all the programs proposed for cuts had some logic. Cutting meals programs for the elderly or NIH research grants or other proposed reductions and eliminations raised great responses. The administration, in an effort to reduce federal expenditures, needed to make the difficult decisions about what to cut. The need to cut seemed to those decision-makers to be paramount: some things had to go. The classic definition of politics is making difficult choices from among competing, reasonable demands.

Around the Washington, DC metropolitan area, the loss of direct federal employment as a result of the new administration's budget plans ranged from 20,000 to 24,000 positions, some 5.5 to 6.5 percent of the total. And, another estimated 1 billion dollars plus was lost to organizations that provided services on the back of federal grants. The direct impact on the local economies will be followed by a ripple effect on the residents of the areas most affected.

The Washington, DC metropolitan area is home to so many government contractors that the concerns about reductions and job losses were greater in that region than anywhere else in the nation. This leads to the very core of the concerns: no one knew what would actually happen. The greatest problem was one that businesses despise: uncertainty.

When a President presents the federal budget for Congressional consideration, every Senator and every Representative reviews the document for programs they oppose or support. They all want to know how it is going to affect their respective constituencies. Then, the negotiating beings: perhaps if this is cut instead, that can be funded. If you support my amendment, I'll give you my vote on one that is vital to you. No one can possibly look at this process and believe that they truly understand what will ultimately be approved.

In the largest private sector employment base in the Washington, DC region, Fairfax County, the uncertainty was voiced loudly, particularly by the federal contractor community. However, even assuming that the President's budget would be passed as submitted, there was a great deal of uncertainty because cuts to Fairfax County headquartered Department of Defense contractors did not necessarily imply job losses in the region. In fact, in the first round of sequestration, nearly 3 billion dollars of federal contracting dollars were lost by county-based companies, but few jobs were lost by the contractors who were simply passing the funds through to their operations in other states where the equipment was actually being made. Fairfax County, which is an almost entirely office space market, does not manufacture things for the feds. If subsequent rounds of sequestration include cuts in federally funded programs that involved the provision of services, the story could be very different.

Similarly, the President's proposed budget cuts result in the same kind of uncertainty for local business because, although the agencies that have been targeted are known, and even the specific projects being targeted are known, the circuitous path that the process will take leads to an uncertainty of the outcome.

A quick review of the federal contracts that were awarded in Fiscal Year 2016 implies that Fairfax County could actually stand to benefit if the President's proposal goes through as presented, even though there would be some losses of federal contracts. In Fiscal Year 2016, nearly 24 billion dollars were awarded to Fairfax County-based businesses, representing about 5 percent of all federal contracts awarded that year in the United States. Of that amount, more than 71 percent (in total dollars) were received from three agencies that had been identified as getting expanded budgets: the Department of Defense, Homeland Security, and the Office of Veterans' Affairs. Agencies that had been targeted for reductions in the President's proposed budget, including the Departments of Health and Human Services, State, Housing and Urban Development, Education, Commerce, Energy, and the Environment Protection Agency, only accounted for 11 percent of the total contract amounts for the fiscal year. While the news looked positive from that perspective, the general air of uncertainty still hung over the federal contractor community because it remained unclear what would be the final outcome of the Congressional deliberations.

Some uncontrollable external forces are the result of national-level decisions. Sequestration was imposed by Congress to curb its own spending and to begin to control the ever-growing federal deficit. The consequences for local governments were varied. Those that had a large base of federal contractors were affected, although not always as it may have appeared. Because Fairfax County, Virginia is an immediate suburb of

Washington, DC, it is home to many federal contractors. More than 2.5 billion dollars in federal contracts to Fairfax County-based companies were lost in the initial round of sequestration. Jobs, however, did not decline relatively because the reductions were in things that are manufactured. While the companies housed in the county lost funds, the majority of the jobs lost were in other states where the items were made. The county's employment base is much more susceptible to reductions in the services that are procured by the federal government.

Around the Washington, DC metropolitan region, the impact of sequestration was felt in a variety of areas, including housing. Reduced federal spending meant fewer contracts with area companies that provide goods and services to the various federal agencies in town. Average wage decline was followed by the growth of lower-wage positions and the average wage rate across the region gradually declined, yielding impacts on the housing markets. Generally, lower-price housing was in greater demand than before sequestration and high-priced housing sat on the market for extended periods.[5] New construction declined and jobs in the construction industry dropped.

There were many other localities around the country, however, where the sequester did have substantial negative impacts. Certainly, these were not intended outcomes of the decisions but it substantiates that sector diversity in the business base is a critical feature—perhaps the most critical element—of a sustainable economic base. This conclusion has been reached in the greater Washington region, as will be discussed in greater detail in later chapters.

2   Forces Impacting Small Towns and Rural Economies

It would be natural to conclude that suburban and rural communities have unique sets of forces that influence their economic growth, decline, and revitalization. While that is true to an extent, it represents only a partial picture. In fact, many of the same forces that impact the highly urbanized parts of the country also affect suburban growth as well as growth in the small towns and rural area of America.

John McDonald, in his study of urban America, notes the influence of the baby boom years (generally considered to be from 1946 to 1964) on rural economies. During this time, more than 76 million Americans were born and the percentage of American adults who obtained high school graduation rose from 49 percent to 76 percent.[6] As cities, counties, and regions grew, they did so outward rather than upward. And, as employers moved away from cities and into suburban areas to chase the higher-skilled workforce, jobs became available to the now more highly educated rural population. This created a brain drain from small towns and rural communities that was further accelerated by the onset of large-scale farming and the loss of family farms across the country.

Today, small towns across the nation are working to re-create the small town feel that once appealed to so many Americans. In particular, they are seeking to attract their young people, who left town to see the world or to get an education or to begin their careers. Many in small towns today believe that these prodigal children may return to recapture for themselves and their families a quieter pace in a community where everyone knows each other and where life is less expensive and just more attractive generally. To that end, many small cities are in the process of beautifying their downtowns, adding infrastructure, including technology needs, adding the amenities that small cities are noted for, and reaching out to those who had moved on earlier in their lives.

What small towns and large city leadership generally have in common is a vision of where they want their community to go and a plan for how to get there. This is, in large measure, due to increasing efforts by other locations—large and small–to attract their companies away. This has caused small towns within regions to collaborate to bring jobs to their area. That also means that these small towns are building the necessary base of firms that will support and attract employers. This includes accountants, lawyers, personal services providers, higher education institutions, and cultural and recreational opportunities. This has been accelerated in many areas of the United States where farming has been taken over by large corporations, forcing small family farm workers either to seek other employment locally or to relocate.

A report by the Federal Reserve Bank of Chicago highlights the attractive elements of rural living, including lower living costs, access to educated and high-skilled workers, and greater-than-average levels of productivity. For many people, and many businesses, the slower pace and higher output make rural communities sufficiently attractive to locate facilities. The same report, however, also asserts that rural health care—both the availability and the quality—"will remain critical factors in how well rural life is judged."[7]

Given the constrained financial and staff resources of small towns, they typically encourage everyone to get involved. There is a greater sense that "this is my community" and that "I can make a difference." People believe that local decisions more directly affect their lives and those of their families. As such, they are very likely to seek opportunities to provide input and to help determine the best way for their community to grow and yet to protect that which is considered valuable about their home towns.

But, because small towns are small and their budgets and other resources are similarly limited, progress generally comes slowly. Though, progress comes only over time, the journey must begin. The Federal Reserve Bank asserts that "Rural communities have the option to change and survive, or refuse to change and run the risk of perishing through the continued migration of their most productive workers."[8]

The need for constant change in rural communities is paralleled by the need to acquire the assets that will attract firms and workers. And, it is the reason that such communities need to create a list of gaps in their offerings for business and start adding them one-by-one as soon as feasible and in the best of times. This will be covered in a later chapter as it applies to communities of all sizes and all geographic locations. In recent years, many small towns started with the enhancement of the fiber and cabling that enable people to work from locations outside of the immediate community. Many small towns feel they can lure people back who have technology skills that permit them to work from a distance—in their small towns—while still earning the salaries and opportunities that generally come from larger employers in distant locations.

Most small town mayors are not long-time politicians; in fact, many have become involved out of love for their community and a sense that they can be of service as it develops. Many of the small town mayors I have interviewed for previously published volumes have maintained that their greatest strength, as will be discussed in later chapters, is that they had held positions in industry for long enough to understand budgeting and people-management and that they can bring business sense to local government as well.

Further, they have repeatedly acknowledged that they are ever-accessible. They see their neighbors at church, in the grocery store, and at scouts and PTA meetings.

Of course, not all external forces are controllable, especially for communities in rural areas. An interview was conducted for previous research with the mayor of the City of Elmira, New York, which had suffered a flood four decades prior to our conversation! The loss of property and jobs was so severe that many for the mayor's constituents still spoke fondly—and openly of "the good old days," meaning the time "before the '72 flood." For communities that have come back, part of the formula for success must include making political decisions in difficult circumstances—perhaps a core factor of political leadership.

The greatest political issue for small town mayors, council members, and administrators in the pursuit of economic development or revitalization is that they must constantly balance matters. Should we invest in infrastructure for future development or in more school teachers or police officers today? How can we create the best development without damaging the natural scenery in and around the community? How can we further develop the economy without overgrowing, and thereby losing the small town feel that people love so much about these communities in the first place?

Small towns and rural communities have begun to re-populate themselves. In the last decade of the twentieth century, the population of rural America increased, including growth in more than half of the nation's rural counties. More than two million Americans left urban areas for rural communities.[9] The impetus for some of this migration to rural communities may have been the growing availability of technology infrastructure in such communities, thus allowing people to enjoy a different lifestyle while still advancing their careers and income levels.

There is still much to accomplish in terms of extending the technology infrastructure outward from the urban and suburban areas of the country, but progress is being made in that regard. In the meantime, however, men and women living in rural areas are still struggling with the prospects of under-employment, meaning that they are either working several jobs to make ends meet, that they are working in jobs for less pay than that to which they are accustomed, or that they are working at jobs beneath their skill levels and prior positions.

Small towns and rural communities must be constantly diligent to identify and to work toward closing the gaps that exist between what business needs in a community and what can be offered in rural areas. These gaps may be found (depending upon the specific community) in technology infrastructure, roads and transport access, capital availability for investments in new ventures, quality public schools, workforce issues and the availability of higher education for recruiting and retraining employees, support programs for potential entrepreneurs, and adequate housing of diverse styles and costs, as well as strategically designed and well-funded economic development programs.

This is not to say that highly successful small towns in rural areas cannot be found. "Prosperous small towns abound in every region of the country and in every state; oddly enough, they are often a stone's throw away from a town that is dying on the vine."[10] Why some fare well and others do not, and how some have recovered and others have not, will be covered in future chapters.

One thing that clearly distinguishes a small, rural community from their larger, more metropolitan counterparts is the potential for a single event to affect the future dramatically. If a primary employer leaves a small town, not only are jobs and income lost, but taxes leave town and the ability to provide public services can be significantly altered by a single decision. Of course, the reverse is also true. Business relocations to the town can also have life-altering impacts for the community and its residents.

Natural disasters can affect the economies of large cities, metropolitan regions, and small towns. One such example is instructive here not just because of the extent of the damage and destruction, but also because of the manner and relative speed with which the community recovered and redeveloped its economy. On May 22, 2011, Joplin, Missouri—a city of roughly 50,000 residents—was hit by one of the deadliest tornadoes in the recorded history of the United States. More than 160 people were killed and the swath of destruction measured roughly 6 miles long and 1 mile wide right through the city. Thousands of homes were destroyed and hundreds of businesses shut down. In all, 2000 buildings were destroyed and more than 10,000 damaged. The tornado hit immediately after the local high school graduation had concluded. While fortune smiled a bit on the people and there was no one left on the school grounds, the school building itself was destroyed. It was estimated that there was between 1 and 3 billion dollars in insured losses.[11] Business revenues lost as a result of the tornado were immeasurable.

The hit to the City of Joplin was also felt in the tax base as 34 million dollars of assessed valuation was lost across the city.[12] Within 18 months, the city had created a tax increment financing district comprising 3100 acres with more than 800 million dollars to incentivize redevelopment. With a city budget of slightly more than 20 million dollars, federal aid was essential, and was approved quickly.

Against such a background, it might have been understandable for the city to languish in its destruction and to drag in its recovery. However, after just five years, nearly all of the businesses had reopened, homes had been rebuilt, and the city's population had grown to pre-tornado levels. The high school, which had been destroyed on its graduation day in the spring, reopened on time in the fall in a makeshift facility in an unused shopping center. In fact, the redevelopment exceeded pre-tornado levels as the Kansas City University of Medicine and Biosciences opened a new campus in Joplin to help alleviate the shortage of physicians throughout that region (which includes Joplin and seven counties in three states—Missouri, Kansas, and Oklahoma) as well as to conduct biomedical research.

The central position in the United States and its position at the connections of four states (Missouri, Kansas, Oklahoma, and Arkansas) make the Joplin area a strong location for logistical operations, manufacturing and transport, a wide range of agricultural products, and more. One of the city's chief promoters and the President of the Joplin Area Chamber of Commerce is Rob O'Brian. In an interview in June of 2017, O'Brian set the stage for the history by reciting he pre-disaster situation in Joplin.

Originally an area economy based on zinc and lead mining, the area transitioned into a services area for mining the interests that had to move further and further out to locate the elements. This meant that Joplin became involved in logistical arrangements and transshipments of the mined products as well as the retail center for the companies. The Sisters of Mercy built a hospital there to treat the employees of the mining companies and their families, and it became known as Mercy Hospital. But, as the availability of the minerals and the demand for them played out, the city needed to find a new economic base.

The area's slow growth of the sixties and seventies began to change in the eighties when the City Council contracted with the Area Chamber of Commerce to create and conduct a program of economic development for the region. An industrial park was developed and outreach began to fill it and other business areas within and around the city. At this point in time, Joplin had a city population of 52,000 people and a total of 80,000 within a six mile radius of the city. In all, the total catchment area for the city (for retailers, etc.) was estimated to be as high as 350,000 people.

In the aftermath of the 2008–9 recession, the region began to recover and was beginning to reach pre-recession levels of population and employment. In May of 2011, the tornado ended that recovery by damaging 8000 housing units and totally destroying 4000 more. Also lost to the city were the hospital, the high school, a middle school, and three elementary schools; and 536 businesses had been closed. But, within months, 485 of those businesses were back in operation and new businesses that had come to the area to help with repairs and services elected to remain in the area.

Following disasters of such magnitude—or, the relocation of business from a region— many areas continued to decline, in large part due to the departure of their residents and workforce, as well as to the general loss of hope of the people. This was not what happened in Joplin: people stayed and gathered together to rebuild everyone's homes and businesses. The sense of volunteerism and commitment to both their neighbors and their city was the essential foundation for a quick and strong recovery, according to O'Brian. He explained, however, that there were no actions taken to enable that spirit of community or to encourage it. Rather, it had always been the case in Joplin and it served them well in this crisis.

A real shot in the arm (pun not intended) came within a week of the tornado. The Sisters of Mercy announced that it would rebuild the hospital in Joplin and its administrators announced that all of the staff would retain their jobs, working on other locations until the new hospital was opened. The local Walmart store, which employed 400 people, and others throughout the area, subsequently made similar announcements. A tent hardware store was established to help people with repairs. The immediacy of those decisions and announcements were vital to the spirit of the people of Joplin as they began to believe that they could rebuild quickly and successfully.

O'Brian's Chamber office was able to acquire an adjacent building and converted it into a "one-stop center" for all repair and information needs. Local attorneys and accountants volunteered their time to help their neighbors. The Business Recovery Center also included representatives of the Small Business Administration and the Small Business Development Council. A website was established by the Chamber that listed vacant properties that could be used and when stores and other buildings began to re-open. The local press, radio, and television stations helped to promote the website. The one-stop concept was so well received and so efficient that the federal employees involved have tried to replicate the model in other locations that have suffered similar disasters.

The facility was opened on the Monday following the tornado and, on Tuesday morning, the teams started going out into the field providing services to business owners and residents and information about everything from how to file for insurance, how to request state and federal assistance, and where to get food and clean water. A local vendor supplied laptops for people to use in the Recovery Center and another local vendor set up a phone and laptop recharging station. The city recovered together. Those in the unaffected parts of the city came to help those whose homes and businesses had been destroyed.

O'Brian noted that the lessons learned included the need for better communications networks and redundancy for data and internet coverage but in the end the city and its people benefitted from a long history of the city working closely together with its business community, the schools, and the residents. Every re-opening was a cause for celebration and proclamations.

As a result of the experience, new companies, including Blue Buffalo, Owens-Corning, and others have been attracted to Joplin, thereby enhancing the tax base and the city's provision of public services. The city's reputation has actually been enhanced by its responses to a natural disaster. The new medical center was opened in June of 2017. It will be the tenth largest producer of doctors in the United States, thereby enhancing the region's overall quality of life. Thirty million dollars was raised locally to support that development. Joplin's experience and the way its leadership and its people responded are an example for other communities: the re-building of the local economy, and its subsequent development (not just growth) can be accomplished to the comprehensive benefit of the state and the city, their residents, and the businesses that call a place home.

3   Charlotte

Charlotte, while not as dependent as Detroit or Seattle on a single industry, is indeed dominated by the banking industry. In the 2007–8 timeframe, the major banks (also, the major employers) in Charlotte were struggling to cover their debts. Hurt by the housing and mortgage crises, their stock values had plummeted and the resultant layoffs had been substantial and spread throughout the city and the region.

What the City did have in common with Detroit and Seattle was that the municipal and corporate leadership could not conceive of a time when the banking industry would take the nosedive that had taken place. By mid-2007, "Wachovia's shares had fallen more than 15 percent to $20.13, a level last seen in late 1994."[13] The decline of banking in the city was so comprehensive that the entire region suffered. Every sector of the local economy was affected, whether that meant decreasing purchases or substantial impacts to local tax bases and public services throughout the region. However, the other economic sectors in the region's economy meant that local difficulties did not reach the point of economic collapse and personal ruin that it had in other cities. And, non-profit organizations, although no longer able to realize ongoing levels of contributions either from the corporate sector or from individuals, were able to continue operating throughout the crisis and providing services to their constituents. "In January 2010, the Charlotte area unemployment rate hit 12.8 percent, its highest level in at least twenty years."[14]

Air service through the Charlotte Airport also meant that foreign-owned businesses were prevalent in the region and that helped to bolster businesses during the banking crisis as well. Finally, jobs returned to the banking base in Charlotte, minimizing the impact on the local economy and residents. However, the salaries that were being offered were much less than previously being granted. As such, families lessened their rates of savings as well as their levels of expenditures for non-essential items.

The region did not return to its previous lifestyle immediately upon the re-hiring of the banking professionals but it did not experience the same levels of decline seen in Detroit or Seattle or Pittsburgh, largely because the crisis was much shorter than was theirs, but also because the other sectors of the local economy helped to sustain the community during the crisis. While jobs and (lower) salaries returned, gone were the extremely generous annual bonuses accorded to bank employees above certain levels. That meant that the decline in sales of very high-ticket items such as homes, boats, expensive vehicles, and travel was lost for indeterminate lengths of time.

The region had, decades earlier, suffered through dramatic losses when the textile and furniture industries had gone off-shore, severely damaging the economy of the Charlotte region and the entire State of North Carolina. Perhaps they had learned their lessons about being insufficiently diversified at that time. Charlotte had become dependent on the banking industry for its economic well-being, but not overly so.

As the region began to emerge, local economic development professionals conceived a plan to focus on numerous business sectors in order to further diversify the city and the regional economies. These included motor sports, contractors to the Department of Defense, the film industry, and health care; and, manufacturing still constitutes between 5 and 10 percent of local output, depending on the year and the success levels of the other sectors.

Today, Charlotte remains heavily dependent on the financial services industry, even though it has developed other productive industries as well. A recent article in the *Charlotte Observer* reported on a study that had been done comparing cities of similar sizes to determine how Charlotte compared in terms of the advent of innovation and entrepreneurial development. It noted that "Charlotte is behind the curve on innovation, entrepreneurialism, and investments in startup companies . . . it lags behind similar cities in the amount spent on research and development and new business formation."[15]

The conclusion is that additional investments will be required in university research to spawn the new companies in the technology areas pertinent to tomorrow's economic growth. "Charlotte can't rely on its traditional big businesses to succeed forever, especially as disruptive technologies continue to reshape the economy."[16] One of the explanations often given is that Charlotte lacks one of the key attractors of grants for research and development: a medical school. In part, although not entirely, for that reason, Charlotte-based businesses receive substantially less in venture capital investment than other cities of its size. The per capita average of venture investment in the city reached only 3 dollars between 2011 and 2014. That was the second lowest amount in the list of comparable cities, placing it ahead only of Tampa, Florida. In the same period of time, the research shows that only 388 patents were issued to firms in Charlotte, compared to nearly 2000 per capita in Atlanta and Kansas City, and 2600 in both Austin, Texas and the Research Triangle area of North Carolina.[17]

The lesson from the City of Charlotte is that, while they overcame the economic decline driven by the financial services industry, and did diversify their present economy, there needs to be attention given in these cities to a specific economic diversification: that of the future economic drivers.

The impact of the banking crisis on Charlotte was swift and highly impactful. Immediately prior to the crisis, the purchase of large-ticket items was at an all-time high. Homes, vehicles, boats, and even artwork sales were increasing, according to CNN. Given the new tax revenues, and because banking had made the city and the region careless in establishing reserves, the local governments in the city and the region had built new roads and a new sports arena to enhance the quality of life rather than saving some of the resources.

Then, the external forces that govern banking growth or decline, and that are not controllable by the executives in Charlotte, began to exert themselves. "Wall Street bailouts, buyouts, and bankruptcies were hastily negotiated in Washington and made a quick impact here."[18] Residents interviewed in local coffee shops used the word "blessed" to be employed. People stopped eating out and buying luxury items. "In the 'after period,' Charlotteans—native and new—learned hard lessons about how life can change instantly, how to adapt, and how to rethink the future for their boom town."[19]

The city learned its lesson: it has recognized that an over-dependence on banking is not a surefire way to ensure a stable and sustainable economy for the future. They have turned to energy as a second industry to serve as a foundation for future growth. Duke Energy's recent expansions seem to indicate that the direction is a good one for the city and the region; however, one must wonder whether banking and energy are sufficient to sustain economic development over time. Fortunately, Charlotte has other components of the economic base as well. "Making the city less reliant on a handful of banks would reduce the pain from another gut-wrenching blow from Wall Street."[20]

Summary: Lessons from the Charlotte Case Study

Charlotte has an asset that not many communities have, and they have used it to considerable advantage. Not all regions the size of Charlotte's are proximate to such a well-established international airport. Its presence has permitted the city and the region to attract foreign-owned businesses to locate in their communities. This has provided the city and the region with numerous companies, jobs, and investment dollars; greater economic diversification; and, opportunities to enhance trade for its local firms and thereby to enhance the local tax base.

Despite the fact that the city is one of the nation's premier hubs for financial services companies, there is a great need for venture capital resources that are not present today. The city has recognized this need and must develop a strategy for attracting venture capital companies to the region as well as encouraging local people of wealth to establish local venture capital investment funds.

The availability of venture funds would spur growth in the region among innovative entrepreneurs and would help grow the economic base as well as the tax revenues that will enable the localities to provide high quality public services without placing the entire burden of those costs on residents. Indeed, there has been a recognition that greater venture capital investment would have precisely that effect and the region is attempting to attract and grow such funds. This could also have the effect of encouraging the kind of university, corporate, and individual research that will drive further entrepreneurialism and innovation in the region over time.

4 Fairfax County, Virginia

Fairfax County, Virginia is the largest jurisdiction in metropolitan Washington, DC. It is home to nearly 1.2 million residents and just short of 600,000 jobs. Its citizens enjoy the second highest median family income in the United States and account for one of every four income tax dollars paid in the Commonwealth of Virginia. Its office space represents 35 percent of the state's total and the United States Department of Labor, in 2007, observed that it was the hub of the private sector growth in the region, making it the only region in the country where that was not the center city. Washington, DC remained the hub for public sector employment growth in the region.

The county's economic history really began after World War II when the federal government expanded both its direct hiring and its outsourcing of functions to the private sector. The county, through the 1950s had been the largest dairy farming community in the Commonwealth of Virginia. As the federal government began to hire direct employees, the eastern-most sections of the county—the closest to the District of Columbia—began to grow. The new "bedroom communities" had a problem, however. The federal employees who came to town were highly employed and expected the same of the public schools in their new community. Other public services also were in increasing demand, including police and fire protection, libraries, parks, and human services. Additionally, new roads and other infrastructure needed to be built for the influx of new residents.

The rub was that local governments in the Commonwealth of Virginia can provide public services primarily from the real estate tax base. In 1976, the tax rate was already an enormously high $1.74 per $10 of assessed value. Increasing the tax rate further was not the solution. Neither was relying on growth in the income tax base because in Virginia, all income tax revenues go to the state to support its public services and only a small portion is returned to the localities.

At the same time, a salient point became clear to the elected officials: when businesses contributed a dollar to the tax base, the return in terms of public service equated to roughly 35–40 cents. But, when a resident contributed a dollar to the real estate tax base, he or she took back around $1.60 in public services. The Board of Supervisors appointed a "Blue Ribbon" panel to discuss the solution. It included elected officials—both Republicans and Democrats—as well as community and business leaders. The panel's conclusion was that business attraction would enable the provision of high quality public services of greater quality and broader scope while not over-taxing residents to do so. In fact, the tax rate declined from the 1976 mark of $1.74 per $100 of assessed value to the current $1.13.

The county was able to see the trends that were coming. In 1976, the population of Fairfax County was roughly 455,000. The demographers forecasted the population growth to be dramatic, and to reach 800,000 people by the 1990 census, just 14 years away. In fact, the 1990 census reports showed that the county's population had reached 819,000 people. Any time a jurisdiction sees this kind of rapid growth, it begins to add up the costs of the public services required to serve the marginal addition of residents, including schools, libraries, parks, human services, roads and other infrastructure needs, police and fire protection, and much more.

Additionally, the cost of providing public services to a greatly expanding population was about to increase exponentially (rather than arithmetically) because, as the population of the county grew, it also became increasingly diverse. In the 1960 Census, 96 percent of the residents of Fairfax County were white. Today, the county's population is 48 percent a collection of all minorities, including large sub-population groups from India, Korea, Latin America, and elsewhere. In the near future, Fairfax County will be a majority-minority community. This kind of diversity—and, diversity within the diversity—exacerbates the costs of public education, public safety, public health and welfare, and more, because services need to be provided within the context of many cultures and with many languages.

The county's officials of the day realized that it needed to grow the non-residential tax base so that citizens would not have to bear the entire burden of the growing costs for the growing and ever-greatly diversifying residential community. The county's economic development program was refocused on business attraction and retention and the results have been impressive. Today, Fairfax County is home to nearly 120 million square feet of office space, the second largest suburban office space market in the United States (Orange county, California is larger). Numerous Fortune 500 and other companies call the county home, including the corporate headquarters of SAIC, Leidos, Intelsat, Bechtel, Hilton Worldwide, CSC, CVent, Volkswagen North America, Northrop Grumman, and more.

Fairfax County is perhaps best known for its community of federal contractors; it is home to the headquarters operations of such household names as Northrop Grumman, CSC, SAIC, and General Dynamics. Recently, it added the federal Transportation Security Administration (TSA) headquarters and its 3400 employees to its roster of federal agencies.

For decades, however, Fairfax County's economic development program planned to diversify its economic base by attracting non-federal contractors to the community. In the early-to-mid 1980s, Mobil Oil Corporation relocated its global headquarters from midtown Manhattan to Fairfax County but, for many years thereafter, the economic base of the county continued to rely upon federal contracting for its growth and stability.

In the mid-nineties, the Fairfax County Economic Development Authority shifted some of its focus to the attraction of businesses that had no relationship to federal contracting. In the decade prior to this writing, the county has developed a great opportunity around the business of translational medicine and was able to attract several US and global headquarters operations that were not related to the federal sector, including Inteslat, Bechtel, Hilton Worldwide, Capital One, Volkswagen North America, Cvent, and more. The county did not provide a single dollar of cash incentive or tax abatement to attract these headquarters operations. As a consequence, the economy of the county is today much less subject to the vagaries of federal contracting or actions such as the BRAC decisions of the military or sequestration. While the federal sector, and even direct federal employment still provide the anchor of the economy in the county, the economic base is more diversified and certainly more sustainable. The wisdom of this strategy was evident as sequestration and other cut-backs in federal programs became increasingly threatening to the economic health of the Washington, DC region.

Despite the evidence of the benefits of more than one and one-half decades of remarkable successes in diversifying the county's economy away from only federal contracting, there were calls for that very process to begin throughout the rest of the region. In the last few years, several of the universities and business organizations in the Washington, DC metropolitan area began to announce that the region was in danger of losing its economic stability because it was entirely too dependent upon direct federal employment and federal contracting. Unfortunately, the balance of the region had not followed Fairfax County's lead of a decade earlier to pursue non-traditional industries and had to play catch-up to diversify their respective local economies. The region experienced an even greater need with the election in 2016 of Donald Trump to the presidency. His intention to "drain the swamp" and to make draconian cuts in federal spending threatens the vitality of the economy of a region that has been so heavily dependent on federal employment and federal spending.

The Washington, DC metropolitan area has begun to pursue alternatives to federal contracting in its economic base. Arlington County, for example, was able to attract the global headquarters of Nestle, thus beginning to minimize its dependence on federal contracting. Other examples of economic diversification took place in other northern Virginia jurisdictions and those in suburban Maryland as well. Nonetheless, the entire region still has a long way to go to stabilize its economic base by diversifying away from federal government direct and indirect employment.

The next significant diversification of the Fairfax County, northern Virginia, and metropolitan Washington area's economies will come from the life sciences. In the early 1980s, the Mobil Oil Corporation (coincidentally, the county's first significant diversification announcement) first moved its Downstream Marketing Division, and later moved its global headquarters from New York City to an area in Fairfax County known as Merrifield. Around 2010, the corporation elected to relocate its employees from throughout Houston, New Jersey, Fairfax County, and Ohio to a new campus in Houston. The 117 acre campus is located directly across from Virginia's largest hospital system, Inova, which purchased the land and the buildings, including two already-zoned pads for new office buildings. The plan for the campus is multi-purpose and will include commercial space, retailers, residential, higher education, and life sciences research and commercialization as well as health care and wellness care. Figure 7.1 shows the former Mobil Oil headquarters building, which then successively became the headquarters of the Exxon Mobil Downstream Marketing Division, and which is today the Inova campus for the Schar Cancer Research Institute and the Institute for Translational Medicine.

On the campus, Inova has sited its Cancer Institute and its Translational Medicine Institute. The latter institute will develop means of translating an individual's genetic information to his or her treatment that will be individual rather than treating everyone with a common illness the same way and with the same drugs. More than one hundred researchers—as well as support staffs—are already working on clinical, bioinformatics, and laboratory work focused on individualized analysis and treatment. As the research leads to discoveries, patents on products and processes will be obtained. Ultimately, the discoveries will be commercialized and office space filled both on and near the campus. This will contribute to the established economic development value chain: companies fill office space; a demand is thereby generated for the new construction that contributes

Figure 7.1 Inova Campus in Fairfax County, Virginia
Source: The Fairfax County Economic Development Authority

marginal revenues to the real estate tax base, which constitutes two-thirds of the General Fund expenditures in Fairfax County; and, a high quality and quantity of public services will be provided while minimizing the burden of those costs on residents.

University involvement with the research and ultimate commercialization of research findings is already coming from such institutions as George Mason University and the University of Virginia. Global higher education partners and corporate partners will create a worldwide connection to the research being conducted in Fairfax County. More-over, officials see this as an opportunity to accelerate the diversity of the local and regional economy further away from its earlier over-dependence on government direct employment and federal contracting while attracting the business tax base that will help to offset the costs of public services for the residents of Fairfax County.

Summary: Lessons from the Fairfax County Case Study

Fairfax County, Virginia is a community that emerged from being a farming community to a bedroom community for federal government employees to a one-company town—the federal government—to a premier hub for technology businesses, including those related to federal contracting as well as those not at all related to working for federal agencies.

With the advent of the Silver Line of the Metro system, Fairfax County's downtown, Tysons Corner, began to grow like Topsy. Unlimited density was permitted within a quarter mile radius of all four new Metro stations at a time when interest rates were low. As a consequence, and in spite of already high vacancy rates in commercial office space (in excess of 18 percent, county-wide), developers built out a great deal of additional office product. Clearly, there has been too much built and it will take time to fill the space with new tenants. The lesson here is that simply building more and more office space has both positive and negative consequences. When the owners receive their occupancy permits, they begin to pay real estate taxes. They are thus contributing to the tax base that helps pay for public services and reduce the burden for those costs on residents. But, it also affects the marketability and assessed values of the existing building base. Communities do not want to have too little space available to show clients because they need options to consider; but neither do they want too much space available. The lesson here is to see the future and understand the trends and to moderate the development to be consistent with development and potential development.

A second lesson to be drawn from the Fairfax County experience is that residents demand more in (value) public services than they contribute. The ratio of costs-to-contributions varies with the types of housing and the number of school-aged children in the families. However, it is reasonable to assume that population growth will generate more in demand for public services than the growth generates in marginal contributions to the local tax base. Businesses, on the other hand, contribute far more in public services (again varying, dependent upon the amount of space leased or purchased) than they take back in public service costs. The lesson Fairfax County illustrates is that the population growth can be accommodated—and services expanded in scope, quantity, and quality—by attracting a business base sufficient to offset much of those costs for the new and existing residential base.

5   Plattsburgh, New York

As part of the 1990 decisions of the Defense Base Realignment and Closure Act, the Air Force Base at Plattsburgh, New York was shut down. The community received the land and buildings and established PARC, the Plattsburgh Airbase Redevelopment Corporation, to plan the best ways the community could use the resource as a means of promoting economic development and replacing the economic impact and jobs associated with the base.

The base was officially closed on September 30, 1995. The transfer included 3,440 acres of land, commercial and office buildings, and residences immediately west of Lake Champlain. Given the nature of the usage as an Air Force Base, there were soil and water remediation requirements that had to be addressed before the assets and parcels could be marketed. These challenges needed to be met at a time when the community was struggling with the realization that the base—and its 1000 jobs—had been lost. Until the final announcement, they had been led to believe that the base would be enlarged, even doubled. The announcement that it would be closed came as a surprise to the officials of the city, town, and region.

There was a divergence of opinion at the time about the impacts that the closure would have on the community. An article in the local press 17 years later recalled some of the dread felt by local residents:

- "It was a very difficult experience for the community. Plattsburgh took a real economic beating."
- "Many businesses were devastated. Several of them closed."
- "We have lost our identity as a military town."

The author concluded: "A sense of desperation gripped the community in the mid-nineties."[21]

Another journalist looked back after 20 years (2015) and reprinted the following comments:[22]

- "Along with our pain is anger."
- "It was like losing a member of our family and we went through the entire grief process." (then-Mayor Clyde Rabideau)
- "It was almost a sense of disbelief that this was occurring." (then-Congressman Bill Owens)

How, then, did the community pass through various stages of denial and grief to the point when, 17 years later, the base was thriving with private sector growth, the area's economy had not only stabilized, but had expanded with a diverse set of businesses? Kelley cites the businesses now in the area, including Pratt and Whitney Engine Services, Wyeth Pharmaceuticals, Multina USA, and Bombardier. PARC reported in 2008 that the former base was then home to businesses, non-profit organizations, residential communities, community college facilities, and a new international airport. Ultimately, it is believed that there will be more than 100 million dollars of assessed value in properties on the former base that will pay taxes to the state coffers and to local governments in the region. By 2015, "only six parcels on 33.5 acres remain, and 99 percent of the base has been redeveloped."[23]

Today, the primary sectors for employment include manufacturing, retail, and health/education. And, the community's proximity to the Canadian border represents a consistent source of revenues. In 2013, people from north of the border spent more than 300 million dollars in the area and generated more than 9 million dollars in local tax revenues as a result.[24] This may have been sufficient to help sustain the community through its most difficult economic times, but how did Plattsburgh recover and even grow and sustain its core economic base following such a devastating experience? And, how was it possible to do so that quickly? What lessons were learned that could be instructive for other communities in the country?

Victoria Duley is the Economic Developer for the Development Corporation of Clinton County, New York, which includes both the City and Town of Plattsburgh. A long-time resident, Ms. Duley lived through the time when the Air Force Base was shut down and recalls the reactions and feelings of the people in the region.

The base was closed in 1995 as the result of the BRAC decisions that had preceded it by several years. The redevelopment corporation—PARC—assumed control of the land and properties and were able to procure a federal grant from the US FAA (Federal Aviation Administration) that allowed the corporation to convert the mile-long runways of the Air Force Base to civilian usage. Adjacent to the runways were a 12 million square foot area for parking and staging aircraft, 1.5 million square feet of adjacent industrial space, more than 100 acres of developable land, numerous large hangars, easy interstate and rail access, broadband fiber optic network on site, and sewer, water, and natural gas services already connected. These sites were ready-made and had been maintained in excellent condition by the Air Force. The region was given a primary economic development gift of which it only needed to take advantage.

PARC also received the thousands of acres and the buildings and much of the equipment left behind by the Air Force. Housing was sold off in various ways, but primarily, the non-com housing was converted and leased as apartments and the officers' quarters were refurbished and sold to individual homeowners.

The successes of PARC and of the community have long since passed the point at which Ms. Duley feels they are now even better off as a region than before the BRAC decisions. The initial reactions included what any observer might have expected. The community first tried to marshal the necessary political forces to fight the decision. But, as an area with a relatively small population base, that battle was lost; once it had become clear that their objections were falling on deaf ears, panic set in.

Figure 7.2 Plattsburgh, NY, Air Force Base

Source: The Development Corporation of Plattsburgh

The panic phase was minimal and short-lived. PARC was able to gather the local leadership (which Ms. Duley points to as a critical component of the future success), develop a sound strategy for moving forward in the use of the base and its facilities in the best possible way to benefit the region and its people, create an effective marketing plan, and begin to move forward in its implementation.

The success in converting the base and its assets to civilian applications was, in hindsight, quite expeditious. Ms. Duley reported that, at the time of this writing, only five or six parcels remain to be sold from the original inventory of "thousands" and the original PARC staff is down from its high of a dozen to one full-time and one part-time person to wrap things up. This certainly must stand as one of the shining examples of rapid success in base conversions following closure. That means that there will be lessons to be learned that may be transferable to other communities in similar circumstances.

The airstrip makes Plattsburgh different from most of the base closure case studies across the country. So does its geographic location: right on the border with Canada. That combination of factors, and the fact that flights out of Montreal were both expensive and difficult for travelers due to the overcrowded nature of that airport, led Plattsburgh's officials to realize that there was an opportunity to be exploited. Today, with many Canadian travelers clearing customs at the border crossing and flying out of Plattsburgh, the enplanements are today ten times greater than they were from the local airport before the base closure. The contrast of the field strip, as an Air Force Base and as a public airport, can be seen in Figures 7.2 and 7.3.

Figure 7.3 Plattsburgh, NY, Civilian Airport

Source: The Development Corporation of Plattsburgh

There are always challenges in such situations of economic recovery; for the Plattsburgh/ Clinton County area, there are a few—and some of those still exist today. A 2013 report noted that Plattsburgh is still losing its youth. Nearly one-third of the area's population is 55 years old or older. Employers have difficulty in finding enough qualified workers. When the base closed and the military personnel left the region, the public schools lost a lot of students and needed to downsize their local operations and resource allocations. They also lost the amounts that the federal government had been providing for each student in a military dependent's family.

As for lessons that were learned, Ms. Duley offers the following:

- The leaders of the community reacted quickly and in a positive way. That leadership included all the key stakeholders, such as the Chamber of Commerce, the Development Corporation, and others.
- The population of Plattsburgh, a "highly resilient people," remained in place; few left the area in search of new opportunities. They felt they "belonged" in Plattsburgh and wanted to begin rebuilding.
- The community had some diversification of industry prior to the base closure, but sought to enhance it thereafter. The base today includes a Georgia Pacific facility, several foundries (e.g., pipes and valves production), and manufacturers in specialized areas of transportation (e.g., rails and bus, and more. Plastics and medical device manufacturers round out a fairly diverse economic base given the size of the region.
- The local colleges and universities include a branch of the State University of New York (SUNY) and a local community college that provide invaluable technical training.
- The final lesson offered is to be patient. There will be a time lag but the economic stability of the region is now greater than before. Today, the local unemployment rate is lower than either the national average or that of the State of New York. "Think big."

Summary: Lessons from the Plattsburgh Case Study

Can communities effectively use abandoned military installations to help regenerate an economic base and to jump-start economic development? Plattsburgh did so, and within a timeframe that was surprising given the stunning nature of the announcement. After the initial shock of the decision had worn off, local leaders quickly pulled together— public and private—to plan for the reuse of the base, and that is the real lesson from Plattsburgh. The reaction time was minimized and that meant that there was a shorter interim period before action could be taken and the community could begin to see results. This helped to minimize the impacts on employers in the secondary and tertiary economies and helped the community get over its shock much more quickly.

A second lesson to be taken from this case study is the prescription for patience. It was clear that a lot of work needed to be done and that the results would not be realized overnight. Acceptance of this fact was a first step toward the economic recovery of the region.

Notes

1 Edward Glaeser. *Triumph of the City: How Our Greatest Invention Makes Us Richer, Smarter, Greener, Healthier, and Happier*. (New York: Penguin, 2011): 6.
2 Phillipe Aghion and Steven N. Durlauf. 2005. *Handbook of Economic Growth*, vol. 1B. (San Diego, CA: Elsevier, 2005): 1546.
3 Robert Samuels. Feeling Snubbed but Pushing Forward. (*Washington Post*, August 9, 2017): A-1 and A-16.
4 Alexia Fernandez Campbell. A Suburb on the Brink of Bankruptcy. June 8, 2016. www.the atlantic.com
5 Lisa Sturdivant. The Impact of Sequestration on the Washington, DC Housing Market. (April 6, 2015) www.handhousing.org
6 John F. McDonald. *Urban America: Growth, Crisis, and Rebirth*. (Armonk, NY: M.E. Sharp, 2008): 66.
7 Federal Reserve Bank of Chicago. *Challenges and Opportunities Ahead*. (Chicago, IL: Federal Reserve Bank): 46.
8 Ibid., 47.
9 Jack Schultz. *Boomtown USA: The 7½ Keys to Big Success in Small Towns*. (Washington, DC: NAIOP, 2004): xi.
10 Ibid., xi.
11 William Alden. Joplin Tornado Inflicts Economic Setbacks on Community Still Struggling with Recession's Legacy. (July 25, 2011) www.huffingtonpost
12 Patrick Tuohey. *Tax Increment Financing in Post-Tornado Joplin*. (St. Louis, MO: Show-Me Institute, April 2017): 1.
13 Rick Rothacker. *Banktown: The Rise and Struggle of Charlotte's Big Banks*. (Winston-Salem, NC: John F. Blair, 2010): 93.
14 Ibid., 221.
15 Ely Portillo. Charlotte Lags in Startups and Innovation, Entrepreneurialism Study Finds. (March 15, 2016) www.charlotteobserver.com
16 Ibid.
17 Ibid.
18 Thom Patterson. What Charlotte Learned When the World Flipped. (June 2011) www.cnn.com
19 Ibid.
20 Ibid.
21 Kevin Kelley. After the Air guard: Plattsburgh's 1995 Base Closing May Be Instructive for Burlington. (July 18, 2012) www.sevendaysvt.com
22 Pat Bradley. A Look Back at Plattsburgh Air Force Base Closure Twenty Years Ago. (September 25, 2015) http://wamc.org
23 Ibid.
24 Laberge Group. *Town of Plattsburgh: Economic Development Strategic Plan*. (Albany, NY: Laberge Group, July 2013): vi.

References

Aghion, Phillipe and Durlauf, Steven N. *Handbook of Economic Growth*, vol. 1B. San Diego, CA: Elsevier, 2005.
Alden, William. Joplin Tornado Inflicts Economic Setbacks on Community Still Struggling with Recession's Legacy, July 25, 2011. www.huffingtonpost.com
Bradley, Pat. A Look Back at Plattsburgh Air Force Base Closure Twenty Years Ago. September 25, 2015. http://wamc.org
Campbell, Alexia Fernandez. A Suburb on the Brink of Bankruptcy. June 8, 2016. www.the atlantic.com

Federal Reserve Bank of Chicago. *Challenges and Opportunities Ahead*. Chicago, IL: Federal Reserve Bank, p. 46.

Glaeser, Edward. *Triumph of the City: How Our Greatest Invention Makes Us Richer, Smarter, Greener, Healthier, and Happier*. New York: Penguin, 2011.

Kelley, Kevin J. After the Air Guard: Plattsburgh's 1995 Base Closing May Be Instructive for Burlington. July 18, 2012. www.sevendaysvt.com

Laberge Group. *Town of Plattsburgh: Economic Development Strategic Plan*. Albany, NY: Laberge Group, July 2013.

McDonald, John F. *Urban America: Growth, Crisis, and Rebirth*. Armonk, NY: M.E. Sharpe, 2008.

Patterson, Thom. What Charlotte Learned When the World Flipped. June 9, 2011. www.cnn.com

Portillo, Ely. Charlotte Lags in Start-Ups and Innovation, Entrepreneurialism Study Finds. March 15, 2016. www.charlotteobserver.com

Rothacker, Rick. *Banktown: The Rise and Struggles of Charlotte's Big Banks*. Winston-Salem, NC: John F. Blair, 2010.

Samuels, Robert. Feeling Snubbed but Pushing Forward. *Washington Post*, A-1 and A-16. August 9, 2017.

Schultz, Jack. *Boomtown USA: The 7½ Keys to Big Success in Small Towns*. Washington, DC: NAIOP, 2004.

Sturdivant, Lisa. The Impact of Sequestration on the Washington, DC Housing Market. April 6, 2015. www.handhousing.org

Tuohey, Patrick. *Tax Increment Financing in Post-Tornado Joplin*. St. Louis, MO: Show-Me Institute, April 2017.

8 Over-Dependence on a Single Company or a Single Industry
Case Studies

It is an all-too oft-cited—although frequently ignored—principle of economic development that local and regional economies are unlikely to be sustainable and constant over time if they are overly dependent upon a single industry or a single business.

I was employed by the United States Department of Labor (DOL) as a lowly GS-5 in 1972 when that critical lesson was being learned by the people of Seattle who believed that they were "golden" because of the Boeing Corporation and the aerospace industry in general. Surely, their economy would be secure for the foreseeable future. Boeing wasn't going anywhere.

For personal reasons, I declined to accept the proffered permanent position and promotion to accept an offer to move to the Region 10 Office of DOL. As it turned out, Boeing was not so golden after all. As the war in Southeast Asia wound down, the military was not buying as many aircraft. And, as the national and local unemployment rates, as well as the rate of inflation, both hit double digits, fewer people were flying and the commercial airlines stopped buying aircraft. The tarnish on Seattle's golden economy was evident in the now famous billboard on the highway leaving town asking the last person to leave Seattle to turn out the lights.

A lesson learned? Well, certainly by the people of Seattle and the Puget Sound region who rebuilt the economy around several distinct and diverse industry sectors and businesses. But, it seemed that not everyone learned the lesson. Pittsburgh and Birmingham, Alabama, while not necessarily over-dependent on steel, were certainly *overly* dependent on its production. Lower costs of labor and other factors in Japan and elsewhere caused the same tarnish to appear in those two regions. Like the people of the Pacific Northwest, they too learned their lessons and have diversified the economic base while rebuilding it.

Other major US cities have encountered similar situations and have learned hard lessons. Hartford, Connecticut (insurance), Houston (oil), Orlando (hospitality), Charlotte (financial services), and others have followed suit. And, whoever foresaw the banking collapse that so widely damaged the economy of Charlotte, North Carolina, and the surrounding region? Small towns and rural areas are not exempt from unexpected declines in industries. The region around Bend, Oregon, for example, had been a timber production region for many generations; so much so that the residents of the area believed they would always have logging and mill work to rely upon. Even as the forests were slowly, but steadily, depleted people did not foresee the jobs going away. But they did: "Depletion of the forest resources ultimately devastated the timber industry in Oregon."[1] When the jobs left, people were stunned.

Both business and community leaders in Detroit felt for many years that they were above the fray. Not only were they home to the biggest of the big automobile manufacturers, they had the top three on their roster. The blind eye turned by Detroit to what was happening in the industry worldwide persisted far after the issues were clearly understood and well documented.

Only an economy that is sufficiently diverse can withstand the rises and falls in the fortunes of a single industry or a single company. Such a diverse economy can rely on one large industry to help sustain the area and its employment base even as others are in decline.

The next great example is played out more recently when the federal government's sequester affected the Washington, DC region, which is preparing to learn whether or not its economic base is "sufficiently" diverse to ride out extraordinary and unprecedented spending adjustments by Uncle Sam.

All of this leads to a number of questions:

- When is an economy "overly dependent?"
- When is an economy over-dependent?
- Are there warning systems that can alert local leadership to the onset of dependence?
- What lessons can be learned by the experience of other dependent cities that can be instructive to others?
- Who's next?

Cities, regions, even small towns, cannot afford to become overly dependent upon a single firm—or even a single industry sector—for their sustained economic stability. Too many communities across the United States—both large and small, urban or rural—have learned that lesson with disastrous consequences. The stories of the large cities that were lulled into that situation are dramatic and oft-cited in the literature on economic growth. Nonetheless, they bear reciting because there continue to be cities and regions whose economies are insufficiently diverse to ensure that they will not experience declining economic fortunes in the future. Small and mid-sized towns are equally, or perhaps even more so, subject to immediate disaster if they are overly dependent on a single employer. These stories will be told because their lessons need to be heeded.

Chillicothe, Missouri is an example of a micropolitan-sized community in north-central Missouri. It is located just one hour from Kansas City and slightly more from St. Joseph. Its economy is essentially agricultural but the city has also hosted other employers over time. Its residents generally believe it to be a nice place to live because of its small town atmosphere and sense of community.

One private employer that called Chillicothe home was Hanes, which had a factory in this community for ten years and manufactured various types of clothing. Like the beliefs of so many small towns, this was deemed to be sufficient. There were non-agricultural jobs available and the company supported the community in many ways. The future seemed assured for the good people of Chillicothe, Missouri until 2011 when the Chillicothe plant succumbed to the substantially lower wage rates the company could find in Mexico. Seemingly overnight, 125 jobs that paid 8–10 dollars per hour disappeared.

The experience in Chillicothe has been repeated around the country in mid-size and small cities. The community's sole—or only—significant employer either closes down or departs for other locations, and the community is left with numerous intractable problems. All too often, the event is a surprise to the city's leadership and the employees who are affected.

The impacts on individuals and families are clear. Jobs are lost, self-confidence is destroyed, savings are depleted, and the ability to provide is eliminated. On the surface, one can also imagine some of the impacts that befall the community itself. The tax base declines and, as residents begin to move away for new employment opportunities, the primary asset needed to attract new employers—a quality workforce—is no longer available.

It is, however, the less obvious impacts on a community that can, over time, be the most insidious. Businesses that are the most significant in town are often the also the primary source of support for community institutions: little leagues, scout troops, church groups, schools, the arts, charitable organizations, and more. When the company leaves, so does its financial and human support for the institutions that make small and mid-sized cities and towns special places.

Although there is frequently a lag in these situations before the next level of impacts is felt, they are likely to be even more painful for the community. This is the damage done to, and the ultimate loss of, the communities' basic institutions. The public schools lose enrollments and have to downsize instructional staff, often yielding the elimination of important programs for the youngsters who remain.

The reduced demand for services, coupled with a lower capacity to spend, results next in the loss of vital services. This has included air service, hospitals and medical care, retailers, and more. One very impactful loss can be the local newspaper that, devoid of advertising support, must shut down operations. This leaves a void in the ability to rally citizens, gather public opinion, and distribute news about what is being done to improve the situation in town and nearby.

The final ignominy is what can only be referred to as the "double whammy." The people who leave town to find alternative employment are typically those who are best able to be hired. That is, they are the most highly educated and highly skilled of the populace. This means that the high-end of the salary scale, and thus the greatest con-tributors to the city's tax base, are the first to depart. The city's coffers are depleted and the public's ability to provide greater services and transfer payments to the unemployed and underemployed is further diminished at the very time when the demand is dramatically increasing. Hence, the sense of a "double-whammy" hitting the city.

In short-term situations of job loss or in situations where the departed employer is not the only company or the largest company in town, these communities can often pull together. Neighbors help neighbors and churches and charitable groups provide additional support. However, as time continues, and no new jobs arrive in town, or when all of the jobs have been removed at once, these institutions and non-profits also become increasingly bereft of funding.

Students of public administration courses and public policy professionals clearly understand what happens to large and mid-sized cities when the economic base declines. One can identify unlimited sources that reference the aftermath of economic collapse in large cities where the primary employer or primary industry has collapsed. Volumes abound that discuss what happened in Detroit or Youngstown or Pittsburgh or Seattle, and their stories and lessons learned will also be covered in this volume. But, there is relatively little available information about what happens in smaller towns when employers depart. What can be found are occasional case studies of the experiences of individual communities. While those are valuable, they reveal only circumstances and not trends. Public policy decisions require greater understanding of the effects on larger numbers of communities in a more general sense than can be obtained from individual case studies.

The lives of those who live in affected areas and their livelihoods are at stake. The issues—and the lessons—inherent in these decisions are not just a by-product of today's America. These are issues that will be faced by other communities in the future. It is therefore important that the next generation of public administrators and policymakers learn from the experiences of small towns in the past. They will undoubtedly be repeated.

Students of Public Administration in colleges and universities today will benefit tomorrow from having exposure to these issues and their impacts on small and mid-sized cities and towns in the same way that they can benefit by understanding how larger cities are affected when they lose a major employer or industry segment. And, the losses in small towns and rural areas span a range of industry sectors; consider the list presented in Table 8.1.

Many small towns and rural communities are dependent on their primary employers for more than simply jobs and expendable income. The "double and triple whammies" discussed in an earlier section occur in these communities as well as they do in urban areas, but often the implications are far greater than in those larger cities and regions. The loss of incomes from those directly employed also impacts negatively on local retailers, newspapers, public schools, and more. The loss of income means the loss of income and other taxes which, in turn, means the loss of support for public services in the community.

The smaller local businesses that catered to the needs of employers or their employees begin to shed jobs, and the snowball effect continues. In smaller towns, the ability to come back from such events may be even more difficult because the dependency on the primary business is often greater than in a larger city where the collection of small businesses in unrelated lines may exist to a greater extent than in rural areas. Further, when an employer leaves a larger area, many residents remain in place to look for new opportunities. In a small town without other opportunities, people have to leave and there is no able-bodied workforce left to attract new employers. Their primary asset may be gone.

In the more rural areas, such losses can be even more devastating because, unlike their more densely populated counterparts, rural areas may include distances that are too great to overcome. In a more urban environment, a new job with a commuting time of an extra 30 minutes means that people and families can stay in place. In rural areas, the next job may be too far away to allow remaining in place.

Many of the cities and regions examined here were surprised to learn that it could happen to them. Neither the corporate nor the community leadership in Detroit ever anticipated the day when automobile manufacturing would ever fail and jobs, income,

Table 8.1 The Loss of Primary Employers in Small Towns and Rural Areas

City	Company	Products
Cheraw, SC	Bi-Lo	grocery chain
Chamois, MO	Central Electric Power Coop.	power plant
Cherokee, IA	Tyson	meat processing
Chillicothe, MO	Hanes	clothing
Dawson, MN	Associated Milk Producers	cheese, sauces, puddings
Glen Lyn, VA	American Electric Power	coal-fired power gener.
Hammonton, PA	American Home Products	Advil, Anacin, Prep'n. H
Hutsonville, IL	Ameren	coal-fired power gener.
Lincolnton, NC	Actavis	creams and ointments
Lynch, KY	US Coal and Coke	mining operations
Monongahela, PA	First Energy	coal-fired plant
Moraine, OH	General Motors	SUV assembly plant
Moundsville, WV	American Electric Power	coal-fired power gener.
Oakes, ND	JLG Industries	aerial work platform lifts
Oscoda, MI	Wurtsmith AFB	military base
Ramseur, NC	Ramtex Yarns	yarns and fabrics
Rantoul, IL	Chanute AFB	military base
Rivesville, WV	First Energy	coal-fired power gener.
Trenton, GA	Shaw Industries	yarns
Vernon, VT	Vermont Yankee	nuclear power plant
Wautoma, WI	Cummins	engine exhaust systems
West Plains, MO	Robertshaw	valves and thermostats
Wiscasset, ME	Maine Yankee	nuclear power plant

and security would all be lost and the community would devolve into the crime scenes, areas of extreme poverty, and the sense of utter hopelessness that it did. Prior to the early 1970s, Seattle believed that it would be forever economically stable because Boeing would produce civilian and military aircraft as long as could be imagined; as a result, the local economic base would be forever stable. The winding down of military involvement in Vietnam, paired with the double-digit inflation that affected business and leisure travel and reduced the purchase of civilian aircraft, seemed to come as a complete surprise to many public and private officials in the region.

Did the planners in Pittsburgh ever expect steel production to let them down? Did the people of Charlotte, North Carolina ever believe that a major banking crisis would result in their loss of jobs, disposable income and the impacts that would be felt throughout the entire economic structure of the city? Over and over again, these scenarios are repeated. Only within the past few years, the Washington, DC metropolitan area awoke to realize that being a "government town" also meant an overdependence upon direct federal employment and federal procurement contracting in its regional economic base.

Major cities and regions are often slow to realize—and even slower to accept—that the economic goose that has been laying golden eggs for them may not always be so productive. Smaller cities and towns are even more likely to ignore the warning signs. This has been particularly true in small communities that are overly (perhaps even entirely) dependent upon the presence of a local military installation. Such bases can be eliminated or downsized with the stroke of a pen and can be relocated in very quick order, with communities left behind either to try to find alternative corporate uses for the facilities and to deal with a declining economy.

Rosenfeld summarized the problems caused by insufficient industrial diversification in a local economy: "The economic history of regions is fraught with examples . . . industrial specialization promoted rapid growth but led to rapid decline when new technology became available or market conditions shifted abruptly and the region was too inbred."[2] A close examination of these histories and the warning signs that may portend economic decline elsewhere constitute an important part of understanding economic growth and decline in America. The following section takes a close look at what happened in some of these cities and regions—large and small, urban and rural—so that others may better understand the warning signs. It will also be vital to examine the means employed in those communities to attempt to recover from their losses.

As will be observed in later chapters, a city that is overly dominated by a single industry or a single company suffers much more than job losses and wealth decline. The first consideration however must be an examination of the instances in which such losses were incurred. What happened and why? What should have been done and when? And, what are the best paths to economic recovery?

The following section examines what happened in 11 different communities that had been overly dependent upon either a single employer or a single industry. There is also a look at some areas that are non-metropolitan regions, including one suburban jurisdiction (Fairfax County, Virginia which is a suburb of Washington, DC) and one smaller, rather isolated community that lost a military base (Plattsburgh, New York). The rest of the section considers large metropolitan regions that were heavily dependent upon a single industry or corporation.

Today, most of those regions have successfully diversified away from that dependency, focusing on higher education or the life sciences or other industries that have helped to stabilize the economy by offsetting rises and falls in one industry with growth in another. This has also had the effect of stabilizing tax revenues and, therefore, the provision of state and local public services.

It is important to note that in most of these metropolitan areas, the industries that led first to their growth and then to their decline are still vital, and even dominating, components of the current and future economies of those regions. Seattle still has a very large presence by the Boeing Corporation and aerospace and aviation more broadly. Detroit still manufactures automobiles and automotive parts. Tulsa still produces oil. Even Pittsburgh still has a presence of the steel and other metals industries, although it is considerably diminished from its heyday. The point is that economic diversification does not have to mean starting over or eliminating the earlier strengths. Cities and regions can build upon them while also attracting and growing businesses in completely different economic sectors.

Further, the discussions of these regions indicate that the re-building of the local economies was, at least in part, driven by a workforce with specialized skills that could be upgraded or refocused and translated to the requirements of new industries. That is to say that the engineers were still engineers and those who worked in manufacturing automobiles, for example, still had skill sets that could be employed in other types of manufacturing as well. Despite the losses of industries or corporations, there was an ability to draw upon what was left to begin the process of economic revitalization.

1   Seattle, Washington

For purpose of this review, a diverse industry base for a city or region is understood to mean that it can withstand the periodic growth or decline of the given dominant industry. Thus, if the industry or industry segment in question experiences declining sales, overwhelming foreign competition, or other exogenous factors that result in a general decline, it will not result in devastating losses for the community because other industries will sustain growth or development. At a minimum, the community will not experience extreme levels of unemployment or poverty, and the community will not suffer destructive losses from the tax base, as a result.

Such, however was not the case in the Seattle of the early 1970s. The city and the Puget Sound region were overly dependent for economic development on one industry and one company: aerospace and aviation, and Boeing. A confluence of factors led to the decline of both in the early 1970s: double-digit unemployment, coupled with double-digit inflation, which led to declining leisure travel, and a diminished demand for commercial aircraft; the winding down of the war in Vietnam and the resultant decline in the federal procurement of military aircraft; and, the constantly rising cost of oil, driven by the OPEC cartel, that translated into increasing costs for air travel. Owing to lack of new orders in 1970 from any US airline, in March 1971 further funding from the US Senate to develop Boeing's SST was halted.

Certainly, an area such as that of Seattle and the greater Puget Sound region was in jeopardy because its economic base was overwhelmingly dependent upon the Boeing corporation for it employment, local supplier contracts, and the municipal tax bases. True, there were businesses in the area other than Boeing itself, but they too were, to a very high percentage, dependent for their existence upon contracts from Boeing to supply aircraft parts. Obviously, at a time when Boeing had no contracts for aircraft manufacture, it had no need for suppliers of aircraft parts. "For twenty years, optimists had claimed a growing industrial versatility, but the region's economic health remained stubbornly pegged to the fortunes of the Boeing Company."[3]

Sale wrote: "

> [I]t became clear that the Boeing era was over. The most widely held presumption was that Seattle was over as well. . . . Unemployment rose from being just over the national average to double the national average: the worst in any major city since the Great Depression. One hundred thousand people were out of work.[4]

In a little over one year, from 1968 to 1969, the manufacturer reduced its workforce from more than 100,000 to about 80,000. By late 1971, the Boeing workforce plummeted to about 32,000, and local economic indicators were in freefall. "The economy was still a one-trick pony."[5] The decline of the region's primary industry and employer ultimately meant that the local governments felt a dramatically increasing demand for transfer payments (e.g., food stamps, unemployment compensation, and other welfare transfers) at the very time when the reductions in the local tax bases rendered them unable to provide them.

The City of Seattle came perilously close to declaring insolvency. The layoffs at Boeing were immediately felt community-wide. "Waves of layoffs rippled through the machine shops and industrial suppliers, stores and restaurants. At its height, general Puget Sound unemployment stood at 17 percent." During what became known as the "Boeing Recession," the region lost one-tenth of its total employment.[6]

Compounding these problems for the region's leaders was the absence of any replacement jobs for those who had been laid off by Boeing and other firms throughout the region. The loss of so many of these highly skilled technology workers meant that the region had lost its most vital asset for attracting new employers. In 1972, a roadside billboard appeared at the side of one of the major arterials leaving the city; it, quite famously read, "Will the last person leaving Seattle please turn out the lights?!"

And, the snowball of decline still gathered speed. As the most talented (read highest paid) of the workforce moved away, home valuations declined. This meant that the cities and counties of the region lost real estate taxes; again, at the very time when public services were in the greatest demand ever. In 2004, a local journalist wrote that "Washington's aerospace industry stands as a case study in how the decline of a dominant industry reaches into every facet of a region's economy."[7] And, Roger Sale referred to the city's seeming lack of awareness by asking how Seattle could have "continued for so long to be so nakedly dependent on its one magnificently successful company."[8]

The absence of economic diversity hurt both the City of Seattle and the entire Puget Sound region. But, the damage did not stop there. As is the case in so many states across the country, disproportionately high shares of state tax revenues (often based on income tax receipts), which are the basis for the provision of the state's public services, come from a single primary region within the state. In Virginia, that is northern Virginia, in Maine, it is Portland; in Colorado, Denver; in Michigan, Detroit, and so on. In this case, one can legitimately say that, as goes Seattle, so goes the State of Washington.

As the city's planners worked diligently to rebuild their shattered economy, their intent was first to create economic development rather than merely economic growth. They needed to rebuild not just the economy, but the city itself. It needed to become a place that would attract the best workforce to live there again, and it needed to be a place where the new economy was so diverse that workers would come not simply for jobs but for careers. In other words, they would remain in the region over time, perhaps even over generations. Skill sets that would be in demand for one industry would be in demand by others. In this way, workers would know that declines of Boeing-like proportions would not happen again in Seattle because their skills would be needed by firms in other industries around the region.

By 2004, Seattle had the highest concentration of health care workers in the region, with nearly 75,000 employed and more than 3 billion dollars in annual incomes.[9] The life sciences industry is greatly supported in the region by research under way at the University of Washington and the Fred Hutchinson Center for Cancer Research.

The dramatic growth in the health care industry throughout the Puget Sound region meant that the economy was more stabilized and that the misfortunes of a single industry could not devastate the area's overall employment situation. By 2004, for example, one in five jobs in Seattle was tied to the health care industry cluster. "In terms of local tax impact, healthcare providers generated $29.6 million for the city treasury."[10]

This economic stability is furthered by the additional diversity represented by some of the nation's largest employers in a variety of fields, including Microsoft, Starbucks, Amazon, a major medical center, and very active and productive ports that stimulate foreign trade as well as creating jobs and wealth throughout the community.

In fact, Microsoft, which now employs well over 50,000 men and women, now ranks as the second largest employer in the State of Washington. And, Luis writes that Microsoft's employment multiplier is 6.8, which means that the company, with 50,000 plus employees, is actually supporting around 350,000 jobs.[11] Luis reports that another advantage of the Microsoft presence in the Seattle area is that their revenues remain largely in the state whereas Boeing contracts with out-of-state suppliers, sending more that 70 percent of its aircraft manufacturing work to other locations outside the State of Washington. Microsoft, on the other hand, reported that the company purchased $2.15 billion worth of goods and services in the state economy in 2008.[12]

Following the 2001 terrorist attacks, and a resultant decline in travel—and thus in demand for commercial aircraft—Boeing employees faced layoffs numbering around 35,000. The diversification of the Seattle region's economic base was not yet what it became but it still was better able to withstand these shocks than it had been in the 1970s. "True, Boeing no longer carries 25 percent of the region's economy, as it did 40 years ago. Its share has shrunk, but only because the pie is bigger, more diverse, and less dependent on the one-industry boom-and-bust."[13]

Still, a sense of dependency on aviation and aerospace was felt. "Boeing transferred its headquarters to Chicago. Six months later, the September 11 terrorist attacks dropped the curtain on the aircraft industry. Some 35,000 Boeing employees still in the region lost their jobs."[14] Despite not dealing a devastating blow to the region's economy, the impact was still mighty.

As a result of the region's diverse rebuilding of the local economy, their "Great Expansion" (1982—1990), "Puget Sound employment had soared at a 4.6% annual rate as the region added a total of four hundred thousand jobs . . . over the long run . . . between 1970 and 2015, regional unemployment advanced at a 2.5% annual rate, more than 50% faster than the nation."[15]

Many of the new jobs are held by residents of neighboring counties (King, Pierce, Snohomish, and Kitsap). This means that those counties realize great residential growth and demands from their highly educated residents for high quality public educational systems, safe neighborhoods, and other high quality public services while their income taxes accrue to the state for the provision of its public services. This, in turn, means that the funds derived from those counties are effectively redistributed across cities, towns, and counties of greater need throughout the balance of the State of Washington.

This is a common concern from the wealthier parts of most states, which tend to concur with the need to help the needier regions of their states but often disagree with the proportion of their funds that go elsewhere and are not returned to help with their own public service requirements. On the other hand, those employees are spending their incomes largely at home and thereby generating support for other jobs, notably home-building, personal services, retail outlets, and more, in their home counties. On the downside of the job growth, economists at Washington's Employment Security Department noted that nearly three-fourths of the re-employed reported that their earnings were lower than their previous salaries, and two out of five reported new wages that were at least 20 percent lower than that of their most recent employment.[16]

Suzanne Dale Estey is the President and CEO of the Economic Development Council of Seattle and King County, a public–private partnership that markets the region. The organization, now in its forty-sixth year, was originally established to combat the region's over-reliance on the Boeing Corporation for economic development and stability. The consequence of its operations over the years has been a highly desirable diversity in the economic base, although Ms. Estey notes that it has been the result of both dedicated work to attract an array of diverse industries and a little bit of luck. The luck comes in the form of being the home to such business leaders as Jeff Bezos (Amazon) and Bill Gates (Microsoft). The University of Washington is also part of the overall economic picture and its presence and engagement in the region's economic development certainly predated the 1970s need for greater economic diversity throughout the Puget Sound region.

The city and the region are now free of its earlier over-dependence on aerospace and aviation, but the legacy remains. The State of Washington has an impressive array of aggressive incentives available to stimulate growth in that industry. The commercial space sector is also emerging and the region is now home to 15 companies engaged on the commercial side of space exploration. The region also pronounces proudly that it has the highest density of software engineers to the total population of any community in the United States, and a host of other industries have removed the City of Seattle and King County from an over-dependence on any industry. Clean technologies, virtual reality and augmented reality advances, medical technologies around immuno-therapy and cancer research, big data, cloud computing, and more stabilize the economic base such that problems in no single industry can have the devastating effects that were experienced in the early seventies when Boeing nearly went out of business.

Relatively lower business costs are another big part of the reason for the region to grow and become successful in attracting diverse industries. The costs of living and doing business are roughly one-third what they are in the Silicon Valley area, which is a major attractive feature both for employers and potential employees. Further, the voters in the State of Washington have consistently rejected proposals to create an income tax. Washington is one of only seven US states not to have a personal income tax, which Estey believes is a very attractive feature for businesses and individuals, particularly those with technology skills and greater personal wealth.

Even mid-level wage jobs are growing in the area. This includes the work on the Alaskan fishing fleet, which is receiving a complete overhaul by companies in the city and county. This represents another form of economic diversification by ensuring that individuals of all skill levels and all income levels can find employment well into the future.

As is the case with so many other communities, employers in Seattle and King County are having difficulties in finding enough workers with the requisite technology credentials. The University of Washington has responded to this situation by doubling the number of slots for students in those curricula. However, the presence of such diverse firms as Amazon, Starbucks, Google, and Facebook in the area, both creates extraordinary demand for such employees but also quickly exhausts the available supplies.

Another issue that has the potential to retard economic development in the region is the H1B Visa restrictions and the related issue of immigration in general. As is the case with shortages of technology workers in all other major technology markets around the United States, the ability to attract and retain foreign workers to the businesses in the area is part of their business lifeline. This is especially true in an area such as Seattle and King County where the third most common language—after English and Spanish—is Vietnamese, and where a great deal of attention is devoted to trade and relationships with officials in China. (The State of Washington, with 40 percent of all jobs tied to international trade, is America's most trade-dependent state.) In sum, the City of Seattle and its northern neighbor, King County, have sufficiently diversified their economic base such that no single company and no single industry any longer have the potential to wreak havoc in the local economy.

Summary: Lessons from the Seattle Case Study

Seattle is a prime example of a city, and the surrounding region, that pursued and secured economic development rather than economic growth. Manufacturing functions were first replaced, and then complemented, by jobs in high technology, health care, and marketing. Corporate headquarters have added to that mix, giving the regional economy a great deal more stability than ever in the past. What Seattle illustrates, however, is that efforts to diversify the local economy need to take place while at the top of the economic growth curve, not after the decline has begun. By doing so, the region had to suffer through a period of transition from one economy—Boeing-dominated—to a more diversified base. An early start on economic development may have enabled the region to grow its job base much more quickly than previously had been the case.

On a further diversification theme, it is clear from what happened in Seattle and the Puget Sound region that one needs to consider the lack of diversity in the employment base as something greater than the employer and one industry. Having Boeing and its contractors did not constitute economic diversification. That requires a diversity of *unrelated* industries and firms.

A very high-level question arises from the Seattle case study. The State of Washington, like many other states, has a history of receiving the bulk of state tax revenues from its strongest market, or markets, and then distributing those resources, in terms of grants and services, to the parts of the state that has the more pressing needs. The issue raised is this: should such resources be distributed to areas in the greatest—perhaps even desperate—need, or should they be reinvested in the strongest economic engines in the state in order to generate even greater future revenues? This is a question that every state confronts every time a budget is passed in the legislature. There is, of course, no one answer, and the proper percentage that should be distributed to either purpose must be decided upon by the elected officials of the states. It should be kept, in mind however, that one may sacrifice future opportunities by the types of policies being pursued.

Finally, another lesson learned in Seattle relates to the value of immigration to an area. The city and the region have recognized that one way to increase the number of start-up companies and to provide the requisite workforce for business attraction and business retention relates to bringing new residents to the area rather than simply trying to make do with—or retrain—the people who already live there.

2   Buffalo, New York

Following the loss of manufacturing jobs, people began to leave the City of Buffalo and the surrounding region. Entire neighborhoods were abandoned as those who could leave, did so. As the downtown declined and entire areas of the city were razed, the city became less viable as an economy and less attractive to new employers who might have considered a location in the city. This led to dramatic and obvious inequities between a largely African American populated city and the largely white suburban jurisdictions which, in turn, led to devastating race riots in the late 1960s.

The situation only worsened as Bethlehem Steel laid off as many as 10,000 workers in the early seventies and left the region with 70,000 unemployed by 1974. Factory employment declined to one in ten jobs throughout the region by the year 2010. In many of the case study cities, local leaders came together to begin planning for their economic recovery but, at the outset, no such leader or group of leaders existed in Buffalo. And, the most highly skilled workers continued to the area. The dramatic decline in the population of the City of Buffalo from post-World War II is demonstrated in Chart 8.1.

Tom Kucharski is the CEO of Invest Buffalo. He returned to his hometown of Buffalo to assume this position after years of economic development work elsewhere. Upon his return to Buffalo, he was confronted with the approach that things should be done the way they always had been, which was on a very small-scale jurisdictional basis, rather than an organized, professional, regional approach.

The city and the region had an inconsistent past as related to economic development. Its manufacturing sectors had been very successful for such a long time that the employment had become "generational." People grew up expecting to work in the same factories and

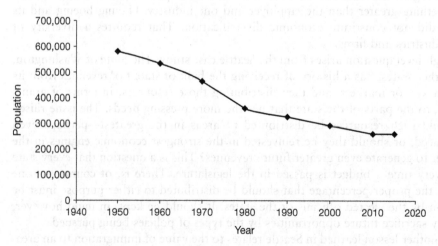

Chart 8.1 Declining Population of Buffalo, New York, Post-WW II to Present
Source: Similarly Sized Cities. www.biggestuscities.com

foundries—Bethlehem Steel, Ford, GM, and others—that had employed their parents and even their grandparents. Indeed, things had been going so well that there was no need to try to attract more businesses; there was "no need to have a Plan B," said Kucharski. In fact, there was no real need to forge strong interactions between the public and private sectors.

Then, "the bottom fell out." Manufacturing employment dried up in the Buffalo–Niagara region and there had been no planning for a way forward. People were "shell-shocked." The city was a great location with a good workforce and work ethic. It had a tradition of good schools and higher education. It became clear to several community leaders that they simply needed to make the effort and they could rebuild their local economic base. In 1995, a group came together for that purpose and they became known as the Group of 18.

The Group of 18 knew they had to do something. They had begun to lose one of their primary assets—their people. The population was moving out. The group put up the initial funds for a program of economic development outreach and set a goal of raising an additional 15 million dollars for expenditures over the ensuing five year period. Instead, they managed to raise more than 25 million dollars.

The group's success in bringing people back to the Buffalo–Niagara region was a long time coming. Today, the population has returned to the high-water mark of 20 years ago but, due to annexation practices of the past two decades, they are spread out over two times the land area. At the same time, the increasing annexation and sprawl has resulted in tremendous expenditures for the growth of the region's infrastructure. This created an increasing inter-jurisdictional competition for funds at a time when regional collaboration to attract new employers was the base requirement.

Kucharski and his team began to assemble public–private relationships on which they could build joint marketing programs. They began by cataloguing the region's assets that would be attractive to potential employers. They developed a regional listing of the commercial land and buildings for prospective businesses. To that time, Buffalo–Niagara had been the last major city or region in the United States without such a listing. Invest Buffalo established itself as "the" point of entry for companies considering a site or office in the region. Previously, there had been no such entry point and there was confusion for companies trying to figure out what to do if they wanted to consider location in the area.

The group then embarked on a traditional strategic planning process. They performed a SWOT analysis to determine their opportunities and what had to be done to overcome the obstacles that stood in their way. They conducted analyses of their optimal industry targets and company opportunities. They began to attend trade shows and meet with companies to establish the relationships that may someday lead to prospect site location consideration. They were able to announce a few small victories that enabled them to survive long enough to gain traction as well as more local allies and regional support for the outreach program. That included assembling a real estate team to help make the sales pitch when companies did come to town to have a look around.

There had been a sense in upstate New York that it had become an afterthought for the legislature and governors. Governor Cuomo however announced a program of a "Billion Dollars for Buffalo," which was designed to spend state appropriations for a variety of projects to stimulate the economy of the region. It has since been used to invest in a medical campus, local business-related infrastructure, workforce development programs, shovel-ready sites, and other projects that will help to generate job growth in the region.

Not everyone, however, agrees that the Governor's billion dollar gambit has been successful in any terms other than political or for public relations. One report calls it "underwhelming." "Real wages in both Erie and Niagara counties ... have been fairly stagnant since the recession." This is not to say that this specific program has been uniquely unsuccessful. Millsap wrote that "grandiose plans to artificially create clusters in older manufacturing cities rarely succeed."[17] Rather, his conclusion is that the state government needs to be supportive of business growth more generally than it has been, citing numerous reports that place the Empire State at the bottom of the lists of the most business-friendly, business tax supportive, and in the overall business climate.

This conclusion is consistent with the earlier section of this book that addresses the means in which state and federal government actions and regulations can stymie, rather than facilitate economic development. Local elected officials across the United States work constantly with their state representatives to ensure that statewide policies help, rather than hinder, their efforts to develop the local economies but, as Millsap correctly points out, localities can control land use, zoning, licensing, permitting, and some other factors, including local tax policies, but "in order to achieve robust economic growth, the city will likely need better cooperation from state officials."[18]

The question all of this raises is: Where do Buffalo and the region go from here? Among the needs Kucharski noted are additional commercial buildings, additional and varied housing, the attraction of talent to the region, and growing demands for infrastructure. The region is struggling to keep pace with the business growth, which is not the worst problem to have, but it does mean that there can be lags in the time of announcement of a company's site-location decision and the time they can be moved in and become fully operational. There are presently four companies coming to the region with an eventual need for 5000 employees; offices, facilities, and housing need to keep pace with that demand.

In such relatively rapid growth, following such rapid decline and loss of both hope and people, there are always lessons to be learned and shared. Other communities in similar situations can benefit from Kucharski's observation that the leadership must trust in their instincts and rely on their established networks as well as develop new relationships and networks of relationships. "In times of tremendous change, you have to be patient and cooperative."

Harvard's Edward Glaeser observed the Buffalo situation in order to consider its future potential. The population loss of the city and the Niagara region is an issue on which he places great emphasis. Following the loss of nearly 55 percent of its residents over a 75 year period stretching from the Great Depression to the first decade of the twenty-first century, the city was smaller and poorer: 27 percent of the residents at that time were living under the poverty level, less than two-thirds of the national average. Today's population stands at a little over 300,000.[19]

The federal government had initiated numerous urban renewal programs that poured money into cities such as Buffalo but Glaeser concludes that the city benefitted while only a relative few residents did, and they were not the poor residents of the downtown communities. For the most part, the federal donations were ineffective in advancing the cause of the residents in greatest need. The city's decline was hastened by the decline of value in locating proximate to the Niagara Falls in order to have access to relatively inexpensive electrical power, the advance of mechanization that meant fewer workers were required for various manufacturing functions, and the region's "dismal weather."[20] Additionally, the state tax rates in New York were excessively high and those costs of living and of doing business were exacerbated by the business costs driven by union demands. The result was that New York companies could be easily lured to warmer, more business-friendly states.

Finally, the fact that housing values in the city had declined so considerably meant that people could buy homes more cheaply than in the past. This meant that the income levels in the city declined among home owners generally. In 2007, the cost of a home in Buffalo averaged slightly more than 60,000 dollars; the state average was 260,000 dollars. The impact of declining home values on a city that constituted its tax base for the provision of public services on real estate assessments cannot be understated.

As people and employers departed the city, the municipal government was left with an enormous debt payment. Estimates topped 430 million dollars at one point in time (Free enterprise.com). This meant that the bonding agencies—Moody's and Standard & Poors—downgraded the city's bond rates, making the cost of borrowing even greater—at a time when they could not afford to pay the debt service on their existing debts.

With the loss of its major corporations over time came the lowering of the general education and skills levels so sought after by employers. Glaeser wrote that "Buffalo wasn't a particularly skilled city in 1970 and it isn't one now."[21] Fewer than one in five of the city's residents hold a Bachelor's Degree. "It had the right skill mix for making steel or flour, not for flourishing in the information age."[22]

The federal government began to fund programs in Buffalo to help its residents but they did not benefit the poor of downtown Buffalo. Nine million dollars was spent in the fifties (equivalent to nearly 70 million dollars today) to rebuild the Ellicott District in the heart of downtown Buffalo. According to Glaeser, low income housing replaced slums, and 2000 of the city's poor were relocated to new public housing projects elsewhere. "Despite millions spent, living conditions for the poor seemed no better and the city certainly wasn't on the mend."[23]

In the late sixties, the federal Department of Housing and Urban Development spent more than 50 million dollars to build a Marine Midland Marina. "While the public money created splendid waterfront edifices, it did little to stem residents' flight from the city."[24] The clear conclusion he reaches is that such investments should focus on the needs of people and not the needs of the businesses in the city. Of course, many would argue that a rising tide does lift all boats and that, as the city becomes more appealing, it will attract more jobs and that will benefit residents both directly and indirectly. And, of course, additional jobs will mean greater tax payments and improved public services and a lesser cost to the city's residents. As many others have concluded, Glaeser felt that "The best scenario would be for Buffalo to become a much smaller but more vibrant community—shrinking to greatness, in effect."[25]

The focus on new industries and the benefits of the presence of higher education has helped Buffalo to recover. The new medical school and several major employers' announcements of new job creation has helped Buffalo to begin recovery and the city to pay off much of its bonded debt which, in turn, has meant that the rating agencies have begun to bump up the city's rating, making borrowing less expensive.

It may be that the patience of the leadership in Buffalo is being rewarded. The press reports that wind and solar power generation may be a real force in the future Buffalo economy. One of the country's leading solar panel manufacturer now occupies an old Bethlehem Steel plant in nearby Lackawanna and Lake Erie has sprouted numerous wind turbines to generate wind power. The relatively inexpensive power that is now available has begun to attract companies, including a large Yahoo facility. "The region, which lost roughly a third of its population of 20- to 40-year-olds over the last 40 years or so, is beginning to see that group rebound for the first time."[26]

Is this a sufficiently substantial cluster on which to base, in part, Buffalo's comeback? It is not, in itself, adequate but, as part of the larger, more diversified growth, it can become a major factor. Cardwell wrote that Solar City, a leading rooftop solar installer that received 750 million dollars to build a plant in the region "is expected to provide 1,500 jobs on site and support 1,500 more among area suppliers."[27]

Summary: Lessons from the Buffalo Case Study

Buffalo first lost jobs and then lost its workforce and general population. Without it, future business attraction became very difficult. This was a time when a community needs to come together—public officials and private executives—to plan for the future and execute those strategies to rebuild the economy. That did not happen in Buffalo, at first because people were "shell shocked" by the losses, and subsequently because there was no plan around which everyone could coalesce. As a consequence, the economy languished and the region gained a reputation as being a place where business did not want to locate.

Finally, after a period that was long enough to result in zero momentum, the public and private sectors did come together and did create an economic development strategy and did begin to pursue a more aggressive path to rebuilding the economic base. The region is now moving forward with its development but did lose much of its most highly trained workforce and is now left with strengths in manufacturing and other more trad-itional areas but does not have the workforce it needs to be involved in new technologies and emerging technologies. The lesson is that coordinated reactions must be immediate and must focus on the industries of tomorrow. If that does not happen, the key asset to attract those industries—the technology workforce—can be lost.

3 Cleveland

In recent years, the City of Cleveland has been noted as a "comeback" city. This is as much a recognition of the city's, and the region's, efforts to rebuild a strong and sustainable economic base as it is a statement of its having arrived at a secure economic position. Clearly, much has happened in and around the city but there is much more to do. But, to what extent has the City of Cleveland actually come back, and from what?

A 2016 report by the Cleveland Federal Reserve Bank expresses a lukewarm endorse-ment of the city's comeback to economic stability and sustainability. It cites a lowering unemployment rate, per capita income growth that has, over a few years, exceeded the national average, and relatively low per capita credit card delinquencies, among other measures. However, it also cites the drag on the city's economy caused by employment growth numbers, flat home prices, and new homebuilding.[28] These industries' slower activity also causes a drag on the city's total expendable income levels and tax base (and, therefore, the quality and quantity of public services for residents and businesses).

The paper by the Cleveland Fed also notes that, in 2016, the fastest-growing sectors in the Cleveland economy were leisure and hospitality and financial services while the slowest growing sectors were professional and business services and construction.[29] The professional services sector includes relatively high-paying jobs while the hospitality sector includes relatively low-paying positions. Employment numbers alone can be misleading.

The City of Cleveland had reached its peak population count in 1930 when it was home to about 900,000 residents. The city had grown haphazardly; that is to say that it had not been planned and simply grew as and where individuals decided to live and work. As a city on one of the Great Lakes, growth today would include an awareness of environmental considerations to keep the waters clean of contaminants and to preserve the areas with clear access and the best views for higher purposes, but neither was that the case as Cleveland grew. The city became home to very wealthy industrialists and a great many areas of considerable poverty.

Clearly, this was driven by the dramatic loss of many of the city's primary business sectors, including manufacturing, wholesale, and retail trade. Chart 8.2 illustrates the precipitous decline of employment in those sectors between 1948 and 1977 alone. Over that period of time, employment in manufacturing positions declined by a total of nearly 46 percent, in wholesale operations by nearly 30 percent, and in retail by nearly 48 percent.

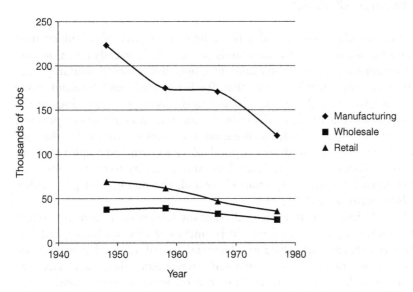

Chart 8.2 Decline of Employment in Major Sectors, Cleveland, 1948 to 1977

Data source: Swanstrom, p. 68

As the city grew to its borders, it experienced the same out-migration and development of suburban areas that occurred in other major metropolitan regions. Ultimately, Cleveland grew to its borders and then found that there was a different situation—as was also found in other major regions of the United States. The suburbs had grown from the border out and left behind no capacity for the city to expand; further physical growth of the city was no longer an option. Covenants established in the immediate suburbs were sufficiently and intentionally restrictive to protect them from encroachment by the city. This ultimately created a barrier to discussions and joint planning. The region had become a place of two parts: the poor in the city and the richer suburbanites.

What followed is what has happened in virtually every other city/suburban growth experience: those who had the resources to relocate, or the skills to be hired by firms now also in the suburbs, did so. By the mid-1960s, there were more people in Cuyahoga County than in the city itself. Then, the inevitable: "the tax base shrunk and the demand for social services grew to meet the needs of an impoverished population . . . the desperate challenges of poverty, the loss of blue collar jobs, failing public schools, and blighted neighborhoods."[30]

Between the years of 1970 and 1980, Cleveland lost nearly 24 percent of its population base, more than any other major US city other than St. Louis. In the following decade, the percentage population loss was, at nearly 12 percent more, more than any other major US city other than St. Louis; Gary, Indiana; and, Newark, New Jersey.[31] As Larkin wrote:

> For a major American city to lose 23 residents in a single day is not big deal. When it happens every day for 43 years, people tend to pay attention . . . Between 1970 and 2013, the city lost just about half its population, tumbling from tenth to forty-fifth on the list of the largest US cities.[32]

According to Sweet, the Cleveland of today is the heir of a legacy of "abandonment and disinvestment: thousands of acres of vacant lands (some of it chemically contaminated by previous use), buildings are closed, thousands of empty and obsolete buildings, . . . tens of thousands of abandoned people."[33] Jonathan Welle reported that Cleveland ended up in the absolute last place in a 2016 study of the most distressed large cities in the country, with "three out of four residents living in zip codes with high rates of poverty, joblessness, and vacant housing."[34] And, the situation continues to worsen for the core city as the affluent suburbs continue to draw the good jobs and strongest employers from the cities to the suburbs, damaging the city's tax base and its ability to provide services. "As businesses have moved further away from Cleveland, the numbers of jobs within 8 miles has fallen 26 percent since 2005."[35]

The Cleveland Foundation took an early and constant leadership role in rebuilding the city. The contributions were both in terms of business executives who stepped forward to work with city officials and substantial financial contributions that were made over decades. This was, of course, in their own self-interest since the central city was where their businesses were housed and the city's workforce was a source of workers for some positions. But, Tittle writes that, to their dismay, "As inner-city neighborhoods have declined, those residents who could afford to have moved to the middle ring . . .

the prospect of an ever-widening core of neighborhoods populated only by people too poor to move out is indeed both plausible and chilling."[36] Urban renewal was considered by the business leadership and that of the Cleveland Foundation of the day to be the most pressing issue confronting the city.

Yet, for many years, the efforts had minimal effects on the inner city. And, the city continued its decline. Cleveland had become the first major American city to default on its loans since the Great Depression and, as a result, was unable to borrow money further for payroll or public services. With little remaining tax base to draw from, the city had to have state oversight in order to continue its operations.

In Cleveland, much of the reason for economic decline and slow recovery can be placed on the problems of inter-regional and intra-city relationships. The political and business leadership were often at odds at the very times when they needed to be in lock-step to rebuild their lost economic stability. Dennis Kucinich was elected Mayor of the city at a very young age, a feat he managed, according to Swanstrom, not by attempting to pull the city's leadership together in a collaborative effort. Rather, he did so by giving "political expression to the resentments and frustrations felt by inner-city ethnics stuck in a declining economy, where they were excluded from the benefits of both suburbanization and the growth of white collar employment downtown."[37] With what is referred to as a confrontational style, he insisted that business leaders and legislators needed to focus first on equitable growth rather than growth in general. Not only did he fail to bring business leaders into the planning and decision-making for a new economy, he deliberately kept them out, refusing to accord them any status with the government, its committees, or its planners. Business leaders had wanted the city and the Mayor to support the redevelopment and the promotion of those parts of the city where businesses were located but there was too considerable political opposition and neighborhood resistance to bearing the costs of projects that would benefit businesses and the residents of the suburbs but not those of the inner city.

The mayor was not inaccurate in his description of the manner in which the political opposition had regarded inner city residents. Swanstrom notes that "conservative elites ... ignored local government which took a passive attitude toward the problems of industrialism."[38] When those problems affected the city and its residents, and calls for cooperation in rebuilding went out, the industrialists resisted reforms. Thus, Swanstrom maintains, the economic problems of the city are all about the poverty of those who remain in the inner city.

The distinction in the economic situation and potential of the suburbs, relative to the inner city, makes Cleveland a particularly volatile environment. Further, the presence of wealthy suburbs as a contrast to the plight of inner city residents, makes the contrast even more obvious. The wealthier suburbs "tend to suck money, businesses, and talent out of the city like a sponge, creating a permanent condition of underdevelopment."[39]

David Ebersole is the Interim Executive Director for Economic Development for the City of Cleveland. Numerous advances were made following the recession in the 2007 to 2008 timeframe. Many of the investments were around infrastructure improvements that were designed to make area more attractive to business start-ups and relocations. One of these improvements was to develop a rapid bus line from the downtown area out to the universities that are located in areas of higher employment.

The funding for the improvements on brownfields sites along the new line were procured from state and federal sources. The effort has been so successful that a recent study of 26 such projects in urban cores across the United States ranked this project as the most successful in creating redevelopment. The City of Cleveland provided nearly 100 million dollars for the project, which was matched by nearly 800 million dollars in private investments, most of which is for flex and other office space as well as offices for spin-off from research at the universities, much of which is health and life sciences-related. Today, there are approximately 4500 jobs along the transit line.

The universities in the city and the highly renowned Cleveland Clinic have, over the past ten to 15 years become more involved in promoting economic development. They have also made significant capital investments and opened up their campuses to appear part of the greater community through a variety of place-making efforts.

Incubators represent another way that the universities have become engaged in economic development within the city. By incubating companies that have spun off from faculty and other research as well as by connecting local private start-ups with university resources, the institutions are a strong part of the city's economic development plans. It is no surprise, therefore, that the city's target economic development industry sectors include higher education and health and the life sciences as well as banking and the traditional regional strength of manufacturing.

Another economic shot in the arm for Cleveland has been the re-population of several older neighborhoods by immigrants: "refugees from Bhutan, the Ukraine, Burma, and Somalia created new jobs and boosted the Cleveland economy by 48 million dollars. Refugee-owned businesses directly contributed more than 7.5 million dollars in economic activity to the city in just a year."[40]

While there is progress being made in the City of Cleveland, there are still challenges to be addressed. In the physical sense, there are still brownfields issues and old and abandoned buildings that either need to come down or be repurposed and there are old manufacturing plants that are outdated, rusting, and boarded up. Figure 8.1 and 8.2 demonstrate one of the restoration projects that have begun to make a difference in parts of Cleveland.

There remain areas of the city that investment has ignored. Ebersole indicated that his greatest hope would be to bring investments and jobs into those portions of the city that have traditionally been behind the rest of the city in terms of economic growth and development. Another area that will require additional attention is the relationship between the city and its suburban neighbors. Ebersole asserts that those relationships have improved over time but that there is still room for improvement for the betterment of the entire region.

Summary: Lessons from the Cleveland Case Study

Cleveland's most important lesson may be about what happens to the reputation of a city after it suffers dramatic losses in jobs and population. In Cleveland, those losses were followed by poor public management and unusual stories of incidents among elected officials in the city. It was easy for Cleveland to become known as "the mistake by the lake." Reputations damage easily, are lost quickly, and are very difficult to recover.

Figure 8.1 Cleveland Street Scene, Before
Source: Department of Economic Development, City of Cleveland

Figure 8.2 Cleveland Street Scene, After
Source: Department of Economic Development, City of Cleveland

Cleveland ultimately began to regain positive renown when the public and private sector began to pull together, along with local institutions such as the Cleveland Foundation. When business executives and others could begin to see that positive efforts were being made, the reputation began to be recovered. When progress was observed, many considered it an impressive "turnaround." Businesses consider locations in communities that are rising up the growth curve, not where the economy is stagnating or declining.

As the city begins to move up the growth cycle, it seeks to ensure that everyone moves forward in an equitable manner. Inner city residents cannot be left behind from the economic growth, so in Cleveland, bus routes were envisioned that would move people from within the city to outlying areas where the job base was expanding. Not connecting jobs and people can be a formula for discord. This was an important lesson for Cleveland as well as any city or metropolitan area.

Notes

1 Nora Johnson, Adhir Kackar, and Melissa Kramer. *How Small Towns and Cities Can Use Local Assets to Rebuild Their Economies: Lessons From Successful Places.* (Washington, DC: Environmental Protection Agency, May 2015).
2 Stuart A. Rosenfeld. Business Clusters that Work: Prospects for Regional Development. *Regional Tech Strategies*, vol. 6, no. 2. (1995): 123.
3 Sharon Boswell and Lorraine McConaghy. Lights Out Seattle. November 3, 1996. www.seattle-times.com
4 Roger Sale. *Seattle: Past to Present.* (Seattle WA: University of Washington Press, 1976): 185.
5 Boswell and McConaghy.
6 Dick Conway. Economic Outlook: We're Slowing Down. (January 2016) www.seattle business.com
7 Boswell and McConaghy.
8 Sale, 185.
9 Rosenfeld.
10 Jill Nish. *Economic Contributions of the Health Care Industry to the City of Seattle.* (Kirkland, Washington, DC: Huckell Weinman, September 2004).
11 Michael Luis. *Century 21 City: Seattle's Fifty Year Journey from World's Fair to World Stage.* (Medina, WA: Fairweather, 2012): 172.
12 Luis, 174.
13 Seattle Buzzes After Buzz: Diversification, Education. October 3, 2007. www.digitaljournal.com
14 Seattle Buzzes.
15 Conway.
16 Dominic Gates. Boeing Says It Can Ride Out Global Recession. (January 28, 2010) www.seattle-times.com
17 Adam Millsap. New York's Buffalo Billion Initiative Has Been Underwhelming. (September 28, 2016) http://neighborhoodeffects.mercatus.org
18 Ibid.
19 Glaeser, 3.
20 Ibid., 3.
21 Ibid., 5.
22 Ibid., 5.
23 Ibid., 5.
24 Ibid., 5.
25 Ibid., 6.
26 Diane Cardwell. The Wind and Sun Are Bringing The Shine Back to Buffalo. (July 20, 2015) www.nytimes.com

27 Ibid.
28 Todd Swanstrom. *The Crisis of Growth Politics: Cleveland, Kucinich, and the Challenge of Urban Populism.* (Philadelphia, PA: Temple University Press, 1985): 68.
29 Cleveland Fed Cleveland Population Loss Dampens Growth. (March 30, 2016). www.clevelandfed.org
30 David Sweet, Kathryn Hexter, and David Beach. *The New American City Faces Its Regional Future: A Cleveland Perspective.* (Athens, Ohio: The Ohio University Press, 199): xi.
31 Ibid., xviii.
32 Brent Larkin. What Population Loss Is Costing Cleveland and Why It Matters. (June 19, 2014) www.cleveland.com
33 Sweet et al., 62.
34 Jonathan Welle. Cleveland's Recovery Never Happened, Report Finds. (February 29, 2016) http://beltmag.com
35 Ibid.
36 Diana Tittle. *Rebuilding Cleveland: The Cleveland Foundation and Its Evolving Urban Strategy.* (Columbus, OH: Ohio State University, 1992): 87.
37 Swanstrom, 7.
38 Ibid., 36.
39 Ibid., 61.
40 Matthew La Corte. Refugees Are Revitalizing Some Great American Cities. (June 21, 2016) https://niskanecenter.org

References

Boswell, Sharon and McConaghy, Lorraine. Lights Out Seattle. November 3, 1996. www.seattletimes.com

Cardwell, Diane. The Wind and Sun are Bringing the Shine Back to Buffalo. July 20, 2015. www.nytimes.com

Cleveland Federal Reserve Bank. Cleveland's Population Loss Dampens Growth. March 30, 2016. www.clevelandfed.org

Conway, Dick. Economic Outlook: We're Slowing Down. January 2016. www.seattlebusiness.com

Gates, Dominic. Boeing Says It Can Ride Out Global Recession. January 28, 2010. www.seattletimes.com

Johnson, Nora, Kackar, Adhir, and Kramer, Melissa. *How Small Towns and Cities Can Use Local Assets to Rebuild Their Economies: Lessons From Successful Places.* Washington, DC: Environmental Protection Agency, May 2015.

La Corte, Matthew. Refugees Are Revitalizing Some Great American Cities Facing Decline. June 21, 2016. https://niskanecenter.org

Luis, Michael. *Century 21 City: Seattle's Fifty Year Journey from World's Fair to World Stage.* Medina, WA: Fairweather Publishing, 2012.

Millsap, Adam. New York's Buffalo Billion Initiative Has Been Underwhelming. June 28, 2016. http://neighborhoodeffects.mercatus.org

Nish, Jill. Economic Contributions of the Health Care Industry to the City of Seattle. Kirkland, WA: Huckell Weinman, September 2004.

Rosenfeld, Stuart A. May 12, 1995. Business Clusters that Work: Prospects for Regional Development. *Regional Tech Strategies*, 6. 2.

Sale, Roger. *Seattle: Past to Present.* Seattle, WA: University of Washington Press, 1976.

Seattle Buzzes after Bust: Diversification, Education. October 3, 2007.

Swanstrom, Todd. *The Crisis of Growth Politics: Cleveland, Kucinich, and the Challenge of Urban Populism.* Philadelphia, PA: Temple University Press, 1985.

Sweet, David, Hexter, Kathryn, and Beach, David. *The New American City Faces Its Regional Future: A Cleveland Perspective.* Athens, OH: The Ohio University Press, 1999.

Tittle, Diana. *Rebuilding Cleveland: The Cleveland Foundation and its Evolving Urban Strategy.* Columbus, OH: Ohio State University, 1992.

Welle, Jonathan. Cleveland's Recovery Never Happened, Report Finds. February 29, 2016. http://beltmag.com

Part III

The Impacts of Insufficient Local Economic Growth

It is perhaps self-evident to say that communities must increase their economic activity over time. Without economic growth or development, communities place at risk their employment base, their tax base, and the expendable incomes that get spent and re-spent throughout the community. The loss of employers and the jobs they control can devastate a city, town, or region.

But, there are even more, and deeper, impacts felt by communities that fall behind or are unable to enhance their economic bases than are generally written about. Some may not be felt immediately and others may have an almost instant impact. This section will consider the many related reactions felt in a community that loses jobs, loses tax base, and begins to lose its quality of life. It will consider the depths to which some communities can fall, while others seem to initiate the recovery process more quickly. This section will also seek to understand why some communities recover and advance while others languish or continue on a path toward further decline.

Part III

The Impacts of Insufficient Local Economic Growth

9 Impacts on the Secondary and Tertiary Economies

We have seen in the case studies that communities across the United States, whether they are large or small, urban or rural, experience ripples in their economic development that flow from the expansion of the primary economy into secondary and tertiary economies. While this has been referenced in the existing economic development literature, the depth and consistency of those impacts has not been well examined. Further, the same ripple effects result in an economy moving in the opposite direction; that is, when in decline.

In one sense, this can be seen as a manifestation of Engel's Law, which was discussed in an earlier chapter and which states that, when salary levels rise, individuals allocate increasingly greater amounts of their expendable incomes to non-essential goods and services. This is relatively unsurprising; people with more income eat out more often. Similarly, when salaries are cut, restaurants may feel the pinch in their revenues.

Now let's consider the same trends across an entire community that has lost a primary employer and has seen its unemployment rate climb either dramatically or over a sustained of period of time. The first impacts are on the non-essentials about which Engel theorized. People stop spending on non-essentials and put any of their reduced income levels aside for savings and for paying for necessities, such as rent, food, clothing, and medical expenses. The first cut-backs in personal expenditures will include the so-called luxury activities and purchases, such as dining out, new furniture, and higher-end purchases. The too-small house will be re-organized to accommodate families, clothes will be let out or handed down, and shoes will be repaired, not replaced. Such cost-saving measures at home affect the livelihoods and jobs of home builders, restaurant workers, and store clerks. New car purchases may be put off in favor of repairs to the current family vehicle. More retail sales decline, more layoffs occur, and less expendable income flows through the community.

What happens to others in the community when such discretionary spending is curtailed? It is clear that the providers of the non-essential goods and services will sustain losses in their revenues: restaurants, theaters, retailers, gyms, and more. Typically, consumers will consider these items to be less essential than food and shelter. There becomes a series of dominoes that usually fall in these communities: restaurants may have to reduce the hours of, or even lay off, their waiting staff, retailers require fewer clerks, and holiday sales decline. That means that there will be even less money being spent and re-spent in the community.

When employment levels decline precipitously and expendable incomes are substantially less, vacancy rates in commercial space and income taxes also decline. This means that the local tax base shrinks and, at some point, public service workers also experience layoffs or salary reductions, the result of which is that the overall quality of life in the community is diminished, thereby making it a less attractive location for new businesses. Even public sector employment cuts tend to be consistent with Engel's law: slots for those who provide essential services (e.g., police officers and firefighters) will be reduced after those who provide non-essential services, perhaps parks or library workers.

In 2001, Seattle approached the point of reductions in even the most vital public services.

> [C]ity tax revenues plunged, and City Hall was forced to make painful cuts. "You were closing community centers ... You were closing pools, you were cutting way back on maintenance, you didn't have the investment in streets or roads like we needed. We actually looked at cutting fire-fighters and police (which led to an absolute war)."[1]

In such circumstances, every line-item expenditure in the local budget will have its advocates, and they will turn out to oppose budget cuts for that program. Some will argue that the public schools are absolute essentials while others will be less supportive as they may not have children in the system. They may argue that libraries are essential in a community while others may maintain that libraries, while important, are not critical to the survival of the community. These kinds of debates leave the decisions to be made about budget reductions (or eliminations) to the elected officials who will try to find the best balance for the community. These are neither easy discussions to hold nor comfortable decisions to have to make.

The most well-known example of a city in extreme economic distress is Detroit. Nathan Bomey, in his recent examination of the resurrection of Detroit, observes that New York and other cities came back from the brink of disaster more quickly than Detroit because the community had the institutions to help fight with the city:

> [T]here were institutions—investors, businesses, universities, hospitals, churches, synagogues—that were dug in and weren't going to abandon the city. The same thing happened in Boston, Chicago, Philadelphia ... You had a core group of civic institutions. They became the center of gravity. There was no comparable group in Detroit.[2]

Impacts of substantial job losses on the community itself can have delayed, often hidden implications as well. In Buffalo, the city's comptroller noted:

> The mass exodus of employers had a stark effect on the region's jobs market, with unemployment steadily rising. It also left the city's finances in ruins ... leading to credit downgrades from rating agencies like Moody's and Standard & Poor's.[3]

The loss of higher bond ratings from these groups translates into higher costs of borrowing for the municipality, yielding requirements in the budgets for higher debt service over time and, as a result, reduced funds for essential and other public services.

School teachers are often the last public servants to feel the budget pinch although they too may experience layoffs if the unemployed move to other communities to find employment in significant enough numbers that the school-age population declines. Class sizes may increase rather than re-filling vacant teaching positions. Presumably, this reduces the quality of educational offerings and diminishes the community's quality of life. It also creates a less attractive situation for the purpose of attracting new employers. In situations of this nature, one thing does indeed often lead to another.

Another important source of a sense of community is the local newspaper. When they are unable to sell enough advertising, they too can go out of business, depriving the community of a primary source of communications at the very time that is most important. But, the loss of economic stability can go still further. In the more extreme cases, communities can reach a point in their economic decline when even essential services must be cut. When that has happened, short-term relief for those in the greatest need has often been provided by family members, friends, local charities, or church groups. The bottom of this cycle occurs when they too are without further resources.

One of the first non-essentials communities tend to lose is support for the arts, scouting, little leagues, boys and girls clubs, community beautification projects, and many of the other activities that, while perhaps not absolutely essential, are among the very things that makes a city or town a community. This is the beginning of a very difficult and dangerous cycle of decline. As the community loses that which makes life enjoyable, it consequently becomes less attractive to new residents and new employers which, in turn, results in less expendable income and local business revenues to provide for and improve those very activities.

An excellent example of how a new major employer can revitalize every layer of economic activity throughout an entire region is the location of foreign automobile manufacturing plants to Alabama. "Spinoff employment included nearly another 34,000 jobs in companies producing automobile components and other companies tied to the industry, while 93,000 more jobs have been derived indirectly from hotels, restaurants, and other businesses that have sprung up."[4] Of course, the same thing happens to smaller areas when smaller companies are attracted. Any economic development professional will complete that thought in the following way: ... but, keep in mind that these positive impacts, when one or more companies come to an area, will also occur when a company leaves. And, the first result of such losses is that the very asset required to attract an employer to replace those jobs, disposable income, and tax base is frequently the first asset lost. People who can find jobs elsewhere will leave the community. Martelle wrote that "When jobs move out of neighborhoods, whether they are well-paying union factory jobs or minimum wage janitorial work, those financially capable of moving go with them, or at least go somewhere else to find work."[5]

This is not just an issue for major metropolitan areas. Six hundred manufacturing jobs were lost in Twin Falls, Idaho when Tupperware and E.F. Johnson moved away. That resulted in an out-migration of the workforce that continued through the 1980s. Those who had been employed by those businesses relocated if they could. The need for job creation and attraction, however, did not abate because those who had lived in the surrounding rural areas moved into the city limits in search of employment opportunities as well.

Thus, the best of the local workforce are typically the first to depart, leaving behind structural unemployment, a diminished tax base, and increasing demands for transfer payments and public services from the state and local governments at the very time the budgetary resources are being lost.

Of course, the connection between primary workers and the secondary and tertiary economies in a community also works in the other direction. That is to say that, when a new employer arrives in a community, it spins off demands—both corporate and individual—that create new jobs in the support industries around town. In December 2011, Daewon announced the location of its latest manufacturing facility near Kinston, North Carolina. It was to serve as a supplier to a nearby Kia plant, with an investment level exceeding 14 million dollars. The employment level was announced to be around 100 jobs over a three-year period. The plant was expected to generate sufficient demand to support several hundred more jobs in the area. This became known in the community as the "Kia effect" because it meant that smaller suppliers would also need to locate in the region and that it would help to generate new businesses in the secondary economy, serving Kia and the related suppliers, as well as in the tertiary economy—jobs not directly related to Kia or its suppliers but that are in the community at large and are supported by that general growth. The lesson learned is that regions in which relocations of this magnitude take place must take specific actions that will accelerate that secondary and tertiary growth. This could mean infrastructure changes or zoning amendments that permit relevant uses or the training of a specific type of workforce. In short, cities and regions can enable such growth based on an initial location announcement.

Once job loss has reached a point of significance, local governments begin to feel the pinch of declining resources and the loss of sales, income, and real estate taxes. This leads to declining local expendable income that causes losses in the local secondary and tertiary economies. This can sometimes be offset by regions in unique ways. For example, Bernalillo County, New Mexico—Albuquerque's home county—saw its population increase between 1950 and 1970 from 69,391 to 480,577. The city increased its area from 3 square miles to 132 square miles, and thus captured 86 percent of the growth and 90 percent of the new tax base over that period. That helped to keep the tax rates low and made the city a "near-metropolitan jurisdiction."[6]

While this is an extreme example of annexation, many smaller cities and towns have done the same as a means of expanding the tax bases. Of course, most cities do not have that kind of opportunity and are simply confronted with declining revenues, diminished levels of service, a lesser quality of life, and fewer or no assets remaining with which to attract new employers and regrow the local economy. In large cities, such as Detroit, the results can be devastating community-wide. As Martelle wrote, "Left behind are the financially isolated and immobile—the uneducated and undereducated . . . Without access to reliable transportation, they (those who live in core cities) also lose access to suburban jobs."[7]

Once the best and brightest leave the area, the results can immediately be observed within the local public education system. Binelli noted that, after the automobile industry collapsed in Detroit, the public schools served

groceries, real estate taxes climb, and more. Groups that support local health causes, the arts, local schools and PTAs, little leagues, and more can also grow.

But, what happens when the reverse occurs: when an employer leaves town? Jobs in the secondary and tertiary economies disappear, institutions have to lessen their offerings, and the community loses some of its quality of life. But, it does not end there. When the local tax base is reduced, services are cut, and those who can find alternative employment elsewhere leave town. Communities are often left with those with the greatest need and the least ability to pay or to contribute to the tax base. Demands for transfer payments increase from a greatly diminished pool of resources.

Ultimately, the greatest remaining need will be found in the parts of the city or region which had always lagged because that is where the lowest income families reside. That is where those with the least marketable skills can be found—individuals with lower skill levels who have a lesser likelihood of finding employment elsewhere and moving on. These are the neighborhoods that decline further and where the unemployment rates will increase. The suburban areas may continue to develop–even thrive—and will still require a downtown to provide some of their cultural and other needs. Sweet wrote:

> The Cleveland region's poverty and their needs are concentrated in the city of Cleveland which has diminished resources or power to help the poor or help them find work. Suburbia benefits from what the city provides but avoids most of the costs the city bears.[13]

The question for these regions then becomes what the neighboring communities are willing to do to help the core city recover. Such a series of setbacks can create a situation that is extremely difficult to reverse because the assets in these neighborhoods are not sufficient to enable them to compete for the attraction of new employers either with other areas within the same region or against other areas of the country. The poor neighborhoods stand to get poorer in these instances, and they tend to suffer through multiple consecutive and related impacts. The suburban communities have their own financial challenges to consider and are generally focused on their own areas of need. Sweet adds that, in Cleveland, for example,

> the region's poverty and their needs are concentrated in the city of Cleveland which has diminished resources or power to help the poor or help them find work. Suburbia benefits from what the city provides but avoids most of the costs the city bears.[14]

How can the core cities in regions recover, when the problems seem insurmountable, the assets are minimal, and the assistance from neighboring jurisdictions may be provided only grudgingly? Does the business community, which professes the need to have a strong core, have a role to play?

3   The Circularity of Declining Public Services

Cities and regions that experience the loss of a primary employer, or employers, or that suffer across-the-board job losses due to national or global recession, can transition through a series of stages of decline. The first stage may be the immediate loss of jobs and the inability of families to meet their financial obligations. This will mean a loss of revenue to those who are the holders of those obligatory payments, such as mortgages and large-ticket expenses such as automobile payments.

The impacts of such non-payments or late payments may not actually be felt if the holders of the liens are nation-wide firms. However, the inability to make purchases will be felt locally as car buying is delayed, retail purchases are kept to the essentials and retailers of non-essential items lose sales. This could include restaurants, electronic goods, some clothing, golf club or gym memberships, and more. The outcome of diminished purchasing in a community will first be the loss of more jobs, perhaps in retail, the decline of expendable income, the loss of assessed value in homes and office space that remain vacant over long periods of time, and the loss of the tax base revenues that help provide the public services that support the quality of life in the community.

With each iteration of reduced expenditures inside the community, the employees of those firms begin to experience layoffs or the reduction of hours or pay. All of this is reflected in the further loss to those tax bases from which state and local governments derive the revenues they use to provide public services, sales taxes and real estate taxes typically being the most prominent. When that occurs, there may not be enough revenues in the state and local coffers to sustain their levels of employment. Thus, public service employees begin to experience reductions in hours, layoffs, or temporary furloughs.

Most communities will forestall laying off what they consider to be core functions for as long as they can manage to do so. These core functions are typically considered to be public education, health services, and public safety workers (e.g., police and fire-fighters). At the depth of these situations, local governments may be forced to lay off even such "essential" workers because the need for specific numbers of teachers, police, firefighters, etc., is sometimes determined by the population of the community. LeDuff noted that, in Detroit, "There are firemen with no boots, cops with no cars, teachers with no pencils."[15]

If there are substantial and precipitous departures from the community, fewer teachers may be required. Conversely, at a time when the remaining residents may require greater levels of public support, social workers may be deemed to be essential employees and therefore more protected. Of course, every community is different and all decision-makers are driven by differing considerations. However a city or a town or a region reacts to diminishing public revenues, the public services of the community will be affected. A decline in the real—or the perceived level or quality—of public services affects the way that businesses will view the community or the region in question. Negative perceptions of the local quality of life—real or perceived—will damage the ability of the local economic development team to attract new companies to create new jobs to replace those that were lost. It may even affect the ability to retain existing employers that may be susceptible to entrees from other localities with a greater real or perceived quality of life.

When this happens, the problem becomes cyclical—firms leave because of the diminished quality of life, which further damages both the ability to bring in new employers and the remaining quality of life of the community. Situations like these can spiral downward rapidly. Martelle noted of Detroit that "Crime travels hand in hand with joblessness, and when Detroit's economic foundations softened then collapsed, Detroit's reputation morphed once again . . . In its worst year, New York City had 31 murders per 100,000 residents, half of Detroit's peak rate."[16]

As has been made clear already, the growth and development of a community's private sector employment and the ability to provide high quality and sufficient quantity of public services are integrally intertwined. As the business community grows, contributions to the local tax base increase, and public services can be financed without placing the entire burden of the costs on the residential community. However, it must be acknowledged that the reverse is also true: as the business community declines, tax revenues decline and the public services they supported must either be reduced or increasingly paid for by the citizens who remain in the community; that is, those with the least ability to do so.

As unemployment levels increase, the tax base is unlikely to be sustainable. The only possible approach has been to reduce public services, usually beginning with those that are either considered to be luxuries rather than essentials, or those expenditures for which there are the fewest voters in support. Of course, the debates that ensue in such situations are about what is considered essential and what are thought to be necessities. Most people tend to agree on including public schools and public safety as necessities. But, not all school programs are unanimously accepted as being necessary. English is and history is, but what about language immersion programs, all-day kindergarten, English as a Second Language, and other programs that may have some but not universal support?

At some point, the budget resources may become reduced so thoroughly that only the basic classroom requirements can be supported. Great debates have ensued over the

Figure 9.1 Scene of a Community in Need
Source: Shutterstock

question of eliminating high school football or other sports in order to accommodate budget cuts. The debate is typically around whether that is an essential component of public education. While most people regard high schools sports as being less important than classroom sizes or textbooks, football programs never seem to find themselves on the chopping block.

As the local business community declines, the tax base is reduced, and budgets are cut and services reduced or eliminated. And, typically, before public safety and public education are examined for cuts, other highly desirable community services have already been impacted, including libraries, parks, and various programs within the human services portfolio. This is an important concern for the residents in the community but it also becomes a problem for economic development. If the most dire situation occurs and public education is cut to bare bones and police and fire services, or other public services that people expect to receive, are affected, it will become increasingly difficult to attract the new employers whose payroll and tax base generation will be vital to reversing the fortunes of the community. What happens in a community when the public sector is incapable of providing even the most basic services? (Figure 9.1)

4   Churches, Synagogues, and Community Support Organizations

In many communities, particularly mid-sized and smaller cities and towns, public services are complemented by non-profit and fraternal groups that solicit funding to support local residents who have extraordinary needs. Their funding comes from men and women in the community—or, perhaps beyond—who have made personal donations, as well as businesses that either contribute directly or that have supported the organizations' events over time. Community Foundations are a nation-wide network of such local and regional groups although there are many others that are nation-wide in their structure or are purely local. Fraternal organizations can also be means of support for families in these neighborhoods, such as groups of individuals who have immigrated to the United States from the same countries or who share a common religion.

The conundrum faced by such communities is that, at the very time the need is greatest due to the departure of businesses and the highest-paid members of the community, the greatest supporters of these organizations may have left the community to accept employment elsewhere. When the local resources of these organizations depart, they may be forced to resort to the use of reserves that have been saved for precisely such a situation. If the reserves become exhausted, there is a last line of resistance.

In many communities, local churches or synagogues reach out to assist their members in times of great distress. They may have funds for such a purpose or they may simply collect donations from the remaining congregants. Of course, at some point, these sources may also have departed the community to seek employment in another location, or the organization may exhaust its reserves for these types of issues.

Major cities in the United States may not follow this pattern quite as directly. For example, the City of New York made a comeback. Why? Because there were institutions—investors, businesses, universities, hospitals, churches, synagogues—that were dug in and weren't going to abandon the city. The same thing happened in Boston, Chicago, Philadelphia and other major cities across the country, where a core group of civic institutions were able to step in and hold on until new employers were attracted. These organizations can become the center of gravity for a community. However, this is not always the case. As Bomey points out, "There was no comparable group in Detroit."[17]

Clearly, the solution for cities and regions is not to find themselves in such dire situations in the first place. The attraction programs of the economic development agencies in such cities are today focused on the diversification of the economy and the ability to spawn and support new entrepreneurial businesses to ensure that large-scale job loss and economic dislocation is less likely. This implies a constant vigilance and an active economic development program before the losses occur.

Notes

1 Paul Roberts. Just How Secure is Seattle's Economy? (2016) http://features.crosscut.com
2 Nathan Bomey. *Detroit Resurrected: To Bankruptcy and Back*. (New York: W.W. Norton, 2016): 14.
3 Andrew Harrer. Silicon Cities: Buffalo and its Remarkable Economic Resurgence. (July 15, 2015) www.freeenterprise.com
4 Micheline Maynard. *The End of Detroit: How the Big Three Lost Their Grip on the American Car Market*. (New York: Random House, 2004): 204.
5 Scott Martelle. *Detroit: A Biography*. (Chicago, IL: Chicago Review Press, 2012): 225.
6 David Rusk. *Inside Game, Outside Game: Winning Strategies for Saving Urban America*. (Washington, DC: Brookings Institution, September 1, 2001).
7 Martelle, 225.
8 Mark Binelli. *Detroit City is the Place to Be: The Afterlife of an American Metropolis*. (New York: Metropolitan Books, 2012): 114.
9 Sherry Linkon and John Russo. *Steeltown USA: Work and Memory in Youngstown*. (Lawrence, KS: University of Kansas Press, 2002): 200.
10 Binelli, 207.
11 Robert Samuels. Feeling Snubbed but Pushing Forward. (Washington, DC: *Washington Post*, August 19, 2017): A-1, 16.
12 Laberge Group. *Town of Plattsburgh: Economic Development Strategic Plan*. (Albany, NY: Laberge Group, 2013): iv.
13 David Sweet, Kathryn Hexter, and David Beach. *The New American City Faces Its Regional Future: A Cleveland Perspective*. (Athens, OH: The Ohio University Press, 1999): 53.
14 Ibid., 53.
15 Charlie Leduff. *Detroit: An American Autopsy*. (New York: Penguin, 2013): 5.
16 Martelle, 17.
17 Nathan Bomey, 14.

References

Binelli, Mark. *Detroit City Is the Place to Be: The Afterlife of an American Metropolis*. New York: Metropolitan Books, 2012.
Bomey, Nathan. *Detroit Resurrected: To Bankruptcy and Back*. New York: W.W. Norton, 2016.
Harrer, Andrew. *Silicon Cities: Buffalo and its Remarkable Economic Resurgence*. July 15, 2015. www.freeenterprise.com
Laberge Group. *Town of Plattsburgh: Economic Development Strategic Plan*. Albany, NY: Laberge Group, July 2013.
LeDuff, Charlie. *Detroit: An American Autopsy*. New York: Penguin, 2013.

Linkon, Sherry Lee and Russo, John. *Steel-town USA: Work and Memory in Youngstown.* Lawrence, KS: The University of Kansas Press, 2002.

Martelle, Scott. *Detroit: A Biography.* Chicago, IL: Chicago Review Press, 2012.

Maynard, Micheline. *The End of Detroit: How the Big Three Lost Their Grip on the American Car Market.* New York: Random House, 2004.

Roberts, Paul. Just How Secure is Seattle's Economy? 2016. http://features.crosscut.com

Rusk, David. *Inside Game, Outside Game: Winning Strategies for Saving Urban America.* Washington, DC: Brookings Institution, September 1, 2001.

Samuels, Robert. Feeling Snubbed but Pushing Forward. *Washington Post,* August 19, 2017.

Sweet, David, Hexter, Kathryn, and Beach, David. *The New American City Faces Its Regional Future: A Cleveland Perspective.* Athens, OH: The Ohio University Press, 1999.

10 Reaction Times and Waiting Until it is Too Late

As has been discussed, several of the larger regions in the nation were slow to accept the loss of entire industries and the subsequent decline of the local or regional economies. This has also been the case in smaller towns across the country. The problem that is caused by either being late in seeing the problem approaching or being unwilling to accept its permanence as a long-term loss from the local economic base, is that it yields unnecessarily slow responses to the problem. This means that there is a gap between the inciting occurrence and the effects of the declining economy during which the community accepts its fate and begins to plan how best to recover and to begin to grow again.

The critical issue for students of public administration and for professionals in the field is to understand what will be lost over the period of this gap between awareness and response. The community leadership often gets so bogged down in denial or in assessing who or what deserves the blame for their problems that precious time is lost. In many cases, communities have devoted their attention to attempts to reverse decisions that are likely irreversible by the time they hear of them. Further time may be lost in dealing with the most immediate needs: how to provide the most essential of public services to the community and its residents, and how to accommodate those needs within the context of declining budget forecasts.

During that time, however, there may be critical losses that will make it even more difficult to attract replacement employers and even to retain other existing companies. The potential exists for an overall loss of the most essential elements of the very quality of a community's life. The loss of the best of the workforce, which is arguably the most important element of what economic development professionals in these communities have to offer new potential employers, diminishes the potential for an economic recovery. The students who complete either high school or college in the area must determine the best places to start their careers and may be forced to consider new locations even though they may want to "come home." Vital components of community life can be lost. All of these occurrences will both damage the community and its citizens, and retard any hope for an economic recovery. Ideally, communities will react immediately and begin to implement programs to accelerate their recoveries and to minimize their losses, but that is not always the case. As typical is the community that delays its response and begins to lose the vital components of a potential economic recovery.

1   The Brain Drain

When a primary employer leaves town either to relocate to another setting or because the business is no longer competitive in the higher-cost labor markets of the United States, the result is that men and women are put out of work. When the employer represents a significant part of the community's overall employment base, the ability of many of those who have been laid off to acquire new positions in close proximity to their homes is minimal. There is but one option available—relocate to an area where employment can be found.

What has happened in cities where this happened is that the first to leave are those with the greatest levels of skills and those who can afford to relocate. The impacts on the communities they leave have already been noted in terms of the loss of expendable incomes and tax base, but perhaps the greatest consequence is that the area no longer possesses the very asset that attracted the company in the first place—the workforce. The brain drain not only diminishes the community but it renders its ability to redevelop its economy ineffective.

A Fulbright Senior Scholarship in 2006 took me to the northern-most region of Scotland. Caithness and Sutherland were sparsely populated counties with a largely agricultural economic base. The exception was a nuclear power generating facility at Dounreay. The facility was old and the evolution of such technology had passed it by, leading to the decision to decommission the plant in the mid-nineties. The plan was for the decommissioning process to take more than ten years and, after the first four or five years, to begin to eliminate the 1200 positions as the various phases of the process were completed. This represented about 20 percent of all the employment in Caithness and Sutherland Counties.

The question I was handed was how to replace this vital source of jobs, expendable incomes, tax base, and contracts for small businesses throughout the region. The good news was that the community had strong leadership and several years to prepare for the inevitable. The bad news was that, once the sting of the announcement had passed, there was no perceived incentive to take action. By continually putting off reacting and planning for recovery, the area was quickly coming face-to-face with the loss of a very large part of their economic base and no actionable plan to replace it.

The urgency of the situation was now being driven by the realization that, in order to attract another employer, or employers, the 1200 engineers, technicians, and other professionals, were constituted the best asset they had to offer. As the deadline for the initial layoffs drew near, the problem became clear. The inevitable brain drain would make it hard to redevelop the economic base in the region.

The only thing that made Dounreay an atypical example of the impacts of the brain drain was that the region had a lead-in period to prepare. The period of 10 to 12 years before the decommissioning of the Dounreay site would be completed was both an advantage and a curse to the region. On the one hand, there was plenty of time to consider, to plan, and to implement a reaction to the loss of the nuclear power generation facility. There was no real urgency to provide an alternative, and the community would not suffer immediate losses of jobs and public services. However, the absence of a sense of urgency was also the curse. It meant that the community's reactions were delayed and that, when the losses did begin, they were in phases. This also minimized the sense of loss and the need to respond to the situation quickly and aggressively.

More often than not, the announcements that lead to the brain drain in communities are much more immediate and leave very little time to react before actions take place. This means that communities are reacting after-the-fact and this makes it very difficult to implement effective plans in a timely manner; that is, by the time action can be taken, even in the best of circumstances, the impacts have already begun to be realized.

In such situations as these, the brain drain renders the area less competitive for future economic development site location prospects. A sometimes unseen impact is that of the loss of the families associated with the employer. Particularly in mid-sized and small communities, the families of the largest employers, with potentially the highest salaries are those involved in community activities, whether that is civic, religious, volunteerism, scouting, little leagues, and more. Further, the employees with greater incomes tend to be those with the greatest levels of education or skills training. When they have departed from communities, it has often been noted that their children were among the highest-performing children in the local school systems, rendering yet another key economic development asset less attractive to potential new employers.

The lessons that have emerged from these experiences are that retention visits with employers—especially the primary employers in any community—are essential. They provide an opportunity to understand and possibly even resolve problems that may result in businesses leaving town. In that way, either local officials can make the changes necessary to retain the firms or they can, at a minimum, prepare quickly to attempt to recover from the coming losses. At a minimum, the intent must be to attract new employment opportunities or to create or attract the necessary assets to enable the start-up of new businesses before the community's key assets of workforce and the leading families depart: before the brain drain begins.

There is some good news, however: a report documented by the Manhattan Institute notes that, while many major metropolitan areas are losing total population, only three have a potential brain drain concern. Those are Detroit; Bridgeport, Connecticut; and, Toledo, Ohio. Out of the 28 metropolitan areas studied, Renn reports that 25, while losing population, are actually gaining in the number of people with college degrees; and, that the rate of increase of degreed individuals in each of those areas was at double digit levels. Detroit gained more than 150,000 degreed individuals between 2000 and 2013. Pittsburgh gained more than 145,000 and Cleveland more than 80,000.[1]

Detroit and Pittsburgh realized the greatest increases in college educated residents, but Cleveland and Buffalo also gained. Even though the population declined by more than 167,000 in Detroit, it gained nearly 167,000 residents with college degrees. The same phenomenon occurred in Pittsburgh, where the population declined by over 67,000 while it gained 148,000 college graduates.[2] In these cases, the ability to attract new businesses due to the stronger workforce has been greatly enhanced while the general population over which the incomes and public services must be spread has been reduced.

As such, one might expect the overall quality of life to be enhanced. The drawback from such changes, however may be that there will not be a sufficient workforce to support economic development. A generally accepted rule of thumb is that a four-year degreed worker in an information technology position spins off three or four more jobs for two-year degreed staff as support personnel, as well as two or three more jobs in the secondary and tertiary economies. In the area of translational medicine and bioinformatics, that ratio has been speculated to be as high as 6–8 to one. Communities that are using university-based economic development as part of their economic development comeback are wise to train the high-end scientists and engineers while, at the same time, ensuring that community colleges and other sources of workforce training for support personnel and other service positions in the community are operating effectively and in advance of demand.

Using universities as the central basis for economic development strategies can be a very effective strategy if they offer the relevant curricula and are supported by other institutions in that endeavor. Part of the change in these cities has been that the older generation had moved out when industry failed. In time, that brain drain was replaced by younger, better educated people. Each generation has gained in educational attainment over the previous ones. As Renn points out, even "cities like Detroit, Cleveland, and Buffalo that are widely viewed as downtrodden . . . are actually catching up with or surpassing the rest of the US in education attainment rates." Renn's conclusion: "a population drain but a brain gain."[3] "As of 2012, roughly 30 percent of adults in Pittsburgh were college grads, 28 percent in Detroit, and 25 percent in Dayton, compared to 48 percent in DC, 45 percent in San Jose, and 44 percent in San Francisco."[4]

The renewal of workforces in major metropolitan areas with younger workers—particularly, the so-called Millennials—has been the subject of much analysis and deliberation. However, the age of the workforce is less of a concern to businesses than is the education and capability of the workforce. Young service workers may not be as critical to an employer as the more seasoned and highly educated. Joel Kotkin observed that most of the places he surveyed that showed the highest percentages of college-educated men and women were in the suburban markets around major cities. "Only two of the 20 most educated counties in the country are located in the urban core: New York (Manhattan) and San Francisco. Virtually all the rest are suburban."[5] This, too may serve as a lesson for communities seeking to expand their economic development. In short, consider education levels and capabilities over age, and ignore assumptions that young people want to live in the cities and therefore, businesses will want locate to return to cities, to the detriment of suburban markets.

Renn's conclusion is that even the cities with the most difficult economic outlooks, such as Cleveland, Detroit, and Buffalo, "are actually catching up with or surpassing the rest of the United States in education-attainment rates."[6] The lesson to be learned here is that the retention of the educated workforce can start at the college and university level. Programs can be put in place to encourage seniors and graduate students to consider fully their future options right where they studied.

Many communities have attempted to staunch their brain drains by providing workshops and other support services to help workers who have lost their jobs to start their own businesses in place. The benefits of incubators for such purposes have been discussed in another section of this volume. Workshops and training programs on topics ranging from how to start a business, fees and taxes required, legal and accounting documents, writing a business and for financing, and more can sometimes help people create new businesses and not leave the area. Such programs can benefit people other than those who have been displaced for established employers. They can also be helpful for people who are planning to retire from one job but who may wish to start a business in the future either to supplement their incomes, pursue a lifelong dream, or to have a means of occupying their time.

2 Underemployment and the Loss of Disposable Income

The immediate and most obvious reaction to the loss of a major employer from a community or an industry relates to the loss of tens, or hundreds, or even thousands of jobs from the workforce. The focus on unemployment normally overshadows an equally problematic, related issue for the community—that of underemployment.

As people lose their jobs, they seek alternatives in the community but, more often than not, are forced to accept a position of lower pay in what has become a buyer's market. In some cases, the replacement job not only comes with lower pay, but may be at a further distance; or, it may only be part time. In many instances, the new jobs come without health insurance which thereby further drives up the costs for families. The consequence is that the breadwinners may need a second job to stay constant to their previous levels of expendable income. In other cases, other adults in the family must also seek employment to help their families make ends meet. This diminishes the overall quality of life for families in the community because leisure time is sacrificed to the need for other family members to work and for the primary wage earners to seek second jobs.

When the most experienced and best-skilled in the community accept lower-paying jobs, the individuals who would normally be most likely to fill those second-tier positions now must accept employment at even lower levels of pay, while those who might ordinarily fill those positions may not have anything for which to apply. The youngsters then entering the workforce may be left with few or no options and be forced to leave the area to find employment opportunities, thereby creating the brain drain discussed above.

Frequently, the remaining employers in the area will either be aware of the departure of other firms, or may see an up-tick in the numbers of applications for vacant jobs, and will realize that they have become the sellers in a seller's market. This may encourage them to lower their wage offerings as they will still be able to attract the community's best as applicants. Lower wages yield lower expendable income and losses in retail sales, and declining sales and income tax revenues. Ultimately, if the tax base losses are considerable enough, they will result in losses in the local budgets and the public services they support, at which point the quality of life in the community is lessened and the competitive advantage for competing for new economic development prospects is diminished.

At the level of the individual, underemployment—whether it means a spouse working or whether it means people working in two part-time positions or whether it means working full-time at lower wages—almost always means the loss of benefits. Of particular concern to the underemployed, especially those with dependents, is often the loss of health care benefits. Typically, it means that the families either go without such coverage or have to purchase individual coverage with fewer benefits at a greater price. In turn, this means that there is less expendable income for purchases in the community and that too leads to the loss of revenues, jobs, and the tax base from which the community can provide public services.

Some of these issues of community-wide concern, including underemployment may be known by a community's leadership. Some of the pertinent issues, however, may be overlooked because they are considered secondary to the community's leadership. In some instances, they are not always immediately apparent. One of these hidden issues relates to state and federal grant programs, particularly those designed to support education and other community services on behalf of those in greatest need. These may supply school lunches or job skills training or transfer payments for those requiring food stamps or general welfare.

When the United States Department of Labor (Bureau of Labor Statistics) and the state employment offices conduct their surveys of localities to determine their rates of unemployment, individuals must report that they are unemployed over a specified number of hours. That only tells part of their story, of course; if the individuals are receiving less income, working a second or even a third job to make ends meet, or if other family members are now also forced to work, that is not reflected in the counts as unemployment—one is either employed (as defined) or unemployed.

Funds that are available under various state and federal programs that are designed to provide relief to individual in communities with distressed economies are often allocated among states or localities or regions within a state on the basis of formulae that include the numbers counted as "unemployed." The numbers of underemployed may not be reflected in such allocations. This means that a community and its residents, if industrious and driven to earn a given income level for their families may actually be negatively affecting the revenue allocations that their communities could otherwise receive if they had merely settled for their lot in terms of employment and income levels.

A further concern for communities with a large amount of underemployed individuals is that the workforce numbers may not be reflected correctly when reviewed by business prospects. They—or their counsel—will look at communities for potential locations and will consider which one provides the asset they need to be successful. The numbers of under-employed may not show in reports as being available for additional work, whereas many of them are working in jobs below their capacity just to make ends meets or are working on two part-time jobs to constitute a full salary. Such individuals may actually be available for different, full-time employment with a new company but it may not appear that way in reports. In effect, a community may have its primary asset masked by definitional issues and reporting processes.

3   Local Newspapers and the Loss of a Sense of Community

Of course, there is a great deal of debate in many communities over the future of print media as electronic forms of communication become more easily available and ever-more popular. People in more populous areas are able to receive their local news and other coverage from these sources. However, in small cities and towns, the local newspaper provides details, coverage of local events, discussions and opinions about what is happening in the community, and other local input and interaction that simply cannot be replaced by social media or other means of coverage. Social media coverage is often spotty and controlled by single individuals. The professionalism is not always evident and fair and honest reporting is not a guarantee. Local newspapers are generally seen as covering topics of local interest, in an unbiased way, on a consistent basis and, as such, are irreplaceable.

The Pew Research Center conducted a survey in 2011 of the role community newspapers play in the lives of Americans. When asked whether the death of the local newspaper would impact their ability to keep up with local news, nearly 70 percent reported feeling that there would be no impact at all. Younger adults were less concerned about losing this news source than the norm. However, when respondents were asked about 16 distinct, specific topics of local interest, the source most often cited for news of 11 of the 16 was the local newspaper. They were cited as the most relied-upon source for such topics as:

> crime, taxes, local government activities, local politics, local jobs, community/ neighborhood events, arts events, zoning information, local social services, and real estate/housing ... The problem for newspapers is that many of these topics are followed by a relatively small percentage of the public.[7]

The report asks the most pregnant question: "What would happen if a newspaper in town were to disappear?" Another survey was conducted by Toronto-based Media Trust. Their respondents and focus groups "want to see and know local journalists, want them to 'walk the beat,' and engage face-to-face. They want journalists, local news, and local newspapers back at the heart of their communities."[8]

The Media Trust report also states that there is a crisis in the provision of local news coverage:

> The crisis is being managed by closing newspapers or shedding staff ... All forms of traditional commercial local news ... are operating with decreasing profits and fewer journalists and/or news professionals covering local areas ... A strong interest in "ordinary" community voices and stories in local media was also in high demand.[9]

The local newspapers, then become a source of community spirit and cohesion. They are sources of news about the places in town, one's neighbors and friends, new happenings, and sports scores from the local high school, and which stores are having sales. The local press helps make a town a community. But, what happens when subscription rates drop and advertising revenues decline? Does the community without the glue of a local press revert to being just a town?

An interview conducted as part of research for a previous volume was with the long-term Editor of the *Raton Range* in Raton, New Mexico. The interview was conducted from her new home in Texas. She had left Raton and had been unable either to revive or sell the paper. In fact, she had forfeited all of her savings and incurred substantial debt just to keep the paper alive and to pay her dramatically reduced staff.

The residents of Raton contributed their support to keep the paper alive but there simply was not enough commercial advertising to make the numbers work. Retailers took ad space that they could ill-afford in a last-ditch effort to keep the paper alive. Why were the businesses and residents of Raton so intent on saving the press? The community gathered around the news of what was happening. Announcements were made, local scores were provided, issues of local concern that could be found only in the Range were important to the community. Without the press, there was no rallying point. No one knew what was happening around town at the very time that people felt they needed to know more. The paper had, for decades, provided the residents and businesses of Raton with a sense of community.

When the paper closed down, that sense of community—of "we're all in this together"— departed with the presses and the paper stands, and the editor. Raton was losing its sense of community. Will an employer want to locate in a town with a deflated sense of community, a town that could not even support the "local rag?" Raton's leadership needed to consider what could be done to rebuild that sense of community and it began with attracting new employers. The question becomes—and will be for some time: Did they wait too long to start the economic development attraction effort? And, should they have initiated an aggressive program of business retention sooner, when it had become clear that the local businesses were either leaving or closing down? Only time will tell.

A smaller survey was conducted in 2015 with the local newspapers in several small towns across the state of Iowa. When the publishers were asked how important it is to report on specific topics, the highest percentage of the respondents answered in the affirmative to matters that were specifically of local concern. They were community events, local people, the schools, local government, agriculture, and human interest.

When asked about the strength of their agreement with given statements, the highest emphasis was given by publishers to these statements:

- "The community would suffer if there was not a community newspaper."
- "Weekly newspapers serve a different role in their communities than large daily newspapers."
- "The weekly newspaper plays an important role in the community's economic development."
- "The newspaper plays a role in integrating residents in the community."[10]

Local newspapers in Iowa, and in other small—and medium-sized—towns across America are an important cohesive element in their communities. One respondent to one of the surveys was a school teacher who reviewed the lists of local offenders so she could be prepared to help her students if needed. Small town newspapers are important for a host of reasons. The local press enables people to come together, to understand and debate local issues, and to join forces to support their home towns. For those who are new to a community, the local press is often the first place they look to learn about where things are and how to access various services. Without them, that element of support and cohesion disappears and the sense of community can be seriously diminished, or even lost altogether. That is not a description of a "community" that is attractive to potential new employers.

4   Business Retention

Any business person will tell you that the best source of business is the repeat customer, not the new client. Economic development is no different. In most communities, if not all, over time, the most substantial component of growth comes either from existing businesses growing in place or from the start-up of new businesses by people already in the community. What captures the attention of local officials and the local media is the attraction of a new employer and, while this is certainly a cause for celebration, it masks the fact that business retention is a far more significant component of local growth.

Existing employers need attention. It is remarkable that companies that are comprised of human beings making human decisions often express their sentiments in human terms. Many are the company executives who have made site-location decisions for personal reasons. This includes a favorite expression: "We left the last town because we just didn't feel loved." This is a cry for local elected and appointed officials to appreciate the companies in their communities, and to make concerted efforts to reach out to them, include them, and celebrate their successes.

The feeling of isolation and exclusion is particularly the case for foreign-owned businesses located in the United States. Communities that want to attract and retain such employers and enable them to grow, will reach out to them and incorporate them into community affairs as much as they do US-based businesses with an office or facility in town. Quite often, economic development officials will work with the local development and commercial brokerage communities to identify potential business relocations from the community. If it is known that existing leases are coming due in the near future, visits can be made to the employers to encourage them to stay in the community.

Business retention visits by local economic development staff and local elected officials are useful for a variety of reasons. First, it is a demonstration of the importance local officials attach to their very presence in the community. Such visits, and other forms of contacts, are also useful in identifying issues of concern to the employer before it becomes a major problem. Some of these issues can be as seemingly ordinary as road maintenance or security. Regardless of how outsiders feel, those types of issues can be very important and nagging to an employer.

Business retention visits are also useful in identifying when a company may be ready to expand or to relocate. In such instances, that kind of intelligence allows the community to make its best retention pitch. Even in instances when a company must relocate away from town—perhaps to find a larger existing facility that does not exist at the current site—there is a benefit to the visit because the exit from the community can be softened. As a company leaves town, a press release announcing the many virtues of the current location can be helpful in attracting a new employer. And, economic developers know that maintaining a positive relationship, especially under such negative or difficult circumstances, could potentially result in a future positive decision by that company.

Business retention visits are critical means of identifying these kinds of issues because local leaders can react and perhaps reverse a negative situation. The Fairfax County (Virginia) Economic Development Authority has a marketing team of nearly 20 professionals. These men and women have a performance requirement to conduct retention visits to local businesses—at their places of business—two times per week. Half of the companies to be visited are selected for specific reasons and the other half are selected at random. This yields a couple of thousand visits per year, and the program has been in place for more than 30 years.

The amount of business intelligence that has been gathered in these retention visits is enormous. Further, over time, local ordinances have been changed as a result of the visits and in order to retain the businesses involved. An example will be instructive. Fairfax County and other jurisdictions in Virginia assess fees for business licenses called BPOL (Business, Professional, and Occupational Licenses). The rates are assessed within state-proscribed ranges and the county decides where in the given range to set the fee for specific types of businesses. The fee is a percentage of the gross receipts of the company.

In visits to advertising and public relations firms, the economic development staff learned that the county was including as gross receipts the payments that advertising and public relations companies receive for the purpose of placing print or electronic ads on behalf of their clients. These were not truly revenues as they were simply passed through to the media for the purchase of space. The intelligence was passed on to the Fairfax County Board of Supervisors which then changed the definition of gross receipts for these types of businesses, and the companies that had announced their intentions to relocate out of the county elected to stay; not a single employer was lost.

A fine line can be drawn between business retention and business expansion. Obviously, a company that continues to grow in a community is one that has been retained in the first place; but, consider the growth potential of companies, whether it is one company growing very large or a collection of small businesses growing and building a large employment base between them. Those are companies that are growing in the same community because they have elected not to relocate. Something was done in the community to make it an attractive place to do business. In 2013, Amazon Web Services (AWS) located its operations in Fairfax County, Virginia. For years, the company was successful enough and happy enough to remain in the county. In 2017, AWS announced a new location and the creation of 1500 new jobs at its Fairfax County headquarters location. Those 1500 expansion jobs only occurred in that community because the company had been retained. Working with businesses to keep them happy—in-place—is a critical piece of any area's economic development strategy.

The expansion of an existing business may not receive the same press coverage as a new business coming to town, but its gains are as vital; and, the losses from a company that is not retained can be even more impactful. Economic development retention visits to local employers have a wide range of benefits for the community and should be given great emphasis in local economic development strategic plans. When existing businesses are lost, much more is placed at risk than the jobs and expendable incomes of the employees.

Economic development professionals can stay in touch with existing businesses in a variety of ways. One has been noted—visits to their offices or facilities—but there are other means as well. By being involved in local chambers of commerce and other business organizations, economic development teams can not only have their fingers on the pulse of the business community, but can become partners in supporting their needs. Creating and hosting events, helping to sponsor others' events, and promoting the successes of companies in the community are other ways to become partners in the business community's efforts to succeed. Many communities host awards dinners for the business community. Again, businesses are comprised of people and people make human decisions. A company that feels that the community cares about it and its success, or a company that feels that the public sector is a partner with them and they have input into the deliberations of the public sector will be less likely to depart. In short, the companies that feel part of the community will be less inclined to leave it.

One successful strategy for keeping the business community satisfied in their present location is to include them in the planning for the further development of the community. An ongoing dialogue between the city or county elected and appointed officials, the business community and its organizations, and the institutions in a community will go a long way to retaining businesses over time and to surface concerns that might otherwise cause them to consider relocation before it is too late.

5 Loss of Vital Services: Travel for Health Services, Retail, and More

When essential services are lost from a community, there is put in place a circular problem. The local newspaper closes, or a post office or school is lost. Retailers close their doors because there simply isn't enough demand to stay open. Without these services and amenities in a community, businesses and workers find it difficult to relocate to the community, and because people and employers do not come to—or stay in—town, there is inadequate demand to support local employers.

When large cities find themselves in spiraling decline, as did the City of Cleveland, the inner city becomes the site of run-down homes of the unemployed, severe poverty, and an ever-worsening appearance and loss of services. At the same time, retail establishments shut down because the population living within a reasonable catchment area for shopping has little to no expendable income and their customer base disappears. In Cleveland, Tittle wrote, "countless mom-and-pop businesses have been forced by the steady drain of customers to move out of the inner city or fold, leaving their neighborhoods without needed services ... many neighborhoods lack a full-service supermarket, a pharmacy ..." Tittle reported a growing awareness of the need to replace the lost retailers with new ones. If that does not happen, it is believed that the inner city neighborhoods will never be able to compete with the suburbs either for new residents or small businesses.[11]

When a city loses its most vital assets, it becomes more of a place than a community; and, when that happens, it begins to lose its best and brightest who can find a better quality of life elsewhere. Residents of a town that has lost its newspaper won't know what is happening around them. Residents of towns that have lost a hospital will now either have to travel many miles for health care services or go without. When the local schools close, children will have to spend hours on buses to get to alternative school locations. When retailers close, costs increase.

But, much more is at risk when a community loses its vital services. People in these communities do not want to drive hours to reach alternative employment and they do not want their children riding on school busses for lengthy periods of time in order to get to the nearest public schools. And, people who have to drive longer distances to reach a grocery or a department store will ultimately begin to consider the many advantages of moving to a point closer to those vital services. Those who can, will. Often, those who cannot are unable to do so because they cannot sell their existing home. No one else wants to buy into such a community, so they remain unhappily in place. As homes on the market do not result in sales, the assessed values decline and the tax generation for the real estate tax base becomes less and less. Public services are reduced and the community loses some of its quality of life. The downward spiral has begun. Now, it is up to the citizenry and its leadership to reverse course.

Notes

1 Aaron M. Renn. *Brain Gain in America's Shrinking Cities*. (Civic Report. New York: Manhattan Institute, August 2015): 3.
2 Richard Florida. Brain gain in the Rust Belt. (August 31, 2015) www.citylab.com
3 Renn.
4 Florida.
5 Joel Kotkin. The US' Biggest Brain Magnets. (February 10, 2011) www.forbes.com
6 Renn.
7 Tom Rosenstiel, Amy Mitchell, Kristen Purcell, and Lee Rainie. Pew Research Center. The Role of Newspapers. (September 26, 2011) www.pewinternet.org
8 Media Trust. Meeting the Needs of Local Government, 3. Freedman, Des (D. J.); Fenton, Natalie; Metykova, Monika and Schlosberg, Justin. *Meeting the News Needs of Local Communities*. Project Report. Commissioned by Media Trust. (2010)
9 Media Trust, Meeting the Needs of Local government, 7, 9.
10 Christina Carolyn Smith. Weekly Newspapering: Iowa's Small Town Newspapers, Their News Workers, and their Community Roles. (Ames, IA: The University of Iowa, August 25, 2015): 44–7.
11 Diana Tittle. Rebuilding Cleveland: The Cleveland Foundation and its Evolving Urban Strategy. (Columbus, OH: Ohio State University, 1992).

References

Florida, Richard. Brain Gain in the Rust Belt. August 31, 2015. www.citylab.com
Kotkin, Joel. *The New Geography: How the Digital Revolution is Reshaping the American Landscape*. New York: Random House, 2000.
Meeting the News Needs of Local Communities. Freedman, Des (D. J.); Fenton, Natalie; Metykova, Monika, and Schlosberg, Justin. 2010. *Meeting the News Needs of Local Communities*. Project Report. Commissioned by Media Trust. [Report]
Rosenstiel, Tom, Mitchell, Amy, Purcell, Kristen, and Rainie, Lee. Pew Research Center. The Role of Newspapers. September 26, 2011. www.pewinternet.org
Renn, Aaron M. *Brain Gain in America's Shrinking Cities*. *Civic Report*. New York: Manhattan Institute. No. 102, August 2015.
Smith, Christina Carolyn. *Weekly Newspapering: Iowa's Small-Town Newspapers, Their News Workers, and Their Community Roles*. Ames, IA: The University of Iowa, August 2015.
Tittle, Diana. *Rebuilding Cleveland: The Cleveland Foundation and its Evolving Urban Strategy*. Columbus, OH: Ohio State University, 1992.

11 Community and Citizen Responses

Community is a word that has been ascribed a dual meaning. In one sense, a community is the physical location, the buildings, the people, the institutions, the geography. But, community also refers to a sense of belonging. It includes not only the residents of an area, but the interaction between them as well. It is one's neighbors, friends, colleagues, fellow church-goers and other soccer families or scout leaders. A community is its people and how they relate to one another. What happens to the inter-personal sense of community when the physical community is diminished?

Complacency and the Loss of Hope

Communities lose employers, expendable income, and tax base. Some recover quickly, others more deliberately, and still others never at all. There is no distinct formula that helps understand why communities fall into one of those categories. Certainly, the assets it has to sell to new future employers is one consideration, as would be local institutions, scenic beauty and the overall quality of life, and other possibly definable, measurable assets.

Not all assets are clear and definable. When Boeing laid off workers in the early 1970s, people left the region for jobs elsewhere but when the steel industry died in Pittsburgh, no one left; instead, they determined to stay and rebuild. When steel left the Youngstown region, many stayed but the community, for a period, appeared more resigned to their fate and less determined to fight back.

In some of these communities—Detroit, Youngstown—people refused to believe that the past ways of life were gone forever and simply waited for a while for them to return. Whatever the response—and whenever it occurs—thee is an indefinable quality that helps to drive the reactions, the reaction times, and the effectiveness of the plans to rebuild. It is a collective attitude that either drives people to fight back, to accept, to give up.

In Seattle, as the jobs left and as the population declined, the new births registered also fell. And, "as the area's birthrate fell, the suicide rate rose dramatically; an anti-suicide net was deployed on the Space Needle, and there were call for a similar safeguard on the Aurora Bridge." There were some who gave up, who did not want to fight on for their families and their communities. In Youngstown, there arose "a sense of failure, loss, and helplessness within the community. Local leaders have often complained that Youngstown has a community-wide inferiority complex."[1] In fact, "Youngstown came to see itself as a site of loss and corruptibility, its sense of hopelessness increased. At the same time, the community refused to take responsibility for its own contributions to its struggles."[2]

Birmingham, Alabama experienced a similar city-wide sense of great loss and slow reaction time. A 2015 interview with Mayor William Bell of Birmingham yielded a discussion about the attitudes of the people of the city in the response to the loss of jobs. Mayor Bell's plan upon coming to office was to elevate Birmingham to the level of a great southern city, in the same vein as Atlanta, Charlotte, and Nashville. Before he could do so however, he recognized that his challenge was to convince his constituents, who had suffered through high unemployment and poverty levels for too long, that they were just as good as those other cities and that Birmingham—and its people—were capable of recovery and economic development. "We need to motivate people about the potential we have here." First, he said, "I'm a cheerleader for Birmingham and its people."[3]

To provide new jobs that are higher paying and offered better and longer-term career paths for all levels of training and education, Birmingham set out to develop the health care industry. The varied segments of that industry soon replaced steel and related products as the region's largest employer. Coupled with increased trade activity and support services, as well as growth in universities and medical research, the city has been able to demonstrate greater diversity in its economic base. Manufacturing and distribution, telecommunications and other smaller industry segments have created an environment that is less susceptible to comprehensive economic decline than at any time in the past. Today, the largest employers in the metropolitan area are in health care, and the city has made great strides in coming back. While there is still more to do in the city, the community has made progress and can look ahead to an economy that is not only growing, but also developing.

A different kind of example relates to the people of Pittsburgh, who reacted differently when the steel industry began to collapse in the late 1970s. Yung wrote: "Don't underestimate the power of community spirit and pride. More than anything else, Pittsburghers' devotion to their city seems to have kept it from becoming a wasteland."[4] Why did the people of Pittsburgh elect to stay in place and fight their way back when the workforce from other cities chose to relocate and rebuild their careers and their lives? Of course, it is difficult to determine why one populace reacted in a certain way while others took different paths. But, if a community is to recover its economic development and its momentum, as well as its very quality of life, it must keep its best people. It is the workforce that is the prime asset that will be needed when appealing to employers to locate to an area. Elected and appointed officials must move quickly to re-establish strength in the economic base.

In smaller towns and regions, an absence of expectations and the loss of hope can be even more profound. For previous research, I interviewed the Honorable Sue Skidmore, who was then serving as the Mayor of Elmira, New York. The town is located along the border between the states of New York and Pennsylvania. An industrial city that seemed to be from a previous time—one in which the manufacturing thrived, and the people thrived with it—had seen those industries move overseas in search of lower production costs. Then, the area suffered through a damaging flood, followed in 1972 by an even more devastating flood. The Mayor acknowledged that people still harken back to "those times before seventy-two." The city and its people have never quite recovered and the city and the area in general are left with relatively high levels of unemployment and poverty. And, there is very little expectation that anything will change in the foreseeable future.

Against a backdrop of such hopelessness, it will be difficult for the community to convince economic development prospects that they will be able to succeed there in business. They will be hard-put to convince prospects that they will be able to find a strong workforce or have the ability to attract others to the region to work for them. Because workforce and workforce attraction capabilities are among the top considerations of businesses when considering their site location options, the revitalization of the local and regional economies are unusually challenged.

Communities should be pursuing additional economic growth long before such a devastating loss of an employer occurs. The community that has diversified its economic base will be less likely to encounter a devastating business loss. Nonetheless, it does happen and it will happen again in other cities and towns. Community leaders—public and private—must react immediately, and they must ensure that steps are taken either to bring new, replacement, businesses to town to absorb the workforce, or to create means by which those laid off can establish new businesses of their own. Once the workforce is lost, the ability to attract new employers is missed. Coming back from those depths is enormously difficult. A population with grit and determination (à la Pittsburgh), and a leader with vision and persuasiveness (à la Mayor Bell of Birmingham) go a long way to making recovery possible and to accelerating future economic development.

Notes

1   Sherry Lee Linkon and John Russo. *Steel-town USA: Work and Memory in Youngstown.* (Lawrence, KS: The University of Kansas Press, 2002): 237.
2   Ibid., 190.
3   Interview with the Honorable William Bell, Mayor of Birmingham, Alabama, September 21, 2010.
4   Katherine Yung. Different City, Similar Story. (April 14, 2008) www.freep.com

References

Bell, William, The Honorable Mayor of Birmingham, Alabama, September 21, 2010.
Linkon, Sherry Lee and Russo, John. *Steel-town USA: Work and Memory in Youngstown.* Lawrence, KS: The University of Kansas Press, 2002.
Yung, Katherine. Different City, Similar Story. April 14, 2008. www.freep.com

Part IV
Enhancing the Local "Product"

One might consider selling a community in the same terms that businesses think about selling products. The firm develops and enhances the product and the sales department does the marketing and sales. The same is true of local economic development programs: some groups are responsible for developing the product (i.e., local government, the school system, the organizations and institutions that help make up the community, businesses, and the people who live there). The product they develop is what can be marketed and sold to businesses seeking locations. The professional economic development team can then promote the community and close deals just as a company sells its products.

This is not to say that the two elements of economic growth and economic success must never interact. To the contrary, just as in a business, the product development teams need to know what customers are saying about the product. For a community, does it possess the facilities, amenities, workforce, and lifestyle that will help it make the decision to buy? These features are the distinguishing features that can be used to market the community in the same way that the Ford Motor Company regularly conducts consumer surveys to assess their preferences for size, interior components, engine power, price, and more. Similarly, the sales professionals need to understand what the community is offering in terms of assets and amenities in order to present them to their clients. In this way, even though the two sets of responsibilities are essentially intertwined, it is helpful to consider them as distinct functions for this volume.

Preparing the product for potential economic development prospects will involve different issues in different communities. The professional economic developer will be adept at resolving any barriers to corporate site location that may arise. In most communities, the available land for commercial use or the available office space may be generally in use. Perhaps there is a marginal amount still available for potential new relocations but there is typically not an overabundance. Of course, there are times and places when there is an over-abundance in the inventory but that is not the ideal situation for communities.

This means that, when a prospect is engaged in discussions with a community, there needs to be some space or available land to entice the company to locate in town. This is a difficult thing to gauge as it usually involves having land prepared or offices built on speculation for the prospect that may consider a purchase or a lease. The formulas for office use are now changing so dramatically that the existing product in many communities may not reflect the actual needs of the companies being brought into town. For example, in Fairfax County, Virginia, in the middle 1980s, the average amount of space required per employee in office buildings was 265 square feet. Today, due to concepts such as hoteling, open space, working from home or other remote locations, and other changes in how business is being conducted, the averages are often around one hundred square feet per employee. Communities and developers must be cognizant of these trends before developing space for new companies on speculation.

Many communities have begun to focus on Millennials who have a different set of views on working than did the previous generations. These young people do not want to be isolated in office parks or similar settings. They want to be located in more dense settings with areas to gather and discuss common problems and issues. Offices with walls have no appeal to them; they want to work in a collaborative setting with casual atmospheres and comfort amenities. As such, the products that communities design and build need to be reflective of those types of concerns. They need to be appealing to these young people, in part because as the Baby Boomer generation leaves the work place, the younger generations are less numerous and wait longer to marry and have families. As such, those who are available for employment are in much greater demand, especially those with up-to-date technology skills. The community that wants to be able to attract the best of this future workforce will need to ensure that their product properly reflects the needs and interests of this next generation of workers.

12 Preparing and Selling the Product

1 How Differences in Local Economies Drive "Product" Development

Local economies are dramatically different across the United States. Corporate real estate executives and site-location consultants are paid to find the best sites across the country for their businesses or their clients to house a new office or a new facility. These men and women look at the differentiators—those factors that make one community a better choice than all the others. In many cases, the costs and other factors will yield several potential communities at the top of the list that are relatively equal in potential as the site for the new business. In such cases, even a minor factor can make the difference.

Major differentiators that are important to the site location decision-maker may include some or all of the following:

- the availability of land and/or facilities at present or for future development;
- the availability, relevance, and quality of the existing workforce and the ability to attract more;
- capital availability for relocation, construction, and ongoing production;
- university and other educational resources relevant to the skill sets required;
- the quality of life in the community, including the public schools, diversity of the population, and things to do;
- the receptivity and business support from local elected and appointed officials, including how that translates into local land use, taxation, and other policies;
- organizations and institutions in the community, including health care; highway, port and air service; and
- local cultural and recreational opportunities.

It is noteworthy that all decisions about site locations are made by human beings. For larger corporations, such decisions tend to be made increasingly on the basis of business factors. However, mid-sized and smaller companies may consider locations that are more in keeping with the personal preferences of their owners. Many examples exist of companies locating near waterfronts because the owner likes to sail or in a given location because he or she has relatives in that community. Disregarding such vagaries, this section will address the means that various communities have chosen to improve the products they have to market and the appeal to business executives and site location consultants and decision-makers.

Many examples can be found of communities that have improved their economic development product through relatively inexpensive projects, such as planting trees, re-paving, or façade improvements in the downtown areas. Of course, not all required changes are either as easy to plan and implement or as inexpensive.

The City of Youngstown, Ohio is an example of a more severe solution being required and it is representative of many Rust Belt cities. Youngstown saw its population peak in the 1950s. In September 1970, the steel mills throughout the region began to close and Youngstown saw its population dwindle from a high of around 190,000 to 95,000 by 1990. The city had lost an average of 16 percent of its population each decade for 40 years. Expansive neighborhoods and entire sections of the city emptied out. Homes were boarded up and businesses sat empty behind rusting, barbed-wire fences. No one lived in sections that were dozens of blocks long and dozens of blocks wide.

Like many such cities, Youngstown harbored dreams of getting it all back. Surely, the steel industry wasn't going anywhere. Once the realization hit that the steel industry was not going to be able to carry the city and its people into the future, some serious soul-searching followed. The outcome was the Youngstown 2010 plan. "This new master plan for the city's future development accepted the reality of population less. It asserted that Youngstown could be a great smaller city."[1]

As Glaeser explained, "Too many officials in troubled cities wrongly imagine that they can lead their city back to its former glories with some massive construction project."[2] Youngstown fell into that pattern as well but, ultimately it became clear that there would be no magic solution, no silver bullet. The vacant structures—both residential and commercial—would never be needed again. They were eyesores and an attractive nuisance for miscreants. They were now housing nothing but drug deals, gangs, and arson. The community recognized that there would be no reversing the fortunes of these areas; there would be no new companies coming to the factories and no new employees coming with them to live in the houses. No employer would want to site a facility in such a down-trodden area. Spending money to clean up and rebuild these areas would be a waste of time and resources. Quite simply put, these entire sections needed to be razed.

Much of the city's crime and fires took place in areas of the city that were, in theory, vacant. Owners of the homes frequently burned down their own homes in order to be rid of the burden. Stories emerged of underground groups making a business out of stripping what valuable components existed in the vacant structures and burning down the rest for a price. This practice, known as scarfing, became rather widespread at one point.

Finally, a new mayor, Jay Williams set his sights on Youngstown becoming a more presentable city to potential employers. Toward that end, he took up a policy contrary to that of many large cities in similar circumstances: rather than trying to rebuild homes and neighborhoods, he decided to raze them entirely, close down entire swaths of the city, and shut off the utilities. By leveling thousands of homes during his tenure as mayor, Williams oversaw the return of entire sections of the town to nature. Those areas became considerably more appealing to potential new residents and companies. Further, it minimized the public resources (largely police and fire protection) that were being wasted in those areas. Glaeser concluded that "it will make the city more attractive, less dangerous, and cheaper to maintain."[3] Many areas of the city, once razed, were allowed to go back to nature; others were used for ball fields or urban farming. All of the new options enabled

Youngstown to present itself to potential new employers as a cleaner, more attractive location. While driving into the city was once a trip through urban blight, it became a much more pleasing ride through fields and woods.

The approach represented a good start, but not a completed project. In 2010, Tavernise reported that "there are 5,249 vacant structures in the city. Together, with the approximately 20,000 vacant lots, that makes about 40 percent of the city vacant in some form."[4] The average price of a home in the city declined to around 17,000 dollars. That impact was felt not only by the homeowners but by the city itself because the overall decline in assessed values meant losses to the city's real estate tax base. This meant that police and fire services were still needed in areas of the city that were producing no tax revenues to help pay for them.

In the early 1990s, Detroit considered following Youngstown's example. In 1993, the city's ombudsman, Marie Farrell-Donaldson, in essence, suggested that "the most blighted parts of Detroit should be closed down ... By redirecting services to more densely populated areas, the city could provide essential public functions at a cost it could afford."[5]

Detroit simply had too much space that had been developed but not maintained, and it was costing the city enormous amounts of very scarce resources to serve, especially with police and fire protection:

> Having experienced a decades-long, ongoing population bleed ... the city was sprawling beyond its means ... Detroit would have to shrink ... in order to survive ... Most recently, Dave Bing (Mayor) made the leveling of ten thousand vacant homes within four years a centerpiece of his administration.[6]

And Detroit came to realize what Youngstown, Ohio had also realized. "The derelict scene depresses property values and repels new investment. Dead zones detach the remaining, populated neighborhoods from each other. In sum, Detroit has gradually reverted to an urban prairie."[7] For businesses to come to the community, these areas simply had to be cleared away in their entirety. As was the case with Youngstown, potential employers now see far fewer slum neighborhoods and can enter the city through much more attractive areas than in the past. In effect, the city has improved the economic development "product" that its marketing teams have to present to potential employers.

Preparing the municipal product for potential economic development prospects will involve different issues in different communities. The professional economic developer will be adept at resolving, to the extent possible, any barriers to corporate site location that may arise. In most communities, the available land for commercial use or the available office space may be generally in use. Perhaps there is a marginal amount still available for potential new relocations but there is typically not an over-abundance.

However, the communities may not make those decisions alone; the owners of the land may elect to develop it as zoned and local governments may not be able to forestall those decisions until the demand is present. Often, landowners will build facilities or office space on speculation; that is, assuming that, if they build something, people will come to occupy it. That is not always the case and it means that landowners and communities need to do their planning together and be in constant communications about trends and changes.

One such recent trend relates to the youngest generations in the workforce, the so-called Generations X, Y, and Z. Many communities have begun to focus on Millennials who have a different set of views on working than did the previous generations and are pursuing the development of future office space and facilities to accommodate what they see as the resultant trends. These young people are not thought to want to be isolated in office parks or similar settings. They want to be located in more dense settings with areas to gather and discuss common problems and issues. Offices with walls have no appeal to them; they want to work in collaborative settings with casual atmospheres and comfort amenities. As such, the products that communities design and build need to be reflective of those types of concerns. They believe that they need to appeal to these young people, in part because as the Baby Boomer generation retires, they will become the largest part of the workforce and, more importantly, they will occupy the decision-making positions.

What communities and developers need to consider is that the workforce of 20- and 30-year-olds today will be making decisions when they are 30- and 40-year-olds. At that time, their perspectives will be different. They may have spouses and children. They may have homes and mortgages, and want good schools and backyards. Things will look very different to them at 40 than they do at 25, including private walled offices and amenities for lunchtime. They may prefer to go home after work rather than hanging around at the local gym or the bar next door. At that point, they will need a car, even though current lore says that they don't want a car and would rather live nearby where they work or near public transportation.

What we can say about the younger generations is that they are less numerous than the Baby Boomers and that they generally wait longer to get married and have families. As such, those who are available for employment are in much greater demand, especially those with up-to-date technology skills. The community that wants to be able to attract the best of this future workforce will need to ensure that their current product properly reflects the needs and interests of this next generation of workers. They may also need, however, to ensure that the future product reflects their future needs in order to retain the companies and these large portions of the future workforce.

As communities consider where and what to construct as part of a product that will be attractive to potential employers, elected officials must consider the ultimate best uses for the land in question. Many are the cities that allowed the uses of prime land for less than ideal applications. Further, many are the cities that wanted to use prime real estate for higher uses that may be more attractive to businesses or may produce greater tax payments. One special consideration has been the land that is located along riverfronts. This is land that could be used for company or high-end residential structures. Land along riverfronts can be used for parks, hiking and biking trails, and more. Elected officials and community planners across the country are constantly being challenged to preserve the best areas in their communities for the best practical uses.

2   Identifying and Developing Essential Components of the Local Product

Economic development professionals market their communities as products in ways similar to corporate marketing. Cities, towns, and regions have facets that are positive and well-received by potential employers and they have asset gaps that need to be updated or filled in order for the product to be more attractive to employers. It has competition for the sale because other communities are trying to win the sale with comparable or better products to offer. The product even needs to be strong enough to retain the employment base it already has as that too is subject to intense competition.

By the time an employer considers buying a given product, that community is likely to be essentially all it has to offer. Coming changes and newly acquired assets and amenities tend to be add-ons to the existing product. For that reason, the community needs to be constantly seeking ways to improve its attractiveness for employers and needs to add or enhance the critical assets for business attraction regularly. Much of this will relate to the physical product: land, buildings, highway and technology infrastructure, hospitals, airports, colleges and universities, and more. Some of it will relate to the less visible elements of the product being marketed, including the availability and relevance of the workforce, the quality of the local public schools, the sense of community, and the relationship between the business community and the elected and appointed officials.

In brief, the community as an economic development product will have some essential elements and some components that are particular to the needs and tastes of individual executives and business clusters. The lesson for communities is to control that which they have the ability to control, constantly review the product through the eyes of the business community, and constantly try to improve and upgrade the product. Economic development is a fiercely competitive business and communities need to put their best product forward for corporate consideration. One less tangible component of a community that is attractive to employers is the relationship between the public and private sectors. A close relationship between the two is critical to both and both will work hard to cooperate on community improvements if given an invitation to do so. Some communities have lost that strategic connection and, sometimes, even the trust that underlies it. When that happens, a "we–them" situation occurs that can be very damaging to all involved.

Quite often, economic development staffs hear from prospective employers that they have plans to move some people to the new location but that they will also need to attract new employees from outside the area. In such cases, the employer will consider how successful they will be in encouraging the most highly sought-after individuals to come to work for them. In many cases, the workers they want to attract are highly educated or skilled and, as such, will want the same for their children.

A public school system that is renowned for its effectiveness in given areas, or that generates high scores across the board, or in which the graduation rates are well above average, becomes a tremendous asset for business attraction. In Fairfax County, which has arguably the finest public education system in the country, this was a frequently offered reason for positive site location decisions. In other areas, employers knew their employees would need to pay for private schools for their children and still would not receive the same quality of education received as part of their tax payments. Indeed, when announcing employers were asked for their top three reasons for deciding to locate their business in Fairfax County, the Fairfax County Public Schools were always included on the list, with the quality of the workforce and the proximity to Washington, DC. Employers always knew that it was a good thing to include in their pitch to young prospective employees. It is difficult to overstate the importance of a high quality public education system as an asset for economic development.

Downtowns and Beautification

Many of the mayors and other community leaders I interviewed in past research noted that the appearance of the downtown is a critical decision point. One mayor referred to it as the town's living room: if it's a mess, a company won't want to stay very long. Other areas that will be discussed in other chapters of this book—including Youngstown, Cleveland, and Detroit—have had to address larger swaths of areas within cities or regions that were so dismal and unattractive that they repelled potential new employers from the community. In those cases, even barren fields that had been returned to nature were more welcoming and attractive. In the best of examples, those areas that had once been unattractive and dangerous and were then cleaned up and replaced with ball fields, wild-flowers, or urban farming, actually became positive attributes that the communities could use in their business attraction campaigns.

Leinberger notes that cities began to decline in the early 1950s as the rush to the suburbs began, causing rampant disinvestment in the cities left behind. He characterizes most US cities at that time as "clinically dead." However, cities began making a comeback across the United States and that resurgence is continuing today. In the last decade of the twentieth century, the number of households in a sample survey of 45 cities across the United States increased by 13 percent:

> [S]uccessful downtown turnarounds have shown that, for every one dollar of public investment, there will be 10 to 15 dollars of private money. The bulk of the public investment must be made in the early years, however, in order to set the stage for private development.[8]

For these reasons, cities today are remaking themselves to be more hip; that is, more appealing to the younger components of the workforce as places to live and work, and to the prior generations in the workforce as a place to visit, enjoy, and spend. Whatever the source, the expenditures create jobs downtown, create a vitality and excitement that can then grow by itself, generate wealth, sales for retailers, and support the local tax base that pays for police and fire protection as well as other public services without placing the entire burden of those costs on the residents of the downtown areas or the cities. The impetus for communities to beautify their downtowns or even entire sections of a city usually comes from the realization that retailers and other employers are far less likely to relocate to a city that is dirty and physically unappealing than to one that is clean, welcoming, active, and vibrant.

Youngstown, Ohio razed major sections of the city and allowed it to return to nature because potential employers had to drive through those sections to consider locations in more attractive parts of town. The dilapidated buildings and boarded-up factories deterred consideration before employers even got to the areas they came to see (Figure 12.1).

The scene was both a deterrent to potential employers and an embarrassment for residents. Once certain areas were razed and others cleaned up and maintained, the approach to the city was greatly improved and became—rather than a deterrent—an attractive zone that included amenities such as parks, bike trails, and ball fields. Even areas that were left to revert to a natural state were a great improvement over the blight and criminal activity that had existed before.

Figure 12.1 Youngstown, Ohio
Source: Shutterstock

Community leaders and elected officials in Baltimore, Maryland reached the same conclusion and for the very same reasons. To look at the areas of downtown that were thriving, one had to pass through the area now known as the Inner Harbor. Once a crime-ridden, unsafe area, the Inner Harbor is now the showpiece of the city, with museums, shops, hotels, restaurants, two stadiums—one for the Baltimore Ravens and the other for the Baltimore Orioles—housing, and office buildings. The city now parades its economic development prospects intentionally through a part of town they had tried to avoid in the past. The city's economy has since grown and much of the credit has been given to the foresight of those who determined to clean up a bad area.

Many communities, large and small, that reside along the Mississippi River have realized that the river areas needed to be cleaned up and that, by doing so, they could turn a large negative into an even greater positive. Snohomish County, Washington reached the same conclusion relative to its areas on Puget Sound and San Antonio, Texas cleaned up the areas along the riverfront and lined it with a variety of mixed uses. Today, the River Walk in San Antonio is an enormous draw and a strong contributor to the tax base of the city.

These downtown revitalization projects were the result of years of strategic planning, fundraising, public relations work, and encouraging of politicians to support these projects rather than using the funds for other public needs. Leinberger notes that the critical components of the planning focus should be the area's essential character, issues related to affordable and other housing, the greater development of local-serving retail and cultural attractions, public infrastructure, and the development of the employer base.[9]

In some communities, it is possible to establish Business Improvement Districts (BIDs) in which land and building owners agree to be taxed an incremental amount that can be used only for designated improvements inside the borders of the BID. These improvements may be to infrastructure, parks, facilities, festivals and events, or other projects that will benefit the area generally.

Downtown areas in small and rural cities, in particular, are important to a community for more reasons than purely economic. They are where people gather and share their days' experiences, concerns, and family news. It is where the children gather and where the community events are held. It is the heart of many small towns and the front door to the community. When potential new employers come to town, the downtown is what they see first. "Downtowns help define community identity through distinctive, often

Figure 12.2 Beautifying Downtown
Source: Shutterstock

historic architecture, shops and restaurants, community gathering places."[10] The first step for many small towns in the rebuilding of their local economies is to beautify and modernize their downtowns (Figure 12.2).

Identifying and Closing the Asset Gaps

Businesses, when searching for a site location, start the process by identifying their various needs, both as a firm and as the individuals who comprise it. Once a list of the required assets and amenities has been completed, the company—either through in-house executives or external counsel—begins the site-selection process to identify the communities that have as many of the requisite needs as possible in one location.

Typically, there are different types of factors the firm will consider. The first type of factor will be those that are absolutes; that is, they are essential to have in their chosen location. These factors may include a ready building or plant, or a site ready to be built on, with all of the zoning and permitting issues already resolved and any necessary infrastructure already in place.

Proximity is not an unusual requirement to be on the list of essentials. This may be proximity to a supplier or a primary client. It may mean proximity to a rail line or port or major highway. It may mean nothing more than proximity to family. As decision-makers are human beings, they often make such decisions on the basis of human factors. If the CEO likes to sail, the company may very likely locate near a lake.

Of course, the items that appear on a specific company's list of essentials will vary with the company. Perhaps natural resources are important and the transportation minimization tactics will be considered. Other cost factors may also be important to the firm, including labor costs, incentive offerings from the state or locality, site or building expenses, and more.

Business amenities may be critical. Local banks that conduct international transactions, venture capitalists or angel investors in the community may be important. Educational institutions and trade schools that provide training in relevant areas could also be considered essential. This often leads firms to consider arrangements made with the local community college or university as part of larger incentives packages.

The ability to attract venture capital or angel investments is an increasingly important component of a community's offering, particularly in areas of technology development or the provision of technology goods and services. Start-up businesses require sufficient capital to begin operations while sustaining the owners and employees. Those who can draw on the resources of friends and family members who might be willing to assist the aspiring entrepreneur will do so, but the time comes in even a small business' growth when larger capital inputs are required. At this point, angel investments are one possibility. This simply means that a person or company supplies operating capital under contract, with specified expectations for return on their capital.

Businesses need access to capital in order to grow. At the earliest stages, entrepreneurs may have limited options because there is no equity in the business to offer a bank as collateral. Individuals must use their personal equity to start a business and to grow it to the point where commercial financing or public supports are reasonable options. This means that they use their savings or equity in the home to grow the business. Another avenue used by many is now characterized as the "three Fs": friends, family, and fools. All of these possibilities are ways to grow a business to the point that it can qualify for commercial financing.

Once the business reaches that point in its evolution, it can access a variety of bank programs and several public funding supports to grow the business. Most of these options can be accessed in most communities. However, when the business reaches a higher growth stage, it often seeks substantial capital investments that commercial institutions are unwilling to take due to the level of risk involved. This is a common situation for technology companies that are working on a new program or a new drug or another new product or service that requires large funding inputs to pass through the research and development phases to the point of marketability. At that point, private funding is needed.

Two financing options that exist for businesses at that point in their evolution are angel investment funds and venture capital funds. These are collections of investors who are willing to take larger risks in exchange for larger potential payoffs. Typically, a venture capitalist will, in exchange for the level of risk he or she is required to take, demand concessions that business people are not always willing to give. They often will expect higher levels of pay-back on their investments and normally will demand seats on the board of directors of the firm and/or equity ownership in the company.

Another expectation of venture capitalist is that they will be able to keep a close eye on their investments. This frequently means that they expect the company to move close to where they (the investors) are located. Thus, if the funding comes from Austin or Boston, the company will be expected to relocate to that community as a contractual precondition of the investment. Of course, communities that have spawned the entrepreneur and the company do not want to have this happen. They would prefer to keep the jobs and the revenues and the tax base in town. As a result, many communities have begun to seek venture capital funds to locate branch offices in their cities and towns, with the objective of being able to support their businesses and not lose them to other cities.

Communities that seek to attract capital to support the growth of their local businesses confront numerous issues. Venture capitalists may agree to invest in local companies but they will only agree even to look if there is a critical mass of possibilities from which to choose. In other words, there must be numerous entrepreneurs, ideas, and businesses worthy of consideration to take their time. Second, if they do fund a few businesses in the community, they typically will spend relative little of their fund capacity in other locations while they spend most of their dollars in their home location.

Many communities have now come to the conclusion that, rather than—or, in addition to—trying to attract the attention of external venture investors, they should seek to grow their own angel investment and venture communities. Often, venture capitalists from around the world who have invested in Fairfax County (Virginia) businesses want to know why they are being asked to do so when the local people of wealth and the local business community are not investing themselves. While growing a local venture or angel investment community sounds like a great solution, doing so is easier said than done.

As a company grows, the need for larger sums of capital grows as well. If equipment purchases are necessary, and larger sums of operating and payroll needs reach greater levels, companies will seek either commercial financing or venture capital investments.

Commercial financing generally comes with very tight payment schedules and leaves little room for flexibility. It is also capped by the level of one's personal holdings that can be captured by the banks in case of a business setback.

Venture capitalists provide greater flexibility in the loans but, because they are taking a higher level of risk, the expected returns on their investments are different. If venture funding can be acquired by an entrepreneur, he or she will likely be expected to sign over a portion of the business and its future profits to the capitalist. Further, the venture capitalist will expect to have a say in the operations of the business and perhaps one or more seats on the board. These higher-than-commercial-bank risk projects yield greater demands from the owners.

Because venture capitalists want to keep a close eye on the businesses in which they have invested, they will often include in their agreements that the business must relocate to a site near them. This means that the community that initially spawned the new business will lose it as it grows and needs to seek alternatives to commercial banking. Thus, a community that is seeking to close critical asset gaps should consider whether it needs to develop an active angel investment community or a cluster of venture capitalists. When considering specific industry clusters, the community must consider whether it is possible either to develop or attract venture capitalists with specific specialties. For example, communities that are actively engaged in research and commercialization of products and services in the bio-medical fields have been successful in attracting capitalists who have experience and expertise in the fields and who are actively seeking potential new clients.

Industry clusters are often a very attractive feature of a community and part of the product it sells. A very good example of an industry cluster is found in Lexington, Kentucky, and is described elsewhere in this book. Localities do not have to have such comprehensive sets of assets to attract a business but the more of it that they can present to an employer, the better will be their chances of attracting businesses for whom those assets are vital to their community.

Incentive offerings of the locality and the state are often very important considerations for larger business prospects. This practice will be addressed in a later chapter but it is important to note at this point that incentives are part of the consideration process for firms because the community that cannot compete on the head-to-head competition and comparison of local assets and amenities can sometimes offset the competitive disadvantageous position by paying the firm for the differences to be provided.

Public education is often at the top of the essentials list. There are several reasons for this: first, the individuals in the firm now want to have their children in good public schools. Second, the ability to attract a strong workforce from outside of the area may depend on their interest in the quality of the local public school system. And, finally, the public schools can be good pools of future recruitment for the firm.

Workforce issues are a primary concern for companies considering locating in a given community. It is frequently the most important consideration and can remove communities from the list for further consideration. Workforce issues do not relate to having people available for employment generally; rather, it means having the necessary numbers of people available who have the specific skill sets the new employer will require or who can easily acquire such skills through available training programs.

In lieu of having the number of people already in place, the employer will want to feel confident that they will be able to attract new workers to the community once they are situated. One possible strategy that has been used effectively has been to present potential employers with plans for attracting and training employees either at a local training facility, institution of higher education, or other program. An alternative is to attract the necessary trainees and conduct the training at the new employer's facility once it is up and running. This enables the training to be more specialized to the employer's needs and often also allows for the training to be conducted on the employers' own equipment and even by the company's staff.

The availability of workforce and the affordability of workforce and executive housing stock are related and important considerations for companies, especially those that are moving the business into existing facilities because they often want to move right in and get started, whereas a company that is building a new facility may have some more time to resolve housing issues for the workers moving with the company. Companies that are constructing new facilities for the company may have time to allow for workers' homes to be built concurrently. However, a business moving into ready space will need its employees to be able to move themselves and their families into existing residential units as well. In Aberdeen, South Dakota, housing shortages were cited as assets that were needed and that were dampening serious site location consideration by potential economic development prospects. Coupled with the fact that the jobs shortages in the region had cost the area its construction businesses, there were too few workers to build homes or offices should a prospect become interested.

This represents a serious problem: without the construction workers and trades people, no homes or facilities can be built. Without the homes, no workers can live there. Without the workers, no businesses can be attracted. In such situations, incremental change must take place and it may require risks to be taken. The community must erect small amounts of speculative office space and homes. While the first businesses and workers are attracted, the next round of construction can begin. While this is a risk because there will be costs attendant to the properties while they are vacant, the costs can be minimized by incremental development, and a product will then be available to offer to site location business decision-makers.

Unionization can frequently be seen as an issue of vital importance to manufacturers or other businesses in which the employees could be subject to collective bargaining groups. The example of Detroit becoming non-competitive, in part due to unrealistic demands of the automobile workers' unions for pay hikes and larger-than-typical pension and benefits packages, has already been cited. There are enough other such examples to assert that companies, given the choice between a unionized location and a location in a Right-to-Work state, often opt for the latter so they will not have to deal with the forces of collective bargaining that can delay processes and raise the costs of production as was the case in Detroit.

Other community attitudes can also be considered essential site-location decision points for companies. For example, businesses are typically willing to pay a fair share in taxes to the state and the community in which they are located. They are not, however willing to pay more than what they consider to be their fair share to alleviate the tax burdens on residents. Moreover, businesses are willing to pay fair levels of taxes if they perceive that they are receiving quality public services in return. If the return is not sufficient, they will locate to a community where the public services are more likely to enhance the quality of life and to support their growth.

Business and site location executives may also elect not to locate in areas that are strongly supportive of one political party or another. Social values are also potential considerations and may include the local or the state stances on political issues relating to the LGBT (lesbian, gay, bisexual, and transgender) community, gay marriage, and more. Companies are comprised of people who make human as well as business decisions. Local residents' attitudes can be considerations at times. More than one company has decided to relocate because the community opposed the nature of their work or because the community had become too conservative or too liberal politically. These are the types of factors that communities must keep in mind if they wish to be perceived as a place to which businesses will want to locate operations.

Because businesses are comprised of human beings, they often respond to these issues, and often even speak in human terms. They want to hear from the local leadership when they can help on an issue or a program and they want to feel generally involved in their communities, but they also want to be contacted for no reason. This is why economic development programs generally include primary efforts at business retention. In this way, local leadership can learn of the issues that are bothering businesses, and businesses will feel as though they are really wanted in the community and that the local leadership will work to resolve the issues of greatest concern to them. It is quite remarkable to hear business executives say that their companies left a given area because they did not "feel loved." Human beings are making human decisions, based at least in part on human factors.

In some cases, the provision of natural resources is a critical consideration, both from the business and the individual perspectives. Such is the case in the American west, particularly the southwest, where the provision of water is a critical asset. Many of the states in the southwestern United States have inter-state agreements regarding the use of water coming from rivers that transvers multiple states. Waters flowing from north to south in rivers such as the Colorado River are critical to the survival of numerous states and their residents. The companies and the communities alike need to be cautious not to overload the supply.

The Colorado River, as an example, serves the water needs of an estimated 30 million Americans. But, as the waters are drawn from the river by the states through which it flows upstream, the residents of states that are downstream are left with precious little of this valuable asset to draw upon. This makes the downstream markets significantly less attractive for business development or relocation and residential growth. The resulting legal battles have not altered the difficult situation for the downstream states or their markets for business development.

In some cases, the community's very survival is in question. Such is the case with the provision of water—at present and in the future—in Las Vegas, Nevada. "The situation is as bad as it can get," said Tim Barnett, a climate scientist at the Scripps Institute of Oceanography. "Unless it can find a way to get more water from somewhere, Las Vegas is out of business. Yet they're still building, which is stupid."[11]

One might imagine the difficulty of marketing business locations to companies where the lack of availability of water is questioned by experts in the rather near future.

> The crisis stems from Las Vegas' complete reliance on Lake Mead, America's largest reservoir . . . it is located 25 miles outside the city and supplies 90 percent of its water. But, over the last decade, as Las Vegas's population has grown by 400,000 to two million, Lake Mead has slowly been drained of four trillion gallons of water and is now well under half full. Mr. Barnett predicts it may be a 'dead pool' that provides no water by about 2036.[12]

And, according to the Bureau of Reclamation (data as of June 2, 2014), "There's never been so little water in the dam since its construction in the 1930s."[13] For Las Vegas to attract—or even retain existing—employers, it must resolve this critical asset gap.

And, this is not just a Las Vegas problem:

> The drought is like a slow-spreading cancer across the desert . . . The effects are playing out over decades. And, as the water situation becomes more dire, we are going to start having to talk about the removal of people from Las Vegas . . . The Colorado is essentially a dying river. Ultimately, Las Vegas and our civilization in the American southwest is going to disappear."[14]

The entire State of California is now classified as being in a severe drought.

Not all asset gaps are so critical or so massive in costs to resolve; many individual considerations are important as well when assessing the list of amenities, as are the firm's non-essential items. The so-called quality of life features of a community are often viewed differently by different site-location decision-makers, but they are almost always part of the consideration. Companies may want to be close to the mountains or the ocean or certain other outdoor activities, they may want to be in an urban or a suburban or a rural population. Even if these kinds of factors are not vital to the success of the business, they can still be important in the decision-making process, if all other things are held equal. It is safe to say that the essential factors must be found first; this however may generate a list of several potential locations, at which point the non-essential factors can become make-or-break considerations.

It is also safe to say that quality of life factors can be deal-breakers more often than deal-makers. Some quality of life factors are less obvious than others, and others, while not typically a decision-making point for firms, do contribute to the overall quality of life in a community that makes it more attractive to businesses and site-location consultants. These may include the arts, the climate, proximity to various outdoor activities, professional sports, fine dining, and more.

To assess their relative position for attracting firms of a given industry sector (or sectors), communities conduct asset gap analyses. These are processes through which the community identifies the types of firms being sought and then assesses the assets and amenities they typically require from a location in order to be successful. It will include all of the considerations discussed above as essential and perhaps even some of those cited as non-essential. The community then identifies those assets and amenities that are present in the area. The missing elements comprise the gaps that communities need to address.

The community then has three options to pursue. It can devise a plan to acquire or develop the gaps in order to be attractive to companies in the sectors it has identified as important to its future economic development. A second option is to assess the list of assets and amenities that are in place and determine the business sectors for which they already possess the necessary assets and amenities. Those sectors become the new economic development attraction targets.

A final option for communities with asset gaps for the chosen industry targets is the most oft-employed strategy. This entails attracting the businesses for which the assets and amenities already exist while also planning to develop the necessary components of the list that will attract a higher level of businesses, thereby leading less to economic growth and more to economic development.

It is very important for communities to conduct these asset gap analyses on a regular basis. The danger inherent in not doing so is that they may develop what was the correct set of assets and amenities for an industry sector, only to find that time and technology have changed the factors on the list.

It is also important for community leaders to realize that companies and individuals from other nations will have the same requirements in terms of assets and amenities as

Figure 12.3 Korean Bell Garden, Fairfax County, Virginia
Source: Shutterstock

domestic companies when considering community as a potential location. They will however, also have additional expectations, including community attitudes, the presence of others from similar backgrounds, the availability of relevant air service, and the presence of schools, groceries, and churches or synagogues, and other amenities that reflect their needs and their culture.

Communities with a large number of foreign-born residents do well to embrace, rather than simply to accept them into the local economy and civic life. This can be done in any number of ways. Fairfax County, Virginia is home to more than 41,000 people of Korean descent (the total population of the county in 2017 was approaching 1.5 million) and hundreds of businesses owned by Korean American residents as well as 64 businesses owned by companies in Korea. As a result, the local Economic Development Authority maintains an office in Seoul which sends Korean companies to Fairfax County when they are ready to enter US markets.

Given the large influence of Korean people and businesses and Korean Americans, the county has created numerous demonstrations of welcome, the most evident of which is the Korean Bell Garden and Pavilion at the 98 acre Meadowlark Gardens. The bell weighs three tons and was made in Korea and transshipped to the United States. A great deal of symbolism is involved in the design of the bell, including the Rose of Sharon, which is the national flower of Korea and Virginia's state flower, the Dogwood. The intention is to make Korean and Korean American people feel wanted in the county and for Korean businessmen and women to consider Fairfax County a great location for their companies as well as their families. Figure 12.3 shows the care with which the bell garden was created and the calming influence it can have.

Notes

1 Edward Glaeser. *Triumph of the City: How Our Greatest Invention Makes Us Richer, Smarter, Greener, Healthier, and Happier.* (New York: Penguin, 2011): 15.
2 Ibid., 2.
3 Ibid., 66.
4 Sabrina Tavernise. Trying to Overcome Stubborn Blight of Vacancies. (December 19, 2010) www.nytimes.com
5 Lewis D. Solomon. *Detroit: Three Pathways to Revitalization.* (New Brunswick, NJ: Transaction, 2013): 50.
6 Mark Binelli. *Detroit City Is the Place to Be: The Afterlife of an American Metropolis.* (New York: Metropolitan Books, 2012): 87–8.
7 Solomon, 6.
8 Christopher B. Leinberger. *Turning Around Downtown: Twelve Steps to Revitalization.* (Washington, DC: Brookings Institution, March 2005): 4.
9 Ibid.
10 Leinberger.
11 Nick Allen. The Race to Stop Las Vegas from Running Dry. (June 28, 2014. www.telegraph.co.uk
12 Ibid.
13 Eric Holthaus. Gulp: The Lake that Supplies Vegas with Most of Its Drinking Water Is Now at Record-Level Lows. (June 5, 2014) www/slate.com
14 Allen.

References

Allen, Nick. The Race to Stop Las Vegas from Running Dry. June 28, 2014. www.telegraph.co.uk

Binelli, Mark. *Detroit City Is the Place to Be: The Afterlife of an American Metropolis*. New York: Metropolitan Books, 2012.

Glaeser, Edward. *Triumph of the City: How Our Greatest Invention Makes Us Richer, Smarter, Greener, Healthier, and Happier*. New York: Penguin, 2011.

Holthaus, Eric. Gulp: The Lake that Supplies Vegas with Most of its Water is Now at Record-Level Lows. June 5, 2014. www.slate.com

Leinberger, Christopher B. *Turning Around Downtown: Twelve Steps to Revitalization*. Washington, DC: Brookings Institution, March 2005.

Solomon, Lewis D. *Detroit: Three Pathways to Revitalization*. New Brunswick, NJ: Transaction, 2014.

Tavernise, Sabrina. Trying to Overcome Stubborn Blight of Vacancies. December 19, 2010. www.nytimes.com

13 Physical Requisites for Economic Development

Workforce and infrastructure represent two primary site location decision factors for businesses, large and small. Communities that cannot provide a prospective employer assurance that the workers are both highly skilled and available will not be able to attract a solid, sustainable employment base. Alternatives such as providing training for new workers can be persuasive to a prospective employer but this is not as strong an offer as the presence of workers who are ready to start working on day one.

Infrastructure is equally essential to employers, from manufacturers who need to bring in materials and move out the finished product, to office users who want relatively reasonable and consistent commuting times and patterns. These are basic considerations not only for attracting new employers but also for retaining existing employers and enabling their growth.

Research cited by Roddy indicates that Pittsburgh's overall economic revitalization occurred in parallel with the dramatic increase of younger individuals in the local workforce. In fact, he notes that of the 471,000 residents between the ages of 25 and 34, 48 percent possessed at least a Bachelor's degree, and that more than 20 percent of those individuals also held advanced degrees.[1] This is not related to their relative levels of energy or their youthful enthusiasm but rather their closeness to the training and technologies of the future.

Research by the Pew Research Center noted that 2015 Census data shows that there were slightly more than 75 million Millennials—defined as those between the ages of 18 and 34 years of age—and that there were slightly fewer than 75 million Baby Boomers (ages 51 to 69) in the United States. Boomers are forecasted to be surpassed by the so-called Generation X (ages 35 to 50) by the year 2028.[2]

The implications that many have taken from such statistics is that businesses, in order to attract these younger, more highly technologically trained men and women, must determine their wants from a workplace and ensure that they can provide them. While there is a certain logic to providing for the interests of these younger workers, employers are being cautious not to upset their desired corporate culture. Communities and employers alike have realized that there needs to be a mix of young, enthusiastic Millennials and seasoned veterans. Research has shown that the older generations in the workplace appreciate the training of the younger people and enjoy their exuberance and enthusiasm, while the younger workers appreciate the experience and wisdom of the veterans.

There are important lessons to be drawn from the research on the needs and desires of the millennial generation. Both businesses and community should take note of the fact that this generation, across the United States, is far more ethnically and racially diverse than its predecessor generations. These workers will therefore be more likely to seek employers that are more than simply open to diversity—rather those that embrace it and seek it out in their hiring programs. Celebrations of cultural, religious, and lifestyle differences will make some communities and some employers more successful in their recruiting of this generation and in their retention once on the job.

Yet, the focus on Millennials has often become redirected from purely business and workforce considerations. And, in some cases, the focus has been on the types of environments and neighborhoods in which this generation wants to live. However, in major metropolitan areas, or in areas with effective mass transportation options, emphasis on the places of residence may be misleading. What businesses want to know is where they should locate if they want to attract this generation to become part of their workforce.

One example can be found in northern Virginia, where jurisdictions compete to be the site of choice for both government contractors and private businesses. For the latter, in particular, the focus on the Millennials in each jurisdiction has been promoted widely. Arlington County has promoted the fact that it is home to the greatest concentration of Millennials in northern Virginia. While true, Arlington County has a population of about one 170,000 people while neighboring Fairfax County has a population that is approaching 1.2 million residents. As a consequence, and by sheer virtue of its size, Fairfax County has nearly seven times more Millennials in its population than does Arlington County. Further, the NAICS codes of those individuals indicate that many are in service sector jobs rather than the highly desired technology positions. Finally, those who are shown to be in technology positions are employed in Fairfax County anyway. The point is that communities and potential employers need to consider the gap between needed workforce and what is available. What is perhaps more critical than where they live is where they work.

The relatively recent interest in having Millennials in the workforce also needs to be tempered by considerations of balance. Employers that are considering locations for facilities are concerned with the entire workforce. They do not want only 20-year-olds; they want a balance of youth and energy and technology skills with wisdom and experience. Filling critical asset gaps needs to be accomplished strategically and only after due consideration of all the factors and all possible implications.

Millennials have created quite a stir because of the size of their generation and because of what some academics and media representatives perceive to be their differences in tastes and "demands," and how that will affect the workforce and doing business in the future in general. Much has been made of the differences between this group, also known as Generation Y, and their predecessors, and the presumption seems to be that, if companies want to be successful, they must bend their policies to accommodate this age group. The extension of that logic has been that communities that wish to attract the businesses for which Millennials are important must ensure that they are present and thriving in the community, and that to do so means creating what the Millennials "want." While there may be some logic to some of these statements, it has been easy for communities to pursue strategies simply on the basis of overreactions to this kind of thinking.

Both communities and businesses need to be cautious in how they respond to the research about Millennials and their preferences. For example, it is often asserted in the literature that this generation has little interest in home or car ownership. Overreacting to these presumptions may be premature, however, as those who express preferences for city living and public transportation today will soon be marrying and raising families and seeking the homes and school systems in the suburbs for their young families. A 2017 Bloomberg report also shows that Americans between the ages of 18 and 34 account for 42 percent of the nation's homebuyers and that nearly half of that generation lives in the suburbs and own both homes and cars.[3]

Every generation of Americans has a different approach to work, family, and life in general. A lot of focus has been placed in recent years on the millennial group because businesses want to attract them to work for them and some believe that, by catering to their preferences, their business has a better chance of attracting them to work for them. Similarly, communities have begun to think the same way and have begun to design offices and plants to be in areas that are walkable and have the various amenities that are of interest to people.

The Millennials are no different than previous generations in the sense that their interests and demands are a reflection of the periods of time in which they were raised. Baby Boomers, for example, were born between 1946 and 1964 and grew up in the fifties and sixties and much of their personal and professional outlooks were shaped by the war in Vietnam, race riots, the cold war, energy crises, and other societal divisions, including young–old, hawk–dove, rich–poor, and suburbs–inner cities. The mothers of many in this generation stayed out of the workforce to raise their families, which certainly had an effect on the girls of this generation.

Some experts believe that this generation had been promised the "American Dream" and, as a result, are generally very materialistic. This can certainly affect the way people in this generation approach work. To acquire the things they desire, they are willing to incur higher debt than their predecessors.

The end of the Baby Boomer generation grew up in the seventies and were children during the presidential administrations of Richard Nixon and Gerald Ford. George W. Bush, Barack Obama, Bill Clinton, and Donald trump were all Baby Boomers. The Watergate scandal influenced a lot of thinking and the reaction of the nation was to replace Ford with President Jimmy Carter, a southern liberal. Conflict in the Middle East became a constant and overriding global issue. Generation Xers, born between1965 and 1980, came of age in the Reagan years and saw the decline of the Soviet Union and the tearing down of the Berlin Wall. Newly formed nations in central and eastern Europe came into being at the same time this generation did.

Many of this generation had been latch-key kids and are, as a consequence, less dependent on supervisors for every instruction. They are more independent and seek to balance work with play. They are highly educated but very informal and think more globally than their predecessors. Experts believe that they tend to be self-starters and are willing to take on greater responsibility more quickly than prior generations.

Generation Y, the so-called Millennials, were born between 1977 and 2000. They grew up with technology, the AIDS epidemic, and the terrorist attacks of 9–11. Mail, research, stories, and games were all quite literally at their fingertips. They were comfortable with technology by the time they were ready for the workforce. On the political scene, they watched the World Trade Center buildings collapse in New York and they have lived through the subsequent "war on terror." This was the first truly tech-savvy generation. They are believed to be focused on and supportive of personal achievements, ethnic and racial diversity, and competition as a means of advancing.

Its successors have been designated as Generation Z. These individuals were born after 2000 and will soon be entering the workforce. They grew up, in part, during the George W. Bush and the Obama years. This generation and the Generation Y (or Millennial) people will soon dominate the labor force. This is why businesses feel they need to cater to their interests and demands which were born of the times in which they were young. Individuals born after 1977 total about 94 million, while those born between 1946 and 1976 total approximately 123 million. At the time of this writing (2018), a person born in 1946 would be 72 years old and may either be planning to retire shortly or have already retired. Thus, it won't be many years before the workforce is dominated by Generations Y and Z.

Businesses are working to appeal to the interests of the younger workers, especially those with greater technology skills. This means that they will locate in areas where public transportation is readily available and places for lunch or other activities are in close proximity. They will even try to locate near affordable apartment buildings and other appealing amenities. These interests are therefore important to communities that want to attract the companies that want to attract the younger members of the workforce.

Millennials are a very diverse population in the United States. There are more immigrants in percentage terms than has been the case for many years. Moreover, the group is very comfortable with that diversity, even insisting upon it for their comfort. That diversity also includes the LGBT community. But their characteristic differences do not necessarily imply vastly different beliefs or business expectations than did their older siblings or their parents or grandparents.

An extensive study conducted by IBM noted that Millennials and older workers possess many of the same career goals. The study compared responses to survey questions between Millennials, Generation X, and the Baby Boomer generation. In response to a question about having a positive impact on the organization, only 25 percent of Millennials replied in the positive. But, only 21 and 23 percent of the others did so.

The well-touted interest of Millennials in working with a diverse set of colleagues yielded a 22 percent positive response from that group, but the same response from the other two. Working on something about which they were passionate generated a 20 percent response from Millennials and 21 and 23 percent response from the others. Financial security and becoming senior corporate leaders also yielded equivalent responses from all three groups.

One of the clearest statements about Millennials and how they differ from previous generations has related to their concern for having a "work–life balance." That is loosely defined as having fun rather than simply working long hours to get ahead. Only 18 percent of the Millennials in the survey replied that such a "balance" was a key issue for them, whereas 22 percent of Generation Xers did so, and 21 percent of the Baby Boomer respondents.

Ben Casselman of fivethirtyeight.com further observed that "The myth of the job-hopping Millennial is just that—a myth. The data consistently shows that today's young people are actually less professionally itinerant than previous generations."[4]

The overall lesson seems to be that a strong and maximally productive workforce really requires a good distribution of the young and enthusiastic and well-trained Millennials as well as the wisdom and experience earned by the other generations.

For communities, the lesson is to build a strong workforce, with the requisite skills companies in the target industry segments require, without being overly concerned about ages, gender preferences, or other irrelevancies. A strong workforce comes in all shapes, sizes, beliefs, and colors.

There is a growing concern in both the United States and around the world regarding the next decade and beyond. The Baby Boomer generation was a very large generation and the workforce of the past 50 years has reflected that bulge in the demographic graphs. There have been plenty of workers to fill the positions that were being created in American commerce. The succeeding generations, however, have been significantly smaller. Men and women have been waiting longer to marry and start families. As such, the American generations that have succeeded the Baby Boomers have become progressively smaller. And, their children too are waiting to marry and having relatively smaller families. This presents a problem for an economy that is booming and a demand for workers that could become increasingly difficult to satisfy.

The concerns about workforce shortages become particularly acute in employment areas that demand skills in information technology and other scientific or technology training. The numbers of jobs that cannot be filled in the future are in the hundreds of thousands today and in multiples of tens of millions in the near future. Great growth in the demand for technology workers is being met by a relatively small group of Americans who qualify for these very high paying positions. Yet, the undergraduate degree most often conferred in the United States today is a Bachelors of Arts in Psychology! American students—as early as kindergarten—need to be encouraged to study science and technology.

There is another solution worthy of consideration: immigration. Immigrants into the United States have always been contributors to our collective innovation, commercial successes, and the everyday workforce. But, today, it appears to be an essential in satisfying the demand for workers in technologies and across the occupational board. A range of policies is available to support and control the influx of immigrants into the United States. Without engaging in the social and political debates here, there is a purely selfish reason to want immigrants to continue coming into—and staying in—the United States. Businesses need them.

What happens when an IT company is unable to fill its positions? They move to locations where the workforce they require is either more readily available or more easily attracted. But, the shortage of technology workers in the United States is a universal challenge, so relocations for workforce needs do not mean that a company will leave Texas to go to Virginia; it means that companies will consider contracts to do the work in India or China or elsewhere. This means that American companies are either losing contracts (or not able to accept work) because they cannot perform; or, it could mean that revenues and jobs may be going overseas. Either way, it greatly behooves policymakers in this country to do two things: 1) identify more ways to direct students into science and technology areas of study; and, 2) identify policies that (at least, selectively) admit immigrants to this nation who have the requisite skill sets.

If such policies cannot be implemented, our workforce will continue to shrink, especially in the critical areas of future commercial growth. Companies will lose revenues and opportunities, communities will lose the potential to grow the state and local tax bases, and public services will suffer. For the national economy (and, therefore, the local economies within it) to continue to grow, a range of forward-thinking policies that will continue to keep America in the forefront of commerce and technological growth are needed. Our businesses cannot wait for the crisis to occur—that is, when workforce shortages are already slowing our economic growth.

Immigrants bear the same relationship to a community's tax base as do any other members of the community. If they are employed, and earning higher than average wages, they contribute to the local tax base from which public services are provided. If, however, they are either unemployed or employed in lower-than-average-wage positions, their contributions to the tax base could be less than the services they demand from it. Lower-income residents are less likely than others in the community to own real estate and are therefore less likely to be contributors to local tax bases. Any income taxes they pay will generally accrue to the benefit of the state's budget.

Immigration as a whole, however, can be subject to many trends and expectations. A lower-than-average cultural history of home ownership translates into lower-than-average contributions to the local tax base (built on real estate taxes), while a higher-than-average number of children per family translates into a greater draw from the tax base than their contributions to it. This is because, for local governments, the public school system often represents at least half of all General Fund expenditures.

The impacts of immigration on American communities where the population has been in decline has been significant. La Corte wrote that "Refugees bolster flagging populations, expand tax bases, and launch scores of small businesses, transforming once desolate areas into thriving neighborhoods."[5] La Corte also asserts that resettling families displaced by war is compassionate but that will be left to the reader to assess. What is more important for this study is his conclusion that "it's also smart . . . to give America's cities a renewed jolt of energy."[6]

Overall, the national experience has been that immigrants have been very positive contributors to local economies. Immigrants to the United States in the recent past are responsible for the founding of more than one-half of all start-up companies, creating an annual value in those companies of more than 1 billion dollars. Further, nearly a quarter of startup companies with a value over one billion dollars have been founded by people who initially came to the United States as international students. Perhaps there is a strategic advantage for communities to establish programs to attract immigrants and to support them as they settle in the United States, establish businesses, create jobs, generate wealth, add to the tax base, and improve the general quality of life.

Infrastructure

Economic development professionals are completely aware of three parts of the local product that they have to market: the current state of the community's physical assets, the plans for improving those assets, and the intangible factors that make a city or town a community. The latter element of their product is very difficult to identify and define, and it is constantly changing. Often, one must live in the community for some time to accurately comprehend the features.

The physical components are another matter. Infrastructure is visible and definable. Roads and trains can be viewed and the various public works can be well understood. It is easy to find out what the technology infrastructure for a community covers and how its bandwidth compares with other competing communities for economic development prospects. In many cases, if not most, the technology and transportation infrastructure is a primary element of a company's decision. The costs of various utilities as well as their forecasted availability and growth over time will be essential parts of decisions to be made by manufacturers. Depending on the type of businesses that are identified in the community's economic development strategic plan, different physical attributes will be more or less critical to potential employers. In order to be maximally competitive with other communities, local leadership must provide these necessary assets as part of the product they have to offer companies.

Transportation

From the perspective of an economic developer, transportation networks are a critical component of the product being sold. But, improving the asset involves more than a simple "more is better." Transportation has many elements to it as it relates to the conduct and success of business operations. The first element that is typically reviewed by a company or a site location consultant is whether or not one's employees can get to and from the office or facility. This is more than a simple matter of the overall quality of life. Longer commutes could mean less enthusiastic employees or requests for alternative, non-rush-hour work schedules. It could result in tardiness or irritability on the job.

In order to attract the best workforce to the community, employers will discuss with prospective workers and their families the elements of the community's quality of life. This will include the quality of the public schools, activities in the area that appeal to peoples' hobbies or interests, and the general ability to get from one place to another with relative ease. Sitting in traffic for extended periods means less time people have for their own hobbies or to spend with their families. If a prospective employer believes that potential employers will be hard to recruit due to the community's quality of life, they will consider looking elsewhere.

Getting people comfortably and easily from home to work is only part of the equation. People need to be able to get from the office or the factory to their meetings or deliveries. If trucks have to fight excessive traffic to make their way to highways before they can move on their delivery points, that time spent will equate to greater costs for the employer and they will likely consider location options. Community economic developers need to use programs of Business Retention visits to unearth these concerns and to help identify solutions. In some cases, relatively inexpensive solutions can be implemented in the form of roads with slightly wider turning radii, and in other cases, more expensive but also manageable solutions such as new entrance and exit ramps to interstate highways can be identified.

Transportation needs and solutions are not restricted to roads and highways. Many employers require ease of access to air service for employees or for cargo. Cargo may also use sea port facilities; ports and terminals that accommodate easy on-loading and off-loading can enable companies to be more efficient in those functions and therefor more satisfied in their present locations. Contrarily, a dissatisfied employer may instead look for alternatives in communities that do offer such amenities.

Transportation elements of the economic development product can be viewed from two perspectives. First, economic developers and local elected officials need to consider whether the asset they have to offer employers reflects the needs of the employers being pursued. If not, the community can either adjust its transportation product or it can re-focus its sights on employers for whom the current asset is adequate. From the perspective of business attraction, as opposed to the retention of a community's existing employers, the questions that must be asked are what employers are seeking and what represents the gap in their asset for those potential economic development prospects.

Solutions to transportation issues potentially come from a variety of sources, including federal programs, state allocations, and local funding. The difficulties in adequately funding such expensive projects imply that there are benefits from piecing together numerous sources to create an overall effective transportation plan. And, because transportation routes often cross municipal borders, and even state lines, the planning must be cooperative and collaborative. A company that needs to move its product by road and then to air or sea ports may use local and state roads as well as the interstate highway system. They will be dependent upon all of those road networks, easy connections, and proximity to port facilities. Clearly, the networks they use must be planned, developed, and maintained so as to be useful over the entire trip rather than in individual segments.

In major metropolitan areas, businesses will locate where the most effective multi-modal system exists. Getting employees to work in the most effective, pleasant, and inexpensive manner possible will be the objective. The confluence of roads, parking, sub-way systems, and bus networks will help designate the most appealing location for an employer who cares about how their employees get to work and how upbeat they are when they arrive. Employers in major metropolitan areas compete quite heavily for employees, especially those with high-demand technology skill sets. They are well aware that, if their employees are offered alternative positions, they could lose them to other companies. The ease of one's commute in a major metropolitan area is a prime consideration for in-demand workers when they decide on which position offer to accept. These decisions are driven for an individual by several factors, including time in traffic, alternatives for their commutes, the cost of travel and parking, and the time taken away from their after-work hours and their families. Smart employers seek to minimize such distractions and concerns for their employees and smart communities strive to create transportation networks that support their employers and their constituents.

Commercial Properties

Another part of the local economic development product is the inventory of available—or, potentially available—sites and buildings that can be offered to an employer. These will include currently available office space, sites on which office space can be constructed, greenfield or brownfield sites on which an employer can build for a variety of different uses, and existing, vacant factory or warehouse facilities. An up-to-date inventory allows the economic development team to provide the information to prospect businesses considering a location in the community. In the absence of an updated inventory, prospects will have to provide the requirements of a site or building and wait for staff to identify and present any sites that fit that list of requisites. In the meantime, the prospect may be talking to other communities about potential locations.

For the inventory to be useful, it must list the location, size, age, ownership, features, technology infrastructure, costs, and previous tenants or owners, as well as access to electrical power, water, highways or other modes of transportation, and more. The more information that the economic development staff can provide, the better. Quite often, business executives will explore site or office availability in complete confidence. The community often will be able to ask only about facility and other needs but not the identity of the firm itself.

Because of the need for a total blackout on any identifying information, executives will often want to tour office or other facilities without the owners, brokers, or their management representatives present. The alternative is to have the economic development team build a relationship with the building owners such that allows them to show the space to prospective tenants or buyers. Again, this will require them to have an available, comprehensive, and up-to-date inventory of buildings, facilities, and raw land at their disposal. This plays to the advantage of the economic development team as well as the owners of the buildings or land. More importantly, it is to the advantage of the prospect.

The economic development organization needs to be conversant with the land and buildings that exist as well as what can be done on various properties and what the length of the process will be. Economic development professionals are aware that companies that are exploring locations in their community are quite likely considering locations in other, competitive communities as well. Quite often, the turnaround time for requested building or site details is relatively short. The time to gather the information that will enable a decision is not after the request has been made; it is prior to the marketing effort even begins so that rapid responses to an employer's request for details on a building or site can be possible.

Finally, companies want to be assured that, if a selection is made of a given property, the zoning and permitting processes have set timeframes on which they can depend. Businesses are highly sensitive to timeframes and the timing for a company to build or retrofit a building—or, even to refurbish an existing office space—must be dependable. All too often, a company concludes a deal on the basis of the timing presumed from the point of sale to the onset of operations in the facility in question. Also, all too often, those timeframes can slip due to onerous or unreasonable delays in the mechanics of the process. When this happens, the company will be dissatisfied and its executives can be unhappy from the beginning of their stay in the new location, and that word will spread.

Communities also may have federal and state instruments that can help lure prospects to specific sites that qualify under statutes as Enterprise Zones or other similar programs. In these designated locations, communities have inducements to attract employers, which may include real estate tax exemptions for new investments, priority for land use decisions, and permitting processes, funding for utility improvements, low interest financing, tax abatements, or other inducements.

As is the case with any profession, site location consultants and real estate executives internal to the company belong to professional associations. Once a community gains a reputation for inefficiency in those processes, the word get out and reduces the possibility of other firms considering the same location. Permitting processes, in particular, are the subject of discussion between these professionals and can seriously damage the future of economic development in a community. On the other hand, a community with a history of adhering to reasonable and stated timeframes for development processes such as zoning and permitting will gain a reputation as a good place to do business. If one competitor community has the reputation for being reliable in its permitting process and timeframes while another has the opposite reputation, a business is likely, all other components of the decision being considered relatively equal, to regard the former community as the more optimal location. Again, business executives, architects and builders, subcontractors, and others in that community talk to each other. A bad reputation among them will spread more rapidly than a good one and will take far longer, once entrenched, to reverse.

Office Parks and Risk-Taking

Communities—especially smaller and rural cities and towns—often find themselves in a "chicken-and-egg" situation as relates to securing the assets needed to attract firms to their communities. There is a basic requirement to attract businesses—they must have the necessary space available for the company to buy or lease. In some cases, the company does not have a need to be immediately settled into their new quarters and will be able to purchase a land parcel and to develop it to suit their needs.

However, more frequently the situation is such that the firm has a deadline for relocation and start-up that precludes building from scratch. In those cases, ready space needs to be provided or the community will lose the prospect to another area. This means that a site must be prepared, the infrastructure must be in place, and the zoning and permitting processes are ready to go. If they are not, the prospect will pass the community by.

This realization has led cities and towns to develop office parks in anticipation of consideration by prospects in the future. This is, of course, a risky business. In order to be prepared for the possibility of demand, the community must spend its scarce resources on a gamble. The results of many such gambles has been that the resources have been spent and nothing has come from it—the park remains empty and the programs that were not funded, or that were short-funded—to allow for those expenditures have gone wanting with no return. These are difficult decisions for elected officials who are caught between the possibility of having a prospect they cannot serve and an expensive asset they cannot sell.

Cunningham believes it is an all-or-nothing proposition: "If a community does not have an available qualified site, it is not in the site selection game, regardless of what other desirable characteristics a location may possess."[7] If one accepts this argument, then communities are in the position of taking greater risk. That is, in order to (maybe!) attract users to business parks, localities must pay in advance for the infrastructure to be in place.

If a user does not appear, or appears much later than anticipated, expected revenues will have been lost and other important budget line items may have been unnecessarily reduced.

But, Cunningham's implication may be correct as well: if you don't have a ready site, the community may never even receive consideration from employers. This means civil engineering costs must be assumed, structural and geo-technical expenses must be absorbed, and any environmental issues must be remediated. He also suggest that the ownership issues must be clear and owners must be prepared to sell or lease, zoning must be clear and appropriate, and that there is a reasonable assumption of the timing required for permitting and related issues to be addressed and approved by the relevant city or county staffers. Finally, the necessary roadwork, infrastructure, utilities, and technology infrastructure must either be already in place or easily connected.

Similarly, a paper prepared by the Federal Reserve Bank of Boston notes that a 2014 survey indicated that "the highest correlates to economic growth" in Massachusetts municipalities was "the availability of sites for development, economic development marketing, and the timeliness of municipal approvals for development projects."[8] Other factors that were cited in the Fed's report included adequate transportation infrastructure, rental and purchase rates, a well-trained workforce, low crime, and favorable tax rates, but the availability of ready sites topped the list of requirements.

Secondary factors that also receive consideration from site-selection executives may include availability of parking, traffic congestion, state and local tax incentives, the physical attractiveness of the area, proximity to suppliers and contractors, proximity to university and other training support, and the presence of trade unions.

A critical piece of the site location process was highlighted most emphatically in the report by the Federal Reserve Bank: along with several measures of the speed with which a municipality deals with site approvals, zoning appeals, and building inspections, "'time to market' was a catchphrase heard often . . . firms need to have the assurance that they can get up and running quickly . . . Any municipal process that appreciably slows the pace of business development is considered a deal-breaker."[9]

The importance of the time-to-market consideration for companies cannot be underscored. The Fed's report noted that municipalities "can affect their own economic destiny by focusing on improving municipal processes and using economic development marketing to change obsolete negative preconceptions."[10]

There can be a middle ground, however, that can protect community interests while also providing enough of the necessary asset to capture the attention of businesses. In this middle ground, the land in question has already been zoned (with minimal, if any, expenses involved), the permitting processes are ready to go and the officials prepared for expedited approvals if and when a prospect does come along. The final element of this middle ground relates to the preparation of the relevant infrastructure. This may include road networks, rail spurs, off-ramps or easier access to interstate highways. There are a wide range of possible infrastructure matters that, if in place before the prospect visits, can enable a positive decision for the community because the time from decision to opening is minimized.

These are not inconsequential matters for budgeting purposes. Infrastructure development can be very expensive. If, however, the sites are connected up to the last mile, business decision-makers can calculate the shorter time and minimized expenses of completing the connections for sewer, water, electricity, and current technology needs. Further, communities can provide each of those connections in different budget cycles; that is to say, the electricity connection can be put in this year and the sewer connections next, in order to spread out the financial impacts. In this way, the community has potential sites to offer their prospective business prospects, and they will have minimized the turnaround time for companies to be up and running; but they will not have had to spend the full amount of site preparation costs without a viable opportunity in hand.

Investing in the site preparation of business parks on the chance that it will be attractive enough to employers that they will locate there is a very risky business. "A Community can easily invest millions of precious public dollars in preparing a site for development, and the consequences of making a poor decision can be devastating for the community and for the decision-makers."[11]

Often, office and research parks can mitigate some, or even much, of the inherent risk by specifying the applications sought or permitted in the parks. Communities have had success in doing so around existing industrial strengths, thereby creating an asset for an industry grouping that already exists and around which other companies may wish to locate. Elk Grove, Illinois provides just such an example. Already an aviation manufacturing hub where businesses have located and grown over time, Elk Grove's economic development planning concluded that a business park specifically for the aviation industry would add an asset to the existing business base and would be an inducement to other companies in the same and related industries to relocate to the city. Today, there are 3600 small and medium-sized businesses in their park. This has made Elk Grove home to the second highest number of manufacturing jobs in the entire State of Illinois, more than 21,000. This is a strategy that other communities can consider, even if on a smaller scale, because it reduces the risk of completely building an office or research park without an existing prospect to occupy some or all of the property. Such strategies are dependent upon the willingness of the community to assume a given level of risk and the financing capability to do so.

Technology Infrastructure

Employers require a range of technology infrastructure to operate. Depending upon the nature of the industry involved, these needs can include sufficient and constant electrical supply, water supply, and infrastructure for data and voice transmission and data storage. High-speed internet capacity can be critically important for many of the businesses that are working on today's and tomorrow's emerging industries.

Smaller towns and rural areas that have not been successful in attracting the technology companies they would like to bring to their communities have an opportunity to support those companies from a distance due to the nature of today's high-speed data transmission. If the community can acquire the necessary infrastructure, it can become home to men and women who live in town and work for companies miles away. A colleague of mine was the President of Federal Services Division of a major corporation. He once asked me how many people I thought worked for him. As I had no idea, he said it was thousands. He then asked where I thought they were located and I said I did not know. He replied that neither did he. It really didn't matter; they did their work and he monitored their output and the jobs got done. Small towns and rural areas can take this lesson and create a great place to live and raise a family while working for companies miles—even continents—away. But, the necessary infrastructure is an absolute requirement.

Notes

1 Dennis B. Roddy. Welcome to the New Pittsburgh: A City Transformed. (January 22, 2015) www.pittsburghmagazine.com
2 Richard Fry. Millennials Surpass Gen Xers as the Largest Generation in the US Labor Force. (May 11, 2015) www. pewresearch.org
3 Lara O'Keefe. Millennials Now Account for Forty-Two Percent of US Homeowners and They're Buying in the Suburbs. (August 23, 2017) www.bisnow.com
4 Bruce Pfau. What Do Millennials Really Want at Work? The Same Things the Rest of Us Do. (April 7, 2016) www.hbr.org
5 Matthew La Corte. Refugees Are Revitalizing Some Great American Cities Facing Decline. (June 21, 2016) https://niskanecenter.org
6 Ibid.
7 J. Vann Cunningham. Open for Business: Industrial Site Readiness. *Economic Development Journal*, vol. 16. (Washington, DC: International Economic Development Council. Winter 2007): 1.
8 Barry Bluestone. *What Makes Working Cities Work? Key Factors in Urban Economic Growth*. (Boston, MA: Federal Reserve Bank of Boston, May 2014): 1.
9 Ibid., 8.
10 Ibid., 18.
11 Cunningham, 11.

References

Bluestone, Barry. *What Makes Working Cities Work?: Key Factors in Urban Economic Growth*. Boston, MA: Federal Reserve Bank of Boston, May 2014.
Cunningham, J. Vann. Open for Business: Industrial Site Readiness. *Economic Development Journal*, vol. 16, no. 1, Washington, DC: International Economic Development Council. Winter 2007.
Fry, Richard. Millennials Surpass Gen Xers as the Largest Generation in the U.S. Labor Force. May 11, 2105. www.pewresearch.org
La Corte, Matthew. Refugees Are Revitalizing Some Great American Cities Facing Decline, June 21, 2016. https://niskanecenter.org
O'Keefe, Lara. Millennials Now Account for Forty-Two Percent of US Homeowners, And They're Buying in the Suburbs. August 23, 2017. www.bisnow.com
Pfau, Bruce. What do Millennials Really Want at Work? The Same Things the Rest of Us Do. April 7, 2016. www.hbr.org
Roddy, Dennis B. Welcome to the New Pittsburgh: A City Transformed. January 22, 2015. www.pittsburghmagazine.com

14 Matching Communities to Optimal Business Development
The "Right Kinds" of Jobs

Communities often take one of two positions when strategizing about industry segments and jobs to pursue for their future economic growth. One perspective has been, "Well, this is what we have always been so let's get more of the same." This is most often seen in manufacturing communities that have a workforce prepared for manufacturing jobs and only believe that's what they can be attractive for in the next iteration of employment. The second approach is more progressive but less realistic. It would be voiced in this way: "We need to consider what the hot industries of the future are and bring them to our city/town/region."

In truth, neither of these reactions to job losses is going to serve the community well. Experiences across the United States have indicated that there is a mid-point between those two outlooks that suggests a two-pronged strategy: while working to attract companies for which our workforce is prepared and for which this community has the requisite assets, we will also seek to develop the assets we will need at some future point to attract other businesses that will be to the longer-term benefit of our local economy. This, of course, requires localities to be highly realistic about which industries are likely to be attracted to the community even with upgrades added, which upgrades are critical and which are secondary, and how the community will pay for the acquisition or development of those assets and what will have to be deleted from the budget to do so.

Not every city or region has unrealistic expectations about the types of employment they are most likely to be able to capture. Quite often, their necessities are the mother of invention, and their leadership logically pursues the types of employers that will both create jobs and expendable incomes, but will also provide vital community services. This is particularly true in smaller communities.

One such city is Watertown, Wisconsin, which was included in prior research. The State of Wisconsin has no local income tax options, which means that the attraction of retail operations is not as critical to the city as the attraction of revenues from new construction. Retail operations that fill the gap needs of the community, including department stores, groceries, and car dealerships, can be as important to the community as office users or light manufacturing because they provide needed goods and services as well as jobs and expendable income. Additionally, the tax impacts are greater on the real estate itself and can be greater than the sales taxes generated by the employers.

In some cases, cities are simply interested in gaining jobs and make no great distinction between types of employers. As is covered in an earlier chapter of this book, this reflects economic growth, but not necessarily economic development. Quite often, this is the result of desperation: that is to say that the need for jobs can be so acute and long-standing that any job will be well received.

In some cases, the "right jobs" are defined by their tax-paying status. One such example is Elmira, New York. In prior research, the mayor of Elmira noted that the economic stability provided by several institutions in the community, including a maximum security prison, a college and a community college, satisfied the need for jobs and incomes but actually impaired the city's ability to provide quality and range of public services because those are public entities and are thus off the tax rolls. This exacerbates the city's already difficult tax base problems because the city is home to more than one 125 churches, which are also tax-exempt. In sum, more than 40 percent of the city's land base is tax exempt!

Those institutions still require a wide range of public services but do not contribute to the coffers from which those services are paid. This means that the City of Elmira is heavily dependent on state aid and formulaic state and federal program disbursements that have been declining and that are unreliable at best.

Another tax base consideration for communities when seeking to attract certain types of jobs relates to the attraction of retirees. While research shows that retirees can bring higher-than-existing pension incomes to a community, they may also bring extraordinary costs. There are nearly 80 million Baby Boomers in the nation today. They are of retirement age—or, at least, semi-retirement age—and control the vast majority of wealth in the United States. Many of those who retire decide to leave the communities of their careers in favor of less congested, lower-cost areas.

Generally speaking, retirees bring in more income and therefore, more income taxes. But income taxes do not always accrue to the locality; in many states those revenues go to the state to support their public services. In many cases, the locality provides public services on the basis of the real estate taxes. Retirees, who are generally "empty-nesters" at that point in their lives, purchase smaller homes, so their tax base contributions locally may be limited. At the same time, retirees do not use the public schools, which often receive the greatest share of local General Fund expenditures. But, the tax base implications do not end there. Retirees use recreational facilities more often, may have greater health requirements over time, and have the time to draw on other municipal services as well. Communities should be cautious in considering the full tax base and other implications of establishing themselves as retirement communities before pursuing that type of strategy.

Many cities derive much of their tax base from sales taxes. Another city included in previous research was Elko, Nevada, which derives between 60 and 70 percent of their general fund expenditures from sales taxes. This means that the city pursues retailers to locate within the city limits as a primary economic development target industry. Interestingly, the bulk of those revenues comes from the construction industry, which represents about 70 percent of the local economy. Thus, in boom times, when people come to work in the mining industry or other fields, home construction—and thus, sales taxes—are higher than when the city is suffering through economic bust times.

Other fluctuations in the economic environment can also result in the types of employers being sought for relocation as well as the best means of enhancing the local tax base. Walla Walla, Washington, for example suffers through inconsistent economic times based largely on external market forces. There are more than 200 wineries within 5 miles of the city's center. The State of Washington imposes an 8.7% sales tax, a large portion of which is returned to the communities that generated the taxes. This means that the budget of Walla Walla is constant or even growing in good years for the grapes and could decline in bad years. It also means that the city needs to pursue economic development prospects that reflect a greatly more diversified economic base in order to level out tax revenues and the ability to provide public services to the city's residents.

Communities across the country have striven to create creative economies either as their primary industry segment or as a component of an otherwise more diverse economic base. Creative businesses are of two types. Some, such as advertising architecture, publishing, television and radio, for example, serve the local residential and business communities. Others, however, can serve as attractions for a community to bring in expenditures from outside the community that then get spent and re-spent locally, as well as helping to provide the local and state tax bases from which public services are provided at a lower cost to residents. These may include performing arts organizations, antiques sales, crafts, and more.

In a recent article, Greg Baeker, of MDB Insight, portrays the arts and cultural communities on a cluster map that includes cultural occupations, community cultural organizations, cultural spaces and facilities, cultural enterprises, festivals and events, natural heritage, cultural heritage, and the intangible arts and cultural assets in a community. In all, he displays more than 50 elements of those eight primary components of cultural resources. In sum, a community can build an arts and cultural economic component but it must either possess or acquire or develop many of those contributing assets to gain the greatest sustainable return from the sector.

The conclusion must be that economic development planning needs to focus on the types of employers that are most desirable for the community and for which the community either now has or will soon have the requisite assets and amenities to be attractive to those employers. Once that is determined, the right types of jobs will be those that such employers require. These analyses need to be realistic and the assessment of the assets that will be needed to attract the right companies need to be both accurate and constantly updated as preferences and requirements for the relevant industries' changes over time.

1 What Do We Want and What Can We Get?

The title of this section clearly constitutes a leading statement. What a community wants to become and what it reasonably can expect to achieve are many times two quite different things. As such, it is critical to be very cautious in the strategic planning process when identifying the targeted industry segments.

All communities want to "stretch" in order to improve their status and the sustainability of their economic base, but appealing to technology companies, for example, without the relevant workforce, training institutions, and amenities that those workers demand is both folly and destined to fail. Nonetheless, the number of US communities that wish to pursue such employers without the requisite assets is stunning.

A proper assessment of what is feasible for a community entails a review of the skill sets present in the community and the employers who require those types of skills. The second layer of analysis will include what potential exists in the community to provide a different sort of workforce in the future through training programs and workforce attraction. That future potential then can be translated into a future asset to attract or grow companies that are dependent upon those skill sets.

There are many variations of processes through which communities' leadership can analyze the job markets and determine whether the industry segments being pursued make the best sense for the community in question. In sum, however, a comprehensive analysis would include the following:

- an assessment of the industry or industry segment;
- the local, national, or global size of the market in terms of sales, jobs, and competition;
- the growth potential for the industry;
- extraordinary requirements for businesses in the industry, such as wet laboratory space or warehouses with high ceilings;
- the asset gaps for the industry within the community in question, and the potential for closing the gaps and the costs of doing so;
- likely strategic partners in the community and existing businesses in the industry within a given radius of the community;
- the availability of workers with the requisite skills for the industry;
- the community's unique selling proposition for companies in the industry as well as nearby competitors and competitive advantages and disadvantages of the community.

Communities need to be realistic in the types of businesses and industry segments they choose to pursue. The city or region must have the assets that are in demand by the companies being targeted. In lieu of possessing the assets, they must plan to acquire or develop them in the community today in order to attract those firms tomorrow. Once a plan has been developed and approved locally, and the financing set in place where appropriate, their economic development professionals can at least demonstrate to the site location decision-makers in that industry segment that the assets they will require are being obtained and will be in place by a specific time. This will also allow the marketing teams to learn more about the companies and their needs in a given location.

Once an industry, or industries, has been identified, the community can make contact with possible employers and begin to sell their product. One of the first things that most employers, and their site location consultants, will want to know about is their ability to find in the community the number and types of workers they will need.

2   Training and Workforce Preparation

The lifeblood of any business is its employees. Companies are increasingly competitive and increasingly aggressive as their employee needs become more tied to a workforce with technology capabilities. Workers in information technology are in great demand in today's economy, and no region of the United States seems able to provide such workers in sufficient quantity. This applies to other skills areas as well and it may be the community that is able to demonstrate the most available, best trained workers that will win the site location competition. For that reason, communities are incorporating in their strategic plans a variety of ways to increase and/or enhance the workers who are most relevant to the existing employment base and to those of the companies and industry segments being targeted for attraction.

Communities are well-advised to be very closely connected to the business community, as well as the local public school system and local colleges and universities. While many students still wish to pursue studies in the liberal arts, it is the student who matches his or her studies with the existing or coming demand who will get the best jobs and earn the greatest salaries. And, of course, it will be the community that can increase the best student selections that may be able to demonstrate the greatest case for business locations.

Community colleges are beginning to play an ever-larger role in economic development. Once seen as either a place for students who could not yet enter a full four-year institution or as a place for training in the trades, two-year institutions are becoming increasingly vital to local economic development. These colleges still play an important role in preparing students for four-year institutions and for the training of welders, electricians, carpenters, and other trades people. But, much of today's information technology workers are coming from community colleges as well. Not all IT functions require four years of training, and neither do they require history, English literature, or biology.

Economic development professionals can recite certain facts universally. They know that a job in a primary company spins off two to three jobs in the secondary and tertiary economies as contracts are let to small businesses and the expendable income of employees is spent in restaurants, groceries, and department stores. Economic developers also know that, as the skill sets of the employees in the primary sectors increase, the demand for support workers also increases and, as the salary levels increase, so does the ratio of demand for 4-year degreed workers to 2-year degreed workers.

In information technology generally, that ratio is assumed to be about four 2-year graduate level jobs to every one 4-year graduate level job. These are good jobs for people to install equipment, run programs, load new programs and help to resolve issues when the computers go down. Other industries can raise the ratio even higher. For estimates in areas such as translational medicine and genomic research, the ratio reaches as high as eight or nine to one. In these areas, the demand is for individuals to conduct experiments, run program, and help analyze the resulting data. Again, the most successful economic development communities may be those that can prepare students for companies and help retrain their existing workforce.

Another component of workforce development relates to the appearance of the community itself. Employers want to be located in communities that enable them to attract the best employees from around the country and perhaps from around the world. They will want to live in a nice community. As the potential recruits are required to have higher level skills and those that are more in-demand, there will likely be an even higher correlation with concerns about the quality of the local public school system. These are areas to which communities must pay attention if they are to attract and prepare the most attractive workforce and thus attract and retain the companies they wish to pursue.

Workforce preparation can be an uncertain proposition at times. It is not dissimilar from communities that develop office parks in order to attract businesses without really knowing whether the businesses will come. On the other hand, if a business needs a location like an office park provides, the community cannot attract them unless they took the earlier risk and made the investment. It is not unusual to hear the expression from the Kevin Kostner movie about baseball: "Build it and they will come." For communities, however, it remains a risk-taking proposition. It may be built and no one comes.

Workforce preparation has a similar cart-before-the-horse consideration. If a community wants to attract high-tech manufacturers, it must have the trained workforce to offer them. If they do not have the requisite workforce, the employers may look to communities with that asset in place. So, many communities train the workforce in order to attract the businesses, but what happens if the businesses do not come to the area? The resolution for many communities is to identify the types of workers that will be required for the desired industry segments, identify the instructors for the relevant courses, and even to identify the location of the training and obtain the needed materials for training.

Then, when an employer is identified, the asset, while not yet in place, can be provided relatively quickly. Often, an employer can make the decision and, by the time the move-in date arrives, the initial wave of trained workers can be ready to start work. In some instances, the employer will prefer to train the new employees with their own instructors and on their own equipment with their own standards. In such cases, a community can best be prepared if they have taken the time to provide the needed numbers of potential employees. Communities often pre-screen the potential hires while the company is moving in and prior to their training. They can be screened for aptitude, soft skills, and experience and reference verification.

This is a situation in which communities or regions can turn a negative situation into a positive asset. Communities with a relatively high level of unemployment can offer a large pool of potential employees who are eager to be fully employed and who can be immediately available for training.

3   Innovation and Entrepreneurship

Entrepreneurs are men and women who take personal and financial risks in order to start and grow their businesses. They are founders and owners of firms in a wide range of economic activities, ranging from personal services to high technology applications and solutions. They can be found anywhere and come in all sizes and shapes.

Entrepreneurs are vital parts of any community, whether it is rural or urban, large or small. They are the shopkeepers and big business initiators. They create jobs and enable the import of resources to a community and its circulation and re-circulation throughout a community. They establish businesses that may start with two or three employees and remain that size for the life of the firm; or, they may grow to host thousands of jobs. According to the United States Census Bureau, using 2014 data, there were nearly 5.5 million US companies with employees, of which 482,000 (about one in 11) had been in business for fewer than two years.[1]

Communities need entrepreneurs for balance and diversity, but their growth does not just occur. It must be supported by the public sector if it is to reach its full potential in the community. According to the Kauffman Center for Entrepreneurial Leadership, there are two types of entrepreneurs: the lifestyle entrepreneur and the high-growth entrepreneur. The former represents new businesses that have been created for the purpose of supporting families or to create careers that are self-managed. In small towns, this is what is found along the main streets and gives the community both visitors and "personality and charm."[2]

High-growth entrepreneurs provide capital for a community as well as enhancing the reputation of the areas as a good place for others to conduct business operations. They also tend to "invest in their communities through schools, community service, and philanthropy." But, these firms, especially in rural areas, typically need greater access to investment capital for their entrepreneurial start-ups. This is an area in which the public sector can enable the further growth of such firms. The federal government and many states often provide low-interest or even no-interest loans for start-ups. Localities should seek to ensure that those funds are legislatively protected and that they are both known to and available to all of their constituents.

Public universities, and especially community colleges, can often be effective in supporting the growth of such businesses by providing both general business skills training and the technical skills in greatest demand by local entrepreneurs. A strong partnership between the community, the educational institutions, and the entrepreneurs can accelerate their growth by ensuring that such training is available both now and in the future in the correct skills curricula.

Incubator and co-working facilities are also excellent ways for the community to spawn and accelerate entrepreneurial activity. These facilities enable like-minded individuals to coexist as they advance their businesses and to share ideas, lessons, and problems, as well as accessing jointly funded, much cheaper professional services such as legal, accounting, planning, and other business needs. A photograph of one such facility is shown in Figure 14.1. In this picture, it is clear that the numerous entrepreneurs are huddling to share concepts, challenges, and solutions. Perhaps the most important aspect of these co-working spaces and the interactions demonstrated in the photograph is the encouragement that one entrepreneur receives from another. A sense that "we are all in this together" emerges. The picture was taken at the Refraction program at the Reston Town Center in Fairfax County, Virginia and is illustrative of the many such programs in all types of communities supporting the growth of all types of entrepreneurs all around the United States.

These programs offer a variety of services that enable companies to grow. Refraction provides space for young innovators to work alongside one another on their own products and corporate plans. This permits entrepreneurs to share ideas and problems and, most of all, to share the trials and challenges of starting and running a business. Refraction offers their tenants a range of services from workshops on a variety of relevant topics, exposure to counsel and new concepts, support for accounting, legal, and other business needs, and much more.

By sharing this space and the costs of the various supports, aspiring business owners can share and minimize their expenses while honing their products and services. Calls are received on their behalf and packages received so that their full time and attention can be devoted to what they need to do to advance their business. From these programs emerge companies that have been guided and developed to the point where they are able to graduate from the facility and enter commercial office space or other facilities.

Recently, many communities have focused their attention on the Millennial generation to be the next array of entrepreneurial business men and women. This has been based on

Figure 14.1 Go Canvas Work Space
Source: Courtesy of James Quigley

the recent proliferation of literature about how this generation tends toward innovation and change. While that may be a distinct trend, there are a few considerations that should not be overlooked. First, a trend could mean that 60 percent of Millennials are entrepreneurial in spirit and, while that may be more than any of their predecessor generations, it is still only 60 percent. One must not neglect the 40 percent that may be more traditional in their thinking about employment in general and their individual attitudes toward work.

Second, the community that focusses solely on what the youngest generation needs in order to be successful entrepreneurs, risks ignoring the needs of other generations to start their own, very innovative businesses. In 2017, as more and more Baby Boomers are retiring from their careers, many, still being young and vibrant enough, are starting their own businesses based on what they did and learned during their work lives. Such entrepreneurs tend to have the skill sets and experiences to be more successful more quickly than new entrants to the labor force.

One final precaution: discussions often link innovation and entrepreneurship as if they were consistent or linked traits. They are not necessarily found to be linked in every situation. Of course, a person who starts a business around a new technology is likely to be both innovative and entrepreneurial. Entrepreneurialism is the willingness to take risks in order to build a business of one's own. Thus, a person who opens a restaurant or a gas station or a lawn service can be considered entrepreneurial in nature. Innovation, on the other hand, requires the search for new technologies or new services.

Innovation and entrepreneurialism can be compatible but are not always found in the same example. The point here is that communities and educational institutions that wish to cater to people with these traits need to be clear about which trait or traits they wish to pursue because the training and preparation required may be very different. Smick called innovation "economy's turbocharger," and noted that "Innovation that leads to productivity growth (doing more with less) is the only way to increase broad-based prosperity."[3]

There is a debate in the current literature about the universal impact of innovation. On the one hand, innovation creates better ways of doing things and increases productivity through mechanization. This, however, comes at the cost of jobs that are replaced by the innovative machines and methods. On the other hand, businesses that discover and market innovative processes and services often result in spin-offs that create higher-paying jobs than existed previously. There is no right or wrong—no ideal solution—but, as Smick notes, it "can be heart-wrenching to those caught in the crosshairs of change."[4] Entrepreneurialism is an important component of economic growth, but it is innovation—even with its attendant costs for some businesses—that creates economic development because it is more likely to contribute to economic advance for all of society.

4   Full Inclusion

Communities can focus on the needs of the largest, most prominent, or most locally involved business in town. Certainly, their needs are important to the economic future of the community. However, a community in which the economy is healthy for some and not for others is only inviting troubles. Further, the collection of all small businesses in the community may have greater combined economic force than the relatively few primary employers. Finally, the small businesses in a community—especially those in small and rural areas tend to be the backbone of the community itself: they are often home-grown and the result of years or even generations of family input and hard work. Without them, the community would be a far different place.

It is important for the community's leadership to ensure that public supports, assets, and amenities exist that are beneficial to the most prominent employers in their midst, but it is also critical that the leadership understand the needs of existing small companies as well as the potential start-ups in the area. They have different needs to support their growth and expansion and those needs must be pursued or funded as well.

Economic inclusion is an increasingly popular topic in the literature about economic development. It typically is a reference to ensuring that all members of the community benefit from the basic economic development of the area. This is a difficult thing to guarantee. The notion that "a rising tide lifts all boats" has some merit but is not truly a comprehensive approach. It has often been employed to mean that, if a large company comes to town with high-paying positions, those workers would be the immediate beneficiaries, but small businesses and their employees would receive increased orders. Then, they would spend their incomes by making purchases in stores that would benefit the sales clerks and others. In reality, however, what this means is that the already well off receive the higher paid jobs and those engaged in lower-wage positions get more of the same. This is not unlike the discussion in an early chapter about the difference between economic development and economic growth.

A 2016 report by the Brookings Institution noted:

> Rarely do we see growth and prosperity benefitting the lower half of the income distribution . . . Indeed, only eight out of the top 100 metros enjoyed across-the-board advancements in the median wage, relative income, poverty rate, and employment rate from 2009 to 2014.[5]

In order to pursue true and full economic inclusion, economic development plans need to address the needs of the lower-paid workers as well. This most typically means the provision of programs that enable such workers to enhance their existing skills sets, thereby enabling them to advance beyond the lowest paid wage positions to gradually higher-paid opportunities. To the extent that such individuals live in lower-cost areas of the community, such programs may be accelerated by locating training programs in those neighborhoods or by providing transportation from those neighborhoods to the places where the training programs are located.

Inclusion in this sense does not mean that there is a guarantee provided to all groups in the community. What it does mean is that the opportunities to engage in the local economic development should be open to all. Programs designed to support small business growth or start-ups are open to the members of the entire community and all elements of the area are encouraged to take part in the growth. Sub-population groups are often well represented through their chamber of commerce. In northern Virginia, for example, chambers exist to support the growth of the Asian American community, the African American community, and the Hispanic community. They very wisely seek not simply to coordinate the members of their own community but rather to integrate their communities into the economic mainstream. They seek to introduce companies to majority companies and majority companies can benefit from knowing of more firms that can provide them with valuable goods and services through contracts. And, in this way, the chambers help their members to help themselves in becoming an inclusive part of the economic development of the region.

Equity, however, can be seen as more than simply a means of reducing poverty and avoiding social conflict. Benner and Pastor found that, "the more equitable a society's access to productive resources, the less likely that society is to seek redistributive policies that can reduce growth by introducing economic distortions."[6] This argument may be seen as somewhat specious because it suggests that localities will implement policies to share wealth and that such policies could potentially result in retarding overall growth. The assertion, however, that an equitable distribution of wealth in a community, however achieved, can result in enhanced growth generally is both reasonable and has been upheld by numerous bodies of research, including one produced by the Federal Reserve and cited by Benner and Pastor: "a skilled workforce, high levels of racial inclusion, and progress on income equality correlate strongly and positively with economic growth."[7]

5. The Revitalization of Older Neighborhoods

In every community, there are neighborhoods that have benefitted more or less from the historical economic growth and development. The areas that lag behind are often the older areas or areas in which there is insufficient land or office space for businesses to acquire. These areas are often referred to as "disinvested areas," meaning that they have blighted properties or obsolete facilities that need to be repaired or replaced.

Communities have identified these neighborhoods as "revitalization districts," in which development is facilitated by a range of additional public services ranging from accelerated processing of zoning and permitting processes to loans, grants, tax abatements, and more. The designation of specific areas as being eligible for either federal, state, or local supports begins with detailed assessments of the areas' current characteristics and future opportunities.

Once an area has been designated as eligible for revitalization programs, localities generally memorialize their decisions in the local land use plans. Programs that may be found within such areas include parking garages, façade improvements in retail areas, pedestrian pathways and parks, cultural facilities, directional signage, street improvements, enhanced mass transportation routes, plantings and other landscaping improvements, and other physical enhancements. In terms of the local development processes, plan reviews, project approvals, inspections, and permitting functions may be subject to modified and expedited processing.

Sets of standards are prepared by the local government to outline the allowed usages and the conditions under which public funds will be expended or tax abatements authorized for projects within the designated revitalization districts. In short, these are provided to enable growth in neighborhoods that are lagging in the general economic growth of the community. Such projects are typically approved after consideration by the local government that there will be a valued return-on-the-investments made. This may be in terms of returns to the local tax base or in terms of improving the neighborhoods involved for existing residents and businesses.

Designated revitalization districts may become eligible for a range of local and other investments to improve or raze properties, build facilities, prepare sites for development, or even to provide replacements for antiquated machinery. The presumption is that these investments will enable the area to be more competitive for new employers and that the programs implemented will catalyze additional growth and development around it. Quite often, economic development representatives will find that no employer wishes to be the first to enter a neighborhood and become the catalyst for further development. Once changes have been made, however, employers may be willing to enter an area that is the scene of positive change and site improvements. In fact, quite often, when a neighborhood is showing clear signs of physical improvement, employers can regard it as an opportunity because the rents will be lower as the community evolves and the local workforce may be more readily available as the jobs will then be closer to their residences.

Notes

1   United States Department of Commerce, Census Bureau. www.census.gov
2   Kauffman Foundation. *Kansas City Resource Guide for Entrepreneurs.* (Kansas City, MO: Kauffman Foundation).

3   David M. Smick. *The Great Equalizer: How Main Street Can Create an Economy for Everyone.* (New York: Public Affairs, 2017): 61.
4   Ibid., 74.
5   Laura Bliss. A New Way to Rank Economic Growth in America's Metros. (January 28, 2016). www.citylab.com
6   Chris Benner and Manuel Pastor. *Equity, Growth, and Community: What the Nation Can Learn from America's Metro Areas.* (Oakland, CA: University of California Press, 2015): 29.
7   Ibid., 32.

References

Benner, Chris and Pastor, Manuel. *Equity, Growth, and Community: What the Nation Can Learn from America's Metro Areas.* Oakland, CA: University of California Press, 2015.

Bliss, Laura. A New Way to Rank Economic Growth in America's Metros. January 28, 2016. www.citylab.com

Kauffman Foundation. *Kansas City Resource Guide for Entrepreneurs.* Kansas City, MO.

La Corte, Matthew. Refugees Are Revitalizing Some Great American Cities Facing Decline, June 21, 2016. https://niskanecenter.org

Smick, David M. *The Great Equalizer: How Main Street Can Create an Economy for Everyone.* New York: Public Affairs, 2017.

United States of Commerce, Census Bureau. Nearly One in Ten Businesses with Employees Are New, September 1, 2016. www.census.gov

15 Institutional Growth and Economic Development

1 Capitalizing on Natural Resources and Other Geographic Assets as an Economic Development Strategy

Across the United States, there is a great diversity of terrain and these geographical differences can have strong appeal for people who live in other areas of the country. People who live in cities are drawn to visit rural areas, natural parks, lakes, ski slopes, and more. People who reside in rural areas or small towns have a natural inclination to visit our great cities and see the famous sights of New York, Chicago, Los Angeles, to visit tall buildings, to go to museums, or to see a show on Broadway.

Many areas with natural amenities have been able to build strong economic development assets around them and to attract visitors who not only enjoy the lakes and mountains but who also stay in hotels, eat in restaurants, shop in local retail outlets and, in the process, contribute to local and state tax bases, thereby supporting the provision of public services. Communities can invest in these natural economic development assets and reap the above benefits as well as show off their community. Research has shown for many years that a visitor who has a positive experience in a community will have a much higher likelihood of making a positive site location decision in favor of that area should the occasion arise. This may include visitors coming to see relatives or a child in college, or visitors who had a positive vacation experience.

The same strength of asset provided by natural amenities can be enhanced by periodic festivals, arts and cultural fairs and demonstrations, various forms of competitions, parades, and more. Some communities have designated arts and cultural districts in which zoning requirements have been structured specifically to attract various types of specific arts uses. This may include artists' lofts, galleries, and performances. One can find numerous examples of very different and very imaginative experiences that draw visitors to town. Chicago has an annual blues festival, New Orleans has the Mardi Gras, Lindsberg, Kansas has Swedish Days, Indianapolis and Daytona, Florida have automobile races, and New York City has the Macy's Day Parade. The possibilities are limited only by one's imagination and the required infrastructure to support such events. The region needs sufficient hotel rooms, restaurants, and other attractions that can provide a day-long or weekend-long experience.

One good example of a community that has taken positive advantage of a nearby natural attraction is Bozeman, Montana. The daytime population of Bozeman is about twice that of its nighttime population. The city bills itself as the "Gateway to Yellowstone."

Another is Killington, Vermont, a winter-season ski resort of considerable renown on the east coast. For a town of about 1000 permanent residents, a typical winter might bring more than 20,000 people to the area. A cautionary concern for such areas will be what becomes of Killington and its thousand residents and shops during the remainder of the year—or, in winters with insufficient snowfall to support skiing.

Regions such as Killington are also very susceptible to external economic forces. For example, in a recessionary period, when expendable incomes are lower than normal, a resort area like Killington will see a direct and immediate loss of business, even at peak seasons. Some areas like Killington have created alternative economies and local tax base revenue streams by attracting retired people or second homeowners.

This can be a perilous strategy, however, depending on how the respective states permit localities to constitute their city, county, and town budgets for the provision of public services. If the municipalities in question are permitted a local property tax, this strategy may be successful because everyone is contributing to the coffers. On the other hand, if income taxes are the prime generator of local budgets, retirees and part-time home-owners maybe a drain on local budgets because they may not contribute as much as they cost. Retirees receive less than they did when they were employed so the tax base potential is less. Second home owners may pay income taxes in the places of their primary residences. In each case, they will require public services despite their contributions to the tax base from which those services are funded. And, as retirees age, their needs for recreational and health services may grow.

Pennsylvania implemented a law designed to attract retirees to the state because the state could benefit from their income tax contributions based on their pension levels. However, the localities in which they lived were unable to collect their income taxes but still held the burden of service provision. The lesson that can be drawn from this is that decisions that relate to economic growth and economic development can have unintended consequences. They must, therefore be thoroughly considered before being implemented.

2   Capitalizing on Local Institutions as an Economic Development Strategy

Many communities possess assets in their midst that can be used to enhance the economic output of their region. These underutilized (at least, in the economic sense) assets have the potential to attract people and revenues without requiring substantial additional outlays in public infrastructure or other services.

Hospitals that are seen as serving the local community may be used to attract patrons (and their funds) from outside the existing catchment area. Their research may be examined for new products that can be commercialized, thereby creating jobs and tax base contributions. Many hospitals have made arrangements with nearby universities to permit some of their pre-med and medical curricula to be conducted therein. This can also attract revenue for communities and import resources that might have to be otherwise procured.

Military bases and universities represent other means of enhancing the local economy through the import of funds. Many communities that have such installations and institutions within their borders have established special arrangements to increase the purchase of necessary goods and services from within the surrounding cities and counties rather than from further away. Again, this can result in the attraction of greater resources and, in the long run, additional tax revenues, without requiring any additional outlays from local budgets around the region. The base and the college are already there; greater commercial interaction may not require any additional roads or schools or police and fire services.

Historic sites, natural wonders, and meeting facilities are just a few of the other types of assets and amenities in a community that can either be enhanced or jointly marketed and that will benefit all concerned. Such collaborative marketing efforts can create jobs, increase visitation, generate additional revenues and individual expendable incomes, provide incremental additions to local bases, and enhance a community's awareness and reputation as a good place to live, work, and recreate.

All of these types of institutions have the local benefit of bringing new dollars to the community which, once spent and re-spent, create the sales and other tax revenues that enable the community to provide public services without placing the entire burden of the costs on their residents. Further, short-term visitors to a community tend not to use much of the public services to which they contribute taxes, most notably the public schools system, which often exceeds half of the local General Fund expenditures.

Hospitals and Health Facilities

The total spend on health care in the United States exceeds five and one-half trillion dollars annually. Some of that growth in expenditures can be attributed to the overall aging of the American population. The 2010 Census reported that there were more than 40 million American "seniors." At an unidentified point in time, experts believe that the number of seniors in this country will rise to double that number, or 80 million people. Health care and illness prevention (the so-called wellness programs) as well as treatment are fast becoming a booming business in the United States.

The American Hospital Association (AHA) reported, in 2012, that the health care industry had added an average of 28,000 jobs in the United States each month. Hospitals alone in that year were the second largest source of private jobs in the United States, employing roughly 5.5 million people, and spending more than 700 billion dollars on goods and services from other firms.[1]

The AHA also periodically publishes a compendium of hospital and medical facilities and their economic impacts by state and region. While they tend to include hundreds of examples, a few would be instructive here. These examples cite data from 2008.[2]

- Louisiana hospitals employ more than 98,000 people and generate nearly 30 billion dollars in economic activity.
- In 55 of 67 Pennsylvania counties, hospitals are among the top five employers.
- Wyoming's health care sector is responsible for more than 10 percent of the state's employment, and the hospitals contribute nearly 450 million dollars to the state's economy annually.

While these are but a few examples, they are indicative of how impactful hospitals and other health care facilities can be on a local economy. Additionally, of course, a range of health care in a community makes it more attractive to both individuals and employers whose medical-related down-time may be minimized.

In a rural community, the same principles apply but the need for health care is even greater because more highly dense areas are likely to provide options, even if not as convenient as would be liked. The National Center for Rural Health Works assessed the measurable impacts of a critical access hospital on a rural community.[3] Among the key findings were that such a facility averages 141 employees, and generates nearly 7 million dollars in wages and benefits, and makes annual investments through construction and related procurement of an additional 4 million dollars. These facilities in rural areas serve catchment areas of nearly 15,000 people.

In many cases, either the largest, or one of the largest, employers in a rural community or region is the hospital. But, there's more to the impact than simply providing more jobs. These tend to be the best jobs because they are the highest paying and typically come with benefits packages that others in rural communities may not receive.

For the community, the benefit extends from the relative rates of pay to the greater expendable income that gets distributed throughout the community and, of course, to the tax base of the city, county, and state. Further, the greater the extent of treatment, the more money that is spent in the local community rather than having to travel to other areas for medical treatment, thereby making those expenditures elsewhere. The Rural Health Information Hub estimates that every ten jobs at a rural critical access facility generates another (approximately) four jobs in the local secondary and tertiary economies.[4] This may be a relatively low multiplier in an urban or suburban area, but it is a significant impact factor for rural areas, particularly those that are somewhat isolated from other more urbanized areas (Figure15.1).

The economic impact of hospitals and health care on a community is not often given full consideration. It is one of those services that many people take for granted in communities. Of course, we have a hospital. It employs a lot of people and provides good care but I don't know what it contributes to the overall economy? That lack of awareness sometimes changes when something happens to the hospital. One such example is the Mercy Hospital in Joplin, Missouri.

A report on the economic impact in the community was prepared by three professors at the University of St. Louis following a tornado that swept through the city and generally caused extraordinary damage, including the destruction of the Mercy Hospital. Because of Joplin's geographic position at the junction of four states—Arkansas, Missouri, Oklahoma, and Kansas—the hospital had been the primary care facility for 19 counties. The tornado, which occurred in May of 2011, resulted in the entire hospital being designated as "unsalvageable."

The staff of the facility, numbering more than 1700, had provided care to a large caseload that included 1500 charity cases. These were people who had neither insurance coverage nor the ability to pay for their treatments. Clearly, the impacts on the region were greater than the dollars and cents payments for various salaries or local contracts for goods and services. Following the storm, the management of the hospital managed to retain all of the existing staff and had them treating patients in various places around the city.

Figure 15.1 Rural Economic Growth
Source: Shutterstock

The authors of the University of St. Louis report noted that the economic impact in the region had included the following:

- 356 million dollars in spending by the hospital and its suppliers;
- 17,045 direct jobs with a payroll of 124 million dollars and the spin-off of an additional employment base of more than 18,050 jobs;
- 10 million dollars in capital expenditures in the fiscal year prior to the tornado;
- 1 million 700 dollars paid annually in state and local taxes;
- 1500 charity patients served; "This is a critical safety net since approximately 914,000 Missouri residents, or 15 percent of the state population lack health insurance";[5] and
- 3900 out-of-state patients served, thereby bringing revenues into the region that are then spent and re-spent throughout the community.[6]

In the aftermath of the storm, the hospital's board announced that it would rebuild the hospital and other facilities throughout the region at the cost of 950 million dollars over a three year period. Those expenditures will generate another estimated 665 million dollars in indirect expenditures in the community. This will mean that contractors will receive work and the salaries that are paid will then be circulated throughout the community. The tax base will be enhanced at a critical time for the community. Employees will make purchases on homes, home repair, cars, groceries, and more, thereby generating incomes elsewhere in and around Joplin.

The non-payroll expenditures approached 40 million dollars and, when the impacts of indirect spending and tertiary spending in the local economy are added, the total spending in the region amounted to more than 356 million dollars.[7] Mercy is but one example in one community but it is indicative of the overall economic impacts a hospital can have on a city, town, or larger region.

Military Installations

Military bases are the sources of jobs, expenditures, and even taxes for a local community. The tax impacts are somewhat less than for civilian employment because federal agencies do not pay taxes to local or state coffers, and because many of the military personnel pay income taxes to their primary state of residence. Nonetheless, military installations are good for local economies, and local communities are generally appreciative of their presence. What they typically do not consider, however, is that communities are often over-dependent upon the local base for economic security and sustainability. But, military jobs and locations can be lost just like the automobile industry or steel. Communities that are home to military installations must absolutely believe that they could be lost. They must diversify the local economy in order to sustain the loss of the base.

Military installations can comprise significant proportions of a local economic base—often, the dominant portion—both in terms of local gross product as well as overall employment. A research paper by Hooker and Knetter for the National Bureau of Economic Research (NBER)[8] states that, in some communities, percentage can reach as high as 33 percent. The incomes earned on base and spent in the local communities can also be significant. Communities that are home to a military installation must incur certain costs to accommodate the needs of the base. On the other hand, they also receive federal impact funds. Sorenson wrote that, as more and more military members move into a community, "funds for schools, sewage and water expansion, road construction and repair, and a variety of other things came in from Washington."[9]

In more populated areas, military bases can generate enormous economic impacts for the community. Fort Belvoir is located a few miles south of Washington, DC and covers nearly 8800 acres. Its economic impact on the region in which it is located includes economic impacts from the use of more than 16,000 contractors, 10,000 military personnel, and more than 24,000 civilians who work on base. Additionally, there are more than 50,000 retirees within the Belvoir catchment area. In all, there are nearly 122,000 personnel involved.

The economic impact of a base the size of Fort Belvoir is staggering. Military pay exceeds 940,000 dollars and civilian pay approaches 3 billion dollars annually. There is a total of 11 billion dollars included in a wide range of contracts for goods and services, and the community benefits from significant federal impact aid payments as well.

Clearly, communities can take advantage of the demand for retail and other services for soldiers and sailors on and near bases. They can attract businesses to satisfy the demands of the military and civilian personnel and their families. They can bring in businesses that can supply base requirements. And, communities with good relations can both take advantage of base facilities and offer those on base access to local facilities.

These may include recreational facilities, social activities, parades and special events, and much more.

These benefits have caused communities to fight desperately to retain these economic drivers when they are threatened through budget cuts or the decisions of the Congressional Base Realignment and Closure Commission (BRAC) processes. The Congressional Base Realignment and Closure Act of 1990 provided for a relatively de-politicized process to govern which bases would be kept open and which closed. The decisions were to be based upon such considerations as the continuing operational effectiveness of the military functions involved, alternatives available to the military, implications for Defense Department manpower and budgets, and the economic and environmental impacts on the community from which the base and the commands involved would be departing.

It was acknowledged at the time that military bases had not been built from the outset with civilian uses in mind. As a result, the closings and hand-overs either to commercial or local civilian control of the bases has never really been either smooth or expeditious, or inexpensive for both parties. But, the outcomes in the long run have most often been positive. A study by the Department of Defense that assessed the overall impacts of 100 base closings between 1961 and 1986 revealed that the loss of jobs exceeded 93,000. However, once under civilian control, the same properties supported more than 138,000 jobs as well as 24 colleges and 33 vocational schools with a combined enrollment of nearly 54,000 students. The vacated military airfields on those bases ultimately supported the development and operations of 42 civilian airports.[10]

Hooker and Knetter argue that, although there may be short-, and even mid-range negative consequences of the loss of such installations, the longer-term impacts may actually be quite positive for the host community, and even the state. The reason for this perspective is that the land on which the base is situated typically reverts to the community when the military departs. The land and the buildings, and even runways, generally have greater value and greater returns when used for civilian developments. "In such cases, local economies may actually be better off after a closure, at least following a temporary adjustment period when some transition and cleanup costs are rarely incurred."[11]

After analyzing 57 base closures, the NBER report states that, just "two years after the closure, counties have on average more than 5 percent fewer jobs than if their employment had grown at the same rate as the state."[12] This can make local leaders nervous; however, over time the growth comes.

> The largest example is Quonset Point Naval Air Station in Washington County, Rhode Island, which officially closed in 1975. The county's employment grew 4, 8, and 8 percent faster than the state's in the years 1975–1977, despite the fact that the closure destroyed over 10,000 jobs, amounting to 32 percent of 1973 employment.[13]

But, these are averages and not all of the outcomes are as cut-and-dried as the growth statistics cited above may imply. Neither is a full appreciation for the art of the possible once the military leaves and returns the land and building to the community. More typically, the announcement that a base will be lost is met with great consternation as not only a vital part of the economy is eliminated but many good and contributing families and friends are lost from the community. "When a new round of BRAC is announced, federal, state, and local government officials actually try to prevent base closures in their respective areas."[14]

In fairness to the communities in question, even if their leadership is aware of the non-military potential for the land and buildings that will be returned to their communities, the forecast is likely far enough into the future that it will still be highly problematic. Hawkins notes that, "the average time for transfer of land can be between three and seven years. Most of the time consuming factors involved environmental cleanup; . . . parcels of base property are turned over when they are ready for use."[15]

Another community effort to save a military installation arose in the State of Utah. The University of Utah, in 2005, studied the potential loss of the subsequent BRAC process that eliminated the operations at Hill Air Force Base. The conclusions included the loss of more than 47,000 jobs—both direct military and spinoffs. Because the military and related federal civilian position paid considerably more than the average of other jobs in the area, the University of Utah researchers concluded that to replace the value of those jobs and the resultant expendable incomes would require more than 68,000 new jobs in the region. The ultimate implications were that 2 billion dollars plus in personal income would be lost, more than 192 million dollars would be lost from the state tax coffers and more than 31,000 people would leave the State of Utah.[16] The potential implications for retail employers, school teachers, and other public service workers were immeasurable.

Further complicating the political and community responses to announced BRAC decisions are the inconsistency of the elected officials in stating the case for closure. Hawkins noted that California Senator Feinstein voted consistently against military expenditures and for base closures, but argued through her web page against the closure of bases in California.[17] This apparently overtly political posture makes assessments difficult, especially when every other Senator, Representative, Governor and local elected official weighs in to save their own piece of the pie. As a result, there is at least great potential for such decisions to be less than effective or efficient. Before any of this occurs, localities need to diversify their economies as though they do anticipate the loss of the local installations.

It is important to note that not all military bases are fit for commercial uses after being turned over by the federal government. Many of these bases have been used to test or store materials that were toxic or munitions that may potentially remain active. The remediation of the soils and waterways may also include non-military issues to be considered, such as the natural occurrence of asbestos. The costs of clearing the soils and facilities of bases may be so extraordinary that the local communities cannot afford to accept the land and buildings without federal assistance. Watson reported in 2010 that the United States Air force and the United States Navy were among the nation's top 100 polluters and that the federal Environmental Protection Agency had designated several such bases as Superfund sites. "Active from 1953 to 1994, Maine's Loring AFB was the second largest airfield in the Strategic Air command . . . large portions of the base were polluted with waste oils, fuel, solvents, polychlorinated biphenyls, heavy metals, radioactive materials and pesticides."[18] Loring contained 54 areas that needed to be cleaned up or sealed off. The military has spent great sums to clean up bases they were closing before handing them over to the communities in which they were located but, in some cases, neither the land nor the groundwater can be deemed useable again for a significant number of years.

A greater problem is the impact on the local community. In the case of Loring AFB, 76 percent of the local population departed and the local economy was dramatically impacted. Housing values tanked and the best of the workforce left when they could to seek employment elsewhere. This meant that homes were left to the banks because they could not be sold. And, once again, a community was left with those least able either to attract new employers or to contribute to the local tax base and the provision of public services. In fact, those who remained tended to require even greater services at the very time that resources had dwindled.

Rural communities that host bases could be completely devastated by the loss of a military installation. If the community's only other source of gross economic product is agricultural pursuits, and the prices decline for the crops being grown locally—for whatever reason—the town or the region could be left without any means of support. Economic diversification before the loss of the base is essential to the long-term survivability of the community.

Higher Education

The presence of one or more institutions of higher education has long been acknowledged by economic development practitioners as a valued community and business asset. Every statement that follows is intended to include community colleges as part of the term, "institution." As economic change increases at an increasing rate, colleges and universities become ever more important to the evolution of a city, town, or region's future economy. But, only if . . .

To begin, the mere presence of an institution of higher learning speaks well for a community and provides it with exposure and renown. The institution may not, however be maximizing its value to economic development unless various conditions are met. Of course, institutions of higher learning naturally attract dollars for the community. Visiting parents and friends, athletic and other events, and a wide range of occasions and sales bring dollars into the community that support retailers, hotels, restaurants, and nearby activities and destinations. These dollars require little in the way of public services but do contribute to the local tax base and help pay for public services.

Faculty and staff of these institutions buy homes and cars and meals, thus also contributing to the tax base of the community in which they reside. The institution itself also procures goods and services in the community and thereby supports local businesses—large and small. This is how the contributions of the institutions are normally viewed, but there is a wide range of additional factors that can also contribute to the community—both financially and otherwise.

Colleges and universities attract sporting events, concerts, lectures, and other activities that are open to the community. This both endears the institution to the community and enhances the overall quality of life in the area.

The University of Pittsburgh reported in 2014 what it believed its economic contributions to the city and the region to be. It estimated its total annual impact on the State of Pennsylvania to be $3.7 billion and to include the following:

- nearly 28,000 supported jobs;
- about one in every 230 jobs across the state attributed to the university;
- about 188 million dollars paid in tax revenues to state and local governments;
- more than 70 million dollars in charitable donations and volunteer services.[19]

The State University of New York (SUNY), Plattsburgh estimated its total impact on its much smaller area in fiscal year 2010–11 to be more than 200 million dollars, including nearly 2300 jobs.[20] The component parts of the economic impact included payroll, the university's purchase of goods and services locally, construction outlays, student expenditures, visitor spending, and attendance at athletic events. The report also cited other contributions it made to community life, including arts and cultural activities, workforce development, business assistance programs, community services, and more.[21]

Additional examples are instructive. The order of magnitude adjusts with the college or university, of course, but the impacts on their home communities—large and small, urban, suburban, and rural—are constant and significant. The Pittsburgh Council on Higher Education reports on the ten colleges and universities that are located in and around that city. The collective economic impact of the ten institutions in school year 2012–13 was 9 billion dollars and they supported 70,000 jobs. The 9 billion dollars reported represented fully one-third of the city's Gross Domestic Product.

Washington University in St. Louis is another institution located in a major metropolitan area. In 2015, it reported that it accounted for more than 2 billion dollars of direct spending in the community, thereby supporting more than 43,000 regional jobs. Its 14,000 direct employees made it the fourth largest employer in the entire region. Its out-of-town students spent an estimated 140 million dollars annually and the university spent more than 249 million dollars on goods and services in that year.[22]

Plattsburgh, New York is a case study in this book because of the closure of the local Air Force Base, but it is also the home of one of the branches of the State University of New York system, or SUNY. In addition to the many financial contributions made to the community and the jobs supported throughout the region, the university also contributes to the area's overall quality of life. A 2012 report from the university reports that its museums, theaters, and athletic facilities attracted 26,000 visitors to the region that year. This means hotel and restaurant expenditures, retail sales, and tax payments. Various university entities provided health, economic development, community, and social services to community residents. Additionally, students from the university provided countless hours in community services that benefitted Plattsburgh and the region. This is highly significant for an institution of fewer than 6000 undergraduates and fewer than 600 graduate students.

SUNY Plattsburgh also contributes financially to the city and the region. Its total payroll approached 74 million dollars, which generates purchases in the community and helps create the tax base that pays for public services for the area as well. More than 30 million dollars in the purchase of goods and services and another 24 million dollars of construction produce the same benefits. And, the average student spent 2600 dollars per year on campus and more than 12,000 dollars per year off campus. Visitors to campus add nearly 5 million dollars per year as well.[23]

Further, the university's academic curricula are aimed at the needs of the community, and include nursing, teacher education, and hotel and restaurant management. Programs of business assistance assist local businesses to start up and grow. Clearly, the presence of this university, and others in their respective communities, play vital roles in their local economies and in the economic development of the cities, counties, and regions in which they reside.

Colleges and universities help to train the future workforce and re-train the existing one (Figure 15.2). Their presence in a community makes it more attractive to business site location decision-makers for whom technology is so rapidly changing that re-training is an important and constant consideration. They also make a region more attractive to businesses whose employees require certifications or continuing education units (CEUs) because the employees will not have to travel to obtain them. Of course, employers also conduct much of their recruiting from local colleges and universities as well.

College and university students and faculty can also provide a valuable asset to the businesses around it. Research conducted by the faculty can be commercialized and contribute to local employment and to the local tax base. And, research being conducted by companies or individuals in the private sector can also be refined and updated by faculty. Outside grants received by the universities represent outside funding coming in, creating wealth and expendable income, as well as additions to the local tax base.

University research parks and incubators are other ways that a region benefits from the presence of institutions of higher learning in its midst. Research parks enable start-ups and

Figure 15.2 Higher Education and Economic Development
Source: Shutterstock

small businesses to access university faculty, research, and equipment more readily than would otherwise exist. And, the community benefits from the spin-off effects of the companies that have been resident in the park. Institutions of higher learning often support incubator facilities that enable young companies to get started and grow while gaining access to shared support resources, such as legal and accounting services and, more.

Thrush wrote in *Politico*, that Pittsburgh is a leading example of a university-led economic recovery. The city's unemployment rate in the early eighties had risen to more than 17 percent of the potential workforce and, at one point, was losing an average more than 4000 residents every week. The city, "after decades of trying to remake itself, really does have a new economy, rooted in . . . robotic, artificial intelligence, health technology, manufacturing, and software industries."[24] Much of this growth emanated from the universities in the city, notably Carnegie-Mellon and its Robotics Institute. The technology and robotics sectors and higher education now account for 80 percent of the highest paying positions in the city and are supporting the growth of other sectors as well as the city's tax base from which public services are provided to the city's residents, workers, and students and educators. When speculating on why Pittsburgh's comeback was so much faster than that of other major US cities, Thrush quite correctly reflected that it was due to the sum advantages represented by the "human capital housed in the city's cultural institutions, foundations an overlooked industrial research sector and, above all, its great universities."[25]

The economic and other contributions of institutions of higher education can be quantified. Cecilia Brain of the Council of Ontario Universities published the following estimates for Ontario's universities during the 2014–15 academic year:

- The impact of university spending was nearly 14 billion dollars in that year.
- Nearly 3.5 billion dollars was spent by students and visitors.
- The impact of all the spending was to support more than 214,000 jobs (full-time equivalents, or FTEs).
- Major capital investments alone supported 7400 jobs.
- The total impact on Ontario's GDP was in excess of 42,300 dollars.[26]

Colleges and universities contribute to the community's wealth, which gets spent and re-spent locally; to the community's renown as a good place to live, work, and visit; and, to the community's overall quality of life. The expansion of such facilities and populations are a valid economic development strategy for communities that possess the requisite assets and amenities, or that can develop a plan to close the asset gaps in order to be competitive for the location of new university settings.

Universities have the potential to translate internal research into commercial applications. Similarly, universities have the internal research capabilities to assist people in the community on the advance of their ideas to the commercial stage. However, this does not always happen in the universities of today. The reason is that many colleges and universities were established as liberal arts institutions and are now trying to pivot to become more oriented to research and development activities. This does not happen overnight. A generation of faculty who were hired to write, publish, teach, and secure tenure have not, all of a sudden, become research-focused. A new generation of faculty has to come in when positions become available, and aid the movement in that new direction. The very culture of the university must shift. As Hill wrote, "University culture and policies can have important effects on the extent to which faculty engage in and develop commercially relevant research."[27]

This is beginning to happen because universities in many states have lost state funding, have had to raise tuition levels, and are looking to commercialization of research as a means of generating revenues for the institution. This means that the number of patents is no long the relevant metric of R&D success for higher education. It means that universities need to hire faculty, encourage researchers, and reward those who can create commercial products, with the potential financial rewards in mind. More universities are making use of equity arrangements when licensing university inventions. Many university-owned patents fail to generate significant income because:

> faculty do not take the time to develop their ideas and concepts into a commercially viable product. When faculty have a financial interest in the performance of the firm that licenses their research, they are more likely to assist the firm in product development.[28]

Universities are making the shift toward commercialization of research and, when they have been successful in that direction, the communities around them will also benefit but, again, this will certainly not happen overnight. In the meantime, communities need to prepare the assets and amenities that will ultimately make the companies that spin off from the university research remain in the area rather than relocating to another city or region. Part of this may relate to ongoing relationships with the university, part of it will relate to workforce availability. But, a very important factor in the retention of the company will be the access to the types of capital-venture and angel investments, for example— that will enable the firms to take the next steps in their own growth.

Industry Clusters

Industry clusters have been studied in great depth since Harvard University professor, Michael E. Porter, initiated his research decades ago. A cluster is a grouping of businesses and support groups that locate close to one another in a given area, and thereby create an increasingly greater synergy. Businesses are able to be more successful because they have common employees and common support business needs. They create an interconnected and interdependent supply of supplier, freight forwarders, universities and other training facilities that are particular to their own industry's needs. As the support structure grows, so grows the community of businesses in the cluster.

The key for a cluster to be successful lies in the interconnectivity of its components, whether public or private, start-up or established firm, non-profit or support, institutions or individuals. One of the best examples cited with some regularity in the literature is the aerospace cluster in and around Seattle, Washington. Boeing is the anchor but hundreds of suppliers and small companies are complemented in the cluster by programs and curricula at the University of Washington, area community colleges, publications, trade and professionals, organizations, conferences, and more.

In communities such as Seattle and the Puget Sound region, the challenge is to develop multiple clusters. This need was made clear in the early 1970s when the combination of the United States pulling out of Vietnam and the nation's double-digit unemployment meant dramatic declines in new aircraft orders on both the civilian and the government sides of the business. Of course, all of the suppliers also ran out of orders. Layoffs and a rapidly declining population spelled trouble for the region. As the industry came slowly back to life, the need for alternatives in the base economy became increasingly clear. Today, Seattle is home to several clusters, including health care and life sciences research and information technology clusters.

The support systems in the cluster are entirely dependent upon the needs of the businesses around which the cluster is formed. They can be small or large and they can contain wildly divergent types of cluster supports. A wonderful example of a cluster and the breadth of the support system that has grown around it is the equine industry in and around Lexington, Kentucky.

> The core of Kentucky's equine economic cluster is comprised of the commercial farms, training centers, show arenas, and race tracks that are engaged in horse-related activities such as breeding, sales, training, racing, showing, boarding, and equine-assisted therapeutic and learning programs.[29]

University of Kentucky Professor Lori Garkovitch also lists the following components of the equine cluster in and around Lexington, Kentucky: sales facilities, mare management, equine veterinarians, bloodstock agents, transportation services, barn builders, farriers, fencing and fence painting companies, pasture mowing companies, pest control, farm equipment sales companies, tack suppliers, hay and feed suppliers, bedding material producers, horse farm tours, publications, organizations, and clothiers. There's more: leather makers, horse care products, barn construction and renovation, landscaping, muck haulers, feed production, pond construction, pasture renovation, insurance agents, advertising firms, equine dentists, horse hearses, sports medicine practitioners, and more.[30]

The point is that a cluster can include a vast network of firms and groups that one might not initially think about as being part of the cluster. As the core industries grow, so grow the support businesses and groups within the cluster. Thus, it is a great economic development practice to create a relevant cluster and to continue to build it over time.

The cluster also serves as an economic development attraction because other related companies around the world learn of the cluster and consider the advantages of being located within the cluster.

Finally, within a cluster, companies and support groups can develop a strong form of interpersonal relationships that Garkovitch refers to as "social capital," that "increases the likelihood of joint ventures, strategic alliances, and collaborative work that builds and strengthens the competitive positon of the cluster" (relative to other similar clusters around the world).[31]

An industry cluster—even one as well known and strong as the equine industry cluster in Lexington—comes with precautions. First, the region must not allow itself to become overly dependent upon a given cluster. As has been discussed in previous chapters, a local economy must be sufficiently diverse to sustain itself through economic growth and decline within a single industry.

Second, clusters of all types require support from the local governments not only to be successful but to serve as an economic development attraction asset to bring other employers into the region. For example, in the case of the equine cluster in Lexington, the land use and taxation policies and regulations of the state and the local governments are very important to the cluster as a whole. Finally, public investments in infrastructure that support the needs of the members of the cluster will mean that the local governments will need to spend tax dollars to build roads, bridges, and more. This, of course, will presume that the expenditures will, in a reasonable length of time, generate even greater returns in terms of tax base and local expendable income.

This cluster is also very important to the State of Kentucky. It incorporates 35,000 operations over the state and includes more than 240,000 animals on more than 1 million acres. The value of the total assets was estimated at more than 23 billion dollars and the related sales and income in 2011 was estimated at more than 1 billion dollars. State-wide, the industry accounted for nearly 41,000 jobs in 2015. The amount of state taxes, supporting state-provided public services was, in 2015, estimated at 134 million dollars.[32]

One of the industries on which Seattle rebuilt and diversified its regional economy is health care. A 2004 report on the health care cluster in Seattle included in the cluster "patient care, medical education, training and research, medical device and instrument manufacturing, biomedical research and development, nursing homes and long-term care facilities, and physicians and other health care practitioners."[33] This illustrates again the breadth of services, businesses, and institutions that can be involved in a cluster.

"Broad institutional support in medical and life sciences are also included within the health care cluster. The institutions and organizations include medical schools, healthcare vocational training schools, medical and life sciences research institutions and professional membership associations."[34]

Another example is the wine growing cluster in and around Walla Walla, Washington. It includes wine growers, agricultural support and research, casks and other materials, grounds-keeping, bottle makers and label printers, shippers, cork producers, training and cooking schools, publications, meetings and tourism, and various public oversight agencies.

Some cluster maps cover an industry segment or a defined part of a larger segment of an industry. As with other industries, manufacturing has many components to it and can cover numerous types of production. Another way to regard a manufacturing cluster, however, is to consider it more broadly and to create a cluster that can support many or all of a manufacturer's needs regardless of the type of manufacturing in which they may be engaged.

Chart 15.1 is an illustration of the cluster activities that are present in St. Louis, Missouri for all types of manufacturing areas and processes. The cluster core highlights the primary industry segments and the inputs, suppliers, and customers that are high-lighted show the industries that sell to and buy from the St. Louis cluster. Supportive institutions in the community are also those that are specific to these types of manufacturers. It is possible that these same components of the St. Louis cluster can be relevant for other types of manufacturing than the automotive, aerospace, and construction industries.

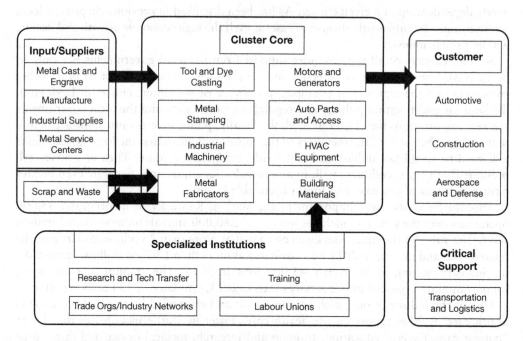

Chart 15.1 St. Louis Manufacturing Cluster Map
Source: Courtesy of the Initiative for a Competitive Inner City

Local economic development professionals can promote the success of the cluster to other forms of manufacturing as well. As that will contribute to economic growth, they may wish to be careful to focus on manufacturing that can benefit from the existing cluster of supports but that also contributes to economic development as well as growth. This may include advanced manufacturing, robotics, and more.

Other communities—even smaller jurisdictions and regions—can also use cluster development as an economic development strategy. It need not be as large as those cited above but they can have relatively similar impacts on a smaller, even more contained, scale.

Notes

1 American Hospital Association. *Economic Contributions of Hospitals Often Overlooked.* (Chicago, IL: American Hospital Association, 2012).
2 Ibid.
3 Gerald A. Doeksen. *The Economic Impact of a Critical Access Hospital on a Rural Community.* (Stillwater, OK: Oklahoma State University, National Center for Rural Health Works, October 2016).
4 Rural Health Information Hub. Community Vitality and Rural Healthcare. August 10, 2015. www.ruralhealthinfo.org
5 Edward Lawrence. Clock is Ticking on Las Vegas' Water Supply. *Channel 8 News.* www.8news-now.com
6 Ibid.

7 Edward C. Lawrence, Jane Qingjang Qu, and Ellen N. Briskin. *The Economic Impact of Mercy on the Joplin Area.* (St. Louis, MO: University of Missouri, November 21, 2011), p. 8.

8 Mark A. Hooker and Michael M. Knetter. *Measuring the Economic Effects of Military Base Closures.* (Cambridge, MA: The National Bureau of Economic Research, February 1999): 1.

9 David S. Sorenson. *Shutting Down the Cold War: The Politics of Military Base Closure.* (New York: St. Martin's Press, 1998): 13.

10 Ibid. 72–3.

11 Ibid., 1.

12 Ibid., 9.

13 Ibid., 11.

14 Kenneth Eugene Hawkins. *Military Base Impact on a Local Economy: A Case Study of Three Military Bases in Two Metropolitan Statistical Areas.* (Tallahassee, FL: The University of Florida, May 2005): 3.

15 Ibid.,13.

16 Rick Mayfield. Utah—Military Operations and Economic Development. *Economic Development Journal*, vol. 8, no. 3. (Washington, DC: International Economic Development Council, Summer 2009): 43–4.

17 Hawkins, 14.

18 Bruce Watson. Cleaning Up the Toxic Legacy of Military Bases. (September 24, 2010) www.aol.com

19 Tripp Umbach. Summer/Fall 2014. An Engine for Moving Pennsylvania Forward: The 2014 Economy and Community Impact Report of the University of Pittsburgh, p. 3.

20 Colin Read. *Regional Impact of the State University of New York, Plattsburgh, 2010–2011.* (Plattsburgh, NY: SUNY, Plattsburgh, Summer 2012): 3.

21 Ibid., various pages.

22 Washington University in St. Louis, Government and Community Relations. https:government relations.wustl.edu

23 Ibid., 12, 14, 18.

24 Glenn Thrush. The Robots That Saved Pittsburgh: How the Steel City Avoided Detroit's Fate. (February 4, 2014) www.politico.com

25 Ibid.

26 Cecilia Brain. Driving a Prosperous Future. *Economic Development Journal*, vol. 16, no. 2. (Washington, DC: International Economic Development Council, Spring 2017): 46–7.

27 Kent Hill. *University Research and Local Economic Development.* (Tempe, AZ: Arizona State University, August 2006): 5.

28 Ibid., 5.

29 Lori Garkovitch, Kimberley Brown, and Julie Zimmerman. We're Not Horsing Around: Conceptualizing the Kentucky Horse Industry as an Economic Cluster. *Community Development*, vol. 39, no. 3 (Rochester, NY: Community Development Society, 2008): 93–113.

30 Ibid., 3.

31 Lori Garkovitch, Lori. Conceptualizing the Kentucky Horse Industry as an Economic Cluster. (October 16, 2009) www.thehorse.com

32 C. Jill Stowe. *The Economic Impact of Kentucky's Equine Industry.* (Lexington, KY: The University of Kentucky, 2015): 6.

33 Huckell/Weinman Associates. September 2004. Economic Contributions of the Health Care Industry to the City of Seattle. City of Seattle Office of Economic Development, p. 6.

34 Ibid., 9.

References

American Hospital Association. America's Hospitals. 2008. www.aha.org

Brain, Cecilia. Driving a Prosperous Future. *Economic Development Journal*, vol. 16, no. 2. Washington, DC: International Economic Development Council, Spring 2017: 45–53.

Doeksen, Gerald A. *The Economic Impact of a Critical Access Hospital on a Rural Community.* National Center for Rural Health Works. Stillwater, OK: Oklahoma State University, October 2016.

Garkovitch, Lori. Conceptualizing the Kentucky Horse Industry as an Economic Cluster. October 16, 2009. www.thehorse.com

Garkovitch, Lori, Brown, Kimberley, and Zimmerman, Julie. We're Not Horsing Around: Conceptualizing the Kentucky Horse Industry as an Economic Cluster. *Community Development*, vol. 39, no. 3. Rochester, NY: Community Development Society, 2008, 93–113.

Hawkins, Kenneth Eugene. *Military Base Impact on a Local Economy: A Case Study of Three Military Bases in Two Metropolitan Statistical Areas.* Tallahassee, FL: The University of Florida, May 2005.

Hill, Kent. *University Research and Local Economic Development.* Tempe, AZ: Arizona State University, 2006.

Hooker, Mark A. and Knetter, Michael M. February. *Measuring the Economic Effects of Military Base Closures.* Cambridge, MA. The National Bureau of Economic Research, 1999.

Huckell/Weinman Associates. Economic Contribution of the Health Care Industry to the City of Seattle. City of Seattle Office of Economic Development, September 2004.

Lawrence, Edward. Clock is Ticking on Las Vegas' Water Supply. *Channel 8 News.* www.8news now.com

Lawrence, Edward C., Qingjang Qu, Jane, and Briskin, Ellen N. *The Economic Impact of Mercy on the Joplin Area.* St. Louis, MO: University of Missouri, 2011.

Mayfield, Rick. Utah—Military Operations and Economic Development. *Economic Development Journal*, vol. 8, no. 3. Washington, DC: International Economic Development Council, Summer 2009: 41–7.

Read, Colin. *Regional Impact of the State University of New York, Plattsburgh, 2010–2011.* New York: SUNY, Summer 2012.

Rural Health Information Hub. Community Vitality and Rural Healthcare. August 10, 2015. www.ruralhealthinfo.org

Sorenson, David S. *Shutting Down the Cold War: The Politics of Military Base Closure.* New York: St. Martin's Press, 1998.

Stowe, C. Jill. *The Economic Impact of Kentucky's Equine Industry.* Lexington, KY: The University of Kentucky, 2015.

Thrush, Glenn. The Robots That Saved Pittsburgh: How the Steel City Avoided Detroit's Fate. February 4, 2014. www.politico.com

Tripp Umbach. *An Engine for Moving Pennsylvania Forward: The 2014 Economy and Community Impact Report of the University of Pittsburgh.* Pittsburgh, PA: University of Pittsburgh, Summer/Fall 2014.

Washington University in St. Louis, Government and Community Relations. https://government relations.wustl.edu

Watson, Bruce. Cleaning Up the Toxic Legacy of Closed Military Bases. September 24, 2010. www.aol.com

16 Building Amenities to Drive Growth

Communities have the ability to create opportunities that both contribute to economic development and, simultaneously, serve to enhance the general quality of life for residents, businesses, and visitors. In many instances around the United States, these "created opportunities" yield ongoing and increasing potential for growth. Events and festivals, the arts, in general, tourism, and more are examples of such opportunities.

1 Events and Festivals

Events and festivals serve the same purpose for communities as other attractions and industries. That is, visitors come to the area and spend money on entrance tickets, meals, hotels, and other purchases, and then leave without placing great strain on the public infrastructure or using other public schools. Much of the revenues derived remain in the local community—or, at least, in the region, and that gets re-spent and taxed. In essence, the visitors are helping to provide the community with both expendable income and tax payments that support public facilities, thereby minimizing the burden for those services on residents.

Festivals and other events also serve to boost the reputation of the community. Studies have shown over the years that, when a person visits a location for such a reason, and has a positive experience, it greatly enhances the likelihood that he or she will make a positive site location decision for a company to go to that community should the opportunity arise.

Events and festivals are particularly beneficial to small towns and rural areas in which the primary economic activity is largely seasonal. In regions where the basic economic asset comes from farming or skiing or some other activity that can only be conducted for part of the year, festivals can be a non-primary-seasonal offset to support that economic activity and to provide revenues both to the city or town and the residents. Typically, this is a beneficial economic activity for an area to supplement the primary activities but it is not sufficient to sustain an economy alone.

Some festivals are not community-wide but rather neighborhood-centric. Permission to close off streets where several restaurants are located has often been granted by local officials. One or two blocks closed off can be a win–win–win–win situation. The restaurants get an opportunity to promote their establishments, their neighboring retailers benefit from the foot traffic, the government reaps additional sales tax revenues, and those who

Figure 16.1 Events and the Economy
Source: Shutterstock

attend have a nice time. If such events grow larger over time, the community has a better chance to show off its assets and the potential sales taxes and revenues are greater.

Ethnic, national, and other festivals have the potential to attract more people from greater distances(Figure 16.1). Those who travel further tend to spend more and thus enhance the coffers of the community as well as having a greater opportunity to see the community's assets and amenities. It should be remembered that, when a traveler has a positive experience in a community—for any reason—it greatly enhances the likelihood of a positive site location decision if the opportunity arises.

The extreme of such examples may be events such as the parades during the Chinese New Year in Washington, DC or the Saint Patrick's Day parade in New York or the Scottish Christmas Walk in Alexandria, Virginia. But, smaller events built around ethnic or national backgrounds can be very effective strategies for smaller cities and towns as well. People will travel substantial distances to see the native dances of Thailand or Peru and to taste their native dishes.

Special events and festivals cannot be insignificant. The International Festival and Event Association estimates the industry to "include some four to five million regularly occurring events (that) have a significant economic impact globally."[1] Irshad further notes that these events impact the community in a wide variety of ways including increased expenditures, job creation, heightened regional awareness and perceptions, the development of new accommodations and tourist attractions, the preservation of local heritage sites and culture, a strengthening of the regional sense of community, an increase in local pride and spirit, and more.[2]

2   The Arts and Economic Development

The arts play a dual role in a community's economic development. Part of what makes a place a nice setting for employers and workers includes things to do. It is one component of what is loosely defined as the local quality of life. Of course, not every individual has the same concept of what a high quality of life means. For some, the arts are an important component of that definition. But, what art is important to him or her? It might be dance (classical or modern), concerts (either classical or country or rock), or performances (plays, operas, or ballet), or it might be museums and fine art, which has too many forms to list.

The point is that few communities can afford to have all of the possible art forms that would satisfy the art component of quality of life for everyone. Most communities have one or a few types of arts to enjoy and that may appeal to some people. It will not, however, cause one to make a business decision to site a facility in a community. It does give a community a certain image as a place where there are things to do in one's spare time. And, Baeker outlines several economic outcomes that a community can derive from a healthy cultural scene. They include the growth of small businesses, expanded employment possibilities for local residents, an enhanced quality of place as a magnet for talent and investment, tourism attraction, and place branding.[3] Further, the expenditures attracted locally from out-of-the-area visitors generate wealth in the community and tax base contributions that support both state and local public services, thereby minimizing the costs of those services for residents.

From an economic development perspective, the greater impact of the arts on the local economy comes from viewing it as any other job-creating, revenue and tax-generating business. The Americans for the Arts reports that the industry as a whole generated more than 135 billion dollars of economic activity nationally. More than 74 billion dollars of that amount came from event-related expenditures by audiences and 61 billion dollars came from related non-profit organizations.

Further, the industry generates about 22 billion dollars in tax revenues for federal, state, and local governments across the United States. And, the typical audience is comprised of nearly one-third attendees from outside of the immediate area. Not only do those people spend an estimated two times the money spent by local attendees, it also means an influx of dollars to the local economy.[4] In this way the arts supports the community, and its public services, as well as enhancing its quality of life.

In Fairfax County, Virginia, the Americans for the Arts reported that, in Fiscal Year 2015, total industry expenditures exceeded 300 million dollars, supported nearly 7000 full-time equivalent jobs, and paid more than 150 million dollars in local household incomes. Further, tax revenues that accrued to the state were nearly 12 million dollars and another 10 million plus in tax revenues went to the local government. Total attendance at arts performances and displays exceed five million patrons. Of course, the spending of attendees at events who came from greater distances was significantly greater than for those who were local. This was due to greater purchases of hotel rooms, meals, and gasoline.[5] This is the reason that many communities have established festivals and performances as part of their economic development strategies.

For the arts to flourish in communities, there need to be facilities—concert halls, museums, and performance spaces. Newberry, South Carolina refurbished an 1882 opera house in order to develop a downtown showplace for the arts and to attract tourists to the community. Hundreds of shows now appear in the opera house every year, generating local retail sales, hotel and restaurant sales, and increased local tax generation. Local shops have since been upgraded and community pride has been enhanced.

Seattle has developed a thriving arts and culture scene in recent years that has attracted visitors and expenditures. A 2004 report by professors from the University of Washington covered the music industry as a component of the arts scene. They noted that the contributions of the music to the city's life involves more than the dollars and cents of expenditures and attendance. It also includes programs at the local public schools and institutions of higher education throughout the region. Yet, it is the economic contributions that are most relevant for this volume. Nearly 8700 jobs were reported as being created by the city's music industry, which totaled more than 2600 small businesses. Just shy of 200 million dollars in wages were paid in 2004 by these organizations, public, private, and non-profit. Total sales approached nearly 650 million dollars annually.[6]

The city's music industry, however, faced some challenges, including the city's tax structure, its perceived isolation, and more. Other communities wishing to create or build upon an existing music scene may benefit from the report's recommendations to improve supports for music programs in the local public school system, to promote the industry broadly, to ensure that the local tax structure is conducive to attracting, keeping, and growing the music industry.

Like any other industry cluster, the music industry can evolve with support groups around it and generate much greater revenues, expenditures, and tax base contributions as a result. Components of such a cluster may include musicians, recording studios, concert halls, legal and accounting services that are attuned to the industry, instrument rentals, agents and promotional businesses, distributors, publications, instrument manufacturers and repair shops, broadcasters, and more.

For larger cities and regions, arts facilities can generate significant attention and sponsorship as well as audience levels. In Pittsburgh, the city created an arts and entertainment hub within the downtown area. It included a $35 million renovation of the Stanley Theater, built in 1928, and the development of the Benedum Center for the Performing Arts. The plan had been developed in partnership with Alleghany International, which had agreed to locate its global headquarters building in that area, contingent upon the development of this adjacent performing arts center. "The intent is to encourage the development of multiple theater and performance spaces; related restaurants, shops, and galleries; park and streetscape improvements; convention business; and, renewed attention to the riverfront."[7] The elected Chairman of the Board of Alleghany County remarked at the time that the district would ultimately become "a key factor in our economic advance, just as surely as industrial parks and industrial development bonds."[8]

The original estimates for the project were that it would generate nearly 6 million dollars annually in expenditures in the area for food, parking, and retail expenditures, as well as over 1 million dollars in annual amusement taxes for the city and the generation of an additional $2.5 million dollars in real estate tax payments. These estimates were made in 1985 so today's values will be much higher, but the numbers do give credence to the value of the arts not only in creating entertainment and enhancing the general quality of life, but also in terms of economic development and returns on the investments made.

The greater Philadelphia region has realized significant revenue generation by a related industry—film, television, and video (FTV) production. Vilain wrote:

> There are two dimensions to measuring the economic benefits of regional FTV production [film, television, and video]. The first . . . is in terms of the economic impact attributable to the expenditures associated with the film production itself . . . The second economic benefit derived from film production is that of image.[9]

These are all valid businesses that support the local economy and tax base in many, often unexpected, ways.

A recent study provided for Fairfax County by Americans for the Arts indicated that the annual jobs supported by arts expenditures over one year (Fiscal Year 2015) equaled 6200, and that the revenues to the state's tax coffers exceeded 10 million dollars and to the county coffers more than 9 million dollars. It further examined the expenditure of attendees at arts events and estimated the average expenditure per patron to vary between local residents and those who traveled to the area for performances and shows. A local resident on average paid nearly 22 dollars per capita on meals, souvenirs, and other items. A visitor to the community for an arts performance or show paid 23.5 dollars per capita because there were greater expenditures for transportation and lodging. And, those figures do not include the cost of admission to the shows. In short, the arts are not only an important element of a community's quality of life but they also contribute to incomes, business revenues, and the state and local coffers from which public services are provided. Again, with visitors from outside the community, the expenditures are paid with relatively little return in the form of local public services. These are great dollars to attract because they contribute to the ability to provide public education, public safety, and more without the residents of the community having to bear the entire burden of those costs.

As a side consideration, municipal leaders need to be somewhat cautious when serving as the setting for films. All too often, for example, films portray New York City as the home of despair, drugs, and homicides. Fear and organized crime rule the mean streets and innocent individuals may suffer the consequences. Another example is that of western cities that were once known to foreigners only through their movie images: cowboys, Indians, and hardship. Such images make it difficult to market the city as a great place to live or to locate a business.

Still, the types of expenditures generated by film production in the greater Philadelphia region (1992–2005) included such diverse sources of revenues as employee wages, food and beverage operations, transportation and car rentals, hotels and lodging revenues as well as any associated transient occupancy taxes, construction and tear-down services, location and filming rents, as well as the daily costs of laundry, equipment rental, protective services and security, photo-finishing labs, and much more. Clearly, filming is good business not only for the community but its small businesses as well.[10]

From the perspective of the community, any tax revenues thereby generated help the community to pay for vital public services while not requiring the regular business and residential populations to carry those burdens alone. Total state and municipal tax revenues attributable to feature film, television, and video production in the Philadelphia Region in 2000 were estimated by Vilain as follows: $2,090,000 in total municipal tax payments and $3,482,200 paid in State of Pennsylvania taxes for a 2000 total of $5,571,000 in all tax payments.[11]

The arts can also become the representation of a community's spirit. Following a devastating May 2011 tornado that tore a wide swath of destruction 6 miles long through the City of Joplin, Missouri, the community had to recover and rebuild. Within a few months, a mural project grew spontaneously by people who wanted to show their determination in rebuilding their city and its economy. "The area of 15th Street seemed a good fit given its central location and proximity to the areas that needed to be rebuilt."[12]

More than 300 people became involved, including children. Focus groups were conducted to

> figure out what we wanted to say to the world, trying to figure out how we wanted to present Joplin. We didn't want Joplin just to be remembered as this tornado town, but wanted it to be remembered . . . for our spirit and our resilience.

After the tornado, pop-up murals, sculptures, and drawings began appearing on other buildings in the area. "People weren't told to make creative changes, they were moved to."[13] Clearly, the display of public art helped the people get over what had happened to their community.

Beyond the initial cathartic effects of the preparations of public art, the community had made a statement: We are strong and will get stronger. Businesses took notice and began to rebuild and relocate into the area. Housing was rebuilt and the population grew to levels greater than those of the pre-tornado times in just five years. The arts and peoples' creative expressions helped the city recover and proudly display its spirit and to rebuild its business community, jump-start its economy, and recover its tax base and public services.

3   Conference and Meeting Facilities

In the same way that television, film, and video production generates revenues from outside the community that help to pay for local public services, so do meetings, conferences, trade shows, training programs, and other gatherings of people from areas outside the community. In each case, people come in to the community and spend dollars in hotels, restaurants, and retailers throughout the community.

Along with those expenditures, they pay transient occupancy (or, hotel) taxes, meals taxes, and sales taxes. And, the facilities pay salaries and real estate taxes. As the revenues from participants come from outside the community, they are helping to pay for someone else's public facilities and public services while using very little of the infrastructure and services themselves. They do not, for example, use the public schools, the libraries, or the parks, or most other public services.

While such facilities do import revenue into the community and do pay taxes, there are some potential downsides as well. These kinds of facilities must be booked fairly constantly in order to make money. Quite often, they need to be subsidized and that often means local governments must dedicate funding to offset the differences between the costs of operations and the revenues generated by the users. In many areas, the primary beneficiaries are asked to pay for that gap, including the hoteliers and restaurateurs in the vicinity.

Clearly, there are opportunities and costs inherent in operating such facilities and those must be analyzed and understood in advance of opening. Those who will make up the gaps in funding must be fully aware of their obligations for as long as the facility remains in place. With that in mind, meeting facilities are a legitimate strategy for growing an economic generator in the right place and time.

Finally, it is not unusual for people to attend a conference or event in a community they have not previously visited. This means that people from all walks of life, including a wide range of business men and women, are being attracted for a brief visit. During that time, if they have a positive experience, they may wish to return. They may even consider the location as a possible site for an office or other business facility. For this reason, communities often "roll out the red carpet" for mid-size or larger conferences. The Mayor may make welcoming remarks and tours and activities are arranged for the attendees. Anything that can be done to ensure that those who participate—and their spouses—enjoy their visit can later translate into positive site location decisions.

4   Tourism as Economic Development

If one accepts that economic development is designed to increase a locality's employment base, create expendable income that is then re-circulated throughout the community, and generate an additional tax base for public services, then tourism can be a vital component of an economic development program. Visitors to a community accomplish all of the above, and do so without drawing on many public services.

People visit communities for a variety of purposes. They may be visiting friends or a child attending a local university. They may be in town for a business meeting or to attend a convention. They may be attending sporting events or visiting historic sites in the community. Their trip may last for an afternoon or a week. Many communities take pains to train those who receive and provide services to visitors because they know that a positive experience as a visitor may yield more positive consideration as a location for an office of a site for a facility for that community. This training may include the importance of providing service with a smile, having knowledge of how to get around town and what to see and do, or just knowing who can help with other types of questions or needs. The training may be provided by the convention and visitors' bureau and it may include people who work at the airport, taxi drivers, hotel service personnel, restaurant receptionists, and others. The impressions of these representatives of their communities can have many positive effects in later decision-making.

While in town, people will enjoy a meal, shop in the local stores for souvenirs or necessities, and purchase gasoline. By doing so, they will make purchases from local retailers that will support local jobs and the expendable incomes thus created will then be spent and re-spent around the community. The sales taxes they pay will help to pay for local public services for the residents of the community.

Different communities assess a variety of fees on travelers, all of which become part of either the state or local tax bases, or both. The result is a greater ability to provide state and local services while minimizing the burden of the costs on the residents of the state and community. In communities where tourism is either the primary industry or one of the leading industries for the area, the taxes assessed can be higher and more varied. Scottsdale, Arizona assesses a 1.65 percent transaction Privilege Price as well as a 5 percent Transient Tax Rate on transient lodging renters, defined as rentals of 29 days or fewer. Major cities that receive a lot of business and leisure travelers—cities such as Washington, DC, New York, or Los Angeles often charge hotel taxes in the high teens as a percentage of the room rates in hotels. These fees help to provide public services in those cities while tourists require far less in public services returned than they contribute to the local tax bases.

But, visitors don't just stay at local hotels and eat at local restaurants. They purchase gasoline and visit shopping outlets, where they also pay the going sales tax rate. And, depending on the community, they may be assessed a meals tax or an addition to the hotel charge for transient occupancy taxes. These generally accrue to the local governments and help them to provide local public services, thereby minimizing the costs of those services for the people who reside in the community year-round. The return-on-investments made by communities for tourism marketing programs can easily be measured in the form of tax base returns and jobs being supported by the industry. Communities that are fortunate to house tourist attractions will have an added benefit from them because the fees that they charge for admission will also be subject to sales taxes. They also create a demand for restaurants, gas stations, hotels, retailers, and more.

Travelers to destinations also support the demand for new transportation networks. Local residents and businesses can enhance their arguments for new roads, road maintenance, and highway maintenance if there are additional travelers using those transportation networks. Frequently, leisure and sporting destinations provide greater support to the case being made with various airlines for an enhanced air service. That, in turn, provides ease of access to new markets and to better connections to new markets, which is a selling point for economic development professionals when dealing with prospective new businesses. In a 2011 survey by Development Counselors International, 9 percent of site location decision-makers reported that their perceptions of an area's business climate were formed in part by leisure travel and 27 percent said it was informed by business travel to a location.[14] In sum, conventions and trade shows in an area contribute to the community's exposure to decision-makers. Hopefully, one day, one of those individuals will remember the community enough at least to consider citing a facility there. Thus, it behooves economic development organizations and destination marketing organizations within the same community to understand where there may be potential opportunities in either program from which there can be mutual benefit for the programs and for the community.

Barry Biggar is the President of Visit Fairfax, the Fairfax County, Virginia destination marketing organization, and a long-term industry leader. He noted in an interview that the field of tourism and destination marketing had changed and become much more professionalized in the past 15 years. It was after the terrorist attacks of 9–11, travel declined to communities and vacancies in hotels rose dramatically; and, the awareness of the importance of tourism as an element of economic development became far more clear. Communities came to realize that travelers spent money in their hotels, restaurants, attractions, stores, gas stations, and more. And they did so without placing great burdens on the public services of the community. In brief, they left money behind and did not cost anything in terms of tax base.

Biggar noted that, if a community had access, a reason for people to visit, and a desire to have travelers visit, they could be successful in this component of economic development marketing. Years later, President Obama announced plans to increase foreign tourism to the United States. This gave a shot in the arm to the industry but it also lent credibility to its importance to states and communities across the country as an economic development tool. Tourism is a clean industry, it imports dollars to a location, and it helps to diversify local economies.

A study done by Visit Fairfax (now being updated) demonstrated that every hotel room in the county (a total of nearly 19,000 rooms in 120 hotels in 2017) generated about 5000 dollars in local tax revenues every year. This helps the local government provide public services for residents while minimizing the burden of those costs for all constituents.

In some communities, tourism can be the prime driver of economic growth. In others, it is a complementary adjunct to economic development. For example, the City of Scottsdale, Arizona has a thriving economic base and a tourism program with several assets to market. Danielle Casey wants to market them more collaboratively and wants to demonstrate the strong connection between tourism destination promotion and economic development marketing. Casey is the Director of the Economic Development Department, an agency of the City of Scottsdale, Arizona.

Scottsdale, a city of 230,000 residents, attracts more than 9 million visitors per year, many of whom visit as part of golf outings. These visitors spend a lot of money to travel to the area's many beautiful golf courses, to stay in the hotels and eat in the restaurants, and to play golf. Not only do such trips represent revenues for the businesses but they also generate tax revenues. Casey sees great opportunity to promote the city as a business location with these groups as well. Given the costs of the travel, the stay, and the rounds of golf, one may conclude that these visitors possess wealth and they may include numerous business executives. If they are impressed with the area when they visit, they may be willing later to consider it as a business location as well. To push out that message, Casey wants to get her message to golfers in unobtrusive ways: brochures, messages on the hotels' in-room television channels, and short presentations when appropriate. All that needs to be done sometimes is to plant a seed that can germinate later.

Why is Scottsdale a natural tourism destination? It boasts 200 golf courses under 300 days of sunshine. There are 70 local hotels and 600 restaurants. There are trails to hike and shopping to enjoy. Expenditure levels do indeed imply that there will be senior business executives in the mix. There are presently a range of businesses that have seen the advantages of the city and the region, ranging from health care to information technology to financial services, and more. Several major league baseball teams conduct their spring training in the area and that attracts even more possible economic development audiences. All visitors to the area in 2015 paid an estimated 37 million dollars in taxes, according to Choose Scottsdale, the Visitors Bureau.

The city's strategic plan includes, as a goal, "build a Scottsdale business location brand on par with Scottsdale's tourism brand."[15] Casey sees this as a primary opportunity to grow the business base by attracting more firms from the west coast, from around the United States, and from around the world. Scottsdale is also proximate to the City of Phoenix, which means it can offer ease of access to the resources of the city without having to be in a city environment. Five percent of the population of greater Phoenix resides in the City of Scottsdale, as well as 17 percent of the region's corporate headquarters.

The City of Scottsdale generates 9 million dollars in bed tax revenues annually. By law, that entire amount must be spent on tourism broadly, and 50 percent of that amount must go to tourism marketing. The city contracts with the Convention and Visitors Bureau to provide those services. Casey advocates a closer relationship between the Convention and visitors Bureau and the Department of Economic Development. She notes that "Business is driving hotel uses and bed taxes." When people visit the area for business meetings or conferences, they are helping to promote tourism and raise the revenues that help to do so. She wants to promote the tourism message to business travelers and the economic development message to golfers and other leisure travelers.

In some communities, the nexus between the two promotional arms is more obvious than in others. Economic development professionals like Casey are trying to demonstrate the mutually beneficial value in such collaboration. "We need to change the dialogue. We are not in competition with one another. We can benefit each other. We are having the conversation about how to relate." A further point made was that tourism is highly dependent upon variations in the national and global economies. More business, more Class A office space, and promoting the message that the region has an unparalleled quality of life will help economic development; destination marketing; the city, its tax base, and its range and quality of public services; and, ultimately, the residents of the city of Scottsdale.

Notes

1 Irshad, D. *Events*. (Boise, ID: International Festival and Events Association, 2017).
2 Ibid., 6.
3 Greg Baeker. Cultural Economics. *Economic Development Journal*, vol. 16, no.2. (Washington, DC: International Economic Development Council, 2017): 40.
4 Americans for the Arts. Arts and Economic Prosperity. www.americansforthearts.org
5 Ibid.
6 W. Beyers, A. Bonds, A. Wenzl, and P. Sommers. *The Economic Impact of Seattle's Music Industry*. (Seattle, WA: City of Seattle, February 2004): ii.
7 Robert H. McNulty. *The Economics of Amenity*. (Washington, DC: Partners for Livable Places, 1985): 53.
8 Ibid.
9 Pierre B. Vilain. Art as Economic Stimulus. *Economic Development Journal*. (Washington, DC: International Economic Development Council, 2002): 36.
10 Ibid., 37.
11 Ibid., 39.
12 Stacey Lindsay. A Creative Renaissance: An In-Depth Look at the Arts in Joplin, Post-Tornado. (April 21, 2017) http://jrbj.biz

13 Ibid.
14 Oxford Economics. *Destination Promotion: An Engine of Economic Development.* (Oxford: Oxford Economics, November 2014).
15 City of Scottsdale, Economic Vitality Office. Economic Development Strategic Plan. (October 2016)

References

Americans for the Arts. Arts and Economic Prosperity. www.americansforthearts.org

Baeker, Greg. Cultural Economics. *Economic Development Journal*, Vol. 16, no. 2. Washington, DC: International Economic Development Council, Spring 2017: 37–44.

Beyers. W., Bonds, A. Wenzl, A., and Sommers, P. *The Economic Impact of Seattle's Music Industry*. Seattle, WA: City of Seattle, February 2004.

City of Scottsdale, Economic Vitality Office. *Economic Development Incentives*. Scottsdale, AZ, Spring 2004.

Irshad, D. *Events*. Boise, ID: International Festival and Events Association, 2017.

Lindsay, Stacey. A Creative Renaissance: An In-Depth Look at the Arts in Joplin, Post-Tornado. April 21, 2017. https://jrbj.biz

McNulty, Robert H. *The Economics of Amenity*. Washington, DC: Partners for Livable Places, 1985.

Oxford Economics. *Destination Promotion: An Engine of Economic Development*. Oxford: Oxford Economics, November 2014.

Vilain, Pierre B. Art as Economic Stimulus. *Economic Development Journal*. Washington, DC: International Economic Development Council, Spring 2002: 35–44.

17 Rural Communities and Small Town Economic Development

Small towns in rural areas across the United States are dying out, the result of job losses, overseas competition, and the lure for young people of the activities of larger communities and major metropolitan areas. The *New York Times* wrote that, "The American small town, which has long occupied a revered place in the nation's history, and mythology, is becoming something of a museum piece."[1] There is a sense among some that small towns are simply no longer required for American economic growth.

Small towns that lose a primary company take the hit more intensely than their larger counterparts. This is largely due to the relatively lesser ability to recover the jobs, the incomes, and the general economic growth that has been lost. This can be the result of a company leaving, an industry dying, or even a natural disaster. In California, for example, a disaster beyond the control of the local inhabitants occurred at Big Sur. More than 80 inches of rain in a two-month period caused mudslides and rock slides that took out the only bridge to many of the interior residential areas. The resultant isolation was reported in the *Washington Post* to include a loss of 600,000 dollars in revenue for local businesses every day. Businesses closed and staff was laid off.

In the case of Big Sur, the state was slow to move and the predicted time for the opening of a trail that would meet the standards of the state code to allow residents to climb out of the area (the only other means was by helicopter) to be five weeks. In such times of severe trial, neighbors can pull together: "in five days, one hundred locals had been deputized to work alongside state employees to build a trail together . . . they finished the job in a record ten days."[2] But, not all such causes are as easily addressed or resolved.

What happens to the economic condition of America's small towns and rural areas is of vital importance to everyone in the United States, regardless of location. In the United States only 2 percent of the land is covered by urban areas, the remainder being varying degrees of rural areas.[3] The economic development and sustainability of these small towns and rural communities is a concern for the national economy.

Most of the causes for the economic decline of small, rural towns are structural and even irreparable. In Oregon, for example, the loss of timber mills was due to a variety of factors: some lands had been largely denuded from the over-cutting; other issues such as the nesting areas of the spotted owl inhibited further timber activity. The loss of 80 or 90 jobs is devastating for the community and the mills were one of the few local employers who provided family health insurance coverage for their employees. Their closings create tremendous concerns for families and others who lose both incomes and insurance coverage.

When communities in Oregon lost jobs, a prevailing sentiment was that the town "is just going to die out." Retailers closed and the hospital shut down, leaving the nearest hospital as many as several hours away. And, as the younger generation left in search of jobs, the median age levels climbed quickly. In Wheeler County, Oregon, the median age rose from 48 to 56 years in just 13 years.[4] Like Wheeler County, rural America is statistically becoming older, whiter, and less populous. Less than one in five Americans now live in rural areas across the United States and many of these communities are dying. Re-populating these communities is the first step to their recovery, and much of that repopulation is taking place today as the result of the arrival of new immigrants to the United States, which will be covered in a later chapter.

The result for those left unemployed—who are uneducated and frequently illiterate— is, at first, disbelief. The logging industry had always been there and there was no evident reason why it should not be there for themselves and their children well into the future. But, the number of mills in Oregon had declined from more than 520 in 1968 to 111 today.[5] The world had changed for them and they simply could not accept it.

> So many small, rural communities find themselves on the losing end of globalization and economic transition, almost to the point of despondency. Yet, some manage to bounce back from the brink of economic ruin and create a renewed prosperity both materially and in spirit.[6]

What sets one community apart from the other? Why does one succeed in its comeback while the other declines and takes the local attitudes along with it?

Somewhat larger, small cities are also susceptible to quick losses and difficult recoveries. Dubuque, Iowa lost two large employers in the 1980s, John Deere and Dubuque Packing, and the city fell on very hard times. But, Dubuque had a natural resource to build upon: the river. The city estimates that "more than one million tourists visit Dubuque annually to ride the riverboats and see the sights."[7] Isolated small towns—those that are truly small, rural communities—may have nothing else on which to fall back when developing new directions for their economies. They lose a primary employer, and the result is that residents move away, and that is when the most essential services to any community are in peril of being lost.

In 2015 and 2016, John Deere laid off 100 people at its mill in Dubuque, Iowa. Another 75 were laid off later that year. Those job cuts came on the heels of a poor agricultural season, leaving consumer confidence and expendable income levels at very low points. That, in turn, meant that shopkeepers were losing revenues and had to cut jobs as well. The ripple effects ran through the larger community. The company had received state incentive grants that had to be scaled back as a result of lost contracts and the inability to hire as had been planned.

Another rural community that lost its primary employer and was left without much recourse for rebuilding is Lamar, Missouri. Known for its largest employer, O'Sullivan Industries, Lamar "was rooted in the three Fs: faith, farming and furniture-in-a-box."[8]

It's very identity was deeply tied to its employer: "Much like Detroit's identity was synonymous with the American automobile industry."[9] O'Sullivan had peaked as a company in the late 1990s with 380 million dollars in sales and 2350 employees. By 2007, the company had shut its doors and laid off the final 700 people. People lost their health insurance coverage and many would have moved but could not afford to sell their homes at rock-bottom prices. Of course, the people of Lamar suffered but so did the city, its shop-keepers, and its service providers.

In the small, rural cities that lost hundreds or even thousands of jobs, rebuilding the economy has not meant attracting a new employer that would create hundreds or thousands of new jobs. Rather, it has meant the attraction and creation of companies that create a few jobs at a time. Rebuilding small town economies is best supported by many small businesses that grow over time. That however, requires planning, patience, and political leadership.

In Lamar, O'Sullivan Industries was typical of many small towns' major employers. They funded little leagues and scout troops, their employees helped to build the football field at the local high school, and they collected funds for those down on their luck. And, no one in Lamar expected O'Sullivan to close its doors. As late as 2006, the corporate headquarters announced that it would be hiring another one hundred people at the facility in Lamar over a few short weeks to meet growing demands for its products.

Later, when the company did leave town, everyone in the area was impacted. Losing 1700 jobs in a city of roughly 45,000 people was devastating. "Several spin-off businesses were started in the wake of O'Sullivan's success. All around Lamar, businesses enjoyed the spoils of the plant. When it closed, the ripple effect went out across the area."[10]

Lamar was fortunate, however, as the facility was purchased by a company from California that will renovate the building for the Gorilla Door manufacturing business as well as other tenants. The City Administrator of Lamar had earlier noted that, "Our unemployment has been over 10 percent. No one is buying cars or furniture and we have a lot of empty houses . . . The housing industry has collapsed."[11] Gorilla Doors ultimately expected to employ 475 men and women. The impact on the region was the reverse of the sense of loss felt when O'Sullivan shut their doors.

Stefanoni reported on another opportune business development for Lamar. Redneck Blinds was a locally started business that manufactured duck and deer blinds for hunters. In a very short period of time, the new business had orders backlogged and needed to employ more people. Although the former O'Sullivan plant remained boarded up, jobs were not coming to, but being created from within Lamar. Various local leaders who were interviewed noted their belief that home-grown, small businesses were the way back to economic stability for this small town. Attracting another employer of 1500, or even 500, positions was unlikely for a town of its size. There was also a general belief that many small businesses meant greater stability than one large business that could leave and destroy the local economy with one fatal decision, often made in another location.

And, local businesses help the community by contributing to its activities: sports teams, scout troops, church activities, and charitable organizations. In Lamar, there was another benefit felt from the development of new companies: they want to help other small businesses grow with them. Redneck Blinds, for example, purchases various accessories for its product from local individuals and firms. The company's owners purchase "curtains for the blinds from local Amish women who manufacture them in their homes . . . the screen printing is done by clients of Lamar Enterprises, a workshop for individuals with developmental disabilities."[12]

The commercial area of a rural community constitutes its downtown. The downtown is the entry-way to a small town; it is what people see when they arrive and it is sometimes what they come to see. It is where the interesting shops and activities are held. It is the heart and soul of small, rural towns and needs to be as clean and vibrant as it can be, lest the community feel even more considerably the losses that threaten the downtown from primary employers moving away. The downtown is a reflection of what is happening in the community and with its economic stability and sustainability.

The losses of jobs and expendable income and population levels conspire to expose other, vital community services as unnecessary and expendable. The resultant cycle of loss results in an inability to sustain the very community. As population leaves, services are lost; the loss of services results in more people leaving and fewer arriving. Businesses are not interested in coming to towns that are dying or that do not have their own schools, shops, post offices, or health care.

In the past few decades, many students from rural schools, especially those in the midwest, the southwest, and southeast have been bused to bigger schools that are often many miles away. In the name of cost savings, communities have had to sacrifice having their own schools. Of course, towns in other regions have also lost schools, and the reactions of small town residents to the loss of their school are immediate and intense: "This is going to turn Monticello (Maine) into a little ghost town."[13] In Monticello, there were nearly 1100 residents in 1970. By decade, the population declined from 950 in 1980, to 872 in 1990, to fewer than 800 in 2000, at which point the population leveled out. The loss of a school spelled the near demise of this small Maine town.

Schools are, in many small towns across America, where people gather, where they vote, where they see plays and watch their children graduate. But, when a company leaves town or shuts its doors, the residents also tend to move away. And, when the population declines, more schools close. It is a tough cycle to break. "Parents who could take comfort in knowing their son or daughter was just a few miles from home, in a school whose staff they knew and trusted, are now anxious about the future."[14]

Another vital community service that is placed at risk in a small, rural town when the primary employer leaves or shuts down is health care. Eighty rural hospitals have closed in this country since 2010. In Haywood County, Tennessee, the closing of the local hospital meant that people had to drive excessively long distances to obtain critical medical care. The hospital had too many self-paying (uninsured) customers and lost more than 4 million dollars in 2000 and nearly 7 million dollars in 2013.[15] It simply could not afford to remain open.

Goldstein wrote in the *Washington Post* that, with the nearest emergency room being 30 miles away for many residents, "the emergency room is now the back of an ambulance." People cannot access health care because they cannot make the trip. Many people will not go in one of the two local ambulances because the trip to Jackson was 30 miles away and many had no way of getting back home. So, the community has no emergency medical care and the ambulance attendants do their best for patients in the back of the ambulance itself.

The county has been paying for ambulance services from their (12 million dollar annual) budget but they're losing money because people will not take the 30 minute ride to the nearest hospital, opting instead to be treated in the back of the ambulance by EMT's while parked in their driveways. Insurance won't pay reimbursements unless the patient is taken to a hospital. Between those losses and the losses from treating those who simply cannot pay for care, the city is losing a great deal of money from its budget without any hope of reimbursement.

Compounding the problems of missing narrow windows for full recovery of heart patients, stroke patients, and others is the inability of residents to access any pre-screening or preventive care. And, the greatest concerns are how people would be helped in the case of a multiple car accident or an industrial accident. The potential for disaster is considerable and is making local officials very nervous. According to the American Association of Retired People (AARP), there are 77 million Americans living in rural areas that are home to a mere 10 percent of the nation's doctors.[16] And, the Kansas-based National Rural Health Association, which has more than 2000 members, notes that 48 rural hospitals closed between 2010 and 2015. Most of those were in southern states. It also warned that another 283 are on the verge of closing as well.[17] In the light of these circumstances, employers that otherwise might stay in—or, even come to—such small towns, are unlikely to be willing to do so.

In Whitehall, Illinois, where the local hospital recently closed, one businessman was quoted in the *LA Times* as saying, "Everybody's scared to death. What if a kid is run over? Or, someone has a heart attack? You're pretty much left alone."[18] And, Mayor Franklin Smith resides in Haywood County, Tennessee, which has a population of a little over 18,000 people. He recites the history of losing the hospital that served his community and much of the surrounding areas. The Council received notice that their private, for-profit hospital would be closed down within 90 days. At that point, there was nothing that could be done to save it because the official papers of notification had already been filed with the State of Tennessee.

Mayor Smith, who had served as Mayor from 1986 to 1999, and again from to 2004 to the present time, created a local Task Force to decide how best to address the situation. The conclusion was to forget about saving the hospital: "It was done." Rather, they agreed to increase the existing ambulance service by seven additional personnel to allow for coverage by three ambulances for twenty-four hours, seven days per week. Of course, this meant that the budgetary resources had to be found to cover the additional expenses. Mayor Smith initially proposed a 30 cent tax rate increase but the Council members objected. Now, several months later, with no other options available, the Mayor hopes to get Council agreement for the tax hike.

Another option the Mayor wished to pursue was to negotiate with West Tennessee Health Care to buy the public's ambulance service and provide private coverage throughout the community. This too was rebuffed initially by the rest of the Council but is now being reconsidered. Unless this is approved, the current ambulance service will continue to serve as what the Mayor calls a "rolling emergency room."

Budgetary impacts for providing this type of service are significant. Because many of the residents who use the ambulance service in this way are uninsured, and because insurance companies will not reimburse for many things done in the ambulance unless there is also a hospital visit, the costs have to be largely borne by the local government. The most recent year's tally indicated that the cost of running the ambulance service was 1.5 million dollars, of which only 900,000 dollars was reimbursed. This means that the community had to cover the marginal 600,000 dollars of operations without the benefit of any reimbursement. Mayor Smith said that the residents of the community will have to bear the burden of a third consecutive year of tax increases to help cover these extraordinary operating expenses.

One hope for the community lies in the Tennessee Valley-certified, 3100-acre megasite. Numerous prospects have looked at the site and may be deterred from agreeing to locate there due to the absence of a hospital in the community. Nonetheless, the Mayor believes that, if a large tenant does locate on the site, there will be sufficient demand created to justify building an emergency room.

On the one hand, one hesitates to place all of their hopes on attracting one large employer. On the other hand, however, the ambulance trip by road to the nearest hospital, which is in Jackson, Tennessee, can be 2.5–3 hours. For the cases that require immediate attention there is an air ambulance service called Hospital Wings but there are gaps in scheduling and other challenges, which is why the mayor is placing his hopes on attracting a user for the mega-site. One deterrent to this solution is that there will be a 24-month delay between the time an employer signs on the dotted line and the time when the site and building can be made ready. The community is generally skeptical about its ability to attract another employer to the area in the absence of health and other services.

Still another unsupportable service is the United States Post Office. Efficiency dictates that post offices conduct so many transactions per year in order to support the costs of labor, space, and operations. While it is difficult to argue with that logic, the closing of a post office does more than inconvenience the residents of small, rural towns; it also means that businesses will not come to the community because it will bear greater costs for shipping small products and bills from such a location. While other post offices nearby may be within reach, one must consider the costs of transportation and productivity to do so.

Post offices in small towns are often the designated gathering places for new collection and social interaction. In Truxton, Missouri, for example, "When a tornado was spotted in the area, residents gathered at the post office until the threat passed. After the terrorist attacks on 9–11, the town held a candlelight vigil in front of it."[19]

Podkul writes that nearly 80 percent of the post offices under consideration for closing at the time of this writing are "in sparsely populated rural areas, where poverty rates are higher than the national average . . . Moreover, about one-third of the post offices slated for closure fall within areas with limited or no wired broadband Internet."[20] Such communities will be unable to attract new businesses—or, new residents—and will simply continue to decline until they too must close their doors. It is not always a matter of driving a little further to obtain postal services. In May, 2011, the Postal Service announced the closure of more than 40 branches in the State of Iowa alone. Two months later, the Postal Service added 178 more Iowa post offices to the closure list.[21] Broad regions of the state were left without delivery and other services. Given the travel time and vehicle expenses, one report estimated the annual costs to the 337 businesses in the northwest region of the state to exceed 136,000 dollars, and the total costs for residents to be nearly 75,000 dollars.[22] The impact on these communities and their ability to attract—and even retain—employers is immeasurable.

Of course, retailers with insufficiently large customer bases will also depart or shut their doors. This represents a further hit to the downtown and also means that the downtown has less potential to make a comeback because, in a small town, it is typically the downtown merchants who promote the community and its businesses and who represent the only vibrancy in the community. Smaller communities have long recognized that their main street is the first thing that potential employers see. If it is neat and attractive, it will become a selling point. If there are significant vacancies, it will become a detriment when trying to attract someone new to town. For that reason, many communities spend considerable resources on beautifying their downtown areas and on trying to attract small retailers and other employers as well as seeking out large manufacturers or other employers outside of the downtown.

Among the retail establishments that close will be the local banks. Banks require a certain level of deposits and loan activity to remain viable. As the population of the city and the commerce within the city declines, banks pass that point and close. Epstein writes that "Empty bank branches are starting to litter small town business districts across the nation as the financial institutions that own them focus on larger communities."[23] This is one area that is of particular concern for small towns because, while it is true that individuals and companies in small towns without a bank branch can still operate by banking online, businesses tend to want to have a person relationship with their bankers. If that is not possible, the community becomes less attractive to new employers and less able to retain its existing employers.

These types of losses paint a picture of many small towns in rural America beginning to die off with very little opportunity to reverse their fortunes because the loss of services portends an additional loss of population that, in turn, means the loss of more services. It is a situation that will be considered inhospitable to new business formations. Many small towns and rural areas have managed to survive and even thrive and, of course, not all small towns have died away when the primary employer departed so there must be a potential solution, at least for some.

There are a few absolutes when attempting to rebuild a small, rural economic base. First, the public sector cannot do so alone. Small towns are just that—they are too small for the public sector officials to prepare for redevelopment alone. There must be a concerted effort on the part of the entire community: public and private, residents and organizations, and those who live within the city limits and those who live outside of town. And, when several towns or towns and the rural areas outside them collaborate, there may be a better case to be made for the retention of such vital institutions as schools, post offices, bank branches, hospitals and emergency rooms, and grocery and department stores.

The combined effort of the community, and even the region, must then initiate a thoughtful process to plan the approach to redevelopment of the broader economy. It may or may not need to prepare a full strategic plan but it does need to think strategically about what makes sense for the community and how best to pursue those possibilities. Part of that consideration must be the inclusion of outside parties that can be helpful.

Federal and state grants and other support may be obtained to further and facilitate the effort. Local universities often assist small towns with counsel, data analysis, and the preparation of marketing plans and materials.

Downtown associations may also be potential contributors to the thought and implementation process. This will be a vital link because the downtowns are usually the focus of small town redevelopment and such groups are adept at figuring out the most likely markets for small towns. Certainly, the beautification of the downtown will make any community more attractive to potential new employers and residents.

Many small, rural communities are fortunate to be close enough to a natural asset that can be developed or used as a tourism or other type of economic development marketing strategy. This might include lakes, mountains, ski resorts, bike or off-road trails, or historic sites such as battlefields or ancient ruins. Tourism can be a strong economic driver, albeit sometimes highly sensitive to economic peaks and troughs. Once an attraction has been developed or refurbished for visitation, the locality may see an increase in hotels and motels, restaurants, gas stations, artisans, retailers, and tour guides. In the case of historic sites, historic preservation can sometimes attract financial support.

Other rural small towns have started their redevelopment process by cleaning up the downtown, updating building façades, creating activities such skating parks or swimming pools. By making the downtown more pedestrian-friendly, cities can ensure that people will step out of their vehicles and walk around. At the other extreme, parks and open areas— especially along lakes or riverfronts—are attractions to many who live in rural areas.

Many communities have created events to attract visitors and support local retailers. These can range from fishing competitions, kite and hot air balloon festivals, book fairs, and marathon races. Community events create gathering spaces and town squares and downtown areas typically begin to thrive again when these events become successful. This means that towns pursuing such a strategy need to erect viewing areas, park benches, and the various creature comforts required by mid-sized or larger crowds.

In order to accelerate the pace of change in small downtowns, some communities have offered tax breaks for businesses that spruce up their shops or replace aging façades. Others have offered low-interest or no-interest loans for such purposes. Some have determined new uses for old, vacant buildings in the downtown. Some can be used as business incubators or artists' lofts, either of which can promote and spur economic development. The tree canopies that line many small town Main Streets can become overgrown. One simple task that has been employed is to raise and trim those canopies so that downtown can be seen more thoroughly. The re-paving and re-lining of streets can also have the effect of beautifying the downtown, and free, accessible parking can make the downtown feel more friendly and welcoming.

Economic growth issues in rural communities do have some commonalities with their larger colleagues but, of course, they also have distinct challenges and distinct assets to market. The economic development prospects that will be inclined to consider rural or small town locations for their businesses fall into one of two categories.

First, people who grew up in small town or rural environments and miss being in them are good targets for these communities. Perhaps they miss the slower pace of life or the sense of community that one finds in such a setting; or, perhaps they wish to give their children the same kind of experiences they had when they were young. It may also be that they have aging parents or family members to whom they would like to be near. Again, site location decisions are made by human beings and quite often more for human than purely business reasons.

The second type of economic development prospect that will seek locations in small town or rural settings are those who do so for purely business reasons. Manufacturers or distribution facilities that are focused on lower-cost labor pools or land may consider these locations. Ease of access to suppliers or transportation routes might be reasons for rural locations as well.

Rural communities also have image issues to overcome when appealing to businesses to consider them as a location for facilities. Poverty rates in rural areas are often believed to be very high; however, the National Research Council reported that when a cost of living factor is introduced to the equation, "rural poverty rates go from being 25 percent higher than urban rates to 12 percent lower."[24]

But, small towns and rural areas also have issues to confront when selling their communities that larger urban centers do not. To some extent, the very size of the population within a given catchment area defines the size of a business that can be supported. However, as important as the numbers of potential employees available in the existing workforce will be the ability to attract additional workers, with the relevant skills, to the region. This will be dependent upon the overall quality of life, the quality of the local public school systems, affordability, spousal employment opportunities, and other personal and family factors.

Businesses will also be concerned about the quality of the workforce. Does it possess the necessary skills—both hard skills and soft skills—for the business prospect's operations? What has been the experience of other local businesses with the existing workforce? Are their institutions nearby that can support the training and retraining needs of the company? Potential employers will be very interested in the relative education levels or the workforce. They will also seek information about the workforce performance and work ethic from existing employers. Lower levels of education in the local workforce can often be offset for a potential employer if there are relevant training options in the region.

For many businesses requiring technology capabilities, younger workers are particularly attractive. What are the demographics of the community and does it have the types of assets and amenities that will help attract such individuals? And, even if the community does have young people in the workforce who may or may not possess higher levels of today's technologies, the region will still need to have the technology infrastructure that enables those men and women to perform efficiently. Many businesses thrive in rural areas by applying technology to their production and distribution functions (Figure 17.1).

Businesses that are engaged in manufacturing and transshipments will need to be assured that the community will be sufficiently proximate to the required suppliers and that they will be able to store and transport their products once ready for market. Are there facilities for storage available? Are the distances to highways or shipping options or air freight services convenient and reasonably priced?

There is always a human element involved in site location decisions. Employers who move to a new location will need to be assured that their employees will be comfortable and happy. Further, they will want to be able to attract additional workers from outside the area, and they will have the same requirements. Are the schools good enough? Are there

Figure 17.1 Rural Technologies to Support Growth
Source: Shutterstock

things to do nearby, including outdoor and indoor activities, shopping, and dining? Are there the types of churches we need? There are as many of these types of questions as there are decision-makers. A rural community can put its best foot forward by beautifying its downtown and ensuring high quality public services for residents, especially public education.

Housing represents a special consideration for rural areas. Quite often, the issue of housing for a large city or region relates to affordability and proximity to the site of the business. For small towns and rural settings, the issue is more often related to availability. Several of the interviews conducted in previous research indicated that small towns are simply not prepared to receive hundreds of new employees because they have no homes for them to rent or purchase. With adequate advance notice, communities can sometimes erect sufficient housing over the course of a year or more but that may be inadequate if the company expects to get in and get started more quickly. In circumstances where the new employer is planning to build a facility, there may be more time available for the planning and construction of homes but that also requires a builder who is both willing and able to build the homes that quickly.

This is a tricky matter and has been a serious problem for business attraction from many rural and small town communities. And, a related problem is the inability of the local governments to staff up the public schools or to provide additional utility access and other technology infrastructure to the new areas. Many stories have been told by people who grew up in small towns and couldn't wait to move to the "big city." Carr and Kefalas address this:

> The flight of young adults is a natural occurrence . . . with devastating consequences for the communities left behind. Scattered throughout the nation, thousands of towns find themselves twenty, ten, even five years away from extinction because there are too few taxpayers, consumers and workers to keep going. For many locales, the final death knell is when there are too few children to keep the doors of the area schools open.[25]

As some families leave small towns in search of better employment or better schools for their children, it often becomes clear that those who have left were the best and most skilled. They departed because, given their skill sets, they were able to find better opportunities. This means that the workforce that is left behind is often less educated, less skilled, and perhaps less driven to succeed.

If one accepts the notion that there is typically a direct correlation between the education and skill levels of the parents and the educational performance and attainment of their children, one can imagine difficulties for the schools after the exodus of workers and their families. Renfro wrote that "Rural areas struggling to rebuild their economy are challenged by low educational attainment among their population, limited financial resources, and a lack of infrastructure."[26] But, Renfro also observes that: "rural areas matter, this generation of workers matters, effective community development involves the entire community . . . informed, healthy communities focus on their assets, and change is difficult and takes a long time."[27] The lesson for other communities is that the public schools in the area are an economic development asset, demanding, in even the most difficult budgetary times. Companies will review the quality and performance of an area's public schools before even considering a site in the community relative to other areas. Not only will the site location decision-makers want their children in high-performing schools, but they may want to be able to attract a strong workforce to their facility from other locations, and they too will want to know about the schools their children will attend before considering a position.

Small towns have numerous challenges to growing and sustaining their local economic bases. The inability to develop new businesses in small towns may be widening the gap between them and their larger metropolitan counterparts.

> From 2010 through 2014, US counties with 100,000 or fewer residents combined to lose more businesses than they created . . . In the recovery that began in 1992, by comparison, those counties created a third of the nation's net new businesses.[28]

Net business losses in these smaller communities ran about 20 percent in the 1990s but rose to about 40 percent in the first decade of the new millennium. Between 2000 and 2014, the total ran up to about two-thirds of all businesses in the small communities.[29]

One particular concern that has been aired has been the impact of chain stores such as Walmart. When the stores entered small communities, they drive out the small, so-called "Mom and Pop" stores. Small independent businesses cannot sustain lower prices for long periods of time. Walmart can do exactly that; then, once the others have gone out of business, they raise their prices back to where they wanted them to be. However, in 2012, Walmart announced the closing of 269 stores across the country including more than 100 of their Express stores, smaller ventures that served rural areas. This left many small towns and rural areas without access to necessary foods and other items. "Walmart's decision to storm into rural areas and destroy the competition before abruptly pulling up shop has arguably decimated entire towns."[30]

Other charges have been leveled at the large retail chains. They are unattractive and take up large parcels of land, much of which is for parking. The profits do not stay in the community. Rather, they return to the home offices of Walmart Incorporated. Further, the loss of main street, home-grown retailers means the loss of community-based shops and employers. These are people who support the local churches, schools, scout troops, little leagues, and more. Finally, the community loses its charm and its appeal to travelers who may come to visit little specialty and other shops.

Small towns also lose essential services when a Walmart leaves town. According to the Institute for Local Self-Reliance, "The loss of locally-owned stores and the pace of retail consolidation is staggering. Eleven thousand independent pharmacies have shut their doors since 1990" and "local hardware stores are on the decline, while two companies have captured 30 percent of the market." An Iowa-based study indicates that a new Walmart store takes 84 percent of its revenue from existing stores in the community.[31] And, perhaps most devastatingly, when the Walmart leaves town, "The town is left with a dead Main Street and nothing to show for it."[32] The very identity of the town has been indelibly altered and even the community's sense of self-worth has been jeopardized or sacrificed.

Dave Nichols is the Mayor of Monticello, Mississippi, and has been for nearly 20 years. His small town lost a primary employer at the very end of the 1990s. A Killwood plant that had manufactured dress shirts for L.L. Bean and work pants for J.C. Penney's and Sears closed its doors, laying off its 400 employees. For a small town such as Monticello—in a rural area of southwestern Mississippi—this was a devastating event. And, as a small, rural community, there was little political clout to bring in to help advance the city.

Many of the people who lost their jobs remained in place and some were able to find new positions. A Georgia Pacific plant manufactured materials for cardboard boxes, and other employers were in and around the city. But, it was not sufficient for the mayor simply to sit back and hope that things would work out. He established an economic and community development office to work on business attraction and community improvement projects. Over time, there were a few new employers lured to the area and retailers began to re-open along the main thoroughfares of Monticello.

When asked about landing one major employer or attracting and growing a number of small employers, Mayor Nichols opined that "landing a large fish is unlikely; I think we can pull in a few minnows." Small towns are indeed unlikely to be able to attract one major employer and are much more likely to develop a cadre of smaller businesses that will grow over time. And, certainly, the economy would be more stable well into the future with numerous employers rather than one major employer which, like Killwood, could eliminate 400 jobs practically overnight. The city's tax base was also hard hit by the company's departure but it did not raise the tax rate; in fact, it did not have to do so.

This is where the city benefitted from a bit of good luck and keen insight. Mayor Nichols examined county records and discovered that several businesses had been listed as being in the county when they were actually within the city limits. As such, the city was able to recoup from the county the past three years of taxes paid and that held them over until new businesses could be attracted to town.

Despite the good fortune of having back tax payments coming in from the county, the Mayor learned a valuable lesson: "Don't sit back and complain, 'Oh, poor me.' You have to become even more insightful than ever before in order to figure out how to come back." A second lesson relates to seeing one's full problems and challenges. Others sometimes see differently that which has been right in front of people all the time. But, they see it through different lenses. Areas of the community that are dirty or falling down, do not help to present the entire community well to others. And, if bad enough, they will discourage employers from coming to town. As Mayor Nichols quoted: "Why should I invest here?"

The State of Mississippi has a program called Asset Mapping through which it brought in outside observers to chart the needs of the city. This is a unique approach to completing an asset gap analysis. As a result, older, dirty areas of the city were cleaned up and land along the Pearl River was acquired by the city and developed for trails and other uses. This helped to drive more traffic to the area and to revive the city's retailers.

Small, rural communities that are reasonably proximate to large metropolitan areas can often play off of the metro area by providing goods, services, and facilities that the metro area cannot itself easily provide for its employers. As one moves closer to a metropolitan area, the population densities tend to increase, yielding greater demand for relatively scarce land. This applies both to housing and office space or other commercial applications. The combination of relatively scarce land parcels for further development and the resulting higher costs for land and buildings yields higher prices. Another consequence is a workforce that is most compatible with the employers in the region.

However, businesses in the region may also require a variety of business support that is more appropriate for the workforce and land values of the exurbs and beyond. Small rural towns, as long as they are within a relatively easy reach of the regional employment, can provide the needed support businesses. What does "proximate" mean in this case? The answer to that question can only come from the employers themselves and will vary depending on the needs, the individuals, and the competition from other communities to provide those services.

Employers that can support the metropolitan-based companies and be located in areas further out may include storage and shipment facilities, a wide range of technology and other back office functions, assembly and distribution, manufacturing and printing services. These cities and towns can provide any office function that does not require the same skills sets or Class A office locations. Such communities can also provide weekend getaways for residents who are seeking a less-stressful location for recreation, festivals, or other day trips.

Notes

1 Dirk Johnson. Population Decline in Rural America: A Product of Advances in Technology. (September 11, 1990) www.nytimes.com

2 Sara Solovitch. *At Big Sur: A Sudden Surge in Isolation*. (Washington, DC: Washington Post, April 14, 2017): A-1.
3 Phillipe Aghion and Steven N. Durlauf. *Handbook of Economic Growth*, vol. 1B. (San Diego, CA: Elsevier, 2005): 1546.
4 Robert Samuels. Feeling Snubbed but Pushing Forward. Washington, DC: *Washington Post*, August 9, 2017): A-1 and A-16.
5 Ed Merriman. Oregon Timber Industry: Pain Lingers. (October 10, 2010) www.bendbulletin.com
6 Jonathan Q. Morgan and William Lambe. Find a Way to Make One. *Economic Development Journal*, vol. 8, no. 3. (Washington, DC: International Economic Development Council, Summer 2009): 5.
7 Nora Johnson, Adhir Kackar, and Melissa Kramer. *How Small Towns and Cities Can Use Local Assets to Rebuild Their Economies: Lessons From Successful Places*. (Washington, DC: Environmental Protection Agency, May 2015).
8 Greg Grisolano. The Factory town that Lost its Factory. (August 20, 2012) www.stry.us
9 Ibid.
10 Ibid.
11 Steve Moyer. California-Based Company Poised to Redevelop O'Sullivan Plant. (October 27, 2007) http://nevadadailymail.com
12 Andra Bryan Stefanoni. Lamar County Finds its Niche After O'Sullivan Plant Closed. (September 12, 2012) www.joplinglobe.com
13 Nona Aronowitz. Class Dismissed, Forever: Rural School Faces Closure. (June 27, 2014) www.nbcnews.com
14 *Bangor Daily News*. Closing Small Town Schools. (Bangor, Maine): February 11, 2011. http://bangordailynews.com
15 Amy Goldstein. Rural America's Dying Hospitals. (Washington, DC: *Washington Post*, April 12, 2017): A-1, A-6.
16 Chris Woolston. Medicine in a Small, Small Town. (June 1, 2010) www.aarp.org
17 Guy Gugliotta. Rural Hospitals, One of the Cornerstones of Small Town Life, Face Changing Pressure. (March 17, 2015) www.usnews.com
18 Sharon Cohen. Doing Without Hospitals: Rural Towns Suffer But Cope Without Care. (Associated Press, December 4, 1988)
19 Jake Wagman. Small Town Post Offices: Going, Going ... Gone? (February 4, 2012) https://parade.com
20 Cezary Podkul and Emily Stephenson. Special Report: Towns Go Dark with Post Office Closings. (February 14, 2012) www.reuters.com
21 Smart Solutions Group. April 2012. *Impact of the Closure of Post Offices in Northwest Iowa*. (West Des Moines, IA: Smart Solutions Group): 3.
22 Ibid., 5.
23 Victor Epstein. Bank Branches Vanishing in Small Towns. (march 2, 2014) www.usatoday.com
24 Richard E. Wood. *The Survival of Rural America: Small Victories and Bitter Harvests*. (Lawrence, KS, MA: The University of Kansas Press, 2008): 17.
25 Patrick J. Carr and Maria J. Kefalas. *Hollowing Out the Middle: The Rural Brain Drain and what it Means for America*. (Boston, MA: Beacon Press, 2009): 2.
26 Bonnie R. Renfro. *Program for the Rural Carolinas*. (Washington, DC: International Economic Development Council, Winter 2005): 18.
27 Ibid.,19.
28 Jim Tankersley. A Very Bad Sign for All But America's Biggest Cities. (May 22, 2016) www.chicagotribune.com
29 Ibid.
30 Ethan Wolff-Mann. The New Way That Walmart is Ruining America's Small Towns. (January 25, 2016) www.time.com
31 Stacy Mitchell. The Impact of Chain Stores on Community. (April 18, 2000) http://ilsr.org
32 Ibid.

References

Aghion, Phillipe and Durlauf, Steven N. *Handbook of Economic Growth*, vol. 1B. San Diego, CA: Elsevier, 2005.

Aronowitz, Nona. Class Dismissed, Forever: Rural School Faces Closure. June 27, 2014. www.nbcnews.com

Bangor Daily News. Closing Small Town Schools. February 11, 2011. http://bangordailynews.com

Carr, Patrick J. and Kefalas, Maria J. *Hollowing Out the Middle: The Rural Brain Drain and What it Means for America*. Boston, MA: Beacon Press, 2009.

Cohen, Sharon. Doing Without Hospitals: Rural Towns Suffer but Cope Without Care. December 4, 2088. http://articles.latimes.com

Epstein, Victor. Bank Branches Vanishing in Small Towns. March 2, 2014. www.usatoday.com

Goldstein, Amy. Rural America's Dying Hospitals. *Washington Post*, April 12, 2017.

Grisolano, Greg. The Factory Town that Lost its Factory. August 20, 2012. www.stry.us

Gugliotta, Guy. Rural Hospitals, One of the Cornerstones of Small Town Life, Face Changing Pressure. March 17, 2015. www.usnews.com

Johnson, Dirk. Population Decline in Rural America: A Product of Advances in Technology. September 11, 1990. www.nytimes.com

Johnson, Nora, Kackar, Adhir, and Kramer, Melissa. *How Small Towns and Cities Can Use Local Assets to Rebuild Their Economies: Lessons From Successful Places*. Washington, DC: Environmental Protection Agency, May 2015.

Merriman, Ed. Oregon Timber Industry: Pain Lingers. October 10, 2010. www.bendbulletin.com

Mitchell, Stacy. The Impact of Chain Stores on Community. April 18, 2000. http://ilsr.org

Morgan, Jonathan Q. and Lambe, William. Find a Way to Make One. *Economic Development Journal*, vol. 8, no. 3. Washington, DC: International Economic Development Council, Summer 2009: 4–13.

Moyer, Steve. California-Based Company Poised to Redevelop O'Sullivan Plant. October 27, 2007. http://nevadadailymail.com

Podkul, Cezary and Stephenson, Emily. Special Report: Towns Go Dark with Post Office Closings. February 14, 2012. www.reuters.com

Renfro, Bonnie R. *Program for the Rural Carolinas*. International Economic Development Council. 18–23, Winter 2005.

Samuels, Robert. Feeling Snubbed but Pushing Forward. *Washington Post*, August 9, 2017.

Smart Solutions Group. Impact of the Closure of Post Offices in Northwest Iowa. West Des Moines, IA: Smart Solutions Group, April 2012.

Solovitch, Sara. At Big Sur, A Sudden Taste of Isolation. *Washington Post*. April 14, 2017.

Stefanoni, Andra Bryan. Lamar County Finds Its Niche After O'Sullivan Plant Closed. September 12, 2012. www.joplinglobe.com

Tankersley, Jim. May 22, 2016. A Very Bad Sign for All But America's Biggest Cities. May 22, 2016. www.chicagotribune.com

Wagman, Jake. Small Town Post Offices: Going, Going ... Gone? February 24, 2012. https://parade.com

Wolff-Mann, Ethan. The New Way that Walmart is Ruining America's Small Towns. January 25, 2016. http://time.com

Wood, Richard E. *Survival of Rural America: Small Victories and Bitter Harvests*. Lawrence, KS: University of Kansas Press, 2008.

Woolston, Chris. Medicine in a Small, Small Town. June 1, 2010. www.aarp.org

Part V
The Process
Initiating and Sustaining Local Economic Growth

If there is one critical thing that has been learned by communities of all types and in all situations, it is this: While economic growth and sustainability can be taken for granted for short periods, it cannot be assumed over the long term. Further, while a community may coast for short periods and sustain an economy, it cannot sit by idly and expect economic growth to *return* to the community once it has been lost.

Not all economic growth simply occurs under its own momentum. It must be envisioned, wooed, and ultimately nurtured. Local officials must do that for which they were elected and appointed: they must lead. It is not easy—largely because it is not always popular, and always because one person's success is another's disappointment. Jobs in a community may mean construction in places where some people do not want it to occur. It may mean new people coming to town; and, some of them may get the best jobs. The local leadership cannot simply react to these concerns. They must foresee them and tackle the most difficult issues before they become targets.

This requires a lot from public officials: vision, creativity, and—most of all—a willingness to take risks that will have long-term potential impacts. Even more importantly, they must be able to take risks for which they will be questioned in the short term and someone else may get the credit in the long term. It may also mean that resources put to projects or economic development marketing now will have to be drawn from other line items in the local budget while, again, the returns on those investments will come back later to be allocated by others.

The considerations of what the community product needs in order to become more attractive to economic development prospects is not somethings that the elected officials and their staffs can assess for themselves. Clearly, if the intent is to build a community that is more attractive to businesses, the input of business executives is vital for the plan to succeed. When communities begin to develop their economic development plans, the counsel of many must be considered: businesses; institutions such as hospitals, colleges and universities, airports; and, of course, the residents.

Once the future has been envisioned and plans decided upon, the implementation phases begin, during which time the expectations of the community must be carefully managed lest people believe that they have been misled and demand more immediate returns than are feasible. For the implementation of an economic development (product) strategic plan to be maximally successful, it will require the entire community to embrace it.

18 Vision, Planning, and Selling the Plan

Envisioning a future for a community is often received the wrong way. Elected officials sometimes believe that, if they can imagine the ideal community of the future, they can make it happen given sufficient time and resources. Regrettably, that is simply not true. Many communities over the past several years have determined that they would become a technology hub, and that they would become the "Silicon Valley" of Kansas or Illinois.

In fact, at one time in the United States there were more than 65 communities that were vying to become known as the "Silicon Prairie." There were so many at one point that several suits were filed to claim the official recognition as the Silicon Prairie. Curiously, because prairies are typically in the middle of the country and silicon is on the coasts, the very term seems to have been oxymoronic.

Those were only the locales that wanted to addend their communities' names to "prairie." There were others that staked their claims to the Silicon—Gulch, Corridor, Glen, Fen, Dominion, and more. Many more. None of these made sense. Vision is not cute. Vision is not idealistic. Vision must be realistic. It must incorporate the most ideal situation that is possible within the context of community assets and needs.

How, then does one define what is possible for a community. There are two ways of planning for the economic growth of a community. One can inventory those present assets that will be attractive to businesses and seek to attract *only* those businesses for which those assets are relevant. Some assets that are present within a community may be attractive to some businesses but not to others. Attempting to use them where they are not an apt fit will just waste time and resources.

The second path to planning is to envision the community one wants and then to complete an inventory and determine the assets that are important to the target businesses that have been identified in the plan. Where gaps exist in the needs of such companies, the community must incorporate into the plan the means of acquiring the assets that are missing. This can be expensive and take extended periods of time but it is a way not only to grow the economic base but to advance it as well.

The critical piece of the visioning element of strategic planning is to recognize that every new activity must come at the expense of something else. Whether the pursuit of the new assets utilizes financial resources or human resources, those are resources that cannot be applied to other line items in the local budgets. Thus, elected officials must be willing and able to make the argument effectively that investments in the future economic growth of the community are worth the short-term sacrifice of funds for public schools, roads, libraries, and all of the other components of the community's overall quality of life.

It is sometimes difficult to convince people to sacrifice immediate needs for longer-term benefit, especially when the element of risk is greater. However, that is precisely what their elected officials must do. It has often helped them to do so in communities around the United States by selling the program in ways that yield more emotional reactions. In other words, an argument that today's investments will yield a given amount of dollars tomorrow will only go so far. Much more appealing to many would be an argument that demonstrates how today's investments can yield smaller classroom sizes in the next five years or a new firehouse in two years or a new road maintenance next fiscal year.

The vision is the beginning of the strategizing. It is critical because it frames all of the conversations that follow, however it represents only the tip of the iceberg. The vision only portrays that which the community reasonably feels it wants to become within the context of what it *can* become. The rest of the process is devoted to the "how." How do we decide what the necessary component parts are? How can we agree upon what is most important and set priorities? How can we manage the costs—both human and capital—without raising taxes? There are innumerable "how" questions to ask. And, finally, when all is said and done, all the community really has is a design and hope.

There is no guarantee that it will be able to make all of this come true. One pundit once said that "Strategic planning is like driving a car while looking out the rear window." All it really represents is an ideal picture of the possible future that is the most likely to be workable only because we collectively thought it through rather than just letting it happen. While it is no guarantee, it is generally the best one can hope for.

And we still haven't gotten to the really hard part: implementation. Now we have a plan and perhaps some resources to begin. But, before getting to the implementation phase, the leadership needs to ensure that all of the relevant stakeholders are both conversant with and in support of the plan and its costs and consequences.

A study of this nature may serve several purposes. The primary purpose of this research has been to document the experience of cities and regions—both positive and negative—so that other cities and regions can gain insights that may benefit them as they move through similar sets of circumstances. It is also possible that communities can learn from this about more than just how to extricate themselves from such situations; there is a possibility that city and regional leaders can become so sensitized to the causes and effects of economic decline and revitalization that they can learn to see the approaching storms and move to avoid them rather than awaiting the devastation they can cause before designing a plan of response.

This begs the question: How can one know economic decline when it is approaching? What is there to look for? If one considers the various sections of this book and the lessons about how to grow and either develop or redevelop a city's economy, part of the answer becomes clear. A city that is overly dependent upon a single industry or a single employer—or even a relatively few employers—is at risk. This is even true if there is such disbelief in the community. If a local economy is based on the production of outmoded products—or, if the means of production are outmoded—it too is headed for an economic decline.

Cities that have thriving suburban economies and economic malaise in the downturn—or cities that have adjoining thriving and declining neighborhoods—are facing certain problems. Cities that have clusters for which competitive locations are becoming more aggressive about acquiring the resources and institutions that support those clusters may see an economic downturn approaching.

Cities that have paid too much attention to the offering of each or tax-based incentives at the exclusion of enhanced public services run the risk of being able to attract—and retain—employees only by buying them, rather than by establishing an environment in which their businesses can thrive. Cities that gain a reputation for being inhospitable to commerce, or that try to maintain a static position in the economy should also be able to foresee disaster.

When the potential pitfalls are observed prior to their local onset, communications can sometimes prepare and attempt to stave off some of the difficulties *before* they occur. This may mean targeting a more diversified set of industries in the economic development outreach programs, or the development of community assets that will help to attract and retain businesses, or the identification of public policies that stand in the way of business growth and expansion. Addressing these concerns before they become issues to be resolved also sends a strong message to the business community—present and prospective—that this is a city that is pro-business and knows how to address their collective needs.

Creating a vision for the community is a critical, though often under-considered portion of the plan and the planning process. In many cases, a vision is put forward to the community by the senior elected officials or the board. In some instances, the vision has been drawn from a campaign statement or promise. This is not what a community needs to help drive its economic development process.

A vision statement is typically a brief description of where the community wants to be in the future; it is the ideal conception of what development can bring to a city, town, or region. Political statements—and, certainly campaign promises—are typically short-term and can sometimes reflect a mid-point on the way to a vision. A candidate—or office-holder—wants to paint a picture either of how a community's immediate problems can be resolved or of what can be accomplished in his or her term of office.

A community vision should look forward to a more distant future. It should not just announce to the residents of Detroit that the east side will be cleaned up or that jobs will be brought back to the city. Nor should it be a lengthy recitation of how the city will overcome traditional obstacles and return manufacturing jobs while diversifying the economy, and more. The vision for the City of Detroit should be something like: Detroit will be return to its historical place as one of the nation's great cities and a great place to live, work, and visit.

For a smaller community, or even a rural area, less grandiose forecasts make good vision statements. A city or town of perhaps 100,000 residents in a less dense region than Detroit might create a vision statement such as Grow and Beautify Springfield; and a small town might envision being a Great Place to Live and Visit.

Clearly, vision statements are not greatly useful in driving progress, but they can be used effectively to create energy and pride, as well as volunteerism toward achieving that view of the future. Because those are potential outcomes from the process that results in a clear vision of the future, it is always a good idea to develop the vision and other parts of the community's strategic plan by encouraging input from a broad group of community stakeholders. Such a group should include residents, businesses and business organizations, institutions in the area, and local government officials. In the absence of discussion leading up to the creation of a community vision, such individuals need to be solicited for their agreement and support.

The critical thing to recall about a strategic planning process for communities is that all steps must be consistent with and lead to the accomplishment of the previous steps. Now that we know what the community's vision is, the mission statement of the organization managing the processes leading to it (typically the local government or governments) can be developed. The mission statement will define clearly what the roles and responsibilities of the local government are that specifically lead to the achievement of the vision.

The critical part of a local strategic plan follows: the goals, objectives, tactics, measurements, and the assignment of responsibilities. These result from a comprehensive analysis of the environments (plural!) in which the community will exist and in which the community will need to operate if it is to move inexorably closer to its vision of the future. Such analyses are the results of a "scanning" process. There are numerous names for this process; my preference is the Environmental Scan. It is noteworthy that the process itself quite often has far greater value than the product. This is not a process best done by an individual, or by a group of individuals (say, local government employees or elected officials) who tend to think alike. To the contrary, the best environmental scanning processes are those that are more inclusive rather than less.

Environmental scans that incorporate people from the business community and the schools and community institutions (e.g., hospitals, airports, colleges and universities) are more likely to result in a manageable and collaborative implementation phase. More importantly, plans that are the result of more expansive groups of participants are better accepted in the community and lead to much greater involvement over time from diverse parts of the community.

The environmental scanning process entails evaluations of every pertinent factor within all of the various environments in which the city or region will exist in the future. Environments might include the city, the region, relevant national and global factors, as well as internal factors including budgets and staffing, potential for volunteerism, and more. Within each environment, a variety of factors should be reviewed, including personnel and budgetary considerations, capabilities, technologies that are available as well as the changing nature of technology that can be applied to future actions.

The scanning process is the component of strategic planning that takes the greatest thought and requires the widest array of opinions. It also typically takes the longest time to complete and is often the least agreed-upon section of an economic development strategic plan for a community. It is appropriate that that is the case because, in short, what is involved is seeing the future and arriving at a consensus as to what it will bring and what that will mean for the community.

How to deal with the future and what strategies to pursue and what tactics to implement come later in the process but they are absolutely based on what the group sees as the future set of circumstances for the community in question. As such, and because different people have different thoughts about what the future will be like, great debates often ensue from this part of the process. Consider that many people from different walks of life and in widely different circumstances are creating a "crystal ball" view of what has not yet happened. Further, because everyone in the planning sessions knows that future strategies will be based on this collective view of the future, individuals tend to disagree. In some cases, participants–whether consciously or subconsciously—argue for a view of the future that is consistent with their individual interests. For this reason, a professional strategic planning facilitator is a useful means of negotiating these difficult discussions. He or she can help to ensure that no one individual dominates the discussions and that all voices are heard. And, reaching compromise positions is not always the objective. Compromises are positions that are mid-way between two opposing positions. The objective is the greatest clarity about what is ahead, not merely something to which every participant can agree.

The environmental scanning process is also a critical piece of the strategic planning exercise because it is the phase during which the greatest degree of strategic thinking takes place. The greatest value of a strategic planning process for economic development is likely to be in the open exchange of ideas and principles that will govern the future economic development of the community, whether large or small.

The essential objectives of a scanning process for economic development are twofold. First, it is crucial to have a great diversity of community stakeholders participate in the review of the forces facing the community that may inhibit the accomplishment of goals leading to the future vision of the community. The second reason environmental scans are conducted is to extract an agreed-upon set of problems and opportunities. This is widely known as the SWOT analysis: What did our scan of the various environments indicate are the strengths and weaknesses of our community and its organizations, institutions, and assets; what are the opportunities we see that will help us achieve our vision; and, what are the threats to doing so?

The strengths and weaknesses components of that exercise are inward-looking assessments. Do we have the right personnel? Is the budget in the best shape to address future needs and gap analyses? What is the community in need of adding or improving or eliminating in order to be able to develop the economy as we wish?

The external view of what is happening is found in the opportunities and threats phases of the discussion. These may be local opportunities or those that the local community can use to its advantage. For example, a growing national economy or growth in a nearby metropolitan area may translate into increased visitation at local attractions. A new highway near the city or town can imply opportunities to attract travelers and businesses. A new program at the local college may mean that there will be companies that could locate nearby to take advantage of the research being done or to hire the graduating students.

Threats have similar implications. Losing an air route at the closest airport may mean that companies that relied on that service to move their people or products will begin to consider other locations for their offices or plants. A brain drain from the community may imply that there will be difficulties in attracting new firms.

These analyses, if done correctly, will make very clear what the potential goals should be. The word potential is very important in this sentence. At this point in the process, there is always a lengthy list of possibilities, all legitimate and all of which could lead to the achievement of the vision. It will become clear later in the process, however, that there are insufficient resources—either human or capital—to do all things at once. It is important to list all the possibilities at this point, however, because it may constitute a list for future planning reference.

The SWOT analysis then yields a list of goals that can take the community in the direction of its vision. Goals are generally broad statements of items to be accomplished although they typically are not measurable and they typically are long-term in nature. Many goals will likely be found in communities of all sizes and descriptions. These might include: expanding the tax base, improving building and permitting processes, focusing new development in designated revitalization areas, working toward eliminating income inequities, lower commercial vacancy rates, low unemployment rates, or attracting specific types of industries and jobs. Examples of economic development goals that may pertain more consistently to specific types and sizes of communities might include some of the following:

- For a region:
  - diversify the regional economy to minimize economic fluctuations;
  - coordinate workforce training among the region's colleges and universities to reflect workforce needs of the future;
  - develop a plan for sharing the costs of a new beltway around the city;
- For a large city:
  - clear land on the east side of town for office development;
  - establish new technology hub zones in revitalization districts;
  - promote greater economic diversification;
- For a mid-size city:
  - extend the rail line to the edge of town;
  - create cooperative programs between the three major employers in town and the colleges, universities, and the public school system;
  - develop an industrial or office park that will serve as an attraction for employers who can move in, build or occupy built space, and be functionally operational in a relatively short period of time;
- For a small town:
  - attract companies to the community that are not engaged in manufacturing processes;
  - generally promote greater economic diversification;
  - work with the community college to create programs of retraining for the former employees of the plant that closed this year;
- For rural areas:
  - design and build a business park near the interstate highway to accommodate distribution facilities and service facilities;
  - seek state or federal funding to develop or improve transportation networks that will facilitate getting agricultural or manufactured products to market.

EDAC/ACDE conducted research with Canadian economic developers and reported that 73 percent of all respondents measured new business openings, 61 percent measured job creation, and 59 percent measured the amount of investment attracted to their communities.[1] There was also an admonition received from those surveyed about what and how to measure economic development success. First, it is important not to try to measure everything; only measure the most important or critical tactics.

Professional economic developers are also very careful not to measure or to take credit for growth or development with which they had no involvement. Jobs in communities grow and wealth is created but not all of that is because of the economic development program; some of it occurs on its own and, as such, should not be measured and credited to the agency. Despite this admonition, many communities measure their economic development performance in terms of direct, indirect, and lasting impacts. A direct impact might be counted when an employer comes to town as the result of working with the economic development team. They may have provided information, conducted a site tour, provided an incentive, or some other distinct and demonstrative service that played a clear role in the employer's decision to select a site in the community rather than one elsewhere.

Indirect impacts are also fair game for economic development programs to claim, as long as they make it clear that they recognize that their role was indeed indirect. For example, a community may advertise and otherwise promote itself as a great location for a given industry segment. Over time, the growth of the industry has occurred and the community's economic development team takes credit for their indirect role in making that happen. Had it not been for their lengthy efforts to inform the industry of the local opportunities and assets, the company may not have considered it as a place to locate. Or, if the community had not identified the asset gaps and filled them in, the company may not have been able to locate there. Such efforts deserve credit for the indirect role in the employer's decision-making.

A third role for which an economic development program can claim a share of credit relates to the lasting impacts of its work. Consider that a company came to town with 50 new jobs in 2010. At that time, the economic development program played a direct role in working with the employer to influence its decision-making. Now, in 2017, the employer adds 50 more jobs. Because the company would not have been in the community in the first place without the efforts of the economic development professionals, its expansion would not have occurred without them as well. In such a case, it is fair for the economic development organization to receive some credit for the second increment of 50 new jobs as long as it does not claim any direct involvement that did not take place.

A second lesson that most professional economic developers understand is that it is important to measure outcomes, not activities. The number of letters sent, calls made, and visits scheduled are important steps to take but they are only valuable if they lead to consideration and positive decisions for the community. Activity is useful in measuring individual performance but, for group performance, a focus on the outcomes, not actions, is essential. In short, the relevant metrics should be the ends themselves, not the means of getting to them.

Planners need to take the strategic plan into consideration and measure that which is included in the plan as critical. For example, if the tax base is priority number one, then those activities that lead to tax generation and the successes with tax base implications are what should be measured. If the unemployment rate is a priority in the plan, then the metrics being watched should be corporate relocations, corporate retention, and new company start-ups, as well as the unemployment rate. Economic development programs need to be sure that they are measuring what is really of primary importance to the community.

Within the plan, each goal and a set of objectives and strategies will need to be agreed upon that will constitute the action plan for the community. They must include who will be responsible for each tactic included in the plan and what resources will be made available for the accomplishment of each item over a specific period of time. Finally, the sum of the actions will define the collective accomplishments for the year, or other specified life of the plan.

The sum of the measurements defined in the plan will constitute the dashboard for the community. In sum, this is what the community wants to accomplish and, over time, it will demonstrate what the community has accomplished over the period of the plan's implementation. Monthly or quarterly progress reports will serve as indicators of interim progress and will enable decision-makers to reallocate human and capital resources to bring the most important components in the plan up to expected levels of performance. This often requires taking resources away, at least in part, from other objectives of the plan. This requires decision-makers to assess the relative criticality of parts of the plan. These are the tough decisions of politics and the decisions that elected officials must face every year at budget time in their communities.

Budgeting for the strategic plan is the point at which many of the hard decisions have to be made. First, the strategic plan for economic development needs to be considered within the larger context of what other needs exist in the community. Public education, public safety, infrastructure and public works, public health, human services, and other mandated and essential services are typically funded first, along with necessary administrative costs and any existing debt service. Remaining funds will be allocated for other community services—the arts, libraries, parks, and more.

Funds that are provided to implement the economic development strategic plan are finite. Almost without exception, strategic planning processes for economic growth in any community will yield many more ways to spend public dollars than the totals available. Once again, elected officials will have to make the difficult decisions about which priorities can be supported immediately, which can be delayed for a later round of appropriations, and which must be shelved indefinitely.

After the decisions have been made and the allocations decided, those who will be implementing the plan must ensure that adequate means exist—or can be developed—to measure the performance against the stated metrics in the plan. This means that, in the planning process, performance measures must be selected that are able to be measured. For example, a goal to reduce levels of underemployment may defy reasonably accurate measurement and therefore it is difficult to know or demonstrate when the plan has been successfully managed.

As has been noted, a plan for a community's economic growth must be based on an understanding of the environment or environments in which the city, town, or region will exist over the life of the plan. The assessment of those environmental factors represents a snapshot in time. Hence, the plan will be most successful when it reflects not only the environmental situations at the time of planning but when the plan is reconsidered and shifted regularly enough to properly reflect the ever-changing environments. This usually means a brief annual review with more in-depth reconsiderations in three- to five-year increments.

Elected and appointed officials will find that strategies that are entirely developed by staff will find a less receptive community audience than those that have included representatives of community stakeholders in the process. The other extreme can also be an issue. There can be a tendency to include as many different groups as possible in an effort to be politically "all-inclusive." The consequence of doing so is to have incorporated into the plan everyone's special interest whether it is critical to the accomplishment of the plan's objectives or simply a luxury or "nice" item for the people of that community. In the public sector, however, that is a common experience, the result of which has often been a dilution of the focus needed on growing or re-growing the economic base.

Having said that, a city or region's economic growth plan needs to be sold to people of influence in the community lest they oppose it later. While the inclusion of key stakeholders in the planning for a community will not guarantee either acceptance or success, it generally does minimize any objections. Many communities have also found that, once the plan, has been formally accepted, there has been benefit in sharing it online, at town meetings, with chambers of commerce and others who might influence public opinion.

The battle for public opinion in a plan for economic development does not only take place over what strategies are or are not included in the plan itself. The most hotly debated matters have quite often related to those things that cannot be funded because of the plan. For example, any appropriations made to new components of the plan will be translated by some as taking funding away from something not included in the plan at all. For example, funds allocated to the economic development plan could have meant more teachers and smaller classrooms or the construction of a new fire station.

Making choices from among reasonable competing demands is the essence of politics. Thus, it is not surprising that some constituents will object to one or more of the appropriations decisions that have been made. Further, at the outset, a plan for economic development success may enjoy a certain level of enthusiasm and support. Quite naturally, over time, that support diminishes and may ultimately begin to turn public opinion against the strategy. There are several ways that have been employed in communities either to avoid or reverse such trends.

Often, communities have used the metrics included in the plan to illustrate that the plan is more than just an expense, it is an investment. And, investments generate returns. As such, a positive means of selling the return-on-investment expected from the plans has often included the conversion of the expectations into that which the community sacrificed for the plan to be implemented in the first place. For example, in a community that needs funding to hire more teachers in order to reduce average class sizes, the expected returns may be expressed in that way: a) we need to hire 100 new teachers; b) funding is being allocated to the implementation of the economic development strategic plan; c) we expect to attract 20 new employers in three years; and, d) in three years, we expect to generate a return from the plan that will enable us to hire 200 new teachers and also enable us to build a new fire station on the south side of the city.

Such illustrations make the temporarily sacrificed need more palatable, at least for a while. Over time, constituents will want to see that the anticipated progress has been realized, that the sacrifices had been worthwhile.

A second means that has been employed to gain and sustain support for the economic development strategic plan has been to celebrate any successes along the way. Constituents can then see how the plan has begun to pay dividends for them. In some communities, plans have included a likely early success—even a relatively minor one—so that the momentum can be assured of being sustained. Once again, the amount of tax dollars generated will not enthuse the general populace as much as will the translation of those dollars into the provision of specific community needs and benefits.

One of the requirements for such a plan to be well-designed and ultimately to succeed is not often reflected in the literature either for economic development or strategic planning. It is really quite simple and evident: elected officials run for office. If they wish to stay in office, supporting an economic development strategic plan that has specific measures of success—especially one that the funding for which requires the sacrifice of funding for other popular public needs—takes political guts! If the plan succeeds, and the returns enable the hiring of more teachers, the decisions of the elected officials who supported it are justified and they are celebrated as visionaries. If the plan is not successful and the public needs remain unmet, those who supported the plan may have staked their political futures on a "failure." Voters often tend to have long memories and political opponents have been known to use such "failures" as campaign fodder. Economic development requires political gumption and a self-imposed drive to do the right thing, often at the cost of other programs.

As a final point, and consistent with desired transparency for the community, it should be noted that not all elements of a strategic plan for economic development need to be made public. This particularly relates to the tactical elements of the plan. It is one thing to announce the vision for the community's growth as well as its goals and objectives, but it is not necessary to release the means by which one intends to accomplish the objectives of the plan. Economic development is a highly competitive field. Even within a given region, where jobs can be shared and local income taxes are assessed where people live, there will be competition. Elected officials can become resentful of the majority of development flowing into one jurisdiction rather than being evenly spread across the region. Elected officials will often feel the need to become more competitive in order to demonstrate their effectiveness to their constituents.

Further, in regions that encompass more than one state, there will be multiple state taxation policies in play. One example is the Washington, DC metropolitan area. In the State of Maryland, local communities can collect income taxes. For that purpose, the location of the employer is less significant than in neighboring Virginia because Marylanders will take their income home to be taxed. In Virginia, however, municipalities provide public services largely from their respective real estate tax bases. In Fairfax County, for example, 64 percent of all General Fund expenditures come from the real estate tax base. Thus, unlike neighboring Maryland, a location on one side of a municipality's border means that residents will still get to apply for jobs and small businesses will still be able to compete to provide goods and services under contract; but, only the municipality in which the firm locates will collect the real estate tax taxes that are the means of providing public services. This makes the practice of community economic development greatly competitive. That competition is both friendly and highly professional, but it is competition nonetheless.

Note

1 EDAC/ACDE. Performance Measurement in Economic Development. (Ottawa, Ontario, September 2011): 1.

Reference

EDAC/ACDE Performance Measurement in Economic Development. Ottawa, Ontario, September 2011.

19 The Timing of the Process

One mistake made by many communities has been to initiate the strategic planning for renewed economic development once a crisis has appeared and it is clear that something needs to be done in order to recover. The instigating event for planning has often been declining world prices for oil or other natural resources, the loss of a primary employer in the community along with the jobs that employer housed as well as those spun off in the secondary economies or, in some more extreme instances, the loss of whole industries (e.g. textiles, steel, automobile, or lumber).

Now, the leadership must act. It gathers the many remaining critical stakeholders to consider how to recoup and sustain their collective economic foundation. Of course, when jobs are lost and companies leave, many of the best and brightest minds depart with them, leaving the community devoid of some of its best thinking about how to recover. The group gathers and considers and drafts a plan of action, it is shared with the community and approved by the local councils and boards of supervisors, and considerable time is spent in calculating how best to recover and how best to involve everyone in the process. Typically, a great deal of time is consumed in the planning process. In the meantime, the remaining residents need employment opportunities and public service cuts begin to represent the revenues that were lost.

The communities that have experienced the greatest success with their strategic planning for economic growth have been those that have begun the process before severe needs arose to force the issue. In this way, a much more positive discussion can be held about advance rather than recovery. And, the planners can enjoy the luxury of time to envision the future and plan for it rather than seeking immediate solutions for the needs people have today.

The good times are also more propitious, and will make an easier sell, for bigger concepts that will drive greater growth, create more and better jobs, greater levels of expendable income, and a healthier tax base. Once decline has begun in the local economy, businesses will be increasingly less inclined to enter such a community. Businesses do not want to be the answer to a needed turnaround; they want to be part of a dynamic market where they can grow along with the rest of the community.

Perhaps most importantly, there will be a period of time during which the situation gets worse while emergency planning is finished and approved. When a crisis does occur—when a company leaves or when an industry collapses due to external, uncontrollable factors—the community can be ready with a plan to implement that can expedite recovery.

Or, even better, the community has already been implementing a plan to offset such potential losses with well-conceived strategies to diversify and sustain economic growth well into the future. The plans must be operational before crises occur in order to be maximally successful.

Finally, communities that can demonstrate to companies that are making site location decisions that they are in growth mode but also prepared for a downturn will appear more business-like. Business executives will consider such preparedness and forward-thinking as a demonstration of professionalism and confidence. It suggests that the local elected officials think the same way they do and makes the community generally more attractive as a location for an office or a corporate facility.

20 Team-Building, Budgeting, and Professionalism

Small communities, particularly those in rural areas, have had varied experiences in who actually implements the economic development strategic plan. The typical paucity of tax dollars available for local government staffing has often resulted in the responsibility for economic development being assigned to an existing employee in addition to his or her existing duties. That is a good recipe for economic development becoming an also-ran activity. Further, the individuals who have been assigned this function in some of the communities whose leaders were interviewed for prior research had no previous experience in the field. As they were then placed in competition to win prospective employers for their cities or towns, they were at a disadvantage.

For the same reason, other communities' attempts have failed when they assigned the function to a group of concerned citizen volunteers. Volunteerism is a wonderful thing but it is not professional and, while it can effectively supplement a professional's efforts, true economic development professionals need to be at the helm of the organization and process. Economic development is a professional field that requires training before being able to compete effectively on behalf of one's community. In previous research, interviews with local elected officials revealed a propensity to assume that a "smart person" can pick this up quickly and, that way, we can save resources. In short, we don't have to create a new position—with salary, benefits, and operating costs—and can make do with what is already in place. The feeling was that marketing is, after all, an art, not a science. It can be easily learned.

The realization soon came in many of those case studies that, while such individuals indeed had "the makings" of a good economic developer, and could ultimately pick up the details of the work, the community was at a disadvantage when regularly competing with a trained, experienced economic development professional. Such an employee is one part manager, one part marketer, one part salesperson, one part politician (even if with a small p), and three parts other components.

They understand the business decision-making process and inter-jurisdictional competition. They understand the multiple intricacies of incentives negotiations with senior business executives who are themselves highly skilled negotiators. They know how to bluff, and how to read a bluff. Economic development professionals must have a basic understanding of buildings and construction. They must understand a little bit about how finances work in such deals. They need to be able to estimate values of office space, land,

and facilities. They need a business sense of workforce issues, finance issues and, as of this writing, immigration policy matters.

Economic development professionals must have thick skins and patience. Far more deals are either lost or just never happen than can possibly be won. Even the deals that do take place can be the result of months or even years of negotiations. Sometimes, there are so many intermediaries that the economic development professional may have absolutely no idea of the company they are negotiating with. And, most importantly, the true economic development professional knows how to develop and nurture relationships. Economic development is, above all, a relationship-building exercise!

Joe or Alice down the hall may be smart people, and may indeed have the makings of great economic development professionals but many communities that have elected to proceed along that route soon realized that they did not have the time for Joe or Alice to gain the experience that would make them—and their communities—competitive with others. An experienced economic developer will advance the process immediately, and he or she will do so initially by bringing in all the other available resources in the city, town, or region to build the best team for business attraction and retention programs to be maximally effective.

Budgeting for an effective economic development program is a difficult discussion for many local elected officials to have. It becomes infinitely more difficult if the city or county has waited until a crisis to act, but even in good times it is a difficult discussion for local government because it is different from virtually all the other functions of local government. This is because an effective economic development program will have a budget that includes line items that are found in other areas of municipal budgets. There will be the more "normal" salary and benefit line items, there will be desks and chairs, and there will be rental costs and contracts. However, there will also be non-local (maybe even international) travel expenses, advertising and public relations costs, expenses for glossy publications, and more.

Public officials are not generally accustomed to appropriating funds for such purposes. And, if the municipality has learned anything at all from private sector marketing principles, it should be that, the tighter budgets get, the more—not less!—one needs to spend on marketing and outreach. This means that, while reducing other line item municipal departments' budgets, economic development budgets should be increased!

The Board of Supervisors in Fairfax County has taken such an action on at least five separate occasions over the past three decades, the result being that companies took notice of the "unusual business-mindedness" of the Board of Supervisors. The long-term result was a tremendously enhanced image with private sector site selection professionals and consultants. As a consequence, Fairfax County is home of the leading private sector economy in both the Commonwealth of Virginia and the metropolitan Washington, DC region. In one instance, while the county was struggling with a very difficult budget situation, a quarter million dollars was added, unannounced, to the budget of their Economic Development Authority. As its President, I received a phone call a mere three weeks after the announcement of the allocation that 320 employees of a major corporation just across the Potomac River in Maryland were relocating to Fairfax County. They were just waiting for a sign, and that was it.

Engaging economic development professionals and properly funding and staffing the effort, and providing that team with the flexibility to do things that are atypical for local governments will pay off in the long run. Economic development needs to be regarded as an investment by local governments rather than purely as an expense.

Many economic development organizations around the country are funded, in part, by private sources. The benefits of receiving private funds are that local governments receive support in supporting the outreach to businesses both in financial terms and in terms of business acumen. The latter should not be underestimated; receiving counsel from those who understand business and how and why their decisions are made can provide extremely valuable insights into how programs can be planned and implemented.

There are concerns about accepting private funding for local economic development programs that are also frequently cited. Fundraising in the community puts the economic development organization in direct competition with other organizations that also raise their budgets from community sources, including chambers of commerce, the local arts organizations, health causes, the local schools systems, and more. Often, local elected officials state that the economic future and sustainability of their communities are public responsibilities and that they should not abrogate those responsibilities in any way. Associated with this sentiment is the concern that, if funds are received from private sources, the local government may lose some of the control over the program. And, of course, when local businesses contribute to an economic development program, they may expect, even to a slight extent, the plan of operations to reflect what is best for their businesses rather than the community at large.

In many communities, the businesses and wealth are concentrated in certain areas. This will mean that those are the areas that most likely to make contributions to the program's budget. Will that mean that the developers of those areas, who may contribute will focus more heavily on the marketing of certain neighborhoods? How likely will the neighborhoods with the strongest economic bases be to support a focus on the neighborhoods with the greater needs?

Perhaps the most significant objection to private funding comes from a consideration of the timing of the contributions. The budget of an economic development organization must be stable so that promotion and outreach can be consistent and constant. Spikes and losses of funding will make it difficult to have a consistent message about the community being a great place to live and work. It is the most difficult of economic times for communities that the economic development program must be maximally effective. Unfortunately, those are the exact times when private contributors can be expected to withdraw their support. If a company is faced with laying off employees and cutting back on its own marketing, it is reasonable to expect that contributions to the economic development program will get pulled first.

21 Creating Strategic Alliances for Growth

In an effort either to be all-inclusive or to give the appearance of being all-inclusive, municipalities often engage every possible element of the community in planning for economic growth. While this is laudatory in some respect, it can also result in groups that are too large to make the most difficult decisions in the most effective manner. It can also result in a lack of focus as every interest group involved insists upon having their special interest recognized and provided for in the resultant plans.

In planning for economic growth, there are two primary groups that need to have seats at the table. When regarded in this way, the groups can most often be constituted in a way that will facilitate rather than distract from the process. The first group of individuals who need to be involved are those who have relevant assets to offer in the subsequent growth activities. In other words, what is the community able to offer businesses either for attraction or retention? This may include those who prepare the workforce, such as the public school system, colleges, universities, and trade schools. Or, it may imply those who own or market commercial real estate. It may include those responsible for airport, rail, or trucking operations.

The second group that needs to be at the table includes those whose actions will be needed to implement the resultant conclusions of the planning group. This may include local government officials with responsibility for land use or transportation planning as well as the community's elected officials. Also necessary will be representatives of local sources of commercial and private investment.

In every instance of community planning for economic growth, executives from private businesses should be included. All too frequently, growth objectives for the business sector are imagined by people from the public sector who have little or no real experience in what makes businesses grow or decline. More recent examples around the country have included public and academic representatives developing plans for enhanced programs to export local or regional goods and services. This is a positive opportunity for many areas around the United States but the planning has too often been attempted without the benefit of having those at the table who have actually conducted such programs and actually know what works and what doesn't, and why.

Other vital economic development assets in communities may not be profit-making businesses but organizations and institutions that also contribute to growth and stability. This may include military installations, airports, universities, hospitals, and more. These are groups that attract contractors and suppliers. They spend money in the community and attract others who spend money in the community. As such, they are important to local growth and need to be included in the planning. Local governments and state government agencies—even federal offices—also have economic impacts on communities. They too bring dollars into an area and issue contracts for small business procurement, and more.

In recognition of the lapse, some groups have developed survey instruments and conducted surveys and interviews to solicit some statistical data about why some companies do export and why others do not. Delivering the results of survey instruments that have thus engaged the private sector, or direct one-on-one interviews, may have some limited value but it is certainly not a substitute for having those with actual experience involved in the discussions from the start. Only the private sector understands how corporate growth works and why. Academic studies and statistical analyses can sometimes be useful, but are absolutely not a substitute for direct involvement throughout the entire process.

This is not to suggest that others should be excluded from the planning process for economic growth. Many of the most successful processes of this sort occur in phases, the first of which includes representative of the essential stakeholders indicated above. Subsequently, the plans may be opened to a broader comment process. This allows everyone to have input and to buy into the plan when it is time to implement it but it also starts the plan off on a more focused path.

Once the plan has been accepted, there may be an opportunity to engage others in the implementation process. This may include those who promote the plan or who support the objectives of the plan by volunteering or by serving on various committees. The selection of the team to address a given prospect situation greatly depends upon the needs of that specific company. Are public schools of great importance to the company's decision-makers? If so, the superintendent finds a place on the economic development sales team. It must be a fluid process of selection. Another prospect may need strong connections with the engineering school of a local university. Along comes the dean.

If the site for the prospective business is going to require a great deal of zoning or permitting approvals, then the local government manager responsible for those areas might be included. All within the confines of retaining the necessary confidences, and with the overall management of the local economic development professional, the team needs to be assembled to reflect the specific needs of the prospect. Selecting the best strategic partners for community economic development is a logical process of:

- determining the goals and objectives to be pursued;
- making an inventory of all the organizations in the community that have consistent missions and whose connections align with the vision for economic development in the community;
- assessing the mutual benefit that exists in collaboration between the entities involved;
- making the case to the relevant organizations and building a plan to move forward together;
- concluding who is the best person to present the case and the best means of approaching the discussion; and
- over time, assessing the benefits to all involved and redesigning the plan and programs as appropriate.

Ultimately, organizations develop an ease of cooperation that benefits all parties. In Fairfax County, Virginia, for example, the relationship between the Economic Development Authority and the more-than-one-dozen Chambers of Commerce in northern Virginia and its various sub-markets, as well as the local Technology Council, has been operational for many decades and is broadly regarded as mutually beneficial. In this case, the economic development team attracts and retains companies and the various partners help coordinate, service, and grow them once they are in the community. Such relationships are easy to form and, once trust is established, can be very comfortable and mutually beneficial for many years. Businesses that regard such inter-organizational community relationships find it to be a positive attribute of the community and another reason to consider a site for a facility in those communities.

22 Image, Awareness, and Selling Communities to Employers

Image and awareness are two distinctly different objectives, and there are two distinctly different approaches to achieving them. Awareness relates to whether people know about a business location; image is more about what they know. Site location decision-makers and consultants point their companies in the direction of locations about which they know. Awareness promotion campaigns are designed with the objective of getting a city or town placed on the consideration lists for business locations. Enough information needs to be communicated in the campaign to make people want to know more but it needs to be communicated in short bursts so that, over time the audience recognizes the name and has a given perception already in their minds.

Awareness is a much easier task to affect than image. Image campaigns entail driving home the strong points of a community while explaining what is being done to improve other areas. Image campaigns cannot be used to convince people that the flaws do not exist. But, all too often, a community's flaws can overshadow its strengths and, as such, the image is poor. Or, a community may have a lingering image problem from past experiences. For many years, the City of Dallas was best known for being the site of President Kennedy's assassination. Later, the Dallas Cowboy Cheerleaders and the television characters of the Ewing family became the Dallas images that people best understood. Seattle was best known for many years as the home of the Boeing Corporation—not a bad image to have but woefully short of the city's character. Detroit was, for some time, known as the nation's murder capitol even though the city had many positive attributes to offer. Colorado got a bad name in the convention and meetings industry for its early position on gay marriage, and North Carolina received a similar black eye for positions on transgender individuals. Reputations can be damaging to an area's ability to develop if not carefully managed.

Fairfax County, Virginia is home to nearly 600,000 jobs—about the same level as neighboring Washington, DC. The county is the driving force of the metropolitan Washington private sector economy. But, in the beginning of its economic development push (in the late 1970s) the county had no awareness among site location decision-makers as a business location. Those who did know of the county knew of it only as a bedroom community to Washington's federal government agencies.

In the beginning of a now nearly 40-year advertising campaign, planned and implemented with the Richmond-based advertising firm, Siddall, the objective had to be to announce to business executives that the county was adjacent to the District of Columbia and was open for business. A few of the ads from that initial campaign are shown below.

Over time, Fairfax County gained awareness in the minds of decision-makers as a place for businesses to consider site location if they wanted to do business with the federal government. While continuing to drive home awareness messages, the program began to shift to campaigns that emphasized image-building. Promotional subjects then focused on the available land, the extraordinary workforce, and the nation's best public school system. Some of those advertisements are shown below.

As noted in the section on strategic planning, the multiple environments in which a community develops are ever-changing. As the Fairfax County business base changed over time, the campaigns shifted to reflect those changes. Some of the advertising in those campaigns is shown below with a description of how the ads were consistent with the community's awareness among the executives of the day.

The first round of print advertising showed pictures of the nation's capital with historic buildings and connecting the county, an immediate suburb of Washington, DC, to the city. Proximity to the District was the greatest strength that Fairfax County had to offer businesses of that time (the late seventies and early eighties). Over time, the county began to acquire an image as a good business location of its own. It still had the benefit of proximity to the federal government but it had also developed a very strong workforce that could attract companies to the suburbs. One of the ads of that time period (middle-eighties to the early nineties), focused on the workforce strengths of the county by citing the number of PhDs in the county (Figure 22.1).

As time progressed, businesses in the county achieved significant accomplishments and, in the mid-to-late nineties, the Economic Development Authority's ad campaigns turned to announcements of the scientific and technological accomplishments that had been achieved within its borders. The theory behind the campaign was to advise companies that they, too could be successful in Fairfax County, "where the twenty-first century is just an hour away" (Figure 22.2).

Over time, the county's economy grew to that of a sizable city and the growth came in the form of some of the nation's finest technology businesses. The ad campaigns turned to announcing the solid business base that had emerged over time, again as a way of showing site location decision-makers that they, too could find success here. The ad in Figure 5.3 illustrates workers, including robots, on the Metro going to work.

In the new millennium, the focus of many employers turned to the creative workforce. It was felt that creativity was at the heart of technology business growth and that the community that could offer the creative workforce was the community that would be able to grow and sustain their economic base well into the future. The advertisement reflected the availability of that asset in Fairfax County by asking everyone in a room in Fairfax County who knows the answer (Figure 22.4).

In recent years, print advertising has been dropped in favor of internet banner advertising. At this point, the ads are building on the economic development that has occurred over time. The banners still speak to the ability of companies to be as successful as those already in Fairfax County (Figure 22.5).

Along the way, decision-makers needed to be disabused of the fact that the county was predominantly a government town that was overly dependent upon government contracting for its economic development. Indeed, the corporate headquarters of SAIC, Northrop

20,000 PHDs AREN'T THE ONLY REASON FAIRFAX COUNTY IS A SMART MOVE.

It takes no genius to figure out that well-educated employees are critical to success in business. In and around Fairfax County, you'll find a greater concentration of them than anywhere else.

But the quality of the people who will work for your company is only part of why you should consider moving here.

Washington, D.C. is right next door. And many companies, including Mobil, AT&T, TRW, EDS and Rockwell International, capitalize on the government's need for information and analysis.

Washington Dulles International Airport, located in the County, offers 1,897 flights per week to 76 domestic markets. And 108 flights per week to 14 international locations.

The State of Virginia is another compelling reason to move to Fairfax County. A sense of fiscal responsibility and sound management dominates both, the County's AAA bond rating being a perfect case in point.

And perhaps most critical to the people who work here is the way of life the County offers. The neighborhoods are beautiful. Public parks are many and inviting. The school system is one of the nation's best.

For more information, call us or send us the coupon.

You'll find that a move to Fairfax County is smart, if not downright brilliant.

FAIRFAX COUNTY, VIRGINIA

Please send me more information on the business advantages of Fairfax County.

Name_____ Title_____ Company_____ Address_____ City_____ State_____ Zip_____ Phone_____

Fairfax County Economic Development Authority, 8300 Boone Boulevard, Suite 450, Vienna, Virginia 22182. Telephone (703) 790-0600. Fax (703) 893-1269.

Figure 22.1 Fairfax County Economic Development Advertisement
Source: The Fairfax County Economic Development Authority

Grumman, General Dynamics, and CSC (all, at least in part, federal contractors) had all been attracted, but the county had also attracted headquarter operations of Volkswagen (North American headquarters), Capital One (global), Intelsat (global), Cvent (global), Bechtel (global), Hilton Hotels (global)—none of which were at all related to federal contracting. The campaigns began to reflect that, as is shown in the image campaigns below.

Another consideration for awareness and image campaigns to target site location consultants and decision-makers is that those individuals change over time, just as do the environments in which communities will operate. It is prudent therefore to ensure that the message being conveyed and the channels through which those messages are directed also change over time. Finally, local economic development efforts are often supported

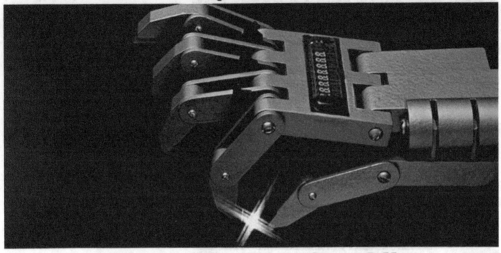

The 21st Century Is Just An Hour Away.

Fairfax County, Virginia. The 21st Century Is Here.

For information about relocation or expansion, call the Fairfax County Economic Development Authority: 703-790-0600.

Figure 22.2 Fairfax County Economic Development Advertisement
Source: The Fairfax County Economic Development Authority

by the economic development outreach of their state governments. Thus, it is important for the localities to advise their state counterparts of the images they are trying to convey. State economic development professionals are trying to accomplish the same types of objectives for the entire state; individual communities will have different approaches and interests; the state professionals can help to further the objectives of the local campaigns.

In Pittsburgh, it was felt that an enhanced quality of life and an enhanced awareness of that new lifestyle would help to attract the best technology workers to the region:

> developing and promoting the cultural, recreational, and environmental advantages of the region were essential to overcoming one of the greatest obstacles to economic development—the longstanding negative image of Pittsburgh as a smoky inferno populated by Philistines and drones. In fact, these negative perceptions were regarded. . . . . . as a serious obstacle to economic development . . . Clearly, creating a new image was vital to the success of the modernization process.[1]

A mid-1980s report by the Alleghany Conference on Community Development had cited the very low perceptions of Pittsburgh as one factor retarding the development of the local economy and the attraction of the workers who could accelerate its growth.

Fairfax County is home to more than
2,000 leading information technology companies.

In a world where technology changes overnight, there's one place where the conditions for change never change
a bit. Where companies like Cable & Wireless, Oracle, Nextel, Concert and Network Solutions can count on access
to three major airports. Where the schools are among the nation's best. Where the world's largest customer for
information technology, the federal government, is right next door. Want to change the face of information technology?
Then change your business address. Call 703-790-0600 or visit our Web site. And join us in Fairfax County.

FAIRFAX COUNTY, VIRGINIA. HOME OF THE 1998 WORLD CONGRESS ON INFORMATION TECHNOLOGY.
www.FairfaxCountyEDA.org

Figure 22.3 Fairfax County Economic Development Advertisement
Source: The Fairfax County Economic Development Authority

From an economic development standpoint, the single greatest problem facing the region is not an aspect of the quality of life at all, but rather negative perceptions about the area's livability ... Time and time again, Pittsburgh's negative image was mentioned as a barrier to recruiting talent, attracting businesses, and giving the Pittsburgh market area the stature it deserves ... The Pittsburgh area has still not successfully communicated its many assets, and it lacks a clear, new identity with which to replace the old label as a smoky, steel industry town.[2]

Youngstown, Ohio faced a similar situation after the closing of the steel mills in September of 1977. In the first few months, 5000 people lost their jobs and, in the ensuing five years, more than 50,000 people had been displaced. Unemployment soared to 20 percent and remained in double digits for more than a decade.[3] By the end of the 1990s, the community faced a struggle to recreate its image: would it be remembered as a "site of loss or as a place of struggle, a symbol of failure or an image of resilience?"[4]

SURROUND YOURSELF WITH A COMMUNITY OF CREATIVE THINKERS,
AND THE ANSWERS ARE EVERYWHERE.

COMPANIES IN FAIRFAX COUNTY, VIRGINIA, RECEIVED NEARLY $11.6 BILLION IN 2005 FEDERAL CONTRACTS.
THOSE DOLLARS BOLSTERED A BUSINESS COMMUNITY THAT INCLUDES 4,900 TECHNOLOGY FIRMS. WHEN YOUR
PEERS ARE THIS WELL-FUNDED AND ENTREPRENEURIAL, THE ANSWERS ARE ALWAYS WITHIN REACH. TO SEE HOW
YOUR COMPANY CAN BENEFIT FROM A MOVE TO FAIRFAX COUNTY, VISIT E-COUNTRY.ORG OR CALL 703-790-0600.

FAIRFAX COUNTY. THE POWER OF IDEAS.

Figure 22.4 Fairfax County Economic Development Advertisement
Source: The Fairfax County Economic Development Authority

WE ARE THE PROUD HOME OF 34,000 COMPANIES.
WE WOULD BE EVEN PROUDER TO MAKE IT 34,001.
We invite you and your company to join the thriving business environment of Fairfax County.

FAIRFAX COUNTY
VIRGINIA

THE POWER OF IDEAS
Click here to learn more.

Figure 22.5 Fairfax County Economic Development Advertisement
Source: The Fairfax County Economic Development Authority

The city became something of a poster child for what happens when the major employer
or industry picks up and leaves. A number of major print publications and television news
shows—even movies—ran pieces about what had happened in Youngstown and portrayed
the most negative of stories about crime and corruption and drugs and boarded up
buildings and deserted neighborhoods. To some extent, the image of the city and its woes

was being created by the media, which had no real interest in showing the efforts that were being made to re-establish the city on the basis of its proud history. "In the years after the mills shut down, Youngstown found its identity . . . up for grabs."[5]

Youngstown's Ohio neighbor, Cleveland, ended its default on its municipal bonds one year after Dennis Kucinich's election as Mayor. Area banks agreed to re-finance more than 36 million dollars in short-term debt. The city has emerged from those dark financial days to a great extent but the image as a city that was so dysfunctional and so poorly managed that it had defaulted on its debts remains in the minds of many Americans.

The city's image with corporate executives, as well as the population in general, has gone through numerous iterations since the onset of its economic decline in the sixties. Many still recall the images of riots in the city that grew out of the loss of the steel and automobile industries, and burning flotsam on the Cuyahoga River. Those impressions are a far cry from the city that claimed prior to that to be the "Best Location in the Nation."

Poverty and discontent replaced that image. The burning of materials on the river was so overblown and continuously reported that it became a story that it was actually the river that was on fire. As the public image of Cleveland as an economically sinking city became legendary, gallows humor arose at their expense. "What is the difference between Cleveland and the Titanic? Cleveland had a better orchestra." These are devastating impressions that are hard to shake, even over time; and, they do not go away just because the situation improves. Rather, it takes a concerted, extended, and often expensive program over a significant period of time.

For Cleveland, that effort was based on downtown office construction complemented by cultural and recreational opportunities and lakefront improvements. No longer wishing to be known as "the mistake on the lake," Cleveland set out to become the "comeback city." This was supported by new jobs and new residents coming back to the city. But, the attitudes of people who have deeply ingrained impressions are very difficult to alter. We become conditioned.

Milwaukee is another city that has made the attempt to rebrand itself, despite having one of the same situations as Cleveland to overcome: shiny new developments and new jobs in one part of town while other parts of the city still display poverty, boarded-up homes, and crime. One reference to Milwaukee, as they tried to revise its image, was "islands of renewal, surrounded by seas of decay."[6]

Brands are difficult and often quite expensive to design, and even more challenging to use. A brand is intended to cause those who see it to understand immediately what product it represents and what defines that product. Consider for example, the symbol of the Mercedes Benz automobile. When most people see it, they are immediately aware that it is the Mercedes Benz symbol. They will also generally identify it as a high-quality vehicle, with German engineering and luxurious seating and other nice options.

Can communities create such lasting images that are immediately recognizable as representing that community? Slogans alone are not sufficient to do so. It is very difficult; the only visual image that even comes close is the apple that represents the "Big Apple," New York City. Can communities develop tag lines that can engender the same response? The Big Apple, the Big Easy, Big D, Hot-lanta, and the Silicon Valley come to mind, but it is hard to think of many others. Part of the reason for that is that the brand must be something to which the entire community subscribes and uses in their own letterheads, publications, and other materials. And, they must do so for a long time so that it becomes recognizable and accepted.

Despite the costs and timeline for establishing a brand that fixes in the awareness of the public, communities can get started. The process can either entail outside contracting for professional counsel or local stakeholders can conduct the process internally. It is a good idea to start with research into what the intended audience knows at present about the community as well as what they think of when they consider the community. This research may take the form of interviews, surveys, or focus groups. The research may have numerous audiences and may include business executives, site location consultants, potential workforce, local residents and other stakeholders, and more.

A series of potential positioning statements can then be drawn from the research and a primary statement selected. For example, the positioning statement selected by the visitor's bureau of the City of Scottsdale, Arizona following such a process was: "Scottsdale's desert location and stirring beauty offer out visitors a getaway that promises relaxation, excitement, and discovery. A trip to Scottsdale leaves our visitors feeling effortlessly revitalized."[7] The statement was then tested and received a 59 percent approval rating, with another 34 percent being neutral. Its strength was felt to be that it would make people want to know more about the area. Next, three possible logos were tested; one of the three received nearly two-thirds of the respondents' support and was selected. The resulting advertisements—both print and televised—were then based around the new logo and the new themes inherent in the positioning statement.

Typically, when new campaigns with new brands are embarked upon by the destination marketing program, local hotels, restaurants, and others also begin to use the same images and statements. This reinforces the messages and enhances the brand over time. Brands of this nature must be used over a great deal of time. Changing the brand periodically could have the effect of confusing the target audiences. However, a successful brand and image for a city can leave lasting impressions on the intended audiences. The reader might consider what he or she thinks of when they think of a tower above a bay (Seattle), an arch by the river (St. Louis), or even a shiny red apple (New York City).

Building the right tag line for campaigns is just the beginning. The real challenge is to build into the phrase an image of what the place is. The Washington, DC region struggles with creating a brand because it must not only advise people that the region is not just a government town, but also acknowledge that it is the home of the federal government, which is the world's largest buyer of goods and services of virtually any description. How can one build a brand that captures two, somewhat competing messages? This is a challenge the metropolitan Washington, DC area has yet to solve, despite numerous efforts by different groups over many decades. Branding and the promotional campaigns that apply them are both difficult and expensive to design and even more difficult and expensive to use effectively, particularly over long periods of time. While they can be useful, they are not essential.

1   Economic Diversification and Seasonality

Many communities are dependent upon economic drivers that have the ability to produce during just part of the year. These may include agricultural pursuits, outdoor and sporting activities, and other seasonally dependent activities. In those types of communities, one of two options are available: either the community can find alternative economic activities for the off-season or they can determine to earn enough income during the relevant seasons to allow them to coast for the remainder of the year.

Local governments' tax bases also struggle from such seasonality and must plan a full year of expenditures for public services based on revenues derived from the quarters that are in-season.

Even with good planning and sufficient part-time resources, some seasonal economic activities are uncertain. Perhaps the best example of that are the nation's skiing areas that are completely dependent upon the year's snowfall, for which, of course, there can be little real forecasting certainty. More recently, as the result of climate changes, generally warmer winters have meant disaster for some in the more than 12 billion dollar winter tourism industry. Burakowski and Magnusson reported, for example that, in the winter of 2009–10, nearly 90 percent of all US resorts needed to use snow-making equipment simply to remain open. The average usage of such equipment cost the businesses one-half million dollars, plus the costs of the required electrical power.[8]

Not only did the loss of revenue hurt the slope operators, but also the hotels, restaurants, gas stations, local shops, bars, and even the local first aid stations. Winter sports in the United States reportedly account for 212,000 jobs and pay more than 7 billion dollars in salaries, nearly 1.5 billion dollars in state and local taxes, and more than 1.3 billion dollars in federal taxes.[9] Moreover, many small towns and rural communities are dependent for their semi-annual revenue streams for their economic survival.

Communities that are located at the entranceway to national parks, monuments, or other natural phenomena that attract tourists may have two concerns about the evenness of visitation to the sites and, therefore to their communities. The first is that visitation is probably greatest during the summer months when children are out of school and families are more able to travel. In such cases, and even if there are some visitors during the rest of the calendar year as well, the revenues and tax base generation accumulated during the strong months must hold the community and the retailers over through the balance of the year. A particularly hot season or a particularly wet year may depress the seasonal visitation and reduce the revenues from which to survive through the remainder of the calendar year.

A second consideration for such communities is the occasional economic down cycle that drives up unemployment or underemployment, as well as reducing expendable incomes. In bad years, even the strong seasons can produce marginal revenues. In communities that are dependent upon seasonal revenues, economic development professionals will endeavor to find employment that will supplement the attractions by providing employment in the off-season months or by diversifying the local economy with other, year-round industries. This type of strategy will require special attention by local officials to the assets the community has to offer employers.

2 Product versus Promotion

In an earlier chapter, the distinction was highlighted between economic development and economic growth. There remains, however, confusion about the term economic development and what it encompasses in a given community. And that confusion is well-founded, because economic development can mean any number of things to different communities, and even at different times in the evolution of their economic base.

For many communities, there is a clear definition of roles for the local economic development organization while in others the responsibilities overlap. This is not to suggest that either approach is better or worse for any given community. Communities and their leadership change over time and every one is different from every other, so the right allocation of roles and responsibilities needs to be that which best suits the local application.

There are clear differences between preparing and selling a community, whether it is large or small, urban or suburban or rural. It is often useful, therefore, to consider the practice of professional economic development in the same light that private companies market products. A company that sells computers will have one division that designs the computer and another that is constantly seeking to improve its appearance and functionality. Another division will then manufacture the product and another still may test the end-product. Some of the computers will be blue and others will be red. Some will have more functions and be larger, so they may cost more, while others will be "starter" models and will have relatively less functionality but cost less as a result.

The equivalent processes in a local government can be considered those that constitute the development of the product. These will include the appearance of the community and its zoning and permitting functions that enable or disallow specific uses within certain areas of the locality. Other components of the community "product" will include the airports, the business community, the chambers and other organizations that facilitate business, public safety, public works, public education, and so much more. These are the elements of the product to be sold in the same way that color and functionality are the elements of the computers that can help sell that product.

When a computer has finished being designed, built, tested, and has its software loaded, it is ready to be marketed and that is when the sales people begin their efforts. They promote the computer as faster, prettier, bigger, smaller, and less expensive. They negotiate contracts to place the computers in stores and the sales people close the deals. In the economic development profession, the marketing function includes packaging and promoting the various sales features of the community, getting attention from prospective businesses to consider their community "product," and close the deal.

Both the private example and the economic development processes have feedback loops. "No one likes the red computers; they just aren't selling" yields a decision to produce only blue computers. "The Acme Computers are selling faster than ours because they're cheaper" yields a redesign process to enable the production of computers that are less expensive because they have different features.

In the community feedback loop, the statements may be "Their office park already has the needed infrastructure and ours is not ready," or our workforce falls short in terms of the following skill sets." These shortcomings can then be addressed by those who develop the local "product."

Cities may undertake massive projects over great lengths of time, and at great expense, to improve the product they offer the business community. Mark Pendergrast writes about such a project taking place in Atlanta. Work on the Beltline entails connecting several rail and high-speed rail systems throughout and around the city in an effort to connect the entire community. By so doing, it is believed that the city will enable the development of people in areas of greatest need with the rest of the region, thereby facilitating growth in the former areas and providing much greater access for the residents of those areas to higher-paying jobs and other opportunities. Pendergrast argues that the development, once completed, will have the potential to reduce dramatically the inequities between neighborhoods and population sub-groups.

This is an ambitious project: in Atlanta, "suburban sprawl impaired the environment even as it eroded the urban tax base and exacerbated a long history of racial injustice." Pendergrast believes that the city is prepared to emerge as a major metropolitan area, with "opportunities for people in the most troubled neighborhoods to break the cycle of inter-generational poverty."[10] Atlanta is a city surrounded by highly segregated suburban areas. The city has high levels of poverty and rather poor schools.

The Beltline will cost somewhere north of 4 billion dollars to complete. It will require federal, state, city and other local dollars as well as private support. Ultimately, it will be a 22 mile ring through 45 neighborhoods around the city. Twenty-two percent of the region's population lives along the route of the Beltline. It will be lined with parks and bike and pedestrian pathways, and will serve as a symbol of the city and its people's resolve to rebuild the region in a way that benefits all. How important is it to the existing and potential business community that the city and the region complete this project? Without it, Pendergrast maintains, the city will very shortly "risk slowly dissolving into an amorphous urban shell, leaving isolated communities powerless to attract business, fix infrastructure, solve huge health problems, or resolve racial prejudice and income inequality."[11]

Projects of such a magnitude as the Beltline project in Atlanta can reverse a city's economic fortunes because employers will want to be part of a community that can accomplish such projects when they see the need. It also is an expression of the ability of the city to work with its regional neighbors, the business community, and the people.

Again, none of the various possible allocations of roles and responsibilities in implementing the plan effectively is, by definition, wrong if it is the most effective and most efficient for the community in question. However, what often happens is that the term economic development is seen to encompass all of the matters that relate to selling the community. If infrastructure is needed in the local office park, the economic development team may be assigned to make that happen whereas the group may not have the necessary capabilities or there may be other units of local government that are more adept at such assignments.

Other assignments of responsibilities may fall on the economic development organization because "they are good at marketing." This has often included the marketing of agricultural products as well as land, buildings, and facilities, the marketing of tourism opportunities in the community, or the marketing of events and celebrations. While these are indeed examples of marketing and not product development, they are unique and require experience in marketing those specific opportunities. Again, this is okay if the right people are in place to do the marketing. In sum, if it is properly understood, planned, and properly staffed, any allocation of the marketing versus product responsibilities can be successful;

what does not work is an unplanned illogical assignment of either product or marketing functions for the purposes of economic development.

Of course, there needs to be a strong nexus between the development of the product and the economic development marketing of a community. First, those who market a community are aware of what will sell, so their input will be invaluable to those who are creating the new assets of the community. A distinction may be easily identified by observing the verbs being used in the different action plans. When one is developing the product, relevant verbs tend to be "create" and "improve." In this sense, community leaders will create assets, improve infrastructure, beautify Main Street, and so on. These are essentially investments made to enhance what has become known as the local "sense of place." In may include the development of hiking and biking trails, arts and cultural presentations, a variety of housing options, modes of mass transportation, gathering places, and more.

McCarney (University of Toronto) notes that "A city rich in . . . assets and attributes retains and grows its skilled labour [sic], enhances its business attractiveness, and expands its economic base for innovation and prosperity."[12] She highlights the contributions of city services, public schools and universities, hospitals and health care, public safety, public works and clean water, diversity, housing variety and availability, and the general vibrancy of neighborhoods as components of the product that make cities "become platforms for sustainable prosperity."[13]

She also suggests that cities can become "logistics platforms" where all the component elements of successful marketing can be found, including that which is needed for global distribution. She includes in this part of the product, commercial and other capital sources, logistics support, and multi-modal transportation hubs. In many cities today, clusters have been formed that bring other supporting components to the product that are specific to a given industry or industry segment. These become almost natural attractions for other businesses in the same—or, even allied—business segments.

Economic development marketing professionals then have multifaceted products to sell that will receive consideration by site location consultants and corporate executives. Their actions may use verbs such as "promote," "provide," "encourage," and others. Tactics will include: promote economic diversity, market to firms in our technology target areas, assist companies to find space, engage partners in the selling process, promote tourism opportunities, support the growth of local businesses, and so forth.

In short, those who market communities to business executives are aware of what businesses require. Thus, their input into community land use and amenity planning is vital and should be included. They know what businesses require in terms of public education offerings in the K through 12 system as well as their educational needs from local colleges, universities, and trade schools. They are aware of the needs businesses will have for air and rail service, highway access, and amenities including hospitals and technology infrastructure. All of this intelligence should be incorporated into community planning. Conversely, those marketing the community (the product) need to be fully aware of existing and planned infrastructure development, zoning plans, and more.

It should be noted that the "product" being marketed by economic development professionals includes more than the local government, the business community, and local institutions. Business executives and site location consultants consider a community product to include quality of life elements as well. This may include symphonies, museums, and other cultural offerings; trails, parks, libraries, and outdoor activities; active scout troops, little leagues, and other activities for children and families; dining options and nightlife; a wide range of housing alternatives and walkable neighborhoods; diverse communities; health care; community events; and, more. These are all components of the product that can be marketed by the local economic development professionals.

3   Marketing Outreach

Marketing outreach for communities can be conducted in many different ways. For most economic developers, the planning for outreach begins with the budget available. From that point, the art of the possible can be defined. A more reasoned process is the one that begins with the best strategies that will reach the ideal outcomes in terms of job growth, wealth continuation, and business attraction and retention. Ultimately, of course, budget considerations are essential but by planning first and budgeting second, it is possible to consider the same projects over longer timeframes or to consider alternative means of financing the outreach programs. This bottom-up approach to planning may even help to build the case for additional public support. This will be especially so if a return-on-investment calculation is included in the argument.

The planning must, however, begin with the fullest comprehension of the environment in which the outreach is to be conducted as well as the desired industry segments to be pursued. The first thing that must be done is to understand the assets and amenities that the community has—or, will soon have—to offer prospective businesses. Second, it is vital for the community's leaders to identify what it can reasonably acquire over the near future. From that point, one of two approaches can be taken. Either the community can pursue those businesses and industries that find that array of assets and amenities appropriate for their type of business.

The second approach is to conclude what types of industries and firms are desired by the community, and then assess what additional assets and amenities will be needed to attract them to this city or region. Then, the community needs to devise plans to pursue those missing assets. What is not a realistic approach is to try to attract business segments that will not find the community properly prepared for them. This does far more damage to reputation than communities generally can imagine, yet it is a practice pursued by far too many communities across the nation.

Assuming that the set of assets—either currently in place or realistically obtainable—matches the targeted businesses and industry segments, the actual marketing outreach to those businesses can begin. There are many ways to capture the attention of the decision-makers in the relevant industries. A logical sequence, albeit protracted and not inexpensive, is first to identify the means by which those decision-makers receive their information. Is it through trade journals, the general press, social media, word-of-mouth, or through their professional associations? Are there other ways to get one's messages across to decision-makers? Once this is known, a program can be established to provide the maximum contact at the best cost. Now, the plan includes the target audiences and the best venues through which to speak to them.

The next step is to determine what the best messages should be. "We have land and facilities" is one such message. Another is that "our workforce is what you need and it is both abundant and highly competent." Now, the communications plan is ready to be funded, at which point the community will have in place the target audiences, the best messages, and the most effective vehicles for reaching them. Now, they have been prepped: they will know what your city or region has to offer; and, if it is properly tailored to their specific industry's needs, they will be more likely to understand and, perhaps, be ready to learn—and see—more.

The preparations described above only bring the prospective executives to the table. Economic development outreach is a people business. Quite often, successful business attraction is the result of many years of relationship-building and contact such that, when a decision is to be made about where to locate the business, your community receives consideration. This means that a highly focused target list of companies needs to be developed and contacted variously and consistently until the decision-making process is engaged. This phase of outreach involves constant phone calls, mailings, updates about the community, follow-up research on the company's needs, and advice to the company about the new assets and amenities being acquired by the community. Such outreach by professional economic developers can be discouraging. Nothing may happen for a long time. And, sometimes, when there finally is action, the company makes a negative decision for their community. The best that a professional economic developer can hope for in these situations is to receive full consideration when the time does come and to have an opportunity to present the case for their communities.

Community marketing by economic development professionals involves a great deal of contact by email, snail mail, social media sites, and so on. It is a highly competitive business because communities are focused on the potential for additional tax base, job creation, and wealth generation. Each community and each professional marketer is up against another community—or communities—that are just as anxious to reap the same benefits for their locations. The best communications are not necessarily the ones that cost the most money. Effective communications are all about getting across the desired message in the most memorable way; they need to incite interest and, ultimately, action.

Publications must highlight the assets that are in place and that are of greatest interest to the industry. There will be some that are in common to all industries and firms. These will include good schools, safe neighborhoods, attractive communities, diversity in business and population, and more. Many of these matters can best be conveyed through pictures depicting school scenes, downtown and side streets, public events, and more. Rather than listing data on every page of a brochure, charts and graphs can often be more effective in getting attention as well as making the point. Above all, all collateral material must be prepared professionally. This is a business-to-business piece and must speak to a business person as a business person.

Other avenues of outreach to business executives exist and can be used quite effectively. These may include attendance at trade shows, sponsoring relevant events, networking at events sponsored by chambers of commerce, technology councils or industry groups, and more. Travel to company sites can be expensive but excellent ways to maintain a strong connection until it is time for site locations decisions to be made. Becoming active supporters of the trade and professional associations of the designated industries is also a good way to build relationships within an industry. The objectives of these involvements are to convey information, stay in touch and, potentially to receive consideration for a positive site location decision at some time in the future.

The construction of an effective economic development program typically involves the following steps. At the onset, the community must develop its strategic plan and determine the best courses of action to communicate with and to attract, retain, and grow businesses in specific industries that make sense for that community. The relevant assets that will be needed to support such growth also need to be identified in the plan, as do the budget and policies to be developed.

Subsequently, the community must lay out the specific budget and staffing structures that are required to achieve the goals of the plan. This must be done, of course, within the limitations of the budget available and, as a result, the goals of the plan may need to be tiered to allow for some objectives to be accomplished more immediately and others over greater periods of time, some of which will have to be lengthier.

One of the first tasks for a new economic development program is to develop materials and websites that can be used as handouts at meetings and as means of attracting attention as well as providing vital information to potential prospects. This collateral material must be attractive to the reader and provide important information and data without being so long or cluttered that readers lose interest. Photos, charts, and brief tables are often means of transmitting information relatively quickly, whereas columns of writing are less likely to retain attention. It must be remembered that business executives and site location consultants receive many of these materials and are likely to appreciate brevity, clarity, and appearance. These "leave-behinds" represent the community after the representatives have departed.

The tactics sections of economic development strategic plans must identify target markets by both location and specific industry segments as well as identifying the means of approaching specific businesses. Marketing representatives should not go into meetings with employers to discuss site location without having done substantial research. As a result, he or she will understand the nature and history of the business and its fit for the community being presented, as well as having a practiced presentation prepared for the prospect. Conducting visits to targeted businesses is not something that is done without preparation. The marketing representative is presenting a case for location to a new community—or, perhaps a presentation making the case to remain in place. This requires a well thought out case, supporting documentation, and a tailored statement of how the community in question is the best possible choice for the company.

Business retention programs are critically important to communities and economic development professionals will know to develop and implement business retention strategies. That strategy will guide research into which companies are considering relocation, whose leases are coming due, who has had a variety of issues in their current locations, and what the key issues are in terms of keeping them in the community. Are their employees unhappy? Are there asset gaps that need to be addressed? Who needs more space and who might want to take less space? Are there matters that can be addressed by the local government that will make them more likely to remain in the community?

Once business retention prospects have been identified, the economic development professional needs to conclude how best to make the case and who is best to do so. In many locations, having the mayor or the local council representative call or visit the place of business makes a very big difference. Numerous businesses will address concerns about locations in purely human terms. This should not be surprising, given that companies are comprised of human beings with human as well as business, needs. On numerous occasions, business executives have expressed that they did not "feel loved" in a given location. That can easily be avoided by having phone calls, mailings sent, visits to the business, invitations to events, and by the simple inclusion of executives and other business people in community activities. A company that is part of the community is much less likely to want to leave. Economic development professionals are constantly making it easy for businesses to become involved, thereby making it increasingly difficult for them to leave.

Another hallmark of an effective economic development plan is that it develops strong and consistent local reporting strategies. Local elected officials are much more likely to support the budgets of economic development organizations if they see evidence of their success and the returns on investment that can be expected. Local voters are much less likely to criticize expenditures if they get regular announcements of activities and outcomes from the program. This can happen through community events, articles in the local media, and announcements of companies attracted, new business start-ups assisted, and especially, jobs retained in the community. The latter affects people in the community who hold those positions, their families, and the contractors who provide goods and services to those companies under contract. Keeping a business in the community that had been considering their locations is a great way to build local support.

A complimentary plan for a community's economic success will outline strategies to close asset "gaps" that had been identified in the economic development strategic plan. It is not sufficient to say to the public or to a business prospect that we have identified the gaps and are aware of their importance to companies. That does nothing more than to highlight the negatives of a location in the community. In any event, businesses that are considering a location will have done their own studies of what is missing from their list of requisite assets and amenities. What they want to see is what is being done about it, or will be done about it. Are there transportation plans in place to address the highway or rail connections that are needed? Are there funds identified to make these changes? What is the timeframe for the improvements? What accommodations can be made while those improvements are under way? Moreover, if the employer introduces new gap needs, is the local government willing to consider addressing them and over what period of time can those improvements be expected?

Strong economic develop programs will also begin to measure changes in awareness in their identified target markets. Have our public relations, advertising and outreach programs begun to penetrate our targeted industry segments and our targeted geographic markets? Do business executives and site location consultants know anything about our community? Is it the information we want them to have? Do they have perceptions of our community as a good place for their business improving? Are there negatives in peoples' perceptions that we need to address?

One precautionary note concerns the manner in which advertising and other promotional programs measure their effectiveness. Often, the effectiveness of such outreach efforts is measured in terms of the number of people reached. In advertising terminology, this would be called "impressions." For events, one might count the number of attendees. In a sense, however, it does not really matter how many people see an ad, or hear a spot on the radio, or attend an event. The critical questions are more specific: Who, not how many attended the event? Was it the right audience? How does that audience help move us toward the objectives in our strategic plan? How many of those who saw or heard an ad, or attended an event, took an action? Did they go to the website? Have they become contacts or prospects?

The outreach and promotion programs of economic development organizations are intended to create an effect or cause an action. Is that what we are accomplishing or are we simply counting numbers of people without a full sense of what they have done as a result of the connection? Outreach should be designed to cause a desired action and the performance measurements for those programs should relate to whether or not the desired actions occurred and to what extent and at what cost. From that point, one can determine the return-on-investment for those programs as currently designed, and compare them to the returns-on-investments from other outreach programs. Ultimately, one can allocate resources to the most impactful outreach programs and/or modify or redirect those that are less effective or less efficient.

Special events can also be an effective means of reaching the desired audiences. If marketing to a specific industry group—say, medical device manufacturers, communities can attend their trade show, host booths at the shows, meet the executives of the industry at such events. By sponsoring the events of industry groups, a community can put its name in lights before the executives in attendance. Ultimately, a community may be able to sponsor events and bring one of the trade shows to its area. If that occurs, then the executives in the audience will have an opportunity to experience the community and begin to consider whether it might make a good location for a facility.

Other special events can attract the industry's key executives by assembling a program that they will be willing to travel to attend. In 1998, Fairfax County, Virginia hosted the World Information Technology and Services Alliance's major program, an every-other-year event known as the World Congress on Information Technology. Part of the appeal of the event to the world's IT community was that it brought topics to the table that they wanted to hear from the leaders in the business. Part of the draw, however, was several notable speakers on different topics and who were magnets for an audience of leading business executives from around the world. These included President Bill Clinton, Mikhail Gorbachev, Margaret Thatcher, and others.

By hosting the World Congress on Information Technology, the county had the privilege of hosting just shy of 2000 men and women from 94 countries who were executives in information technology businesses. This was regarded as more than simply a large meeting—it was seen as an opportunity to state the case for Fairfax County locations for thousands of IT corporate executives. In the following two or three years, numerous companies opened offices in Fairfax County who might not have done so had they not seen what the area had to offer.

The county has repeated this formula often. An event entitled. "The Urbanization of Fairfax County" included speakers such as the well-known futurist, Alvin Toffler and the author of theories on the creative economy, Richard Florida. Hundreds of attendees got to hear the speakers and see what Fairfax County had to offer as an economic development location. And, in 2017, the county hosted a conference called Cybertech, the speakers list for which was also star-studded and headed by the former Secretary of Homeland Security, the Honorable Michael Chertoff, and that attracted more than 700 attendees from the cyber security business sector.

Advertising, public relations, events, and other such programs for economic development are designed to enhance the awareness on the part of executives of the community and its competitive assets and amenities. They can be seen as "stage-setters" because they are only a means to the ends stated in the economic development strategic plan. Once the impressions and the attendance create sufficient awareness of the community, the economic development professionals begin to visit the targeted industries, companies, and executives. There is absolutely no substitute in economic development to meeting corporate executives face-to-face, making the pitch, and establishing and nurturing those relationships over time, until a site location decision is in the making.

Once employers have been identified for economic development visits, the best contacts need to be identified. Who is the best person within the company to meet? It may be the owner or the CEO, but it may also be that the best person to meet with is the Chief Financial Officer, who often gets involved in site location decision-making. Larger firms often have a person responsible for corporate real estate or a facilities manager. Other points of entry into a firm can be developed as well and, once nurtured, such contacts can often be a means of meeting other, more senior people within the company. Those relationships can then be enhanced over time through the conduct of mailing and phone campaigns, invitations, and other regular connections. Economic development professionals will then schedule meetings with the companies in their targeted industries and follow up on those discussions with additional information, and will remain in contact with prospects to build relationships over time. They will meet with local companies whose leases are nearing expiration to retain them in the community share with prospects of the existing land and buildings in the community that can satisfy. At its heart, the profession of economic development is a relationship-building business!

Customer service is the hallmark of any great business and economic development is no different. Prospect servicing includes receiving business prospects and touring important components of the community, viewing potential space or land for locations, meeting other local business people and community stakeholders, and following up with additional information after the visit.

Once a positive decision for a community is announced to the economic development team, of if there is a preliminary need, economic development professionals will need to work with the relevant state and local officials to finalize the final points of the decision. If this takes place prior to the final decision, it will often be done under an agreement of confidentiality, frequently solidified by a Non-Disclosure Agreement (NDA) signed by all involved parties to memorialize the agreement to hold the information and all names in complete confidence. During this phase, if appropriate, local economic development professionals will work with any relevant sources of incentives that may be available to the firm as an inducement to locate in the state and/or community.

Another well-known practice of most successful businesses is known as service-after-the-sale. For an economic development organization, this may include the facilitation of local permitting and zoning processes for the company, helping to announce the company's decision to locate or remain in the community, holding press announcements or a grand opening, helping the company become integrated into the community, perhaps helping new residents in the community who came with the company to get adjusted, and continuing to serve in an ombudsman role vis-à-vis the local government and other community stakeholders as needed.

4   Successful Business Retention and Business Attraction Strategies

The business of economic development is one of building, nurturing, and exercising relationships with executives and others who can influence site-location decision-making. Ultimately, the employer will pick the best site from their perspective for a wide range of reasons. But, unless they are aware of the community and unless their impressions of the city, town, county, or region are accurate and positive, that consideration may never come. It is a relationship-building business!

A community can advance job growth in one of several ways. It can improve the product being marketed by adding or increasing the value of relevant assets and amenities that firms require. Second, it can work with new companies and entrepreneurs to create new employment opportunities in new and expanding firms. Community economic development organizations most frequently focus their efforts on business attraction and retention/expansion.

Companies can remain in a given location and stay at the same number of employees; this is generally considered to be a business retained. In some cases, companies will remain in place and add to the number of existing jobs. Such cases are referred to as retention and expansion. Of course, a business that is new to a community is generally referred to as having been attracted. In much the same way that businesses will acknowledge that most of their work comes from repeat customers, so will communities generally realize that business retention and expansion generate greater employment growth than does business attraction. Many of the communities' leaders who were interviewed in prior research, however, acknowledged that they were intent upon attraction when they might have spent a greater level of effort on retention and expansion. Perhaps part of the reason for such emphasis is that communities expend valuable resources for economic development outreach and a company attracted will generally have greater newsworthiness than one retained.

Cities and counties and states need to demonstrate that the money they spent on economic development rather than police and fire, or public schools, was a wise decision. Constituents are likely to be more impressed by a big announcement and ribbon-cutting for a new facility or office building than for the press release that a give company has elected not to leave. Not surprisingly, when communities fail to retain companies, it can be argued that those who lose existing jobs are impacted to a much greater extent than when a new company creates new opportunities to hire people.

Any economic development professional will maintain that a balanced program of job attraction and retention/expansion is the best way to ensure the sustainability of their local economic base. They will also invariably point out that one should not lose sight of the growing significance of new business start-ups as generators of employment growth and economic stability. This has become even more significant in recent years as young people entering the workforce (as well as others) have been encouraged and have been given training to be entrepreneurial. By starting their own businesses, people can be their own bosses and reap the rewards of their own risks and hard work. And, this growing trend is further enabled by the advance of technologies that allow people to work from home or in shared working spaces, and to grow at their own pace. As a result, many economic development programs are placing greater emphasis on training people in entrepreneurial skills and providing the support services that can accelerate the growth of such companies. This may include shared working spaces and incubators, legal and accounting help, no—or low—interest loans or grants, and a variety of other supports.

The attraction of businesses to an area can provide multiple benefits. A company that creates 100 new jobs in a community, for example, typically generates the spending that results in the creation of new jobs in the secondary and tertiary economies. The general rule-of-thumb that is accepted is that a primary job can create an additional 2.5–3 new jobs in the support economies. For example, 100 new workers in town buy homes and cars and groceries and send their children to schools. That means new retail workers and teachers and police and fire employees are needed. Further, the company itself will buy supplies and raw materials, and that creates new job opportunities as well.

If one accepts that 100 new employees in the primary business results in another 200–300 job opportunities, the community just added 300–400 jobs, and they all pay taxes. That means that the public services the community provides are being funded by more people. That may mean that more can be accomplished or that the tax rate can be reduced for everyone.

The announcement of a new business to a given community also makes a statement to the business community that this is a location that a competitor found to be of value. Perhaps we should look into this. Such positive notoriety cannot be over-estimated in the economic development business. In the early 1980s, the Mobil Oil Corporation announced that it was moving its global headquarters from New York City to Fairfax County, Virginia. As a result, major corporations worldwide began to consider Fairfax County as a potential site for their operations as well.

A large business attraction announcement also benefits the organizations in a community because it—and their employees—contribute to community causes in their new home. This may include everything from health and social causes to churches, little leagues and scouting programs. For all of these reasons, business attraction often receives greater attention than do business retention efforts or programs to help grow new businesses. The bottom line is that a well-conceived economic development program includes an appropriate balance of strategies aimed at attracting new businesses, retaining and expanding existing companies, and helping the new start-ups to grow over time.

It is remarkable that companies, which are comprised of human beings making human decisions, often express their sentiments in human terms. Many are the company executives who have made site-location decisions for personal reasons. This includes a favorite expression: "We left the last town because we just didn't feel loved." This is a cry for local elected and appointed officials to appreciate the companies in their communities, and to make concerted efforts to reach out to them, include them, and celebrate their successes.

Commentary: Bon voyage, Exxon Mobil

By Gerald L. Gordon

July 1, 2012—Not long after I arrived at the Fairfax County Economic Development Authority in 1983, Mobil Corp. announced its headquarters relocation from New York City to the Merrifield area of Fairfax County. It was an enormous shot in the arm for the county, as much for the renown it brought as for the number of jobs and the tax base impacts. It created exponential changes in our economic development efforts. It put the county on the map as a business location and especially a location for corporate headquarters.

Exxon merged with Mobil in 1999 and the new company located its "downstream"—refining and marketing—headquarters in Merrifield, with just more than 2,000 high-paying, highly skilled jobs. It has been one of our largest employers, and its presence has given us prominence in what is for us a "nontraditional" industry.

I have now observed the company's entire life cycle in Fairfax County. On June 6 ExxonMobil announced that it will pull out all of its Merrifield-based employees and relocate them to Houston in 2014 and 2015. On behalf of Fairfax County, I have

this to say to ExxonMobil: Thank you for all you have done for this community.

We have been extremely fortunate to have had Mobil and then ExxonMobil in this community for all these years. The corporation has been an exceptional corporate citizen, contributing to all manner of community activities and organizations. And it did so not just in terms of dollars of support, but in human resources as well.

Mobil and ExxonMobil employees have participated in—and funded—many organizations around Fairfax County and the Washington area. The Fairfax County Economic Development Authority Commission, to cite one example I know well, has benefitted over time from having four senior Mobil and then ExxonMobil employees as members, including our current chairman, who retired from the company just a few years ago. We thank the company for its contributions to the county economy and quality of life. We are absolutely sorry to see it go, but feel most fortunate for having had it in our community while we did.

Today, its departure is regrettable, and it comes as many Fairfax County companies wonder how they—and their payrolls—might be affected by federal budget

cuts. But ExxonMobil's departure will be hardly as devastating as such a loss would have been all those years ago. By different counts, Fairfax County is today home to between 600,000 and 620,000 jobs. We will lose 2,000 jobs—not good, but something that this community and economy can withstand.

Yes, the ExxonMobil facility is large—the two buildings have more than 1.3 million square feet of space and sit on 117 acres. There could be a number of good uses—corporate, government and institutional—for the site and we will work to find another excellent employer for the location.

We wish ExxonMobil and those employees who leave the best in Houston and thank them for calling Fairfax County home for 30 years.

Gerald L. Gordon is president and CEO of the Fairfax County Economic Development Authority.

Figure 22.6 Letter to the Editor of the *Washington Post* re Exxon Mobil
Source: With permission from *The Washington Post*

The feeling of isolation and exclusion is particularly the case for foreign-owned businesses located in the United States. Communities that want to retain such employers and enable them to grow will reach out to them and incorporate them into community affairs as much as they do US-based businesses with an office or facility in town.

A final note to this discussion of business retention programs is a reminder that sometimes companies do leave town. It may be due to circumstances that are completely out of the control of the local economic development professionals. In 1980, Mobil Oil relocated its Downstream Marketing Division headquarters from Manhattan to Fairfax County, Virginia. In 1984, it brought the remainder of the Mobil Oil headquarters to Fairfax County as well. This was a critical moment in the economic development history of the county because it put Fairfax County on the map—and into the thinking of American and foreign CEOs as a potential location for their companies. In 2014, the remaining 2300 employees of the Downstream Marketing Division of Exxon Mobil were relocated in Houston, Texas. There was nothing that could be done locally to prevent the move as the new leadership wanted to build a campus in Houston for all of its employees.

When the company announced its decision to leave Fairfax County, no one was happy about it, but everyone was grateful for all that the company had done while it was there. I wrote a letter (Figure 22.6) to the editor of the *Washington Post* thanking the corporation for their excellent corporate citizenship and for their many contributions to the community. This too can be seen as a retention action. Perhaps, someday, the company will need a facility or office space in the region again and will keep Fairfax County in mind.

5   Global Marketing Strategies

Communities seeking to advance their local economies through global strategies have a number of options available. The most oft-considered is known as Foreign Direct Investment (FDI) and involves programs to attract businesses from outside of the United States to open locations in the United States. They may do so in order to conduct business in the immediate vicinity or in order to establish a landing point from which they can enter other markets in the region or elsewhere in the country.

For communities, there are several advantages of attracting foreign-owned businesses. First, even though the company may bring executives from the home country, they primarily employ American workers, pay salaries, purchase goods and services in the community, and pay federal, state, and local taxes that help to provide public services. Second, a foreign-owned business helps to diversify both the business community and the surrounding neighborhoods. Business leaders frequently express the benefit of an economic base that has people from different places in this way: no one business problem has but one solution. There are many potential solutions, some of which are faster or prettier or last longer or cheaper. There is a business benefit in having a range of solutions from which to choose. The global economy offers greater potential solutions because people from different cultures or educational backgrounds see things in different lights. Finally, companies from overseas are subject to different external environmental forces, meaning that they can help stabilize the local economy if the domestic firms are differently affected by change.

Communities that wish to attract companies from overseas must be realistic about their potential for doing so. Foreign-owned businesses have the same requirements a domestic business will express. They seek appropriate space, a pro-business community, a cluster of companies in similar industry segments, a qualified workforce, and an acceptable quality of life. They will also expect to find assets and amenities on which domestic businesses may place somewhat less importance. These may include direct flight access to their home city, a cosmopolitan community in which foreign-born people are welcome, and possibly the types of churches, restaurants, and groceries to which they are accustomed, and possibly a small community of people already in place from their home countries. While these may or may not be essential components of attracting a foreign-owned company, they will almost certainly enhance the likelihood of success in bringing them to the area.

A second manner in which global economic development benefits the community is by bringing to it the investment of foreign capital. This brings new expenditures for plant and equipment to the regional economy that can complement the investments made from domestic banks and businesses. And, once a company from a country comes to a city or region, it increases the likelihood that another company from the same country will also feel comfortable in locating a presence there.

Trade programs are another global-facing strategy for growing a local economy. Trade can actually refer to overseas marketing of a community's products or services, or to the export of goods and services from the region to the rest of the country. In short, the value of trade programs for the local economy is that they bring money into the community that gets spent and re-spent around the area. As companies trade with external markets, they also create jobs and pay taxes at home. Further, as trade exposes executives from other markets to the home location, there is an enhanced potential for that person to make a positive future site location for a facility in that community as well.

Focus groups conducted by the Fairfax County Economic Development Authority have repeatedly revealed that diversity is very important to its highly educated workforce, many of whom move to the area specifically for that reason. Men and women have discussed their interest in raising their families in environments that reflect the future world. They want their children to grow up around people from other nations and of other beliefs. Fairfax County is 48 percent a collection of all minority groups.

Over time, there have been a variety of tactics that communities have employed in marketing overseas. In terms of FDI, overseas marketing efforts have typically been the domain of states because these programs are more expensive than those of domestic outreach. Travel costs are greater, exchange rates are variable, and materials and staff must be able to communicate in multiple languages. Fairfax County, Virginia has a 20-year-old program of overseas marketing, and now has six external offices with permanent staff. They are in London, Seoul, Bangalore, Tel Aviv, and Berlin, as well as southern California. As has been noted elsewhere, economic development is a relationship-building business. It takes several years to establish the necessary relationships and to achieve sufficient awareness in the market place to attract attention and develop true prospect situations. During that time, there will tend to be minimal returns on the investments.

Some states and localities have attempted to market overseas using staff that are housed in the home headquarter. This has not proven to be as successful as having employees who are indigenous to the markets in which they are working. Such individuals know not only the people and the right organizations to join and meetings to attend, but they under-stand the culture and can create the relationships needed more quickly. They may even have the relationships already established, thereby accelerating the time to garner returns on the investments. The overseas offices of the Fairfax County Economic Development Authority are manned by a native German, Korean, Israeli, Indian, Brit, and Californian respectively. This also means that travel to and from the headquarters is minimized because the work is being handled by the employees of the overseas offices.

Once a presence is established in an overseas market, the process of prospect develop-ment is not greatly different than marketing to an American business in the United States. Attendance at, and the sponsorship of events, cold calling, and relationship nurturing are all part of the process. Over time, there will be companies that are interested in expanding in the United States and the process will be similar to speaking to a US-based executive.

Increasingly, the language of business today around the world is English. Often, busi-ness can be done in other countries either by speaking English or through professional interpreters. However, even if the corporate counterpart speaks and understands English very well, he or she will always appreciate any efforts made to fit into their culture and use their language rather than expecting them to do everything the other way. The use of peripheral materials in multiple languages, business cards in various languages, and learning a few key words in other languages are always winners in foreign negotiations.

Attention to details is vitally important when working with executives from other cultures. Japanese executives have distinct ways of welcoming people, bowing as well as shaking hands, and other cultural practices. It is wise to respect their ways and to do one's best to demonstrate them as it will further discussions. Other cultures have certain colors that designate death or infidelity. Clearly, materials need to be developed with those considerations in mind.

Notes

1. Roy Lubove. *Twentieth Century Pittsburgh: The Post-Steel Era.* (Pittsburgh, PA: The University of Pittsburgh Press, 2004): 31.
2. Robert H. McNulty. *The Economics of Amenity.* (Washington, DC: Partners for Livable Places, 1985): 103.
3. Sherry Lee Linkon and John Russo. *Steel-town USA: Work and Memory in Youngstown.* (Lawrence, KS: The University of Kansas Press, 2002): 131.
4. Ibid., 132.
5. Ibid., 188.
6. Michael Broadway and John Broadway. Cleveland Reimagined: Changing News Media Images of Cleveland, 1985–2015 (August 17, 2017) www.researchgate.net
7. Brand Strategy. Project Roadmap. (2016) www.experiencescottsdale.com
8. Elizabeth Burakowski and Matthew Magnusson. *Climate Impacts on the Winter Tourism Industry in the United States.* (Manchester, NH: The University of New Hampshire, 2012).
9. Ibid.
10. Mark Pendergrast. *City on the Verge: Atlanta and the Fight for America's Urban Future.* (New York: Basic Books, 2017): ix.
11. Ibid., ix.
12. Patricia McCarney. Building High Caliber City Data. *Economic Development Journal*, vol. 16, no. 2. (Washington, DC: International Economic Development Council, Spring 2017): 10.
13. Ibid., 10.

References

Brand Strategy. Project Roadmap, 2016 www.experiencescottsdale.com
Broadway, Michael and Broadway, John. *Cleveland Reimaged: Changing News Media Images of Cleveland, 1985–2015*. Marquette, MI: Northern Michigan University, August 1, 2017.
Burakowski, Elizabeth and Magnusson, Matthew. *Climate Impacts on the Winter Tourism Industry in the United States*. Manchester, NH: The University of New Hampshire, 2012.
Linkon, Sherry Lee and Russo, John. *Steel-town USA: Work and Memory in Youngstown*. Lawrence, KS: The University of Kansas Press, 2002.
Lubove, Roy. *Twentieth Century Pittsburgh: The Post-Steel Era*. Pittsburgh, PA: University of Pittsburgh Press, 2004.
McCarney, Patricia. Building High Caliber City Data. *Economic Development Journal*, vol. 16, no. 2. Washington, DC: International Economic Development Council, Spring 2017: 7–18.
McNulty, Robert H. *The Economics of Amenity*. Washington, DC: Partners for Livable Places, 1985.
Pendergrast, Mark. *City on the Verge: Atlanta and the Fight for America's Urban Future*. New York: Basic Books, 2017.

23 Managing Internal Expectations

Economic development in communities seldom generates overnight results. It is a process by which corporate consideration may build over time before actual announcements can be made. For a variety of reasons, communities can gain unrealistic expectations about what and when returns might be expected. Perhaps it is because the political leadership needs a win to show the electorate. It may simply be that the planning has led to the build-up of a certain level of enthusiasm in the community and that has given rise to a heightened level of expectations. Or, it may be that the budget for marketing was provided at the expense of other line items and programs, giving way to greater scrutiny of the performance of the economic development program.

For whatever reason, there may have been unrealistic expectations created about the timing and magnitude of the returns on the initial investments. Many communities have put plans into place to manage their community's expectations about the benefits of economic development.

1   Communications

Professional communications from economic development organizations are entirely dependent upon the objectives laid out in the community's strategic plan. Generally, the purpose of communications planning by EDOs is to identify the various audiences that need to be reached, identify the best means of reaching those individuals, and finally, to craft the messages that will accomplish the objectives of the plan. It will be beneficial to consider each of these three purposes separately.

The beginning of an economic development communications plan is to identify the numerous audiences that need to be reached. These will range from local elected officials who ___ of the activities their funds are supporting to local business ___ he purposes of business retention; local residents who, in ___ become opponents of the plan; and, business site-location ___ ts who need to be educated about potential business a___

___iences have been identified, it will be important to con-clu___ ___diences. There are a range of print and electronic media that ___ r advertising on relevant websites. Whatever the means of communication selected, the audience needs to be pinpointed. That is to say that, if one is trying to speak to manufacturing facility managers, the best means of reaching them might be their professional association's newsletters or other publications they tend to read. If the target is a technology company, the executives will be interested in other publications and websites.

In many cases, the best information source for business executives could be trade shows. Hosting a booth with community information is one method of reaching these executives; another might be to sponsor events as part of the larger trade show. Again, the method being employed needs to be tailored to the desired audience in order to be maximally effective.

Crafting the messages is a very difficult step in the process because the decision-makers one wants to reach will be bombarded regularly with similar messages from competing communities. This means that the messages must be relevant, consistent, and have the ability to capture the target's attention, even if briefly, in order to make an impression. For that reasons, pictures, graphs, and visuals are often more important than the text of an advertisement or announcement. Once the outreach campaign has begun, it has to be consistent and ongoing.

The ideal outcome if for the decision-maker, when he or she is actually considering a facility or office location, is to know the name of the community and perhaps a little about it. Ignorance of the community will most often mean that it will not receive consideration. The advertising, public relations, mail campaigns all need to be similar, with a consistent logo and message; they need to complement one another.

Finally, economic development professionals and their boards must allocate their scarce resources for these purposes. Without any doubt, the range of possible ways to reach specified audiences will exceed the amount of funding available for the communications plan. The key question will be: What will make the most effective and lasting impact on the most focused audience? (Table 23.1)

Creating catchy slogans for economic development marketing materials and websites is a treacherous practice. Too many communities have attempted to label themselves by something memorable or catchy only to learn that the process has pitfalls that they had not foreseen. In the 1990s, the use of websites for economic development marketing purposes first became in vogue.

Suddenly, it seemed, there was a spate of communities that developed slogans and catchphrases that they believed would drive interest in the location as a place to do business. At a minimum, it was felt that tag lines and branding slogans would help attract the attention of site-selection decision-makers and consultants. Of course, the hot technology center of the day was the Silicon Valley in northern California. That caused communities and states—even nations—to want to play off of the term silicon. As a result, there was an overnight dearth of communities applying the term silicon as an adjective to describe their location. At one point, there were more than 60 American cities and counties calling themselves the Silicon Prairie, many of whom went to court to sue and counter-sue the others over the use of the name. The area around Cambridge, England became the Silicon Fen. States were not immune to that effort. Virginia tried to brand itself as the Silicon Dominion. Even countries get involved, as Scotland tested the Silicon Glen.

Table 23.1 Targeting Advertising and Public Relations

Audience	Vehicles	Possible Messages
local political leaders	local press, radio, and television	economic development is an investment
local orgs' newsletters	businesses	pay taxes for public services
local businesses	chambers of commerce consumers local and external media	development yields consumer growth and spending
local residents	local media	economic development will mean better public services places of worship elected officials' newsletters
external businesses (general)	state, regional, and national media	this is a great place to live, work, and raise a family statewide and national chambers
external businesses (specific)	trade and professional organizations	we have the following assets . . . trade shows and exhibitions travel to external markets special promotional mailings
workforce	industry-specific sites and events	this is a great place to work and own a business general industry sites and events colleges and universities

Economic development tag lines have the same basic requirements as product tag lines. They must be basic and clear; they must relate a story or create a lasting impression; they must be sufficiently catchy that people will pay attention; and they must differentiate the community from others while reflecting its personality and attractiveness. Not an easy task! Furthermore, the line must be enduring. Constantly changing an area's tag line defeats the purpose of making an impression on peoples' minds and reminding them of it repeatedly. One of the most difficult challenges in developing a tag line is to ensure that everyone in the community uses it as well. Four different images being created by four different groups all in the same location is simply noise and will be self-defeating. Instead of clarity, it will create confusion.

Many communities have made the mistake of picking tag lines for their economic development programs that are too commonplace. Simple Google searches for overly used tag lines yield the following results:

- "the best place in America for business"   36,000 results;
- "we're open for business"   650 million results;
- "explore the possibilities"   84 million results;
- "a great place to live"   920 million results;
- "America's hometown"   637 results.

Clearly, these phrases are too ordinary to make a community stand out from the others. The Washington, DC metropolitan area has long had a different problem with branding. Over time, as its regional economy has become diversified away from the historical over-dependence on federal contracting, the misperception remains outside of the region that the city and the region are still little more than a government town. This is, of course, not an accurate understanding but that is the case in terms of peoples' perceptions. The conundrum is that being a government town has always been a good deal for local economic developers. It is very difficult to tell the story in a single brand that this is a government town, that being a government town is a good deal, and that, while we are not just a government town, we are indeed a government town and that that is a good thing. If it is that tiring to read the last sentence, it is impossible to create a brand that incorporates all of those thoughts and that is both concise and memorable.

2   Establishing Performance Metrics and Return on Investment

There are a wide range of possible metrics for economic development plans. Some relate to the improvement of the product being marketed and others to the success of the marketing itself. Other than job creation and lowering the unemployment rate, communities often measure their success by tax base generation, increased visitor counts, or even wealth generation. Other measurements include private sector investments, the number of new business start-ups, and more.

Some communities have made a distinction between that which makes the area more attractive to businesses and that which is the result of the actual marketing of that product. The product will include buildings, land, and office space for promotion, infrastructure, community assets, and amenities, the workforce, community institutions, and more.

Many communities with economic development surprisingly do not measure performance of the program on a regular basis. A study by the International Economic Development Council (IEDC) concluded that more than 30 percent of all economic development organizations do not measure their performance on a regular basis.[1] This is most peculiar since their local governments obviously must make difficult choices about what and how much to fund programs. To justify expenditures for marketing, one would imagine that the elected officials in those communities would require something more than anecdotal evidence that a program was producing what it should be producing. Furthermore, such performance measurements help managers decide whether existing programs are being successful and whether there are areas that should be re-examined or re-planned.

Another key for economic development measurements is to use measures that reflect outcomes rather than simply process or mere activity. For example, the number of letters sent or the number of companies visited are means to an end. The "end" is the productivity that comes from the process elements. Outcomes include announcements of new companies, new jobs created, and so forth. One good example that can be found in a great many annual reports of economic development programs is the number of delegations hosted and the number of attendees at hosted events. These are clearly process metrics; what's important is what came from the connections established in those events.

Did a company locate in the area as a result? Were new trade deals concluded and how much of that will stay in the community or its tax base? Objectives must be measureable and the outcomes and the systems for measuring must be understood and accepted as legitimate by those who fund the programs.

It is not always critical that the programs of the economic development organization can be tied directly to the outcomes, but this must be understood as part of the original plan. An example would be announcing that "1000 new jobs came to the community." Was all of that activity the result of economic development activities or were some of those jobs created incidentally? It is valid to measure either the universe of new jobs or only those that resulted directly from the outreach efforts of the economic development program. Either measure is valid, as long as it was understood that way at the beginning of the program. A lower unemployment rate, for example, is a valid and typical measure for economic development outcomes. That does not mean that a lower unemployment rate can be entirely attributed to the program. The program however, helped to enhance the community's awareness, positive perceptions, and connectivity. It is thus reasonable for the economic development office to claim that it influenced the improvement in the rate.

One key lesson in measuring the performance of an economic development organization relates to accountability. It is absolutely essential that the objectives against which an economic development program is to be measured are things over which the professionals have a significant degree of control. Lowering the unemployment rate or enabling diverse populations to create and grow businesses are certainly laudable goals but it would be unfair to criticize an economic development program because it was not effective in performing well against such goals, both of which may have extraordinary external factors that may present challenging barriers. Objectives for economic development must include only those factors over which the managers of the program have a substantial degree of control.

One objective that is very difficult to measure is the perceptions of business executives to locating and operating in a given community, or even a specific state. This can be evaluated through ongoing surveys that look for increasing or decreasing indicators of awareness and perceptions, but that requires a long time to determine trend lines, and a great deal of expense. Communities should be very cautious about the use of such measurements as objectives. Open statements such as "increase the vitality of ..." or "accelerate the pace of innovation" must be used sparingly as they tend to defy measurement. At the end of the planning period, constituents and funding sources will want to know whether their programs have returned greater value than the costs that went into them. This means that the metrics used—and the means of measurement—must be well defined and completely above any questions of manipulation or reporting uncertainty.

It is prudent for any program that expends public dollars to produce some indication of how the funds were expended and what the results from those activities were. Most especially in today's situation of local budget shortfalls, programs must justify not only their appropriations but their very existence. This means that every dollar must be maximally applied to the achievement of strategically derived goals and objectives. Economic development organizations must be able to demonstrate that logic was inherent in all expenditure decisions and that that logic is consistent with the community's overall goals.

Local budget oversight committees and elected officials will not only be interested in demonstrating the returns they received from the expenditures but must be able to justify the expenditures on economic development outreach instead of other community needs. For example, if there is only a marginal return from these economic development activities, might the same funding be better used to reduce the local teacher-to-student ratio, or to increase police protection in high crime areas, or to rebuild aging infrastructure, or the many other necessary items under consideration for local funding?

Quite often, economic development organizations will demonstrate their returns-on-investment for local allocations to their budgets not in dollars and cents but in terms of what the outcomes can buy. For example, an increase to the local real estate tax base of a half-million dollars is less impactful than a description of the eight school teachers or the six police officers or the road project to which it equates. Such matters have a great deal more appeal to voters and make it easier to make the case for continued or even expanded funding. Taking that approach a step further is also an effective manner of expressing the value of economic development. Stories can relate how individuals or families were affected. People who have been unemployed or underemployed for extended periods tell a convincing story for the community.

The need for justification of investments in economic development organizations applies not only to the public dollars invested. Nationally, many economic development organizations receive private donations for their programs. Newspapers invest because they expect more companies to come to town and begin advertising. Grocery chains expect to have new customers. Residential and commercial developers expect to have more clients so they invest. Consequently, those investors will expect results; they will want to know how many new potential advertisers or customers they can expect. And, over time, they will begin to divide the new customers by their total investments in the program to determine whether the effort was worth it. Did we spend more than we can reasonably expect to recoup in sales?

For the examples of grocery stores or newspaper publishers, that may be a hard number to reach. And, of course, many will invest for other reasons as well—to be a team player in the community or to be a leader in economic development. In many cases, however, the major contributions may come from builders, land and office building owners, or developers. This is where the big money is more likely to come from and that is where the largest potential return on the investments may come. In such case, one large commercial tenant or several new residential owners or renters may be sufficient to justify the initial outlays. Although such sources may have a longer timeframe for expecting outcomes, they will still expect results to be forthcoming and to be reported fully on a regular basis.

For these reasons, it is somewhat surprising that more EDOs are not more active in terms of reporting their outcomes or to relating them back to the levels of expenditure and the overall returns-on-investment. The expectation of returns must relate back to the strategic plan. If employment growth is the objective, then new jobs must be reported. If wealth accumulation, or visitors to the community, new company start-ups, or new homes sold are the expected outcomes, they dictate the reporting elements. There are two difficulties associated with such outcomes reporting. First, the typical community strategic plan for economic development has multiple objectives; and, second, the expected outcome is quite often an enhanced real estate tax base, and that is difficult to measure accurately.

Most communities' economic development plans are focused on multiple anticipated outcomes. They may hope to create new firms, attract investment dollars, create jobs and reduce the unemployment rate or the underemployment rate, attract workforce increase patent outputs, or enhance the level of the community's awareness as a good place to live, work, or visit. Reporting the year's results to public and private investors will require a number of elements to be measured and, the greater the number of metric components, the more complex will be the reporting tool. And, as the tool grows increasingly complex, the ability to communicate it effectively to all parties becomes increasingly unlikely.

Thus, a conundrum: how to develop a multiple-metric reporting tool that can be easily understood by others. One conclusion is to create an index of factors—such as a balanced scorecard—with weights that demonstrate the relative value of each metric against the whole. While this can be an effective tool for internal use, it may have limited practicability for sharing with investors or the general public. The ideal tool will be easily communicated to all. Often, charts and graphs are effective ways of showing results in an understandable way.

The second issue is that many economic development plans are designed to generate increases (beyond the costs of the programs) to the tax base from which public services are provided. The reporting of the relevant outcomes for that objective would include the marginal increases in the tax contributions made by individuals or companies and much of that information is confidential and cannot be released. It is sometimes possible to acquire the information in aggregate form but it is not entirely accurate because not all marginal additions to the real estate tax base will be as a result of the efforts of the economic development organization. Often, people and companies move in or out without having been influenced by the outreach efforts of the program and they should not be included, lest the validity of the reporting be drawn into question.

Perhaps due to the difficulty in providing accurate and fair measurement reporting, many economic development organizations throughout the United States only report on that which they can find reliable information. Often, the reliability is best guaranteed by ensuring that the source is a third party. In other words, if one is quoting an external source for the data, there can be no suggestion of inaccuracies in one's reporting to make the program look more effective than it might really be. In fact, many organizations report only the barest of information about their outcomes. The possibility exists when doing so, however, that questions will be raised in future funding cycles about why continued funding for economic development marketing should be approved.

In any scenario, it is important to manage the expectations of the investors—both public and private. Economic development is a relationship-building exercise so it is vital that investors appreciate the timeframe required for the potential returns on their investments. Companies are cautious about where they make their location decisions and individuals are similarly intent upon cautious decision-making. The returns they might reasonably expect over a five-year timeframe may not be realized for the first few years. Economic development professionals must become adept at investor relations and reporting.

Ultimately, the ideal situation is one in which economic development marketing is understood by the providers of funding—whether public or private—to be an investment in the future of the community rather than simply an annual cost. Once that understanding has been reached, decision-makers may exhibit a greater propensity to appropriate funds and to be reasonable in their expectations of returns and the periods of time over which they might be provided. It might even bring community leaders to the realization that businesses are right in marketing more aggressively when sales are slow rather than pulling back on marketing budgets. The community that spends more on marketing in difficult budgetary times will likely leapfrog over many of their competitors who have reduced their marketing expenditures. During these times, even though businesses may not be active in relocation decisions, their site-location executives and consultants are still scanning the playing field. To be absent from the game is to lose ground to other communities.

There are two types of performance metrics that have been used by economic development organizations generally: those that measure process and those that measure outcomes. It is my firm belief that process measures are valuable for measuring individuals' performance only, not that of programs or organizations. The number of letters sent or calls made are noteworthy if that is a person's job. Presumably, there will be others in the group who are responsible for culling the responses and following up on leads. Other such measures used by economic development organizations often include testimonials, media contacts, trade show attendance, website hits, and awards received.

Some will assert that there are "new" ways to measure economic development success in a community, and that these means include relationship-building, an analysis of how satisfied customers are with the economy and their servicing, the benefits that accrue to parts of the community that have been left behind, environmental impacts, collaborations, and more. While these are clearly benefits of economic development and do increase the quality of life for all in a community, it is often more important to those who provide the funding for the programs to create jobs, generate wealth, and expand the tax base.

Some communities have the specific need to grow the residential population. For them, there will be strategies put into place that will accomplish that aim. The metrics will then reflect the outcomes of those strategies. Other observed metrics for economic development performance have included the narrowing of income gap disparities, decreases in the poverty rate, reductions in the vacancy rates in office buildings or other commercial properties, changes in median education levels, or an increase in the number of start-up businesses.

Regions have more and different means of measuring their economic performance. Measures of Gross Regional Products are available and have been for some time which enables one to regard trend lines and determine whether the region is moving its overall economy in the right direction. The Brookings Institution in Washington, DC periodically releases rankings of the nation's top 100 regions which enable local planners to assess performance relative to other similar-sized regions across the country.

For an organization whose mission it is to attract and retain businesses or grow the local tax base, there are more vital measures that actually address the purposes of the program. The program is not likely funded to call on companies or mail brochures. The purposes are to create jobs, retain jobs, sell or lease land or buildings, attract investments, attract venture capital and angel investments, grow the real estate tax base to support public services, redevelop brownfield sites or revitalization districts, and more. If these are the outcomes that are expected, and are built into the economic development strategic plan, then those are the items that should be measured to assess performance. If jobs are not created, no one will care about how many meetings you attended.

The country's most populous regions have more comparative economic data available to them, and the same is true of the nation's primary cities that can more readily find data on job generation, increases in average wage rates, and a wide variety of trends that measure the growth of patents, technology companies and technology production, levels of expendable income, gross product, and more. Indeed, a variety of indices that combine a range of factors are often much more readily available to primary cities and regions than to smaller cities and towns. Such comparative indices are also available over time and provide a sense of how one city is either improving or declining against its peers and competitors for economic development.

One means of measuring impact for economic development programs is to assess the marginal revenues generated for the state or local tax bases. Indeed, this is often the primary reason such programs are established and funded. As such, it would make great sense to be able to say our announcements generated X amount of new tax dollars this year. When added to the tax dollars of past announcements that are still paying into the city's coffers, one can reach a total of tax contributions generated by the efforts of the economic development program. At that point, one need only to divide the total tax returns by the amount of dollars spent on the program over time. If the former exceeds the latter over time—that is, if the returns exceed expenses—the program can boast of a positive return on investment, or ROI. Over time, the ROI should grow because past announcements, if still in the city, are still paying taxes. If the total returns (taxes paid) are less than the costs of the program, the ROI is less than one-to-one, and there will be questions about whether the program should continue or should be restructured.

However, there are two problems associated with what would, on the surface, appear to be a very logical approach. The first is the most critical: tax returns are confidential in nature and companies will not release that information. The local tax assessor is also bound by that confidentiality. Simply put, the returns part of the calculation is seldom made available.

The second problem with such an approach is that it is only a valid measurement if the announcements of new companies and the tax generation that results are directly tied to the efforts of the economic development program and that such involvement can be documented. A great deal of economic development in a city or region occurs outside of the economic development program's direct involvement. Therefore, thorough documentation in the form of emails or other communication must be maintained in the files. If performance bonuses or continued funding is contingent, at least in part, on the outcomes presented, it is always wise to have an outside auditor or individual confirm the numbers.

Because ROI calculations are so constrained, other approaches can be more useful. For example, several representative examples of announcements and leased space can be selected and assumptions made about number of employees and the amount of space they take, the assessed value of the building, the company's share of space used and their relative tax burden for the building. Based on such assumptions, an overall tax contribution—and therefore an ROI—can be estimated. Because the estimates would then be based on numerous assumptions, there will almost certainly be debates about the accuracy of the return projection. However, if the conclusion was that the ROI was four-to-one and others argue that it may only be three-to-one, the conclusions must still be positive. On the other hand, if the calculation yields an ROI of 1.5:1, then any questions of the accuracy of the estimates are entirely reasonable. Economic development and elected officials need to devise performance metrics that accurately record true impact and means of using the information for future planning.

3   Describing ROI in Terms of Teachers and Police Officers

When citizens examine the expenditures of their local elected and appointed officials, they want to know what they will get for those costs. They may not be imagining an ROI calculation, *per se*, but they will expect to know outcomes are expected. This will especially be the case when the community is expected to forgo funding for other activities. Thus, when funds are spent for economic development marketing instead of smaller class sizes or a new fire station, they want to have a clear and valid explanation.

Officials and economic development organizations often take great pains to display models indicating that expenditures for marketing have generated a given amount of dollars in return, usually measured in terms of marginal revenues contributed to the tax base. Perhaps some of the constituents will understand and appreciate the inherent logic of such demonstrations. However, more successful approaches have been used around the country to illustrate the returns in the guise of what line items had to be overlooked in order to support the economic development program. Thus, if the community saw a need for smaller classrooms, it may have been willing to fund economic development outreach instead if it had the understanding that the return would allow the community to have smaller classrooms and other things.

One way to ensure that the returns on investment are understood and fully appreciated is to characterize them to constituents in terms of the foregone projects and needs. For example, in the case of a community interest in smaller class sizes, the solution is to hire more teachers. If that was delayed until the returns from the investments in economic development marketing come in, it is instructive to describe those revenues in like terms. Rather than showing charts with increasing revenues of 100,000 dollars, constituents will be likely to be more receptive if the returns are shown to enable the hiring of two new teachers.

As real estate tax revenues are not only collected in the year of the location decision, but rather in each successive year as well, the returns on the investments in economic development cumulate over time. Thus, if companies add 100,000 dollars to the tax coffers one year, and other companies do the same in the second year, and so on, the number of dollars compounds in successive years. Another way of looking at this is that the companies in year one provides the costs of two new teachers. In year two, the funds are still contributed for those two new teachers and additional revenues are collected that will support two other teachers. In year three, new revenues are added to the repeating contributions, and so on.

Constituents who feel they have "given something up" for an economic development marketing program, and who have been told that the return will be greater than the investments, will expect local leaders, upon the receipt of those returns, to come back to the funding of their issues. Elected officials explaining the impacts of those returns in dollar terms will likely have far less reception than descriptions of the returns that they can better understand and appreciate.

Note

1 Swati Gosh and Jess Chen. *Making it Count: Metrics for High-Performing EDOs.* (Washington, DC: International Economic Development Council, February 3, 2014): 7.

Reference

Gosh, Swati and Chen, Jess. *Making it Count: Metrics for High-Performing EDOs.* Washington, DC: International Economic Development Council, February 3, 2014.

24 Managing Inter-Jurisdictional Relationships

When corporate site location executives, and their external counsel, consider a given location as a potential site for an office or plant, they typically do so in comparison to several sites that may suit their firm's needs. Those competitive locations may be distant. St. Louis may be competing with Dallas and Seattle. Or, the competition may be closer to home.

When a company is seeking a location in a specific region, the component jurisdictions find themselves in competition with each other. There may be a location in the core city and two in the suburbs; there may just be three in the suburbs. When intra-regional competition occurs, and one jurisdiction is successful, it may result in a competitive spirit between the leadership of the various jurisdictions that were involved. If one jurisdiction is repeatedly successful in the competition for economic development prospects, there can arise a competitive nature that could possibly interfere with other inter-jurisdictional programs and activities.

1 The Concentricity of Regional Growth

The pattern of economic growth in regions across the United States has been similar for generations. Initial business and residential development was located at the heart of the central city and, over time, spread throughout the city. As was noted in previous chapters, the post-World War II generation sought more spacious lots for homes and moved out of the cities to acquire them, thereby creating the suburbs. Initially, the suburban communities served as "bedroom communities" for the employees that were located in the central city but, once the employers realized that their best workers had moved out to the suburbs, and that land was cheaper for businesses too, they began to move their facilities out of the cities as well. This, in turn, accelerated the movement of those who had the resources and skill sets to follow the trend out of the cities.

This meant that the inner suburbs—those closest to the central city—became employment centers. Over time, of course, those close-in suburbs became both older and time-worn. This is when employers—and residents—began to move out to the next concentric ring of development around the core cities, giving rise to the so-called "outer suburbs." And, that pattern has continued over time in the same way: concentric circles of growth moving ever further away from the central city, leaving older cores and inner suburbs.

There are perhaps several lessons for economic development that can be drawn from this pattern. First, the center cities of this country need to be mindful of what businesses are moving to the suburbs and to be prepared to replace them with businesses for which the assets and amenities of the downtown are relevant. Second, the suburbs that are home to the businesses of today need to realize that the next concentric circle of development will be their competition in the future. This means that they will need to build the assets base in their communities that will encourage their businesses to remain in place. And, for the next circle of growth, the need will be to put into place the assets and amenities that will draw businesses to their communities rather than to other communities within the circle.

To some extent, middle rings of the development can also develop economies based on companies that provide services to businesses and residents looking in both directions—inward to the central city and outward to businesses in the next ring of development. What communities need to avoid is becoming the bedroom community in a state in which local governments are reliant on real estate taxes for the provision of public services. This creates a situation where residents must pay for the preponderance of costs of providing public services. Businesses help to offset the costs of public services for residents because they tend to take back far less in public services than they contribute to the real estate tax base. Residents, on the other hand, require more in public services than they contribute to the real estate tax base. Communities need to plan to develop both residential and business bases regardless of the concentric rings in which they are located.

In some regions, the initial—and, therefore, the older—development—occurred in the core city. Subsequently, bedroom communities grew in the first concentric ring of development outside the city. As business growth moved out into the suburbs, away from the city, it did so in a second concentric ring, skipping over the first ring which then became a bedroom community looking both inward and away from the core city. This creates a middle ring of suburban areas that have little or no tax base other than that which supports a bedroom community (e.g., retail and persona services). Cities and towns in that ring may face tax base issues because residents will have to pay for the full range of public services without the benefit of a significant private sector to offset those costs. In such cases, the bedroom communities must seek business growth that either supports growth in the other rings or develop new businesses that prefer that type of environment rather than more traditional business settings.

2 Neighbors and Tax Base Considerations

As the suburbs in this country grew, and people and firms moved outward to the suburbs, the bulk of tax base revenues also shifted. In the Washington, DC metropolitan area, northern Virginia:

> transformed itself from a residentially-based economy to a diversified technology-intensive and knowledge-based economy and it also transformed the Washington metropolitan area economy from one that was DC-centric to one in which job and income growth was driven by private sector expansion.[1]

In regions across the country, the post-World War II move from cities to suburbs by those with the greatest skills created competitive markets for business relocations as well. As a consequence, poverty grew in cities that now had the least capacity to support poor people. Meanwhile, the suburbs grew in employment, wealth, and overall quality of life. This, too had consequences: relationships between cities and suburbs, between mayors and county boards, and between a region's poor and its more well-to-do reflected tensions. While those tensions were, at their origins, driven by economic conditions, they soon spread to socio-political factors as well. Racial conflicts and other negative perceptions of one another grew as the cities became increasing poor and the suburbs increasingly successful.

The Washington, DC metropolitan area is one region in which this clearly occurred. Northern Virginia's population growth accounted for 65 percent of the Washington metropolitan area's total population. It also represented 61 percent of all new jobs added in the metropolitan area. "But, more important than rapid job growth alone has been the shift in the quality of the jobs being generated by the northern Virginia economy compared to the other portions of the Washington area."[2] Initially, this did create the very type of situation described above; however, inter-jurisdictional cooperation on a variety of issues has, over time, reduced much of the tension between city and suburbs. That is not to say that it has been eliminated. The city has begun to develop an economy, much of which is based on the federal government, and the disparities between it and the suburbs has diminished somewhat. There is still a long way to go but it should also be noted that the disparities of wealth and job base that exist between the city and the suburbs also exists from one suburb to another.

There is no reasonable expectation that all communities or all people will progress evenly or that their economic bases will grow at the same relative pace. Nor is it entirely reasonable to expect one jurisdiction to slow down so that others may catch up. Inter-jurisdictional cooperation can help lagging areas grow but it may or may not create total economic equality. And, inter-jurisdictional collaboration will go only so far: the bottom line is typically drawn when a prospective economic development company must make a choice of location. Tax base considerations and first priority attention to one's own residents is usually the point at which cooperation turns into competition.

The dominant growth of one jurisdiction within a region can give rise to a degree of envy on the par of neighboring jurisdictions throughout the region, including, to some extent, the center city. Elected officials throughout the region have been careful not to allow such developments to become flash points or for competitive jurisdictions to interfere with inter-jurisdictional relationships that are as strong and collaborative as possible.

In the Washington, DC metropolitan region, the greater economic development competition has come not from the center city but from the jurisdiction immediately to its north, across the Potomac River and in a different state: Montgomery County, Maryland. Fairfax and Montgomery Counties are comparable jurisdictions in many ways. Both are highly diverse communities with excellent public education systems and attractive and safe neighborhoods. The two states are different in other ways, some of which have affected their economic development successes. For example, Fairfax County is a Right-to-Work state and Maryland is not. However, the primary difference over time has been that Fairfax County has been consistently aggressive about economic development programs and has always had very pro-business Boards of Supervisors and benefits from being in a similarly very pro-business state.

In recent years, Montgomery County and the State of Maryland have become increasingly active in their economic development efforts as well, but the reputation as being pro-business will take time to build. And, the effort must be consistent for a long period of time; businesses expect certainty in the level of state and local support they will receive as long as they remain in a given location. That certainty must appear and be expected to remain in place for many years to come and must be reflected in policies related to zoning and permitting, taxation, infrastructure improvements, and more.

Montgomery County's elected officials have, on several occasions, conducted surveys to compare their standing in economic development and community assets with those in Fairfax County. On at least two occasions, those surveys were released to the public and reported in the local press, including the *Washington Post*. The survey results reflected rather negatively, in a comparative sense, on Montgomery County, thus further damaging its reputation for business attraction, and creating some ill will and concerns. The damage done to inter-jurisdictional relationships can come from within and, at least for purposes of economic development and collaboration, need to be very carefully managed by all concerned.

3   Urban–Suburban Tensions

One of the laudable goals of economic development is that it is generally felt to be all-inclusive; that, in some way, all parts of the community will benefit. Where there is not unanimous concurrence is how that equity is applied. The literature includes assertions that the community has an obligation to ensure that everyone benefits equally from the local economic development. There are even those who maintain that it is an absolute requirement of development.

But, as the balance of population between urban and rural areas and urban and suburban areas began to shift, the balance of power and taxes, and economic development shifted with it. "population in the nation's metropolitan areas increased from 36 million in 1950 to 74 million in 1970, . . . 74 percent of total population growth . . . over those two decades."[3]

In a more practical sense however, the economic development of a large city, small town, or metropolitan region will yield unequal advance. That will mean not only that some individuals will fare better than others, but that either neighborhoods or parts of larger regions will fare well while others will advance more slowly. CNN noted that Charlotte's recovery from the banking crisis "masks difficult times for many people who live there . . . Racial inequality, poverty, and segregation in housing and education have relegated many residents to the sidelines while the rest of Charlotte thrives."[4]

In Cleveland, suburban governments have been more open than most about what they feel their responsibilities to the center city to be. Swanstrom writes that they have "used every power within their grasp to capture the positive externalities of metropolitan growth while foisting the negative externalities on the central city."[5] While this may be a somewhat unbalanced characterization, the central city–suburban municipality relationships must be nurtured over time and must have some two-way components to them.

Economic development is a means of moving the local economy forward. It is a means to an end, that being the enhanced opportunities for all to pursue. Those with higher education levels, greater experience, more relevant skill sets, backers for business start-ups, and maybe just plain luck, will be the first to improve their economic standing. However, as primary businesses grow, small businesses will thrive because they will supply goods and services to those companies and to their employees. The workers will earn greater pay and, as described in the chapter on economic growth theories, those employed will begin to spend more on non-essential items (see Engel's Law, Chapter 1). This supports local retailers and restaurants. The resultant increases in the local tax base will provide for more teachers, firefighters, and other public services in the community.

While the economic development will not be entirely equitable for all people and all firms, it will have the effect of spreading the benefits and elevating all. Where the greater difficulty arises is in the equitable distribution of development across the entire geography of a community, city, or region. It should not be surprising that market-driven economic development will locate in the sub-markets that contain the greatest resources for business growth and expansion. This will mean the most and the best office space or other facilities, the highest concentration of primary workforce or training institutions. The agglomeration theory described in the first chapter asserts that the additional development will occur most efficiently where the most complete cluster of support entities exists.

If one considers any major metropolitan area, one will find that greatest economic development takes place in a relatively few nodes while other parts of the region expand more slowly. Such areas would be wise to take advantage of the development elsewhere in the region and build a community of businesses that support the primary industries growing throughout the region. Over time, with the addition of workforce, technology, and capital, they can develop primary industries as well. In fact, the Product Cycle Theory of economic growth (Chapter 1) states that their advance could be accelerated by the development or attraction of new technologies that leapfrog those of the primary markets that will ultimately become obsolete. That, however, is a very long-term play and requires substantial inputs of capital and an ability to compete with those agglomerations where capital and workforce already exists. By providing the support businesses for primary industries, they establish a cluster that can sustain growth over time.

There is always an "on the other hand . . ." In this case, that relates to the plight of many of the inner cities in America's larger regions. Sustaining a movement that began after World War II, people with the financial wherewithal moved out to the suburbs. These were the best-educated and most highly skilled residents of the region and those who wanted continued access to that part of the workforce took the businesses with them. That left behind in the center cities a less desirable workforce and businesses for which they are appropriate. As that trend continues, the choicest elements of the tax base also moves to the suburbs, leaving behind fewer and poorer public services that make those communities even less desirable to businesses for location decisions.

Economic development will never be entirely equitable across entire communities, especially larger regions, although the trends of development and improvement can be spread more equally over time. This requires the political will to enact public policies that will spread the benefits to those communities over time. There are two inherent difficulties in these kinds of policies. The first is that regions are generally comprised of multiple jurisdictions that have elected boards or councils and that are empaneled by their constituents to improve their quality of life, not that of the residents of other neighboring jurisdictions. This is not to say that elected officials turn a blind eye to the needs of their neighbors, but they must be aware that, in the eyes of those who put them in office (and can take them out of office as well), charity must begin at home.

Regional economic development is a particularly challenging process. Inevitably, the urban cores in this country have lost many of the primary employers to the suburban business centers. This was the result of the post-World War II movement of those who could to suburban residential communities where they could afford single-family homes, backyards, and better public services. As the higher-skilled people moved, the companies moved to them, leaving the cities to deal with the needs of the lesser-skilled, lower-income individuals with ever-diminishing local budgets. Because it benefits no one in a region to have the center city fare poorly, regional jurisdictions work in tandem to spread the benefits of economic development; however, the bottom line for all jurisdictions is the provision of public services to their own communities. This often leads to unequal development that can generate resentment or conflicts in other areas.

The further challenge to spreading economic development across a multiple community scope is the perceived need to fuel the engine that creates the greatest development. That is to say that, even when larger multi-jurisdictional regions collaborate and intend that all should benefit from the economic development in one or a few of the component areas, a dilemma arises. Should the benefits of growth be spread out so all will benefit a little bit, or should the benefits of that economic development be allowed to, or even be encouraged to, cluster together. In theory, such agglomeration provides an impetus to further development. And, those greater rates of growth provide higher salaries that residents of the entire region can access. In turn, that means a greater tax base in the neighboring jurisdictions as well that can enhance public services, increase the general quality of life, and thereby make that community more attractive to future economic development as well.

There has been a recent trend that should give hope to the center cities in metropolitan regions. Many large companies have begun to move their headquarters operations back into the center cities in order to take advantage of good real estate deals and the amenities of the downtown areas. Examples include Quicken Loans (Detroit), GE (Boston), Cadillac (New York City), and McDonald's (Chicago). Large city elected officials and their economic development professionals should seize upon this trend and try to understand what was behind those decisions. Perhaps there are similar opportunities in other parts of the United States.

As relates to large versus small cities and the development of their economies, the tendency is for larger cities to become highly diversified as smaller cities move toward specialization. Aghion and Durlauf explain:

> Diversified cities have some of all types of workers . . . New firms have a choice. They can locate in a diversified city with low localization economies in any one sector. But in a diversified city, they can experiment with a new process . . . until they find their ideal process. At that point, they can move to a city specialized in that process."[6]

This notion can be prescriptive for smaller cities as they try to define their ideal business base; such strategies will be revisited in a later chapter.

Since the 2010 Census reports were issued, however, there has arisen a sense that the cities are beginning to grow again and, surprisingly, that the nation's suburban areas are generally growing at a slower rate. The Brookings Institution reported that these spikes in city population growth were due to the young workers preferring downtown life styles, empty nesters moving into cities, and new immigrants preferring those environments.[7] This movement provides a sharp contrast to the post-World War II mass movements to create and reside in suburban environments. Further, trends are that the youngest workforce generation—Millennials—prefer not to own vehicles, are marrying (and requiring homes, backyards, great schools, and safer neighborhoods) later in their lives, and don't have an interest in large living spaces.

Through the mid-2030s, more than 70 million people in the Baby Boomer generation will retire and there will not be enough of the younger workers to fill all of those vacated jobs. Localities and the business community must find technology applications and other ways to ensure that the job demand does not so dramatically exceed what will be the overall supply of workers. Gatto reports on a McKinsey Global Institute report that suggests that, by 2020, "the world could have 40 million too few college-educated workers and, in advanced economies, up to 95 million workers could lack the skills needed for employment."[8] This means that communities will need to become very competitive for the relatively few workers available. The locations that can offer a workforce will attract and retain the companies in the future. Universities, communities, and businesses must work together to address these issues if they want to survive.

If current trends of population growth in the cities exceeding the rates of growth in the suburbs continues into the future, there will be severe implications for employment, transportation, housing, tax bases, and public services for both the nation's cities and its suburbs. The leadership of communities across the United States must take notice and begin to plan now. Multi-family housing is on the increase and home ownership for people between the ages of 18 and 34 declined from 43 percent in 2005 to 37 percent in 2013.[9] These trends are changing the dynamics for land use planning, zoning, transportation issues, public service provision, and commercial office and plant development. It has also led to an increased interest in the notion of multiple jurisdictions within the same region in working together to attract, retain, and grow new employment opportunities.

4   Regional Promotion

Proponents of regional economic development marketing offer two primary arguments in support of collaborative promotion. First, they observe that companies are concerned about the labor force, the buildings, and the quality of life in an area, not which jurisdiction they locate in; and, second, that the collection of assets across an entire region is more attention-getting than those of each individual jurisdiction displayed separately. The extension of that proposition may be that, by combining the resources of several jurisdictions within a given region, the outreach program can be more robust and far-reaching.

To establish regional economic development organizations requires that several jurisdictions sacrifice some degree of local authority. It also means that the outcomes must be spread over time somewhat fairly across all of the component communities. Most typically, the regional organizations provide outreach and prospect identification, Once prospects for the region have been found, they are handed off to the respective jurisdictions for servicing and, hopefully, locating. The more communities that are included in the regional organization, the greater the difficulty in collaboration and sharing the outcomes. And, the greater the diversity of the constituent jurisdictions, the greater will be the difficulty in establishing a plan for business attraction because every community will want something very different.

This was the case in the greater Washington, DC metropolitan area. A regional program was established that included more than 20 different jurisdictions across two states, Virginia, Maryland and the District of Columbia. Added to the mix was the federal government, whose presence dominates much of the economic discussions in the region. Of the various municipalities, there were several that were highly urban, with high income levels and excellent public schools. There were also several that had less to offer in terms of assets and amenities. Some were quite large: Fairfax County has well over one million residents. Others were small towns and rural areas that had greatly different needs and interests. Finally, the larger jurisdictions put more into the budget of the regional organization and, thus expected more decision-making authority and results that suited their requirements.

Added to the public sector contributions were private sector supporters, each of which was interested in their own bottom lines: newspaper advertising purchased, groceries sold, or homes bought. To market such a diverse region was extraordinarily difficult and, because the focus was spread over so many distinctly different needs and interests, the outcomes were limited and the program closed. A final problem was that, even when the regional organization was able to identify a prospect about which everyone did not already know, the localities closed the deal and the regional program received little recognition. As a result, fundraising was always difficult. Much of the CEO's time is engaged in fundraising rather than the more directly economic development objectives of the program, and as much as one-third of the money that was raised represented the cost of the campaigns required to do so.

Not all regions are suburban and metropolitan. In the case of large rural regions, it is often clear that small towns will be unable to thrive on their own. Despite long distances, times between small towns may be small enough to enable close cooperation. In order to constitute enough of a population to represent a viable workforce or a sufficient demand for institutions such as hospitals, community colleges, and more, small towns in rural areas may band together to demonstrate their potential for the location of a business facility.

There tends to be a presumption that regions should conduct cooperative marketing campaigns for economic development prospects. The argument goes something like this: businesses don't care where the borders are between jurisdictions, the labor force doesn't care which side of the line the company is located in, and the effort, if regional in scope, would eliminate inter-jurisdictional competition, thus yielding much more efficient campaigns.

While much of that is true, those arguments ignore some very important considerations. Economic development is a very competitive business, even between neighbors in the same region. There are a few essential reasons for this. In some states, localities are legislatively enabled to impose local income taxes. In those states, municipalities may be less concerned about where a company actually sites itself; if the company lands on the other side of the boundary line from Springfield, its companies will still be able to compete for contracts to provide goods and services. And, its residents will still be able to compete for the jobs. Then, when they bring their incomes home to Springfield, the city will tax it. Their purchases in the city limits will still be subject to sales tax and their homes to property taxes.

However, not all states have local income tax options. Northern Virginia is a good example. The Commonwealth of Virginia collects 100 percent of the income taxes generated in the state and uses it to fund state services. Localities in Virginia build their local public service budgets largely on the basis of taxes on real property. Their residents will also be able to compete for jobs and their companies will still be able to compete for contracts, but only one of the jurisdictions will be collecting those valuable real estate tax dollars! If you are an elected official in a Virginia jurisdiction, no matter how important being a good regional neighbor is to you, your first obligation is to build your own tax base and enable the provision of public services to your own citizens without raising the residential tax rates if at all possible. Thus, even in the most tightly knit communities, there will come a time when one must draw a line and tend to one's own issues above regionalism.

This inherent competitiveness is further encouraged when the region in question incorporates more than one state. In the example of northern Virginia, there are three entities involved: Washington, DC, northern Virginia, and suburban Maryland. Each of the states has both an obligation to its citizens and a political commitment to ensure that their state wins the competition for any given economic development prospect. Similar regional strains occur in other regions that cross state lines, including St. Louis, Kansas City, and others.

Proponents of regional economic development outreach indicate that the current trend is in that direction. In fact, most of the regional economic development organizations are of relatively recent vintage. That, however, is an observation of a trend and not an argument for doing so. Further, the trend is matched by a larger number of communities that have elected to continue as single-jurisdictional programs. The fact is that the best approach is the one that makes the most sense for the community—or communities—in question.

Economies of scale, so goes the argument, enable greater outreach and issues such as workforce naturally cross borders anyway. That's all, true, but the taxes will only accrue to the jurisdiction in which the office or facility is ultimately located. Often, that is the bottom line. Sweeping generalizations about regional collaborations for economic development are not applicable in every locale. Another argument in support of the regional approach goes like this: "This requires all parties to set aside sentiments of 'turfism' and begin thinking about individual mandates."[10] This represents an extremely unrealistic statement in many areas because it means that elected officials need to forego the opportunity to compete for the tax base that improves the quality of life for their constituents and their community. Quite often, the best that can be expected is for communities that exist within the same region to be friendly competitors—but, still competitors! In some regions, collaboration in marketing works well and in others it does not.

A report by the IEDC indicates that 80 percent of the regional economic development partnerships were created in the last two decades of the twentieth century.[11] The driving factors for regional collaboration for economic development are generally cited as interjurisdictional commuting patterns, industry cluster components, and other factors that support corporate growth regardless of their location within a specific jurisdiction within the region.

In many cases, regions are primarily dependent upon the functioning of the core city in order to succeed economically. For that reason, the neighboring jurisdictions may be very happy to cooperate for economic development purposes because they "need" the core city as a partner to be successful. This, however, is not always the case. Consider once again the metropolitan Washington region. The United States Department of Labor, in 2007, released a report that characterized the Washington, DC metropolitan area as the only large region in the nation with two distinct nodes of economic growth: the core city for federal jobs and Fairfax County, Virginia for private sector employment. Additionally, there are numerous other very strong sub-markets in the region, including Crystal City and Ballston in Arlington County; Reston, Tysons Corner, and Merrifield in Fairfax County, Virginia; and Rockville and Bethesda in Montgomery County, Maryland.

This abundance of strong sub-markets means that the region is not as dependent upon the core city for economic growth as elsewhere in the country. Thus, it may be that the concept of regional promotion for economic development can be most successful in regions with a primary business district—typically, the center city—and other sub-markets throughout the region that are wholly dependent upon that primary market. In such cases, there would be a greater proclivity to cooperation for economic development and less natural competition for the resultant business prospects.

Of course, not all regions are urban/suburban in nature. Regions also exist in rural areas, and encompass several counties and cities or towns. In these instances, regional may make sense because there are relatively few resources available for marketing separately. Also, the assets and amenities that may be attractive to businesses may be collectively impressive while they are not as attractive individually. This often encourages rural regions to market themselves as such. The key to this practice is to ensure that the partner communities agree up front to represent the whole, and not its parts, to business prospects in a fair and open manner. And, when a prospect does land in one of the region's component jurisdictions, there must be a universal acceptance and celebration.

Of course, even in highly competitive regions, there can be regional collaboration for economic development. However, this generally works only if there are protocols in place that permit joint marketing and a fair distribution of any resultant prospect opportunities. In regions that have had successful regional economic development entities, careful structuring of the process and an ongoing relationship–management practice has been engaged.

Regional economic development organizations fall, in one sense, into one of three categories. In the same way that local economic development programs can be either: 1) focused primarily on marketing; 2) focused entirely on preparing and enhancing the local "product" to be marketed; or, 3) a combination of the two, so too can regional organizations.

Regional groups that pursue the option of being primarily a marketing body on behalf of the entire region can be greatly effective if the component jurisdictions are all in agreement on the need for joint promotions or if those communities have such limited resources as to be either limited or ineffective on their own. In rural communities, there are too few resources in each hamlet to market themselves and there may be too few assets for economic development when standing alone. In such cases, regional economic development may make great sense.

Regional programs can also be a logical strategy when the assets and amenities for economic development all reside in one of the component jurisdictions. That is to say that, in most regions, the core city is the site of that is most attractive to employers. The surrounding communities may need to collaborate on marketing because, alone, there is simply not a strong enough appeal for employers.

Regional programs may be less likely to succeed when one of two other conditions are present. The first is when there are numerous strong markets throughout the region. In a metropolitan area with five or ten strong markets in the suburbs, there will be considerably less willingness to market jointly because the various markets are intent upon attracting companies to their own jurisdictions. Of course, the jobs and sub-contracting opportunities may be shared in any event, the tax base goes only to the jurisdiction in which the company sites itself.

A second situation in which regional cooperation in marketing is less likely to succeed is the region in which there is more than one state involved. In northern Virginia, for example, its jurisdictions also compete with those in the neighboring states of Maryland and Virginia and the District of Columbia. The Commonwealth of Virginia, for example, provides its public services on the basis of the state's income taxes. It wants to see companies located in Virginia rather than Maryland because the income taxes accrue to the benefit of the state in which the people reside. While people certainly do cross borders to go to work, the chances are presumed to be greater that the workforce will locate nearer to the company and more than likely in the same state.

Collaboration of regional bodies in these cases tends to be more effective when they focus on one of two strategies. The first is related to promotion but ends with the advertising and public relations of the region as a good place to live and work and to locate a business. Once prospect companies have been identified, the regional body is no longer involved and the localities that are relevant for the particular business take over the relationships. This sounds good in theory but does not always work smoothly because it is never quite clear when the regional body should let go and the localities take over.

A second situation in which regionalism for economic development works well is when it is focused entirely on those assets and amenities that every jurisdiction in the partnership markets together and separately and that benefit every jurisdiction and every local economic development program. These will include transportation issues, clean air and water issues, workforce training, and more. These are regional assets from which every jurisdiction benefits.

Many states are now organizing programs that encourage regional collaboration for economic development. In Virginia, for example, Go Virginia is a recent program that has been enacted and funded, in part, by the General Assembly. The program requires regions to work together in order to receive any state funding. The region must design a program that will advance that region's economic development and it must include financial contributions from more than one of the component jurisdictions as well as other funding. That latter category of funding may come from universities, institutions such as hospitals or airports, or the business community. Once the program is approved by the Regional Council, application is made to the State Go Virginia Board for approval and funding.

The advantage of a regional program such as Go Virginia is that each region can identify its own needs and work collaboratively using state and local money to improve its economic development posture. In parts of the Commonwealth, regions may regard this as an opportunity to raise the awareness of the region through marketing and promotion. In other parts of the Commonwealth, such as northern Virginia, where several jurisdictions have substantial and very effective economic development programs of their own, it is far less likely that the funding will be used for joint marketing. More likely projects will be based on improvements in regional infrastructure needs and workforce preparation.

A nascent regional effort is the One Region program that incorporates the City of Charleston, South Carolina and the surrounding counties of Berkeley, Charleston, and Dorchester. An organization has been formed with 80 board members from throughout the region. Some are elected officials while others are educators, business people, representatives of non-profit organizations, and others. The collective focuses have been placed on global competitiveness, competitiveness, unified regional actions, and the varied regional dynamics that make that area a great place to live, work, and visit.

Specific areas that will be addressed by One Region include infrastructure, talent, affordability, momentum, equity, and innovation and entrepreneurship. The key to the success of these endeavors is the willingness of all to collaborate and to ensure that all areas—and all the people—of the region advance the collective cause and all benefit equally. The essential underlying belief is that the area will progress more expeditiously together than it can as a region of separate component jurisdictions.

Notes

1 Stephen S. Fuller. *Northern Virginia's Economic Transformation.* (Fairfax, VA: George Mason University, November 2011): 1.
2 Ibid., 17.
3 John F. McDonald. *Urban America: Growth, Crisis, and Rebirth.* (Armonk, NY: M.E. Sharpe, 2008): 85.
4 Chris Isidore. Charlotte's Economic Success Masks Deep Black–White Divide. (September 22, 2016) http://money.cnn.com
5 Todd Swanstrom. *The Crisis of Growth Politics: Cleveland, Kucinich, and the Challenge of Urban Populism.* (Philadelphia, PA: Temple University Press, 1985): 68.
6 Phillipe Aghion and Steven N. Durlauf. *Handbook of Economic Growth*, vol. 1B. (San Diego, CA: Elsevier, 2005): 1575.
7 William Frey. City Growth Dips Below Suburban Growth, Census Shows. (May 30, 2017) www.brookings.edu
8 Richard M. Gatto. Changing Workforce Demographics. (Spring 2015) www.naiop.org
9 Ibid.
10 Richard E. Wood. *Survival of Rural America: Small Victories and Bitter Harvests.* (Lawrence, KS: University of Kansas Press, 2008): 19.
11 Louise Anderson. *Opportunity for All: Strategies for Inclusive Economic Development.* (Washington, DC: International Economic Development Council, 2016).

322   *The Process*

References

Aghion, Phillipe and Howitt, Peter. *Endogenous Growth Theory*. Cambridge, MA: MIT Press, 1999.

Anderson, Louise. *Opportunity for All: Strategies for Inclusive Economic Development*. Washington, DC: International Economic Development Council, 2016.

Frey, William. City Growth Dips Below Suburban Growth, Census Shows. May 30, 2017. www.brookings.edu

Fuller, Stephen S. and Harpel, Ellen. *The Washington Area 2030 Economic Outlook: Standard Forecast*. Fairfax, VA: George Mason University, March 2009.

Gatto, Richard M. Changing Workforce Demographics. Spring 2015. www.naiop.org

Isidore, Chris. Charlotte's Economic Success Masks Deep Black-White Divide. September 22, 2016. http://money.cnn.com

McDonald, John F. *Urban America: Growth, Crisis, and Rebirth*. Armonk, NY: M.E. Sharpe, 2008.

Swanstrom, Todd. *The Crisis of Growth Politics: Cleveland, Kucinich, and the Challenge of Urban Populism*. Philadelphia, PA: Temple University Press, 1985.

Wood, Richard E. *Survival of Rural America: Small Victories and Bitter Harvests*. Lawrence, KS: University of Kansas Press, 2008.

25 Business Incubation and Entrepreneurialism as an Economic Growth Generator and State Development Programs

Many communities have developed incubator facilities (or shared-work locations) to generate the growth of new businesses. There are a variety of models for such programs but, generally, most provide access to shared support services and rent at considerably reduced rates because they are shared by the many businesses in the facility. They also provide training and workshops on, and often access to, such topics as starting a business, accounting and legal services, legal and licensing requirements, writing a business plan, obtaining the necessary financing, finding employees, marketing and sales, and more.

For start-ups, incubators also enable close proximity to other small start-up companies and their owners. This allows for the exchange of ideas as well as simply having support networks with whom one can commiserate. Solomon writes that Detroit found this approach to be very productive for those who had been laid off from the automobile industry and who wanted to start their own businesses as alternatives. "Besides discovering the entrepreneurial spirit and finding a niche, an unmet or under-met need, would-be entrepreneurs require capital, space, and training for their business start-ups."[1] Incubator facilities proved to be in great demand in the northern Virginia region when there were a lot of layoffs (either from the dot-com bust or sequestration) and some of those who had been laid off wanted to start their own businesses. It has also had an appeal to Baby Boomers who had completed their primary careers but who wanted to remain active and saw a new business as a means of doing so. Another group that showed an interest in business start-ups was from the millennial generation, for whom research suggests this is a desirable career path. Finally, many new Americans have expressed an interest in space in incubator facilities to launch import–export businesses to trade with their home countries.

For whichever of these reasons a community—or individuals in communities—elect to create incubator spaces, it is something communities have been doing to generate new business growth from within.

State Economic Development Programs

Every state in the United States operates economic development programs. At the state level, economic development has a broader meaning because the states are so inherently diverse and the communities within them are extremely different and have divergent needs. Each state has both urban and rural communities, some poor areas and others that have enjoyed greater economic development success. This often yields a dichotomy that can be challenging for state-level programs.

In many states, an effort is made to place the state's economic development resources in communities that need the help. This may be either urban or rural communities but the typical scenario is for those states to support the economic growth of the rural areas and small towns that lag in economic well-being and potential and that may not have the resources to conduct successful economic development programs for themselves. This is certainly a laudable use of state resources but it does not contribute support to the growth of the state's primary economic drivers.

In some states, the decision is made to spend the economic development programs' resources to enable the further development of the most productive cities. These are not always politically acceptable positions because it appears that those states are enabling the rich to get richer while the poor are left to their own, minimal devices. The logic behind this approach, however, is that, by fueling the engines of economic growth in a state, the returns will be substantially greater, and that those areas will generate significant tax revenues as a result. The resultant tax revenues then enable the state to provide increased public services to the less advantaged areas.

In Virginia, for example, 25 percent of all of the state's income tax revenue comes from one jurisdiction in northern Virginia, Fairfax County. Northern Virginia as a whole, contributes 44 percent of all the state's income taxes. Fairfax County receives only 19 cents back in the form of programs and services. The rest of the state benefits from its contribution. The question then becomes: Should the Commonwealth of Virginia focus its state-wide economic development strategies on northern Virginia in order to generate greater future tax revenues, or focus on the southwestern portion of the state where the unemployment rates are very high and the economic prospects limited?

Indeed, most states try to create a balanced program that accomplishes both takes: generating additional tax revenues and assisting those parts of the state in the greatest economic need. But, beyond the distinctions between the have jurisdictions and the have-nots, other great distinctions exist in most states. Rural areas may wish to see more manufacturing plants attracted while urban areas will likely seek office space users. Even different urbanized areas will have different strengths and will be interested in having the state seek to attract firms in the industry segments that are most advantageous to them.

A 2013 report of the National Governors Association highlighted some of the more recent trends in state economic development programs. They include a greater emphasis on job creation from companies already within the state as opposed to business attraction efforts, a new focus on strategic partnerships that help businesses address current workforce shortages, placing higher demands on in-state colleges and universities to translate their research discoveries into products that can be commercialized, and developing programs to support the expansion of exporting by companies within the state. This latter approach is designed to increase revenues coming into the state, which generates new jobs as well as attracting dollars that can be taxed by both the localities and the states in order to help pay for public services.

Most counties and towns do not have enough budgetary resources to conduct global marketing for economic development. Typically, that is the domain of the states that each select overseas markets in which to market or to locate an external office. The markets are selected because they are the most likely to generate interest by companies that have similar industry strengths and are sufficiently funded to take their companies outside of their native countries.

States also conduct most of the programs designed to develop foreign trade. Trade between the businesses in one's communities and people or companies overseas is an important economic development strategy. By selling either goods or services externally, companies bring revenues into the community and pay greater taxes in the process. Trade creates jobs and generates wealth. State trade offices face the same dilemma stated above. What are the best items to trade and where are the best trading partners?

One area of involvement for state economic development agencies is incentives payments. While there are some municipalities that also have incentive programs, it is more typically at the state level that one finds the real incentives programs for business attraction and retention. This means that the state economic development organizations are usually charged with managing the incentives programs, including accepting requests, working with the relevant local governments, negotiating the contractual agreements with the companies involved, overseeing the returns-on-investments, and even recovering funds when the businesses do not meet the required outcomes specified in the agreements. These responsibilities entail legal, accounting, auditing, reporting, and other management functions for state economic development agencies.

There are a variety of funding models for state economic development programs. Some are funded entirely from the state's budget while others are joint partnerships between public and private entities and are thus funded by both as well. One of the issues attendant to a state economic development organization that is funded entirely with state monies is that the strategic planning and the process of marketing can become more political than needed. In such cases, the Governor or the legislature may direct attention to areas of the state or to industries that have a greater return in political benefits for him or herself or for the party.

State economic development organizations that are jointly funded by both public and private entities can sidestep much—although certainly not all—of the political nature of marketing and targeting industries but may have others issues to address, including focusing on industry segments that benefit only the most successful economies of the state and do not pay enough attention to the needs of the poorer areas of the state. The managers of the public–private state partnerships also find out that they have multiple bosses: the governor, hundreds of legislators, and a council or board with members both from the private sector and those who have been politically appointed. Again, different perspectives must be melded into a common vision and a common set of strategies.

In either model, the economic development organization needs to be managed on the basis of agreements that have been in place prior to its establishment and that take into consideration all of the needs of the people of the state. This is a logical conclusion and one that is easily stated, but not necessarily easily implemented.

Note

1   Lewis D. Solomon. *Detroit: Three Pathways to Revitalization*. (New Brunswick: NJ: Transaction, 2014): 105.

Reference

Solomon, Lewis D. *Detroit: Three Pathways to Revitalization*. New Brunswick, NJ: Transaction, 2014.

Part VI
Sinclair Lewis Redux
It *Can* Happen Here

In 1935, the already well-known author, Sinclair Lewis, wrote a novel entitled *It Can't Happen Here*. The story was essentially a warning that the fascist dictatorships that arose in Europe could happen anywhere, even in the United States. At a time when Americans remained essentially oblivious to what was becoming increasingly serious on the continent, the book made a statement: regardless what people think, if it can happen in one country it can happen in another.

In the early 1970s, Seattle's erstwhile economic powerhouse faltered and ultimately declined to the point of damaging a major city and region for years. It was very clear at that point that no city or region can sustain its economic viability, let alone growth, on the back of a single, dominant industry or major employer. A hard lesson for Seattle but one from that other municipal leaders across the nation could learn.

However, other cities, counties, and regions seemed to believe that although, the decline of the aerospace industry nearly destroyed Seattle and the greater region, it certainly couldn't happen here! Not in the automotive industry! Not in the oil and natural gas industry! Not in banking and financial services! Not in federal contracting. It couldn't happen here!

But, repeatedly it happened in each of these industries. The fact is that it can happen here—anywhere. The Washington, DC metropolitan area is home to 16 of the top 20 contractors to the federal government. Fairfax County, Virginia alone is home to most of the large federal contractors. Certainly the federal government isn't moving and certainly it will continue to buy goods and services; it has to. Therefore, this region really is recession-proof; we are different. It really can't happen here . . . until it did.

The region had weathered reductions in various federal programs as well as cutbacks in federal direct employment numerous times. It always meant that one business or some people were affected. It sometimes even had spinoff effects in the secondary and tertiary economies. But, it never had overwhelmingly negative industry-wide or region-wide impacts. Recovery was always possible if you could ride out the storm. Nothing more disastrous than that could ever happen here. After all, the federal government isn't going anywhere. The Pentagon is here. NIH is here. All of the federal agencies that procure goods and services are here. And, they always will be here. We're the exception in the Washington, DC metropolitan area.

In 2011, a new term of art became a regional warning: sequestration. However, even as the sequester was discussed in the local media, it was still not really believed. Congress had actually designed it to be so onerous that matters would be resolved before they were ever be implemented. It was to be implemented at the end of 2013, but only in the most dire circumstances. The sequester?: it'll never happen!

But, according to the George Mason University Center for Regional Analysis, expenditures through federal procurements declined between 2010 and 2014 by $11.2 billion, or roughly 13.6 percent. At the same time, cutbacks in direct federal employment hit the region. And, that is just in the federal contracting business community; direct federal employment was also impacted by sequestration.[1]

From its high employment mark in 2010, direct federal employment in the region declined by a little more than 6 percent, or roughly 23,700 jobs. The corresponding decline in the federal payroll equated to nearly 6.5 percent, or 2.5 billion dollars. In the metropolitan Washington, DC area, that meant that fewer homes were built, fewer cars were purchased, fewer groceries were bought, and much more.

Research conducted by the Fairfax County Economic Development Authority revealed the following about the impacts of sequestration on the Washington, DC metropolitan area (FCEDA, 2016):

- Federal procurements declined in value by more than 11 billion dollars from federal fiscal year 2010 to 2014. That represented a decline of about 13.6 percent.
- Direct federal employment declined by more than 6 percent over the same period, equating to nearly 24,000 jobs.
- The loss of payroll was about 2.5 billion dollars.

The loss of payroll in that order of magnitude to a region means that fewer dollars are being spent in everything from retail establishments to higher education. Moreover, the effects on the psyches of both individuals and communities can be seriously damaged, from which recovery can take some time. This too may translate into reduced revenues for retailers and others.

The impact of federal losses must be understood in the context of the history of the region. From 1980 to 2010, there was a steady increase in federal procurement levels in the region. A decline of this nature post-2010 means not only jobs and revenue losses but also a significant cultural shift as communities and their leaders began to realize that this region's dominant line of business was not going to be what it once was.

The economic impacts are substantial. In Fairfax County, Virginia alone, federal procurement in 2016 reached nearly 24 billion dollars. Of that amount 58 percent came from the Department of Defense and the remainder came from all of the other federal agencies combined. Forty-six hundred vendors in the county received 5 percent of all federal contract dollars. This includes the following Fairfax County-headquartered companies: Northrop Grumman, CSC, General Dynamics, SAIC, Leidos, MITRE, and more. (FCEDA Federal Procurement)

The realization that it could indeed "happen here" struck the region hard. Some of the component communities were prepared and had begun to diversify their economic base while others did not heed the warnings and began preparing for economic diversification too late.

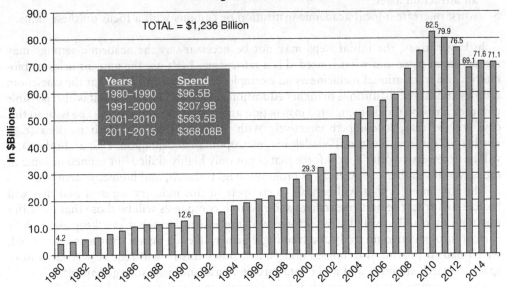

Federal Procurement in the Washington Metro Area, 1980–2015

TOTAL = $1,236 Billion

Years	Spend
1980–1990	$96.5B
1991–2000	$207.9B
2001–2010	$563.5B
2011–2015	$368.08B

Chart VI.1 Federal Procurement in the Washington, DC Area

Source: The George Mason University Center for Regional Analysis

Despite numerous examples of cities or regions that had failed to learn the lessons of insufficient economic diversification, it seems to recur. It happens again and again in small cities and large. My own research has shown that small and mid-sized towns, particularly in rural or semi-rural areas, are indeed aware of such perils but those communities are likely the least able to pursue effective diversification strategies due to their size and location.

Frequently, economic diversification in a community or region will be less the result of business attraction than the phased implementation of a long-term strategy designed first to attract the necessary assets that will, in turn, later attract the companies requiring such assets. In other words, if software developers are a targeted, diverse industry segment, the provision of a relevant workforce, and the necessary training institutions for upgrading technical skills over time are essential.

The implications of this realization are twofold. First, a software developer will not even consider a community that does not have both of these assets. And, second, the attraction and development of such assets requires time and resources. It does not however, need to be accomplished in one great, expensive action. It is most feasible to work toward these ends in small stages:

1 work with a community college to establish classes in the necessary skills areas; if a college is not nearby, work with one in the state to establish a few classes to start;

2 begin to develop a small group of qualified employees;

3   begin to attract or grow local small software developers and companies;
4   use this growing base of companies to attract larger businesses, using the classes as an attraction asset;
5   work to create a local academic institution or campus with a focus on these skills.

In larger areas, the initial steps may not be necessary as the academic settings may already be in place and what is needed is a refocusing. Let's use the nascent fields of biometrics and translational medicine as an example. Not only is it likely that the classroom settings and larger institutions of higher education are already in place but it is also possible that they already offer some related instruction and certificates or degrees. The issue in this case will be that, to compete effectively with well-established research markets (e.g., northern California, Boston, Philadelphia, metropolitan Washington, DC, and others), it will be necessary to offer a workforce that is not only highly skilled but trained in some of the newer and rather exotic areas of programming, research, and biometric analysis.

The communities that will be able to compete in this industry segment and that will be able to attract the best researchers and research companies will be those that can offer this type of readily available workforce and the institutions that can keep their skills current through ongoing study and training. Further, like the manufacturing sector of old, which had to provide warehouses and plants, this industry will require wet laboratory space, research support, and a big data business base and data storage capacity.

Once a community has concluded that, although the local economy is presently sound, there should be concern about a potential overdependence on a single industry or a single dominant employer, it needs to establish a detailed plan for economic diversification. Such a plan must be developed through a deliberate process that includes the key elements of the community, most especially representatives of the present single dominant industry. It must be focused on the identification of the existing assets and which industries will find them necessary components of their success as well as what missing assets need to be developed in order to attract the targeted industries the community wishes either to grow or attract. An alternative approach is first to identify the assets that can effectively be developed or attracted and then to identify the industries for which they are essential components of success.

Such assets may include the educational institutions and workforce assets that are noted above but also will include the kinds of things that will make these companies want to locate in a community and that will enable them to attract people to work for them there. For companies, this will mean supportive state and local tax policies, appropriate land use and permitting support, a positive labor or union setting, and more. For individuals, this will include a wide range of issues typically listed under the general heading of "quality of life," and include strong public education systems, safe neighborhoods, outdoor activities, and more.

The economic diversification strategy must then be focused on which additional assets to acquire and which existing assets to enhance, and how to do so, especially given the necessary resource allocations, over what period of time. Further, it may need to prioritize the assets acquisition plan so as to use scarce resources most effectively and to use the initial asset development to build upon itself and even to create a momentum in the acquisition of additional assets.

Over time, as the evolution of the asset base for economic diversification becomes more evident, business attraction plans can also be implemented that will now have a firm basis for discussions with companies and executives in the targeted fields. All of this must first be based upon a collective community realization that such over-dependence exists and that what has happened in other cities and regions can indeed happen again—here.

There are far too many examples of cities and regions across the United States—both large and small—that have presumed long-term economic security because their primary industry or company was golden. Surely, Boeing will never go out of business; it almost happened. Surely our steel will always be needed; the industry died out. Certainly, the American automotive industry will always be strong; after all, we invented the automobile and started the industry. That assurance turned out to be insufficient. Certainly, banking is secure; we will always need banks. Yet, Charlotte learned that they may not always be able to rely on the industry to the same extent as in the past.

And, not just large industries and large regions have repeatedly missed the point. Surely, our timber industry will remain strong. Where else will timber come from? Certainly, our textile employers will always be needed; people have to have shoes and shirts.

But, perhaps the greatest disillusionment of all is this one: we, in the Washington, DC metropolitan area's economy will always be stable and secure because the federal government is here and it will always be here. Perhaps this false sense of security was even fortified when Donald Rumsfeld was the Secretary of Defense and announced that the agencies of the federal government should be moved from Washington and relocated in other parts of the country in order to "disperse the target." But, because that didn't happen, it supported the notion that it never would.

Over time, events have proven otherwise.

Sequestration has demonstrated that not only could federal contracting be cut back, but that direct federal employment could also be reduced in the region. Washington, DC and the rest of the nation also learned that the various rounds of the Base Realignment and Closure Commission (BRAC) decisions could remove military personnel and their contractors from their communities, costing jobs, income, local expenditures, and the state and local tax bases that provide public services to residents.

In 2016, Donald Trump was elected President of the United States and, immediately upon his inauguration in January of 2017 began to implement his campaign promises, some of which related to the size of the federal workforce. Further, he had announced plans to eliminate various units and some entire federal agencies, such as the Environmental Protection Agency. All of a sudden, it became clear that having the federal government in the region was not a guarantee that the employment levels would remain the same. Even though the federal agencies will still be a large part of the local and regional economies, large-scale reductions-in-force (RIFs) could have highly damaging impacts on the economy of the entire region as well as its component jurisdictions and, of course, its residents.

Even if the total federal contracting expenditure levels remain the same—or, even increase—it appears that the sources may be shuffled around. A contract with one company from the Commerce Department is not the same thing as a contract with an entirely different firm through the Defense Department. Companies will lose contracts and people will lose their jobs; a great deal of economic dislocation will occur.

Finally, even if you are not among the groups of companies or people who are directly impacted, there will be a dampening effect on the economy at large. Consumer confidence indices will drop and expenditures will decline. The snowball effects are hard to predict, but they will be there.

Maynard wrote:

> [A]s the steel industry discovered, as the airline industry found out, as retailers learned, as dozens of names in American business know from painful experience over the past few years, no company is immune from demise, no matter how storied its history.[2]

Clearly, it can happen anywhere!

Notes

1   George Mason University, Center for Regional Analysis. (Fairfax, VA: George Mason University, May 2016).
2   Micheline Maynard. *The End of Detroit: How the Big Three Lost Their Grip on the American Car Market.* (New York: Random House, 2004): 232.

References

George Mason University, Center for Regional Analysis. Fairfax, VA: George Mason University, May 2016.
Maynard, Micheline. *The End of Detroit: How the Big Three Lost Their Grip on the American Car Market.* New York: Random House, 2004.

26 Preparing Communities for Economic Development

1   Seeing It Coming; Admitting It's Coming

A study of this nature may serve several purposes. The primary purpose of this research has been to document the experiences of cities and regions—both positive and negative—so that other cities and regions can gain insights that may benefit them as they move through similar sets of circumstances. It is also possible that communities can learn from this about more than just how to extricate themselves from such situations; there is a possibility that city and regional leaders can become so sensitized to the causes and effects of economic decline and revitalization that they can learn to see the approaching storms and move to avoid them rather than awaiting the devastation they can cause before designing a plan of response.

This begs the question: How can one know economic decline when it is approaching? What is there to look for? If one considers the various sections of this book and the lessons about how to grow and either develop or redevelop a city's economy, part of the answer becomes clear. A city that is overly dependent upon a single industry or a single employer—or even a relatively few employers—is at risk. This is even true if there is disbelief expressed in the community that that industry or employer could ever be in jeopardy; in fact, *especially* if there is such disbelief in the community. If a local economy is based on the production of outmoded products—or, if the means of production are outmoded—it too is headed for an economic decline.

The City of Vallejo, California declared municipal bankruptcy in 2010. Before finally doing so, its unemployment rate had climbed over 15 percent. Local businesses were failing because they had fewer and fewer customers. Between 2006 and 2009, the value of all housing in the community dropped by two-thirds.[1] Taxes for residents had been climbing steadily. Should the leadership have seen greater problems on the horizon? Could they have reacted more promptly by cutting budgets and then raising taxes to reduce debts rather than continuing public service levels? Could they have been more aggressive in terms of new business attraction or sought the assistance of the state's economic development program? Could they have avoided municipal bankruptcy by acting more aggressively more quickly? Can other communities see the problems coming far enough in advance to react more quickly, thereby recovering their fiscal stability more quickly? Can communities see it coming?

Cities that have thriving suburban economies and economic malaise in the downtown—or cities that have adjoining thriving and declining neighborhoods are facing certain problems. Cities that have clusters for which competitive locations are becoming more aggressive about acquiring the resources and institutions that support those clusters may see an economic downturn approaching.

Cities that have paid too much attention to the offering of cash or tax-based incentives at the exclusion of enhanced public services run the risk of being able to attract—and retain—employers only by buying them, rather than establishing an environment in which their businesses can thrive. Cities that gain a reputation for being inhospitable for commerce, or that try to maintain a static position in the economy should also be able to foresee disaster.

When the potential pitfalls are observed prior to their local onset, communities can sometimes prepare and attempt to stave off some of the difficulties *before* they occur. This may mean targeting a more diversified set of industries in the economic development outreach programs, or the development of community assets that will help to attract and retain businesses, or the identification of public policies that stand in the way of business growth and expansion. Addressing these concerns before they become issues to be resolved also sends a strong message to the business community—present and prospective—that this is a city that is pro-business and knows how to address their collective needs.

Much has been made in this volume—as well as elsewhere—that cities and regions should have seen their respective problems approaching and should have been better prepared to react. That would be great in the best of worlds, but seeing is not always believing. Surely, the executives of the automobile companies in Detroit and the elected officials of the city saw their problems coming. They could see their revenues decline. Ditto Boeing and the officials of the City of Seattle. They could clearly see what was occurring; they simply could not believe that the changes were permanent, that the old boom times would not return. Or, at least, would not return right away.

Critical to a positive response is a rapid response: before long-term damage has been done to the local psyche and to the locality's reputation as a good place to locate a business or for individuals to work, and before the best of the workforce departs for other regions where employment opportunities are greater. Economic development officials need to be prepared for such downturns and have a plan in place to address them when they occur.

2 Laying the Foundations for Growth in the Best of Times

Communities all too often wait until a disaster occurs before starting to consider how best to extricate themselves from it. What they have learned from these types of experiences is that, once the disaster has occurred, it is far too late to figure out what to do. The best contingency plans allow for recoveries that may yet come—or, may not ever come. But, once the occurrence takes place, plans in place enable the community to come together, to recover, and to do so as quickly as possible. Of course, not every contingency situation can be anticipated, but many can. The primary situation for economic developers to prepare is the loss of a major company or industry from the community. It isn't important to know which company will leave; it is only important to know beforehand who will do what and how the community's leaders and other stakeholders will interact if and when the time comes.

Community leaders should lay the foundations for economic development during the best of times, when resources are available and there are fewer competing needs that can serve as distractions from building or promoting the assets of the community or the region. By doing so, they can be assured that, if a downturn does occur, they will not be scrambling for solutions and resources at the time when positive actions are needed and the business and residential communities require reassurance.

To prepare the foundation, communities must regard their economic development strategic plan and consider the needs of companies in the identified target segments. If the requisite assets for such companies are in place, improve them, create more of them, refurbish them. If they are not in place at present, those asset gaps should be addressed. To build roads or buildings or to develop the workforce requires funding, and that funding will be more available while the economy is driving forward on all cylinders. Assess the costs of plugging the asset gaps and solidify the financing. Then, build and develop the asset base so that, if an economic decline does occur, for whatever reason, the city or county will be ready to approach other employers about possible facility locations.

This activity in preparation for an economic decline should include advertising, promotion, public relations, events, and visits to employers and trade shows. Economic development is a relationship-building exercise. Decisions about site locations are made over time and they favor sites and communities about which they already have some information. When a company is ready to make a site location decision, it is entirely too late to start building a relationship and passing on information about the many attributes of the community. Preparing decision-makers in advance and providing them with information consistently over time goes a long way to receiving consideration. It does not guarantee a win, but, at least the community will be in the game.

3 Tax Base Considerations

Economic development, for community leaders, has a variety of objectives. Residents who are constituents need jobs and constituent businesses not only seek growth but will locate in, or relocate to, cities, towns, or regions that are perceived to be generally pro-business. This includes, among other policies, taxes that are fair and services that represent a fair return for their tax contributions.

The adjective "fair" was not used incautiously in the sentence above. Businesses in my experience have not argued for there to be no taxes; rather, they expect a reasonable rate to pay that is comparable to what their colleagues and competitors pay elsewhere. This ensures that they are not placed at a competitive disadvantage when it comes to pricing their products or services. Further, they are quite willing to pay such taxes if they feel that the returns they receive in the way of public services are acceptable to them. No one wants to pay taxes and not see high quality public services as a result. At the national level, businesses that debate tax issues do so largely because they do not agree with how those revenues are used. At the state and local level, public safety, public education, the public welfare, and other services comprise tangible evidence of the value of their tax payments.

There is a growing number of examples of communities that, in cooperation with local business leaders, took positive action to increase the local tax burden. Because the business executives were able to identify specific infrastructural investments, the taxes are agreeable to all. This is an example of the neoclassical theories described in Chapter 1: an influx of capital to increase assets that are important to the business community will result in economic development.

In the case of metropolitan Denver, Colorado, the collaboration yielded the resources necessary to convert what had been an economy primarily based on natural resources into a fast-growing technology hub.

> It's transformation, noted the *New York Times* . . . was led by local business leaders and government officials, who took advantage of existing assets while also raising taxes at times to invest in critical transportation links, development-friendly policies and a network of colleges and universities.[2]

Even higher taxes were acceptable because there was an understanding on the part of the business community about the returns and benefits they would reap. These included a "new rail line that will connect the airport to the downtown and serve outlying industrial parks and a push to support cultural institutions."[3] States that are generally regarded as being high tax states find it difficult to attract new companies, and even to retain existing businesses. This creates a real conundrum; in order for those states to attract and retain businesses, they must provide quality public services. That requires tax revenues; however, due to the relatively inadequate public services, in combination with the relatively higher tax rates, businesses are less likely to come to, or stay in, the state than they are to locate in states with lower tax rates. At the end of the day, higher taxes have a negative impact on a business' bottom line. As we observed in the discussion on economic growth theories, cost minimization is a critical component of any company's site location decision-making process.

As Shaffer et al. state:

> [T]axes and fees/charges are the predominate source of revenue for nearly all levels of government: they include the individual and corporate income tax, property taxes, sales taxes, excise taxes, and dedicated payroll taxes . . . The sales tax is a significant source of revenue for most state and many local governments.[4]

The sources of taxes for local governments—large or small, rural or urban—are different in each state. Some get to keep locally generated taxes, some get a return of a proportion of such taxes after the state collects them and takes its cut. In some cases, the tax structure is felt to benefit certain areas of states, or to benefit cities rather than rural areas. As such, general statements about the tax base and economic development must be made very cautiously. The essence of all tax base structures is an estimate of the best means for all levels of government to provide quality public services without either overburdening residents or making the state or locality or region unappealing to businesses. Of course, such a balance is very difficult to maintain and is at the very essence of leadership. One of the classical definitions of politics is that it requires the allocation of scarce resources over competing, legitimate demands.

Another principle that underscores local tax rate decisions is that residents typically cost more than they contribute. The cost of public education, public safety, human services and more generally cost more than localities are able to collect from their residents. This is one of the reasons that economic development is so vital. In addition to creating jobs, generating wealth, supporting small businesses, and more, economic development means that the private sector is helping to offset the costs of the public services being demanded and enjoyed by local residents. It is generally accepted that businesses, after having paid a tax dollar, require less in public services than they contribute to the tax base.

4 Taking the Long-Term View

Economies grow in one of several primary ways. Communities can establish programs either to attract, retain, or grow new businesses. At the same time, they can develop the assets and amenities that make the community more attractive to employers. This latter approach may include good schools, safe neighborhoods, a strong workforce, improved infrastructure, and a higher quality of life.

None of these occur in a hurry. Business attraction takes many years of laying the groundwork, developing the promotional pitch and materials, and building the strong relationships with corporate decision-makers, site location consultants, and others that may ultimately result in prospect identification and site selection. There can be a tendency to anticipate results in the short term. Economic development professionals are aware, however, that their efforts will take time to come to fruition. Connections need to be made and relationships nurtured over time in order to receive consideration. Business executives need to know about the community and have a reasonable understanding that it is home to the assets their firms will require in order to be successful. Building the necessary reputation to be successful in attracting new businesses to the community takes some time, especially as economic development strategies take aim at new markets, emerging industries, and firms for which the competition is strongest.

Business retention is also a relationship-building exercise that results in businesses being approachable before deciding to depart from a community. In this way, problems can be resolved before they become too difficult. These relationships take time to nurture. Growing new companies takes enough time for entrepreneurs to decide to build a company, select a line of business, secure the necessary financing, improve the product or service, begin to market, acquire a clientele, and open the doors.

It is necessary for local decision-makers and constituents to take this type of long-term view toward economic development. All too often, economic developers have reported that they are under the gun to produce immediately. Some of that pressure comes from the elected officials who may have been criticized for spending scarce resources on marketing when the funds were desperately needed by the local school system or the police and fire departments. Sometimes the pressure comes from the constituents directly for the same reason.

In communities where the resources that are available for the economic development budget come in part from the private sector, those investors may also apply pressure for more immediate results. Home or office builders who invest in the program do so to sell homes and ease office space. Grocery stores want to sell product, newspapers want to sell advertising, and other types of investors also want a return for their contributions. There will be a natural tendency to want to see results in an unreasonable timeframe.

For these reasons, economic development professionals must learn to manage local expectations at the same time that they conduct their outreach programs. This means encouraging the local elected officials and their constituencies to be patient in waiting for the initial results. Consider the major cities and regions analyzed in an earlier chapter: Seattle, Detroit, and Pittsburgh, for example. In none of those cases did the turn-around occur quickly. Decades went by in the cases of Seattle and Pittsburgh before the post-aerospace dependency and the post-steel era passed and the economy was revived and sufficiently diversified to ensure sustainable and positive economic development. "The long-range time-frame is a challenge. Decades don't fit into election cycles very well. The political benefits of politically difficult situations and regional issues don't usually occur before the next election."[5]

5   The Use and Overuse of Financial Incentives for Economic Growth

The term incentives covers a wide range of financial and non-financial inducements designed to encourage companies either to come to, or to stay and expand in, a community. They are often offered by states or localities or the two in tandem. They might include one or more of the following:

- cash in the form of grants or funding for R & D;
- tax abatements for a specific time;
- low-interest or no-interest loans;
- support for customized training either for existing or new employees;
- infrastructure improvements that are specifically related to the company's site.

The purpose of incentives is to push a prospect past the point of indecision, to "sweeten the pot." Rarely does the payment of an incentive create the decision. Second, incentive programs are designed to attract or retain a business whose presence in the community will ultimately generate far more in return than the initial costs of the incentives. These are the public purposes of incentive programs. On occasion, however, there are other motives: a state or an area really needs the win, or can ill afford the loss, or a given administration either needs the glow of a victory or does not want the embarrassment of a loss. This has made the practice of state and local incentives a highly competitive practice. The justification for increasing state or local incentive pools has often been that the competitor jurisdictions have done so.

Ruth Simon wrote in the *Wall Street Journal* that "These days, the competition isn't Mexico, China, or some other country promising cheap wages and low taxes. It's coming from nearby competitive cities offering incentives to companies to select their location over others."[6] Especially in the large Rust belt cities, very large incentives are offered because it is all they can do to lure employers.

One means of considering the magnitude of incentive offerings by states and local areas is to calculate the cost per job gained through the total incentive package. In previous research, one of the most expensive costs per job found was the result of an incentive package totaling more than 500 million dollars given to IBM in 2000. United Airlines received more than 450 million dollars in 1991 and Alabama gave Mercedes a total of more than 250 million dollars in 1993. While these seem like massive payments, the cost per job seems truly overwhelming: Mercedes, $168,666; IBM, $504,000; and, United Airlines, $71,587.

One might question whether the State of Alabama, for instance, could afford to forego so much in tax revenues in the future. One might also question whether such well-established companies as Mercedes or IBM should be provided so much funding from the coffers of state and local governments when those funds are so desperately needed for education, law enforcement, and infrastructure. The final argument comes from those businesses that helped to pay the tax revenues that enable these jurisdictions to provide such incentives. A constant refrain heard from opponents to incentives is that the "little guys" pay into the tax base for many years and the "big guys" are given tax holidays and grants.

The counter arguments are based on the long-term impacts of the incentive packages. The first argument goes like this: do not consider just the initial cost of the incentives packages, but the benefits of those well-paying jobs being in the community for decades. Those employees will buy homes and cars and groceries, and pay taxes, all of which accrue to the benefit of the community as well as the retailers in the area as the money is constantly recirculated throughout the economy. A second argument is that, ultimately, the company will outlive the life of the incentives, and will begin to pay large increments into the tax base of the state and localities that abated the payment for a specific number of years.

An additional argument made is that employers such as Mercedes and Hyundai and Toyota, which also received large incentive deals in the 1990s and early 2000s, are strong community citizens and give back to schools, little leagues, scouting organizations, local arts and health causes, and more. They are good to have in the community and those contributions—both capital and donations of individuals' time—offset some of the public service programs that could not be expanded due to the offsets to tax base revenues.

Clearly, there are various ways of considering the value of the largest incentive offerings. At the conclusion, the decisions must be made on an individual basis and in terms of the short-term ability to support those packages and the long-term benefits that will be reaped from them. Further, many opponents of large incentives packages maintain that the company will live out the timeline in the deal and then seek either similar deals to remain in the community or deals from other areas to relocate there. While there have been some cases in which that has indeed occurred, one might consider that it is more difficult for manufacturers regularly to pick up and move. Automobile manufacturers who build a large factory floor plate and install their equipment may be considered less of a risk to depart later and therefore a more reliable, long-term addition to the local economic base.

One difficult aspect of incentive programs that is not often discussed in the literature has to do with the "slippery slope" it represents. How does a community agree to provide tax abatements or grants to one prospective business and then decline to do so for another? Will this automatically forestall the latter deal because they feel they are less valued? And, how do a community's leaders justify providing financial benefits to a company considering coming in when others have been in the community for many years, supporting jobs, taxes, public services, and even local organizations?

Another concern cited about economic incentives for businesses to locate to, or stay in, a community relates to the notion of a free-market economy. Many public sector officials have decried a practice that is inconsistent with the requests of the private sector in general. For example, business organizations often maintain that the role of state and local government should be to allow business to succeed and that they can do that best by staying out of the way, or at a minimum, creating the right environment for commerce to thrive. Some officials have difficulty in then accepting the argument that government should provide funds and tax abatements to some businesses. This is especially true when other businesses that have been in the community for many years now see their tax dollars paid over time going not only to other firms, but even to their competitors.

There have been numerous situations in which the prospect businesses have asked for incentives from a new location solely in order to negotiate a better deal with their existing location to remain in place. In such instances, the local economic development professional may be uncertain whether he or she is simply being used to the company's benefit or whether the relocation possibility is real. This means that the company will be treated as a real prospect and much time and energy will be spent to try to win a situation that one suspects may not really be in play.

Another objection raised to the use of incentives to lure businesses to a community or state is that they are offered to businesses of a minimum number of employees or that are making at least a given amount of investment in the community. As such, one can argue that they are only in place to attract the larger employers and that is, literally by definition, unfair to smaller firms or businesses that are creating jobs without making large dollar investments in new facilities.

One of the more frequently heard objections to financial incentives is that the foregone revenues, in effect, distract scarce community resources away from health or education or other immediate needs of the residents. An additional concern has been that, if a company locates because of an incentive offering, it is going to a site where it received the best deal while that may not really be the best location from which to operate and be the most efficient. In other words, the business is making a decision that the value of the incentives is sufficient to offset (or even more than offset) the potential loss of efficiency, even over time.

When incentive deals go bad, local and state officials are squarely on the hot seat because the lost revenues could have been used productively for services that would have improved the quality of life, such as education or public safety. The Commonwealth of Virginia had a mis-step with an incentive payment that cost many individuals a great deal of political capital. A 2013 study of Maryland incentive programs revealed:

> Of the 155 companies that were grant recipients, 32 percent moved or went out of business; 42 percent of small businesses that received revolving loans left the county or went belly up. Most of the firms attracted to the county had to pay back their incentives because they didn't meet private investment or job creation criteria.[7]

Counters to some of these concerns include the observation that the formal incentives agreements can be structured to protect all parties and that "claw-back" provisions are typically included to ensure that non-performance under the agreement will result in the return of all or some of the incentive dollars. Another protection for state and local governments is to provide incentives that are not cash but rather infrastructure projects that will benefit the entire area around the prospect's new location.

Essentially, incentives are best used to convince an employer who is on the fence about a given location. They can ensure that the deal is consummated and that the greater area benefits from the arrangements. They can safeguard both the community and the company, and they can, if properly structured, benefit the community and the tax base in the long term.

The critical pieces to incentive deals are to treat them separately and to ensure that the due diligence is thorough and that the ROIs are realistic and truly beneficial to the community. They should be concluded and announced, to the extent possible, in the light of day and they should have economic, not political, reasons for their creation. In sum, it should be possible to regard incentive packages not simply as costs but rather as investments in the future of the entire community.

Clearly, not all professionals are in accord as to the use of specific incentive packages, or even the appropriateness of the practice in general. On the one hand, many communities' leaders argue that they must engage in the practice of granting incentives for business attraction and/or retention. If they do not, they will be placed at a competitive disadvantage because so many others do. Others have justified the use of incentives with a sense of desperation: we so desperately need the jobs, the income, or the tax base that we must do this or the community will suffer. The Mayor of Lansing, Michigan stated that "We would be dead in the water without economic incentives ... Old vacant buildings and contaminated industrial properties can be impossible to redevelop without incentives."[8]

Still other observers maintain that some incentive programs are politically motivated: elected officials with term limits care more about the short-term splash than they do about the long-term implications for the community and its finances. The argument continues to maintain that there are opportunity costs forgone by the granting of incentives that mean fewer dollars to allocate in the present and fewer to allocate in the future. Frequently cited as being hurt by the loss of present and future revenues are the local public education systems and infrastructure maintenance and development requirements.

Fisher and Peters examined a large number of examples of incentive payments in states across the country and asserted that the average incentive provided present and future tax reductions that equated to about 20 percent of the value of the project. Yet, they also concluded that "the effect was too small to affect business location decisions."[9]

For many, there is a greater use of the same funds in providing more long-term and community-wide impacts. These might include training for entrepreneurs who want to start numerous new businesses. Others maintain that incentives should include social benefits; that is to say that the community's standards of living are raised and that those who have historically not benefitted from economic development be brought along as a result of the incentives granted.

The International Economic Development Council states that incentives are essential because they induce companies to "create new jobs in places where they would not have otherwise."[10] This is a serious misstatement: the word "would" ought to be "might." Many case studies have concluded that economic development incentives were extracted from communities by businesses that would have either stayed or come in the absence of such financial inducements. The practice has been, in some cases, abused to receive funds from the community or to save on a business' future tax burden. All of those things impact a company's bottom line, and some businesses have been known to take advantage of jurisdictions and states that are willing to pay an incentive rather than run the risk of losing the prospect company. In fairness, communities may be wise to take such calculated risks because it is difficult to know whether the demands for incentive payments or tax abatements are real and the potential loss of that business may be sufficiently frightening that the calculated risk is worthwhile to a point. That point is the critical decision to be made. How much could be lost? What is it really worth to save or attract the company in the community? What is the chance that the company is bluffing? And, in some cases, the added consideration relates to the need of elected officials either for a visible "win" or at least not to have a visible loss.

The bottom line for these discussions is that each community is different and each prospect situation is distinct. Community leaders must have one objective in mind: the costs must be far outweighed by the ultimate benefits for the community. Those are decisions and calculations that every community must make on an individual basis. And, the calculations change over time and individual case, as well as whether or not the company in question falls within one of the community's specified economic development target industries. In those cases, the calculation changes because there may be multiplier effects to consider.

Critics of the practice of issuing economic development incentives may do so for a variety of reasons. Some objections have been based on pure economic theory. These arguments note that a free market economy would not include such inducements to some because it creates an "uneven playing field." What that really is suggesting is that incentives create inefficiencies in commerce and that companies that receive an incentive may be compensating, at the public's expense, for being less efficient than their competitors. By issuing incentives, the public sector is sustaining that inefficiency in the market place and is potentially causing damage to the more efficient firms who are not receiving the same public investment.

Another objection to the practice of economic development incentives—and, indeed, to economic development attraction programs in general—is that they are used simply to steal jobs from one community to bring them to another. The extension of the argument is that commerce broadly is not advanced, simply shuffled. The counter to that argument is that companies that move to locations in which they can be more productive can hire more employees and create greater wealth, and even pay additional real estate, sales, and other taxes to the communities and states in which they are located.

Another challenge to the practice is that employers might prefer to see the municipality's funds used to improve the community in ways that would also bring them to that community. In other words, businesses are attracted to areas that are safe, have good public schools, updated technical and physical infrastructure, and other assets and amenities that are attractive to both the employer and their workforce and their families. Perhaps, incentive funds and tax abatements would be better used in those ways.

Non-financial incentives are often offered by communities to attract and retain them in their communities. These may include training, workshops, recruitment assistance, and more.

But, typically, these are not really incentives and are not always factors in companies coming to a community. They tend to be services that communities offered anyway and that are then customized to the needs of that particular employer. They do have value but are frequently cited as incentives when they are really standard services. The offer of free space is sometimes noted as a "non-financial" incentive but, even that has a cost for someone—either the owner of the building or the community that absorbs that cost. True non-financial incentives are often very useful in negotiations with prospective employers, but communities must total all of the attendant costs and forgone revenues when making well-informed decisions about the worth of a company and the value of the offering.

Communities must also protect themselves from non-compliance or non-performance by the recipient businesses of incentives. This is actually a simple matter of preparing binding contracts that state clearly the expectations of both parties with time-specific metrics. If those requirements are not met, the contract should be easily enforced. The return of incentive funding as a result of not meeting the stated objectives for job creation or investment in the community is a well-demonstrated practice in economic development circles known as the "claw-back" provisions.

Consider the examples of the automobile industry being offered incentives to locate plants in the southeastern United States. In 1980, Nissan received 33 million dollars to site a plant in Tennessee. In 1987, Toyota received 150 million dollars, and the total package from Alabama to Mercedes-Benz in 1993 totaled about 258 million dollars. Were these massive incentives worth the return received by the states and communities involved? Thirty-seven, 31, and 25 years later, the tax payments, jobs created, total investments, incomes and wealth generated, and small businesses supported through contracts and sub-contracts would argue in the affirmative.

Over the past 25 years, incentive offerings have increased across the country by more than threefold. This has resulted in an offset of roughly 30 percent of the tax revenues that municipalities would otherwise have received from businesses locating in their cities and counties. The annual cost of these incentives had reached a staggering 45 billion dollars by 2015.[11] These are the dollars that could have been used to pay for better schools or the infrastructure that would have also attracted more businesses and improved the local quality of life. In 2016, a report of the International Economic Development Council set the annual spend on incentives in the United States much higher, at 70 billion dollars.[12]

Clearly, one of the great problems for those who design and implement programs of incentives is that the businesses that have been located for many years in a community may be opposed to giving their tax contributions to other companies to locate in their community. Downing wrote that "One of the most difficult arguments in providing incentives for a new business is explaining the deal to an existing business with a similar number of employees that has paid taxes for years in the same community."[13] The practice of incentives may be more acceptable to existing businesses, however, if they are used to retain existing employers rather than to attract new ones. The retention of an existing employer implies the use of tax revenues to keep a business that has contributed over time to the tax base and to the community more broadly. That is typically more palatable than using funds for a new business. Of course, if it can be demonstrated that the benefits of attracting a new business outweigh the costs and may even serve to grow the local or state tax base, some of the objections can be overcome. It is generally not the use of incentive programs that draws criticisms; it is the over-use and the impression that incentives may be used to enhance the reputation of a governor or local elected official rather than merely growing the local economic base that is the more likely target of such criticisms.

Another concern for local and state governments in the use of incentives is that the recipient is obliged to remain in place for the duration of the agreement. In exchange for the issuance of grants and tax abatements, communities hope that there will be a sufficiently strong tie to the locality and the local workforce that the company will remain in place after the termination of the formal agreement. However, a term has arisen to apply to companies that do not do so once the legal requirements have been satisfied. These are called "footloose." These firms are likely at least to consider departing after the agreement's termination, "meaning that even if there is a short-term boost it will be expensive to maintain since the incentives will have to be renewed."[14] Communities must consider these possibilities when designing the original deal and the agreement. This calls for numerous assumptions about the future but these possibilities must certainly be taken into account by the state and local governments that are using incentives to help stimulate economic growth.

Beyond business attraction, many public entities do provide various incentive offerings either to keep a business from leaving or in an attempt to keep a facility from shutting down. These retention projects are particularly problematic because it is extremely difficult to know whether or not the business would really shut down or relocate without incentives. Additionally, if the company is truly in jeopardy of shutting down, the provision of incentives comes at an implied greater-than-typical risk that the tax base benefits will be returned from the investment.

Further, other businesses in the community could potentially make a similar claim to be considering relocation in order to receive a similar deal. An example of this concern relates to the Marriott Corporation which twice received tens of millions of dollars from the State of Maryland to remain at its corporate headquarters location in Bethesda. Questions were raised in the media as to the wisdom of such large payments to the corporation that may not have moved anyway. In both instances, the State of Maryland determined that the investment would, over time, generate sufficient returns to warrant the initial financial costs.

Not all of these decisions are made purely on a financial basis. In the case of the Marriott Corporation, most employers in the area would agree with the retention of such a primary and long-term employer, with such a large employment base and payroll. Certainly, the non-financial implications of retaining Marriott's headquarters were substantial as the firm—and its employees—are exceptional corporate citizens through-out the state, the region, and the local community. Those benefits—although not always quantifiable—would certainly have been part of the ROI "calculation."

The Marriott example leads to yet another consideration in terms of offering incentives to attract a business that is not sure about leaving its existing location. In such an instance, the home community offers incentives and other states and localities also offer inventive packages. The "new" location is in a defensive position and is attempting to out-bid the existing locality for the firm. Because neither side is aware of what the other is offering, a bidding war can ensue that has the potential to exceed any original calculations of worth or ROI. Communities must approach these and other incentive situations with extreme caution. Incentive programs are best managed when there are established, well-publicized criteria to which elected officials and managers adhere. There should be clear contractual obligations for outcomes as well as comprehensive and enforced actions to recover the investment if the company does not produce the agreed-upon number of jobs, levels of investment, or other metrics. In short, incentives have a time and place, but must be used very wisely and in the light of day. Outcomes and shortfalls should be reported and audited, and the programs should be monitored by external bodies on a consistent basis.

Notes

1 Neil Conan. What Happens When a City Declares Bankruptcy. National Public Radio. January 11, 2012.
2 Patricia Cohen. The Cities on the Sunny Side of the American Economy. (March 31, 2016) www.nytimes.com
3 Ibid.
4 Shaffer, Ron; Steven Deller; and Dave Marcouiller. *Community Economics: Linking Theory and Practice*. (Ames, IA: Blackwell, 2004): 177.
5 David Sweet, Kathryn Hexter, and David Beach. *The New American City Faces Its Regional Future: A Cleveland Perspective*. (Athens, OH: Ohio University Press, 1999): 12.
6 Ruth Simon. US Cities Battle Each Other for Jobs With $45 Billion in Incentives. (March 16, 2017) www.wsj.com
7 Michael Neibauer. MoCo's Business Incentives Get Mixed Results. (Arlington, VA: *Washington Business Journal*, April 5, 2013).
8 Simon.
9 Peter S. Fisher and Alan H. Peters. Tax and Spending, Incentives, and Enterprise Zones. *New England Economic Review*. (March–April, 1997): 128.
10 Joshua Morris Hurwitz. *Incentives for the Twenty-First Century*. (Washington, DC: The International Economic Development Council, 2015): 1.
11 Simon.
12 Hurwitz, 1.
13 Mike Downing. Incentives for Economic Development. *Economic Development Journal*. (Washington, DC: International Economic Development Council, 2004): 74.
14 Adam Millsap. New York's Buffalo Billion Initiative Has Been Underwhelming. (September 28, 2016) http://neighborhoodeffects.mercatus.org

References

Cohen, Sharon. Doing Without Hospitals: Rural Towns Suffer but Cope Without Care. December 4, 1988. http://articles.latimes.com
Conan, Neil. What Happens When a City Declares Bankruptcy. National Public Radio. January 11, 2012.
Downing, Mike. Incentives for Economic Development. *Economic Development Journal*, vol. 3. Washington, DC: International Economic Development Council, Spring 2004; 73–80.
Fisher, Peter S. and Peters, Alan H. Tax and Spending, Incentives and Enterprise Zones. *New England Economic Review* (March–April), 1997: 109–30.
Hurwitz, Joshua Morris. *Incentives for the Twenty-First Century*. Washington, DC: International Economic Development Council, 2015.
Millsap, Adam. New York's Buffalo Billion Initiative Has Been Underwhelming. September 28, 2016. http://neighborhoodeffects.mercatus.org

Neibauer, Michael. MoCo's Business Incentives Get Mixed Results. Arlington, VA: *Washington Business Journal*, April 5, 2013.

Shaffer, Ron. Dying Communities. *Community Economics Newsletter*. Madison, WI: University of Wisconsin, May 1995.

Simon, Ruth. US Cities Battle Each Other for Job with $45 Billion in Incentives. March 16, 2017. www.wsj.com

Sweet, David, Hexter, Kathryn, and Beach, David. *The New American City Faces Its Regional Future: A Cleveland Perspective*. Athens, OH: Ohio University Press, 1999.

27 Conclusions and Actions/ Recommendations

There are lessons that can be learned from the experiences of one community that are transferable to other communities. That is not to say that every occurrence in one place will have the same cause and effect relationship in others. However, the actions taken by some to the causes they experienced may demonstrate to others a certain potential for success or failure. One must observe the outcomes of various development strategies and consider the possibility of similar results occurring elsewhere.

The conclusions listed below are drawn from personal experiences and the experiences of the leadership in the case study locations included in this volume. There are macro conclusions listed here that may apply to all communities and some that are more directly attributable to, and more likely to recur in, communities of similar size and situation. In any case, such knowledge potentially yields the power to respond to economic development and decline, and efforts to rebuild local economies, more effectively.

1 Conclusions Regarding Theory

i) Over time, economic growth has been the subject of numerous theories. Some are applicable to certain circumstances. Some have been relevant in certain times. Some rebut others. None are uniquely applicable all the time to every situation. Theories are only constructs for observing and explaining reality, and reality is ever-changing and always different in different communities, with different leadership, and unique opportunities and challenges.

ii) Personal observation and the reporting of experiences in similar communities at similar times may be the best means of understanding economic development, economic decline, and the rebirth of local economies. The study of case studies and interviews with those who lived through the very situations in question can be most instructive to those learning about economic development and to those who led communities—large and small, urban and suburban and rural, through various portions of the growth cycle. Imagine yourself to be the mayor of a city facing economic decline and seeking ideas about how best to kick-start commercial activity in your community. Then, imagine sitting at a table with a dozen other mayors who have already experienced similar situations. The benefits of their counsel exceed the benefits of reviewing a historical theoretical approach to growth. The theoretical constructs have merit but largely in preparing one for the real-world experiences of others.

2   Conclusions Regarding the External Factors that Impact Local Economic Development

i) Local economic development is vitally important for communities of all sizes. Overall, residential growth costs more in terms of public service expenditures than results from the tax generation of its workforce. This is largely due to the need for increased public education expenditures. In many communities, the public school system is more than half of all the community's General Fund expenditures. Businesses are generally believed to contribute far more in taxes to the states and localities in which they locate than they take back in public service expenditures. In short, business growth helps to offset the costs of public services for the residential community. In most communities around the United States, this is the *raison d'être* for economic development and business attraction programs.

ii) Regardless of preparation or the strength of local public and corporate leadership, it must be concluded that most of the forces that influence local economies are either largely or completely outside of local control. This is increasingly true in today's global, interconnected economy where events on the other side of the globe or labor rates on another continent directly influence the growth, decline, and redevelopment of the local economic base in Nebraska, Connecticut, or Texas.

This means that local business executives and government officials need to be constantly scanning the economic situations around the world to determine how best to prepare for coming changes. Businesses tend to be more able to do this; strategic planners and risk assessment officers spend their careers doing so. Community leaders and economic development officials tend to take their lead from the business executives in their communities. The danger in depending on business leaders for global risk assessment is that the company may relocate, shift focus, or shut down to accommodate its own needs and shareholders first. Communities must understand the situations that lead to such decisions long before they happen, so they can prepare rather than react after the fact.

iii) Some of the external forces that affect local economies around the United States originate within federal and state government agencies. These may include tax policies, energy policies, allocations for infrastructure development and improvement, the establishment certification of new hospitals or airports, and much more. This means that localities need to be ever-cognizant of legislative and policy considerations so they can argue on their own behalf before the negative consequences are felt. At a minimum, that will enable localities to prepare responses to any negative impacts before they occur.

iv) No local economy can remain in one place, without either growth or decline. Everyone's local economic future is dependent upon its comparative assets, relative to other competitive economies. If one community becomes larger or more efficient in its production or its growth, its competitors will lose relative position. Companies will grow elsewhere, creating jobs, generating wealth, and paying the taxes that will help to pay for public services without requiring the residential community to shoulder the entire burden of those costs. There is no standing still because everyone else is advancing or declining around you. Community leaders who do not favor growth need to figure out ways to control it without damaging the local economy.

v) It is sometimes very difficult to see economic change coming. It is impossible, however, to do so if you aren't looking. Economic development officials need to be considering events and trends in commerce on a constant basis; they must be as aware of coming changes as possible and attuned to how to react and should therefor scan economic and cultural changes around the regions, throughout the United States, and around the world.

vi) When a local economy is impacted negatively, local officials need to implement prepared plans immediately. The longer the issue persists and the longer it takes to react, the deeper the local depression and loss of hope, and the greater the likelihood that the very best of the existing workforce will depart for locations with better employment options. When this happens, the most important asset for attracting new employers has been lost and the road forward becomes increasingly difficult.

3 Conclusions Regarding the Impacts of Local Economic Decline

i) When jobs are created in local economies, there are secondary and tertiary benefits that are created as well. Contracts are let for supplies and services, and new employees contribute to the local growth by purchasing homes and cars and groceries. When that happens, home builders, car dealerships, and stores hire more people and they too spend their incomes in the community, thereby creating more jobs, and so on. Further, increased spending results in an enlarged tax base that can provide for a greater quantity and an enhanced quality of public services, including schools, public works, public safety, parks, libraries, human services, and more.

Similarly, however, when jobs are lost, there are jobs and contracts lost in the secondary and tertiary economies. Retailers lose business and lay people off. Tax revenues decline and public services suffer. The impacts of job loss are felt throughout a community and it is often those most in need who are the first to feel the pinch and are ultimately likely to be the most negatively impacted.

ii) When people lose their jobs, they turn to anything that will enable them to pay their bills and support their families. They may take two jobs and will take jobs from which they make far less than for previous employment. Other family members may be forced to seek employment as well. This is a reflection of underemployment, which is not easily measured in communities and, because these individuals are not counted as unemployed, may affect the amount of state and federal funds that are provided to economically distressed areas. Further, underemployment often masks the availability of the workforce when the locality is considered as a location by new employers.

iii) As the community loses its high-paying positions and its best and brightest workers, the unemployment rate increases and the overall contributions to state and local tax bases are reduced. As this occurs, the demand for public services increases and transfer payments are increasing due to the need of those who are no longer working full time or are earning reduced wages. This increased demand frequently occurs at the very time that the ability of the local government to provide such services has been dramatically reduced. Many communities, although certainly not all, prepare such contingencies by setting aside reserves in advance of these impacts.

iv) The loss of tax base is immediately translated into a loss of public services, including health care, school teachers, police and fire officers, and more. This, in turn, makes the community a less desirable place for new workers and new businesses. In short, the very assets that make a community a great place to live and work are lost when they are most needed for new business attraction.

v) When community services are eliminated, people turn to other sources of help, whether they are private, non-profit organizations or faith-based groups or fraternal organizations. But, even those sources of support will ultimately run dry, at which point the people in the community have nowhere else to turn.

vi) When hope for a recovery has been drained from the community, it becomes increasingly difficult to rebuild the economic base. This can be considered rock bottom for a community. Economic change is very difficult and discouraging. When employers leave town, many people see their lives changing before their eyes. Perhaps their parents and grandparents had worked there and they thought that they too would have jobs for life there. When a company town loses "the" company, it also loses its sense of itself, its pride. For many communities, it has meant the loss of any will to rebuild their neighborhoods or towns.

4 Conclusions Regarding Strategies for Economic Recovery

i) When a community and its leaders are in recovery mode, the objective must be twofold. First, they need to create an immediate solution that will put people back to work today and preserve the hope and the workforce. Second, they need to plan for a longer-term economic future in which this will never happen again, and that means the creation of an economic base that is sufficiently diversified that a rise or fall in the fortunes of one industry or a single business will be minimized on the community because it has been propped up by other industry segments that are present locally. Economic diversification is always the holy grail for economic development professionals and community leaders.

ii) Economic diversification means entirely different industry segments, not one major employer and its sub-contractors. It means several industry segments that are sufficiently disconnected from one another so that impacts on one will not affect the others.

iii) Economic diversification does not happen overnight. Local leadership needs to be diligent to ensure that constituents are informed through a variety of means and that they comprehend not only what is being done but what the results have been. If those lines of communication are not kept open, and if the messages do not broadcast at least a modicum of hope, rebuilding the local economy is much less likely.

iv) The retention and development of the local workforce is perhaps the most critical piece of economic development for a community that has lost major employers. Without it, there will be no new employers. Localities need to consider retraining programs and support services for men and women who want to start their own new businesses, and they need to do so before they lose employers and are forced to turn to entrepreneurial supports as a last resort. New business start-ups are an essential component of growing and diversifying the local economic base even in the best of economic times.

v) Immigrants are one means of building a workforce that will attract new employers. Immigrants raise the overall number of available workers and have been shown in research to be more inclined than their native counterparts to develop their own businesses. They support local retailers and other businesses by spending their incomes locally and they support public services through their tax payments. Immigrants can not only diversify a community and make it a more interesting place, but can set up new businesses and a workforce that can support existing firms.

vi) Building support systems for individuals to use their innovative talents and their entrepreneurial drive to build new businesses is a vital way to rebuild community economies. Such ecosystems include capital availability, training and support for legal, accounting, and other services that will enable a first-time company owner to get started and become as successful as possible as quickly as possible. This may mean incubation facilities, business counseling, access to capital, guidance on developing business plans and customer development, executive coaching and mentoring, legal and accounting advice, and more.

vii) An important first step for local planners who are trying to rebuild a local economic base is to consider the types of employers you want to attract. A determination must be made about what types of local assets and amenities those employers will want in the locations in which they site an office or plant. Once it is clear what is required to attract the designated industries, it is important to identify the various assets needed and those that are missing. This is referred to as the community asset gap.

A community that has identified the gaps in its current assets now has several options. First, it can pursue the industries and employers for which it has the current asset requirements. Second, it can focus on obtaining the assets needed to attract the industries and employers they have selected. In many, cases both approaches are pursued simultaneously.

viii) When employers come to town to consider sites for the location of their branches, they will fall under the sentiment that "first impressions are lasting impressions." Many mayors have addressed the need to beautify their main street because it is the "welcome mat" for the city. Communities such as Youngstown and others elected to tear down the old dilapidated parts of town rather than trying to rebuild them. By electing to forego being an unattractive big city in favor of being a great small town, these communities have created a better first impression of themselves for potential new residents and new employers considering the locality for a branch or other facility now see a natural landscape or ball fields and hiking trails rather than dilapidated structures.

ix) Regional marketing for economic development is not always a workable practice, especially in regions where there are multiple business hubs rather than just one in the core city or where tax base considerations override the desirability of united efforts. In some circumstances however, regional marketing can be a good way to spread resource requirements and present a larger catchment area for workforce and quality of life factors.

x) As communities rebuild their economies, they are well-advised to keep in mind the concepts of equity. It is not sufficient to provide jobs in one area and not others, or that have access to some people and not others. If that does occur, community leaders need to figure reasonable ways to move workers from the areas without jobs to where the employers have located. It does no one any good to advance the economic fortunes of some but not all and such uneven development is an invitation for crime in some neighborhoods and for inter-jurisdictional conflicts throughout the region. It is true that a rising economic tide can lift all boats but access to employment is a critical piece of "rising." Numerous research studies have drawn a direct relationship between an equitable distribution of employment and income levels, and positive economic development.

xi) In today's world, with communications technology advancing regularly, it is possible to work from great distances rather than being in close proximity to one's employer. As such, small towns can become very attractive to the workforce of tomorrow. Combined with the interests of the millennial generation regarding a work–life balance, and an interest on the part of many families for a slower pace of life, small towns should consider building the amenity base that will help retain their high school graduates in the community as well as help to attract the younger workforce and build their economies around that. Similarly, larger communities can also be attuned to the desires of this generation of workers and continue to develop their economies in that way.

xii) Many communities are located in proximity to natural resources or features around which they can build economic development. This may include oil or other resources, a riverfront area, mountains or other features that can attract tourism, and more. Communities should maximize the advantages that surround them naturally. Clusters that support the development of such businesses can not only help grow the primary employers but also create employment opportunities in the supporting businesses and organizations that want to locate in proximity to the businesses they supply or otherwise support.

xiii) Communities do not always take full economic development advantage of institutions in or around their communities. These may include military installations, hospitals, universities, and other organizations. Much can be done to build small businesses that can benefit from these groups, including businesses that provide goods and services under contract to the base, the hospital, or the college. Community amenities can also benefit from local institutions, including restaurants and clubs, book stores, clothing stores, groceries, and more.

xiv) Just as economic growth and economic development are different, so are economic development and community development two different things. Community enhancement and the development of the factors that attract businesses are the challenges that confront community developers and local elected officials. There are very defined skills sets that are required to create an attractive community. Marketing that product—created by local officials, businesses, and local institutions—also requires a defined set of skills. Professionals in both areas are needed and they need each other as well. Planners need the business insights developed over time by economic development professionals when designing the land use of the community. And, economic development professionals will need the local administrators to operate efficiently on behalf of their business prospects when approving zoning and conducting inspections and issuing permits. But one cannot assume that a good planner can market a community effectively any more than one can assume that an economic development professional can be a productive plumbing inspector.

xv) Creating clusters around an industry or industry segment is a good way to develop an economy, however, one must be careful not to become so focused on the development of a single cluster and its support organizations. By focusing on a single industry, it is possible unintentionally to ignore the greater need for economic diversification into other industry segments altogether.

xvi) Rome was not built in a day. And, neither will be the economic development successes of communities. Before a community can attract businesses, it must either have or acquire what businesses need, and such things take time. Good schools, college classes in the area, available and diverse styles of housing and commercial space, clean and safe neighborhoods, attractive downtowns, and a relevant workforce all take time to develop. This may mean making expenditures that cannot be used for other purposes, and it means being attentive to the established economic development vision for the community for many years until the assets are in place and companies begin to come to the area.

5 Additional Conclusions

i) Investments in business attraction programs involve decisions not to fund other public services. Politics is all about making these difficult decisions between legitimate demands. Therefore, in order to justify allocations for economic development outreach, one must be prepared to present it as an investment rather than merely an expense: by investing in economic development outreach now, there will be a greater tax base available in the future to pay for even more of the other needs of the community.

ii) Constituents expect to see positive outcomes from economic development programs and those outcomes should exceed the costs of the program. Because constituents have tacitly agreed to forego equivalent amounts of spending for other areas—say, smaller classroom sizes or a new fire station—explaining those returns in those terms of the numbers of new teachers or police officers now affordable by the enhanced tax base can be more sellable to constituents than mere dollars and cents explanations.

iii) The commercial real estate business is changing. The younger workers—soon to be the majority of the nation's workforce—have different expectations of work. Those expectations translate into new commercial office locations, new designs of office space, differing amounts of space required, and requests to work from home rather than "coming to work." Amenities that are in proximity to office space will also change as the interests of this generation begin to impact the use and design of commercial office space. Communities need to be cautious about over-building space and designing traditional types of uses in traditional settings. The same can be said of traditional types and locations of residential units.

iv) Ever-advancing communications technology enables employees to work from a distance, including from their homes. This seems to be the interest of many in the new, Millennial generation. If people are enabled and permitted to work more from their homes, one must consider where they will want their homes to be. In their twenties, they may want to be near other 20-year-olds. In their thirties and beyond, they may want to be in smaller towns with good schools and a slower pace of living. Whatever those preferences are going to be, communities and commercial office developers need to take heed of the trends and respond to them. This could conceivably be a boon for small towns, especially those in proximity to larger employment hubs; their leadership should consider these possibilities.

v) Within mid-size and larger regions, the relationships that exist between the core city and the surrounding suburban cities and counties is critical. While joint economic development outreach is not always possible, collaboration on the development of the product is likely essential. The issues that quite naturally cross jurisdictional lines require cooperation and even joint funding. Employers are not interested in areas where some form of cooperation between municipalities is not evident and where squabbles are constant. Those issues that naturally cross jurisdictional boundaries include workforce, transportation, clean air and clean water, public safety, various public works, and more. These are not issues relevant only to elected officials and the residential community; corporate executives and their employees care deeply about these matters as well.

vi) The practice of economic development is comprised of one part reality and one part perception. The reality is based on the "product" being sold. That is to say that the community and its various businesses, institutions, inhabitants, tax and other public policies, workforce, amenities, and the surrounding geography all must appeal to a business executive seeking a site location. That is the reality; however, if no one knows about the reality of the community as a good place to locate a business, it all becomes irrelevant.

Perceptions are everything, which is why economic development marketing and communications are so important. An impression of the community that reflects its positive business and other attributes is critical. A community's reputation lives for a long time in peoples' minds. If a community is known to be the "Crime Capital" or a poor workforce area; or, if it has a reputation as being home to extremist politics or beliefs or if developers know it to be a very difficult jurisdiction in which to build and obtain permits in a fair but expeditious manner, then business attraction can become nearly impossible. If a place is known for its business growth or its pro-business polities or for having a strong and well-educated workforce, business attraction will be accelerated.

Constant repetition of the desired messages to the right audiences through a range of means, using ever-changing technologies is the first consideration in developing the new economy. Positive impressions on the part of workers and business site location decision-makers are very hard to develop and must be nurtured endlessly over time. Negative impressions will remain well beyond the phase of reality and will take a long time to correct. Further, in the absence of an economic development program that asserts a community's reality, executives and others will be left to form their own impressions. When this happens, the impressions can often be horribly misinformed.

vii) When building a commercial base in a community, maintaining momentum is vital. All too often, communities have attracted one or more substantial employers and decided to sit back and let the others come. This will not happen unless the pressure is kept up. Communities must build on the successes and use them to demonstrate to other employers that theirs is a good place to do business. After all, their colleagues and competitors obviously think it is. Resting on the laurels of other announcements not only concludes progress, but it means that, when the community wants to become more aggressive again about attracting businesses, it is starting over again. It will have lost awareness and it will have lost its place in the minds of the relevant business community. It will have lost its momentum!

viii) Communities have all too often waited until they have lost a primary business or industry, and the local economy is in free-fall before preparing a response. Strategic planning is just that—planning. It takes place before events occur. The development of the product that will attract new employers and begin to rebuild the local economic base cannot occur when the tax base has declined and when the demand for public services has declined. The funds are simply not available in bad times to do these things.

Creating the product needs to take place in the best of times, when funds are available to build and maintain roads, invest in high-speed communications and other infrastructure, generally beautify the community, and to attract the assets and amenities that will appeal to businesses. When employment is stable is the time to create training programs to update the workforce on new technologies, to establish encouragements and supports for those with an entrepreneurial bent to start their own businesses, and to provide programmatic support for innovators to commercialize their concepts.

ix) States in which economic growth has either been negative or flat for a period often have to face a difficult decision. In all states, there are areas in which unemployment and poverty are substantially higher than in other areas of the state. The reaction has always been to provide funding to keep those areas alive and to sustain their residents. The funding provides for their schools, health care, and more. But, the funding continues every year because there is not enough of an employment base to offset the cost of local, vital public services.

At the same time, most states have areas that are the economic providers for the rest of the state's public services. In Virginia, Fairfax County provides nearly one of every four income taxes to the state's coffers and all of northern Virginia accounts for 44 percent of all the Commonwealth's income tax base. Fairfax County gets back 19 cents for every dollar contributed. In the State of Washington, Seattle and the Puget Sound region can make the same case. In Maine, it is Portland. And, the list goes on. State legislators will continue to support the more needy areas of the states because that is whom they represent. But, ultimately, there must be some consideration given to sending more of the funds back to the economic drivers from whence they came because, by doing so, they will generate even greater returns that can then help the other areas of the states. This will be an ongoing discussion as US communities face increasing competition from parts of the world where public dollars go only to fuel the fires of economic growth.

6 One Special Lesson

i) Mayors, and even governors, are often term-limited. Sometimes, this means that the vision for the community stretches only so far as that individual's term of office. Sometimes, the strategies that will produce the greatest results will do so after the expiration of the incumbent's term of office. Sometimes, these concepts are ignored because they will accrue to the benefit and renown of the next occupant of that chair. This can be a limiting factor for state and local economic development.

It must be noted, however, that the vast majority of American state and municipal leaders would be highly offended by and horrified at that notion. I have interviewed hundreds of mayors and other local leaders while conducting the research for my last five books and have been immensely impressed by the dedication of these men and women and their love for their communities as well as the personal, family, and business sacrifices they make every day to serve their communities and to make them better places to live, work, play, and visit.

ii) It is always all about leadership! A city, town, county, or region that has all of the necessary assets for business attraction and retention can lose economic development prospect competitions every time if the leadership is taking the community in the wrong direction. Of this, there are numerous examples. Similarly, a strong and effective leader (or leaders) can advance the economic development of their city, town, county, or region beyond any reasonable expectations, given the nature of the assets and amenities possessed, simply by force of will and an ability to marshal the forces within their communities for a common cause.

Index

Locators in *italics* refer to figures and those in **bold** to tables.